The Thinker as Artist

Also by George Anastaplo

Books

The Constitutionalist: Notes on the First Amendment

Human Being and Citizen: Essays on Virtue, Freedom,
    and the Common Good

The Artist as Thinker: From Shakespeare to Joyce

The Constitution of 1787: A Commentary

The American Moralist: On Law, Ethics, and Government

The Amendments to the Constitution: A Commentary

Campus Hate-Speech Codes and Twentieth-Century Atrocities

Plato's *Meno*: Translation and Commentary *(in course of preparation)*

Documents of Liberty *(in course of preparation)*

Abraham Lincoln's Constitutionalism *(in course of preparation)*

Seven Introductions to Non-Western Thought *(in course of preparation)*

Greek Tyranny and American Misjudgments *(in course of preparation)*

Leo Strauss, Teacher *(in course of preparation)*

Book-Length Law Review Collections

Human Nature and the First Amendment

What Is Still Wrong with George Anastaplo?
    A Sequel to 366 U.S. 82 (1961)

Church and State: Explorations

Slavery and the Constitution: Explorations

Freedom of Speech and the First Amendment: Explorations

The Constitution at Two Hundred: Explorations

On Trial: Explorations

On Freedom: Explorations

Rome, Piety, and Law: Explorations

Lessons for the Student of Law: The Oklahoma Lectures

Law & Literature and the Bible: Explorations *(in course of preparation)*

Law & Literature and Shakespeare: Explorations *(in course of preparation)*

The Thinker as Artist

From Homer to Plato & Aristotle

∽

George Anastaplo

OHIO UNIVERSITY PRESS
ATHENS

Ohio University Press, Athens, Ohio 45701
© 1997 by George Anastaplo
Printed in the United States of America
All rights reserved

Ohio University Press books are printed on acid-free paper ∞ ™
01 00 99 98 97   5 4 3 2 1

This book has been brought to publication with the
generous assistance of Loyola University of Chicago.

Book design by Chiquita Babb

Library of Congress Cataloging-in-Publication Data

Anastaplo, George, 1925–
    The thinker as artist : from Homer to Plato & Aristotle / by
George Anastaplo.
        p.   cm.
    Includes bibliographical references and index.
    ISBN 0-8214-1176-4 (cloth : alk. paper). — ISBN 0-8214-1184-5
(pbk : alk. paper)
    1. Greek literature—History and criticism. 2. Philosophy,
Ancient. 3. Rhetoric, Ancient.   I. Title.
    PA3052.A48   1997
880.9'001—dc21   97-2389
                                                      CIP

Ariadne at Naxos

If I could be the world! I would explode
Then smash the dust itself to bits
So I could murder you.

Was it for this I doomed my brother,
Tricked my father, grieved my mother,
And chose your ugly, black-sailed ship?
Coward! Safe, you are fool enough to think
You could have solved the labyrinth,
Killed, and lived—without my help?

I only slept; I was not dead
In Naxos on this rocky bed,
Drowsy with his love and child.
I woke: dear Theseus was gone!
Oh, better to be dead at home,
Where only pity made me wild.

Lucky, high-browed Athens, be ruled by a knave,
A common sacrifice, garbage for the grave.
I deserve the shame of an unroyal choice.
You immortals know me better,
Send my sweet love a letter
For me, in this wise:

"I am still the princess of the royal house of Crete.
I will not, like a peasant woman, weep, rave and sweat!
With salt water, I shall wash away salt tears;
And, relentless, comb the tangles from my stringing hair."
Then I will wait. Dionysus will come,
Who is a god, and handsomer than him.

Contents

Preface

We read a classical text to improve our eyesight.
—John of Salisbury (1115–1180)

I RETURN IN THIS BOOK to some of the greatest works of the mind that have shaped and challenged us from antiquity. Each of these texts invites study on its own terms, instructive though it may sometimes be to weave them together. Vital to what is said in such texts may be the way it is said—that is, the artistry with which it is said. Even more significant aspects of artistry, including some form of inspiration, may be seen at the core of the most profound thinking, if not also in how texts can be said to be related to one another. But, however this book is organized, and whatever its topics and themes may be, it must ultimately justify itself as a collection of separable commentaries upon the ancient works, and workers, of the mind I happen to discuss. We have in this volume, therefore, still another set of reminders of how serious books might be read.

Most of the major Greek authors from Homer to Plato/Aristotle whose texts survive are represented here in a more or less chronological order. One of my principal omissions is Hesiod, whose *Theogony* will be discussed (along with *Genesis* and Parmenides) in an article on *beginnings* that I am scheduled to publish in the 1998 edition of the Encyclopedia Britannica annual, *The Great Ideas Today*. Other neglected authors, such as Isocrates and Xenophon, are glanced at, in effect, in my discussions in this book of Gorgias and of the Socratics.

I conduct inquiries into distinguished texts that can help us to remember who we are—and this, in turn, can help us to discover what we should be and do. Some of the ancient texts drawn upon here are still familiar; others were once far more familiar than they are now. All of them reveal what can and cannot be sensibly said by the thinker in matters divine as well as human. Suggestions are made in this book about what these and like works of the mind have to say about the goodness of life, about the relation of art to politics, about education and morality, about the relation of the noble to the just, about chance and fate, about the relation of reason to revelation, and about the discourtesy of death. There is a concern throughout this volume to bring to light the artistry upon which the greatest thinking often depends. This dependency has been anticipated in my Leo Strauss epilogue to a companion volume, *The Artist as Thinker*.

A thoughtful reader of my manuscript, who is more attuned than I am to contemporary gender and related scholarship, has identified one critical set of arguments of my book in this useful way:

> Ideas of the divine are human attempts to understand the order of human life within the order of nature. A fundamental ground for the natural order of human life is the tension between male and female, which is manifested in religious accounts of gender differences, sexuality, and family life. As popularly understood, ideas of the divine are the work of poets. The most serious poets, however, have philosophic inclinations; and philosophers do not accept popular conceptions of the divine as simply true, although they do see them as images of the truth about nature. Although they have much in common, poets and philosophers differ, because the former rely on particulars, while the latter look to universals. In this respect, the poets are more "female," while the philosophers are more "male," in their inclinations.

The serious general reader wants something less than what scholars are usually obliged to say about such matters, but something more than what popularizers are equipped to offer. Even so, care must be taken not to reduce the greatest texts to an interpreter's argument or theme, but rather to try to read each text on its own terms, terms which can include an awareness of other texts.

Longstanding questions about the relations of thought to art are considered throughout this book, and (it is hoped) are left in a more refined condition. Thus, the Aristophanic critique of Socrates, in chapter 7, part 3, is anticipated by the Platonic response to Aristophanes in the addendum to chapter 7, part 1. One form these questions take may be seen in section viii of that addendum:

> Still, we can wonder, are not the greatest philosophers likely to be poetic? Do they have to be so in order to be able to grasp fully the things that

they investigate? Do they, too, have access to inspiration? To what extent, and in what way, *is* the thinker an artist? On the other hand, what do the poets understand about the fine things they make? That is, are they philosophical? Do they know what they are saying?

A variety of approaches in addressing such questions is on display in this book, suggesting the ways that the most challenging texts might be read. My reader could well begin by consulting part 2 of chapter 8, where there is a detailed comparison of the uses by Herodotus and Plato of the Gyges story. (Another comparison, that of the uses of the Phaedra-Hippolytus story by Euripides and Racine, may be seen in chapter 6.) An even more detailed discussion, turning around a disputed line in Homer's *Odyssey*, may be found in part 2 of chapter 1. It should be instructive to see how varied the approaches to first-rate texts can, and indeed should, be by the reader as artist. I frequently presuppose a general familiarity with the texts drawn upon, just as most of the authors discussed in this book presuppose in their readers a familiarity with Homer. Citations in this book to two dozen of my publications provide guidance to other discussions by me of the authors addressed here, as do the indexes of my earlier books.

I have profited from the suggestions by generous readers of the manuscript of this book (without its addenda), including John Alvis of the University of Dallas, Larry Arnhart of Northern Illinois University, Clifford Bates, Jr. of Coventry, Rhode Island, Keith S. Cleveland of Columbia College of Chicago, Christopher A. Colmo of Rosary College, A. P. David of the University of Chicago, and Stephen J. Vanderslice of Louisiana State University. Also helpful with respect to various parts of this book have been Laurence Berns of St. John's College, David Bevington of the University of Chicago, William T. Braithwaite of Loyola University of Chicago, Leo Paul S. de Alvarez of the University of Dallas, Jules Gleicher of Rockford College, David Grene of the University of Chicago, Elliott Krick of the University of Chicago, John A. Murley of the Rochester Institute of Technology, Joel Rich of the University of Chicago, and John Van Doren of *The Great Ideas Today*. Barbara West and Sherman Lewis, of the Loyola University of Chicago School of Law Library, have long been of assistance in my research. The secretarial staff of the Loyola School of Law, under the leadership of Ellen B. O'Gallagher and Shawn Mercer-Dixon, have helped prepare this book for the press, as has Nancy Basmajian (an excellent copy editor for the Ohio University Press).

It is my hope that both the general reader and the scholarly specialist will be encouraged by what I say here and elsewhere to return to the enduring works I consider—and to do so with renewed interest, enhanced competence, and deepened pleasure. It is also my hope that both my critics and I will learn from the differences between us, keeping in mind a salutary observation by Arthur W. H. Adkins (*Classical Philology*, July 1980), "Where one disagrees [with an author], the need to think out why one disagrees will demand a clarification of one's own presuppositions and reasons for holding them; and this is always a worthwhile activity." Also salutary here is a related observation by Laurence Berns (St. John's College *Gadfly*, May 9, 1989):

> The best dialectical teacher I have ever seen was Jacob Klein [of St. John's College]. He had a way, first of all, of making students feel that their own perspectives and assumptions were of the greatest importance. More than once I heard him say, sometimes to the most outrageous statements, "Why did you say that?" Then he had the great gift of being able to ask questions that remained within the student's perspective, but would lead to exposing the limitations or errors or deeper truths in what the student had said. [His old friend] Leo Strauss admired that ability in Mr. Klein and remarked that he himself lacked the patience to excel in that way.

The "great gift" described here by Mr. Berns exhibits the thinker as artist. Likewise exhibited here, as it is in the following quotation from Xenophon's *Memorabilia* (1.6.14), is the generosity which thinking can both depend upon and engender:

> Just as others are pleased by a good horse or dog or bird, [Socrates said,] I myself am pleased to an even higher degree by good friends. . . . And the treasures of the wise men of old which they left behind by writing them in books, I unfold and go through them together with my friends, and if we see something good, we pick it out and regard it as a great gain if we thus become useful to one another.

I also appropriate for my use in this book sentiments expressed by Mark Van Doren in the preface to his instructive book, *The Noble Voice* (p. xiv):

I have tried to make these [authors] comment on one another as in fact I think they do. For they inhabit the same world, and stand or fall by the report of it they give. To be an expert in them all would be to have a perfect knowledge of the world. I do not make the claim.

Nor do I.

George Anastaplo

Hyde Park
Chicago, Illinois
November 27, 1996

We all feast off the banquet table of Homer.

—Aeschylus

The Graces, seeking a shrine that would never perish, found it in the soul of Aristophanes.

—Plato

Neither according to the classical philosophers [*Politics* 1328b11–12] nor according to Thucydides is the concern with the divine simply the primary concern of the city, but the fact that it is primary "for us," from the point of view of the city, is brought out more clearly by Thucydides than by the philosophers. It suffices to remember what Thucydides tells us about oracles, earthquakes, and eclipses, Nicias' deeds and sufferings, the Spartans' conpunctions, the affair of Cylon, the aftermath of the battle of Delium, and the purification of Delos—in brief, all these things for which the modern scientific historian has no use or which annoy him, and to which classical political philosophy barely alludes because for it the concern with the divine has become identical with philosophy. We would have great difficulty in doing justice to this remote or dark side of the city but for the work of men like Fustel de Coulanges above all others who have made us see the city as it primarily understood itself as distinguished from the manner in which it was exhibited by classical political philosophy: the holy city in contradistinction to the natural city. Our gratitude is hardly diminished by the fact that Fustel de Coulanges, his illustrious predecessors, Hegel above all and his numerous successors have failed to pay proper attention to the philosophic concept of the city as exhibited by classical political philosophy. For what is "first for us" is not the philosophic understanding of the city but that understanding which is inherent in the city as such, in the pre-philosophic city, according to which the city sees itself as subject and subservient to the divine in the ordinary understanding of the divine or looks up to it. Only by beginning at this point will we be open to the full impact of the all-important question which is coeval with philosophy although the philosophers do not frequently pronounce it—the question *quid sit deus.*

—Leo Strauss

Prologue

Simonides the poet came once upon a time to Hiero the tyrant. After both had found leisure, Simonides said . . .

—Xenophon

i

I CHANCED, A QUARTER of a century ago, to find myself conducting seminars in Plato's *Republic* both in an adult education program at the University of Chicago and in the political science department at the University of Dallas. Socrates elicited protests from both sets of students, but for quite different offenses. I attempted in both places to say what could usefully be said on behalf of Socrates' arguments.

Similarly, in this book, I attempt to subject representative texts of a dozen ancient authors to a more or less Socratic inquiry, suggesting thereby how one might usefully read (as well as enjoy) such texts as I

The epigraph is taken from Xenophon's *Hiero* 1.1 (opening lines of the dialogue). See, for discussion by me of the *Hiero*, *The American Moralist*, p. 51.

The epigraphs at the front of this book are taken from (1) Aeschylus: Anastaplo, *The Artist as Thinker*, p. 356; (2) Plato: Aristophanes, *The Clouds* (Loeb Classical Library), p. 264; (3) Strauss: *The City and Man*, pp. 240–41 (concluding passage in the book). For the John of Salisbury epigraph for the Preface, see *Christian Century*, July 5–12, 1995, p. 689. See, also, John of Salisbury, *Policraticus* (Cambridge: University Press, 1995), pp. 4, 159–62. On the Classics, see Anastaplo, *The Artist as Thinker*, p. 284.

Full publication data for books and articles cited in these headnotes (as well as elsewhere in this book) may be found in the "Selected Bibliography."

collect here, texts which illustrate the artistry employed by the greatest thinkers and how they "talk" among themselves across the centuries. I do not presume to repeat the many fine things said about these and like authors, but rather to set forth what I myself have noticed about them, *text by text,* sometimes with the help of others. (I emphasize "text by text," and hence to some degree chance, even though the organization of this book, as well as the themes carried from one chapter to another, recognizes a "system" of ancient Greek literature.) My *Republic* seminars of the 1960s provide a useful point of departure for the introductions I offer in this book to the intellectual treasures of antiquity.

In Chicago, a bastion of "liberalism," the students did not like the Socratic reliance in the *Republic* upon censorship; in Dallas, a bastion of "conservatism," the students did not like the Socratic reliance upon a community of women. On the other hand, the Dallas graduate students did not mind what Socrates had to say about censorship, whereas the Chicago adult education students found somewhat congenial what Socrates proposed about a community of women. All this should remind us how much the responses to and effects of legislative proposals, as well as artistic efforts, can depend upon particular circumstances.

We may well wonder how these two controversial proposals are connected. We may also wonder how playful each of them is, considering both the fatal unwillingness of Socrates to be censored by Athens and his legendary difficulty in dealing with one woman, to say nothing of a community of women. If it is playfulness, whose is it: Socrates' or Plato's or both? Let us put the community of women aside for the time being. What should we say about the Socratic responses to the arts, and especially to Homer? The extended discussions of the arts in the *Republic* are in books 2 and 3 and in book 10. In the first extended discussion, Socrates takes issue with how death, the gods, and hence morality are portrayed by artists. This is in the course of his establishing the political order, or the best city. It is a political discussion of poetry, with the principal concern being the character of citizens.

In the second extended discussion of the arts, in book 10 of the *Republic,* problems with *mimesis* (or imitation) are addressed. Once the political order has been provided for and disposed of, a philosophical discussion of poetry and of its relation to Being and hence Truth is in order. The principal concern in the book 10 discussion of poetry can be said to be about service to the cause of truth and how that bears upon the life of philosophy, especially since the inevitable collapse of even the best city had been anticipated.

How is all of this to be taken, especially since Plato, a first-rate dramatist, is widely recognized as a considerable artist himself? The artist is evident in the Myth of Er with which the *Republic* ends; the dramatist is evident in the dialogue as a whole, with its memorable story about the events leading up to and culminating in a night of wonderful talk. We should also notice that Platonic authors, such as the ever-instructive Plutarch, think highly of Homer, as does that most philosophical of Plato's students, Aristotle. I set aside, for the moment, several distinctions that are typically drawn between Socrates and Plato and, for that matter, between Plato and Aristotle.

ii

In a sense, characters such as Achilles and Odysseus are no more Homer's creations than Socrates is Plato's. Socrates is, of course, a historical figure who is amply testified to by other sources than Plato. But, then, the characters in the Homeric poems seem to be regarded by Plato and others as historical figures also. The Greeks, as may be seen in the opening chapters of Aristotle's *Politics,* drew upon the ancient poets as important sources of history, including political history. In fact, for some critical matters, the poets may have been their only substantial sources. The historicity of Homer's story is reflected in a casual observation by Plutarch identifying a certain day of a certain month as that on which Troy was perhaps taken (*Life of Camillus* 19.4). Plutarch's biographies of eminent Greeks and Romans abound with references to Homer. Characters in his biographies are very much aware of Homer. Pompey, for example, dreaded being called "Agamemnon" (Plutarch, *Comparison of Aegislaus and Pompey* 4.3). Alexander the Great took Achilles seriously as a challenging predecessor. Thus, one of the small frescoes in Raphael's *Stanza della Segnatura* (discussed in chapter 13 of this book) shows Alexander the Great depositing the poems of Homer in the tomb of Achilles.

Not only did Socrates regard Achilles and Odysseus as real people—

however much he disapproved of some of the things reported about them—but it seems as well, from the Myth of Er, that he could even place Odysseus' death (not Homer's telling of his stories) as one thousand years before. (See *Republic* 615A, 620C.)

Homer tells, then, about heroes and episodes that others evidently also knew about and had long told stories about. Some, if not much, of what Homer retells would have shaped the Greeks even without Homer. Still, we must wonder how much, and in what ways, Homer elevated, refined, and otherwise changed what he had inherited.

We must also wonder what the Homer is who is presented by Socrates. If all we had of Homer were what is available in and through the *Republic*, what would that Homer look like? What would the effects of such a poet be? We would suspect that Homer (like, say, Orpheus) had been immense. But could we get a more reliable sense of him than we now have of Orpheus (who is referred to many times in ancient texts but whose poems survive, if at all, in fragments)?

Plato does seem to count upon his reader's knowing the Homeric texts. An effective banishing of Homer from a reader's education would leave some parts of the *Republic* incomprehensible. One can properly see and assess what is said about various matters in the *Republic* only if one does have a reliable sense of what is in Homer.

At the very least, then, to deprive oneself of Homer would be to eliminate much of the "history" of the Greeks available to Plato and his contemporaries. (I consider, in the epilogue of this book, modern hypotheses about who, or rather what, Homer was. It suffices for most of this book to work from the traditional understanding of Homer.) The modern hypotheses can best be assessed after a survey of the "considerable" influence of Homer in antiquity. (See, e.g., Herodotus, *History* 1.1–5, 7.169.)

iii

The radical educational reforms suggested by Socrates in the *Republic* work from what is already there. He looks first to the gymnastics and the music with which Athenians were familiar, just as he relies upon the learning of his day when he begins to develop the sciences that the guardians would need in their education.

The arguments Socrates makes in the *Republic* are directed to and depend upon young men, such as Glaucon and Adeimantus, who are already shaped by poets such as Homer—shaped with respect to their opinions about the noble and the just and about war and peace. Socrates' arguments are made, of course, in the Greek language, to which Homer had very much contributed. Besides, Socrates, in establishing and counseling the best city, speaks with special respect of Greeks and their cities: he disapproves, for example, both of unlimited war between Greek cities and of the enslavement of Greeks by Greeks (*Republic* 469–71).

Even so, an attempt is made, in establishing the best city, to avoid much of what is already present in Greek life. This is the purpose, it seems, of Socrates' revolutionary proposal that everyone over ten years old be evicted from the city that the philosopher-king would take charge of (*Republic* 540E–541A). My argument thus far suggests that this Socratic eviction-proposal is substantially equivalent to the proposal that the poets, and especially Homer, be eliminated from the city.

Would this not be like trying, today, to eliminate Christian influences from the culture of the western world? I was reminded of this upon hearing (on April 23, 1993) the Chicago Symphony Orchestra perform Olivier Messiaen's *Les Offrandes oubliées (Méditation symphonique)*. Consider how the composer described the three parts of his six-minutes-long piece:

> THE CROSS (very slow, grieving, profoundly sad): Lament of the strings whose plaintive "neumes" divide the melody into groups of different lengths, broken by deep grey- and mauve-colored sighs.
>
> SIN (quick, fierce, desperate, breathless): A type of race toward the abyss at an almost mechanized speed. One will note the marked accents (comparable to declensions in grammar), the whistling of the connecting notes in the glissando, the cutting cry of the trumpets.
>
> THE EUCHARIST (extremely slow): The long, slow motion of the violins, which raises itself over a carpet of pianissimo chords in tones of red, gold, and blue (like a church window), to the light of soloists playing string instruments with mutes. Sin is forgetfulness of God. The cross and Eucharist are offerings to God, who gave his body and shed his blood.

The "account" of Sin was most graphic in this performance.

Whatever reservations the modern artist or critic may have about Christianity, would not an effort to eliminate completely its influence in

the West amount to a foolish, probably impossible, attempt to disman-
tle two thousand years of culture? Did not Socrates' proposal with
respect to Homer and the other poets amount to a similar attempted
dismantling in Greece? Does not this suggest that the Socratic proposal
with respect to poets is not to be taken any more seriously than that with
respect to ten-year-olds? What, indeed, does all this say about how seriously Socrates' grandiose political reforms are to be taken? (One might
be reminded of quixotic proposals today to abolish broadcast television.
See Anastaplo, *The American Moralist*, p. 245.)

iv

What does Socrates truly believe about the moral stance taken and promoted by Homer? Must not we assume that Socrates knew Homer at
least as well as we can? This suggests that in order to understand Plato
one has to understand Homer, a Homer whose texts for the *Iliad* and the
Odyssey are evidently much the same today as they were in Plato's time.

This means that Socrates notices Homer's own reservations about
some of the things said in the *Iliad* and the *Odyssey*. How, for example,
does Homer understand what is believed and reported in his poems
about the sayings and doings of the gods? How seriously does Homer
take the more bizarre adventures recorded, those reported by Odysseus
(rarely by Homer, in his own voice) in the tales he tells in the Phaeacian
Court of Alcinous? Among the tales, as we shall see, is one about a visit
by Odysseus to Hades.

What, then, *are* the moral principles that Homer draws upon and
fosters? Is there not something noble, if not even godlike, in the great
poet? He is a wise man—or he could seem to the Greeks to be wise,
not least perhaps in his openness to the Idea of the Good. The quarrel
between poetry and philosophy is, as we shall see, said to be longstanding. That quarrel takes one form in Socrates' banishment of even the no-
blest poets from his preeminently just city; it takes another form in
Aristophanes' ridicule of Socrates. Who is better able—the poet or the
philosopher—to know himself and hence to understand the other? (See
chapter 7, part 3 of this book, and the addendum to part 1 thereof.)

Even if we assume that Socrates personally appreciated the subtleties
and thoughtfulness of Homer, might he have feared that the typical cit-

izen would be moved, to his detriment, by the surface appearances of
Homer? What, then, is the life that *seems* to be promoted by Homer and
how does that relate to the life advocated by Socrates? Homeric characters and episodes were probably as much a part of the everyday life and
talk of the cultured Greek city as, say, sports are today among us. Is not
something that popular *apt* to be distorted, if not even corrupted, eventually? But would not the same risk be run by whatever Socrates nomi-
nates to take the place of the Homeric tradition in a Greek city?

Sparta is looked to by Plato, in one dialogue after another, as a city
worth taking seriously for the care it lavishes upon training its citizens.
Aristotle, too, recognizes this about Sparta. The best city of the *Republic*
can be identified, to some extent, with the city of Lycurgus, the founder
of the Spartan regime. Yet there is a tradition, related by Plutarch in his
Life of Lycurgus (1.2) and by others, that Lycurgus met Homer face to face
and profited from his counsel in preparing the Spartan constitution.

What kind of a human being is one likely to be after long exposure to
the Homeric gods, heroes, and adventures? A sensible answer to this
question could oblige one to recognize Socrates' censorship proposal as
something of an instructive diversion, as is perhaps also his provocative
community-of-women proposal. No one was more exposed to the
Homeric gods, heroes and adventures than Odysseus—and yet he is
shown by Socrates, in the Myth of Er (in book 10 of the *Republic*), as
being very much like Socrates in critical respects.

v

What did Socrates believe *not* about what Homer was truly saying (for
example, about Odysseus' visit to Hades), but rather about what the
effects of Homer were upon the training of Greek youth? Much is made
by Socrates of what Odysseus reports Achilles to have said, in Hades,
about his preferring virtually any kind of life on earth to the most
exalted life among the dead. An underlying question, to which I have referred, is whether Achilles "actually" expressed the demoralizing sentiments that Odysseus reports. Are such sentiments consistent with the
character and experience of the Achilles we know, and know well, from
the *Iliad*?

But we need not settle this underlying question immediately. A more immediate practical question is, What dominates everyone's recollection of Achilles—what is *shown* of his life by Homer in the *Iliad* or what is *said* about him by Odysseus in the *Odyssey*? The career of Alexander the Great is a particularly dramatic illustration of the influence of Homer upon talented young men of spirit well after Socrates. That Socrates is aware of such an influence in the generations before Alexander is suggested by the "rehabilitation" of Achilles exhibited in book 7 of the *Republic* (516D). There Socrates uses with approval the very lines (about Achilles' preference of an ignoble life to a glorious death) that he had condemned in book 3. (See Anastaplo, *The Constitutionalist,* pp. 278–81.)

Socrates had protested that the lament by Achilles in Hades would make cowards of the young. But I suspect that if Socrates has any serious reservations about Homer here it is not this one. Rather, it would make more sense for Socrates to play down Homer because of the tendency of his *Iliad* to make the Greeks more spirited and imbued with *filotima* than is consistent with the restraint required in a just city. After all, it *is* the wrath of Achilles that fuels much of the action in the *Iliad;* even the far less violent *Odyssey* virtually ends with the murderous rage of Odysseus against the suitors. (In both instances, by the way, the community-of-women principle is dramatically rejected.) Thus, aspects of Homer might be repudiated, but perhaps in the hope of having another poet, such as the more pacifist and yet pious Hesiod or the more pacifist and rationalistic Euripides, move into the ascendancy.

However attractive Hesiod is in many ways for Socrates, there is not in his poetry a Socrates-like character such as Odysseus—and it would be a serious loss not to have him. It is hardly likely, in any event, that Socrates would expect most human beings to exhibit that unconcern about death that Socrates himself evidently had. More important for Socrates than a concern about belligerency or pacifism may have been the lessons taught by Homer about the gods. These reservations contributed to the legal condemnation of Socrates. But do not we, as heirs of both the Biblical and the philosophic traditions, stand with Socrates against what Homer apparently teaches about divinity, no matter how a-philosophical we may be personally?

vi

Does our deeper understanding of Homer depend upon distinguishing him from his characters? (We have noticed, for example, that it was Odysseus, not Homer, who reported Achilles' lament in Hades.) Would our understanding of the Platonic dialogues be deepened by distinguishing Plato from *his* characters? Certainly, Plato is to be distinguished from almost all of his characters. But is he to be distinguished from Socrates also?

An effort to distinguish Plato from Socrates might have to begin with distinguishing, as Leo Strauss did, between the performed and the narrated dialogues of Plato. It may be appropriate that the decisive "action" against the poets is taken in a narrated dialogue—that is, in a dialogue nominally shaped in its presentation to us by Socrates, not by Plato.

That there are critical differences between Socrates and Plato is obvious. Socrates did not write anything for publication, so far as we know. Others may have been like him before—but there was no one like Plato (or Xenophon or Aristophanes) to "fix" *them* for the ages. Plato, in presenting various Socratic conversations, is poet-like, working from and with particulars. Yet there *is* something about a Socrates that transcends particulars, lifting him above the shortcomings evident in all others. He is, at least in Plato, somehow reason and virtue personified.

Does Socrates, in his campaign against poetry, recognize the extent to which poetry is dependent upon particulars and hence upon chance? Art, too, may attempt to conquer chance—but it must take the particulars of personality more seriously than philosophy does. For example, we can be reminded of the folly of attempting to establish a community of women when we imagine with the poet what naturally develops when Romeo happens to meet Juliet.

If the Platonic Socrates is indeed without significant shortcomings, then he must recognize as well as we can the merits of Homer—and there are indications enough in the *Republic* that this is the case. Do not the merits of Homer include a thoughtful awareness of the good, the true, and the divine, all of which Homer can present with a terrible yet engaging beauty? Underlying a great poet's presentations is a reliable awareness of *what cannot be*, something that bears, for example, upon how Odysseus' more outlandish tales *are* to be taken. (See, for a primer

on the good, the true, and the beautiful, Anastaplo, *The Artist as Thinker,*
p. 275.)

vii

The fundamental question here may be one that we can barely touch
upon: What is involved in that ancient quarrel between poetry and philosophy that Socrates refers to in book 10 of the *Republic*? That ancient
quarrel may be substantially like the quarrel sometimes discerned between men and women (however much it is moderated in the *Republic*
by what Socrates says about the equality of the sexes). Whether the
quarrel is between philosophy and poetry, or between male and female
as such, its key question in the context of the *Republic* is who is to be in
control. A proper answer to this question in each case requires consideration of, first, the nature of each party to the quarrel, second, what each
party can distinctively contribute to the association in which the parties
find themselves, and third, what the ultimate objectives of the association are. Is the artist necessarily limited or subordinated socially, so far
as the philosopher is concerned, except to the extent that art is guided by
divine inspiration?

Circumstances change, and yet poems, once "published," keep saying
the same things. However impolitic a poet may be, he can still attract
people without regard to moral or other consequences. The pleasure
offered by the gifted poet may be hard to resist. We can see all around us
today how much our sports, our news, and even our politics are exploited and all too often distorted for the sake of entertaining us.

It has been observed that literature spreads suffering around. No
doubt, poets do help us to anticipate, and hence to learn to deal with, the
miseries as well as the triumphs of our mortality. We do need to prepare
for our joys as well as for our sorrows. But when too much is made of
being entertained by the imitations which poetry relies upon, illusions
and images can come to dominate our lives and thoughts. We can even
become addicted to the peculiar pleasure of watching (if not causing)
the suffering of others, to say nothing of the often unbecoming pleasure
of sharing our own suffering with others. Novelty in these matters can
come to be sought, especially in those democratic times which like to

provide something for everybody again and again. This novelty can extend to religious institutions and practices, as may be seen in the innovations in democratic Athens that help account for Glaucon and Socrates being down in the Piraeus at the beginning of the *Republic*. Eventually the sense of wonder is either woefully diminished or callously exploited and corrupted.

This is related to the question of whether religious practices and piety should ultimately be subordinated to justice and the political order— that is, whether the inspired human being (be he prophet or poet) has to be subordinated to the rational citizen (or statesman). This is an issue that such events as the 1993 Waco Branch Davidian debacle and the 1995 Tokyo subway nerve-gas attacks should revive for poets and philosophers alike, and not only with a view to advising statesmen. (See Anastaplo, "Lessons for the Student of Law," p. 187.)

Among the questions left by the *Republic* is whether the philosopher can produce an appropriate religion, with plausible revelations, when there is nothing adequate at hand. Socrates' reliance upon the Delphic Oracle is instructive, as is his recourse to the Myth of Er. The measures resorted to here by Socrates reflect, it seems, his awareness that some form of poetry is needed to help most human beings cope with the sorrows, as well as with the temptations, that flesh is naturally heir to. (The Delphic Oracle is visited in part 2 of, as well as in the addendum for, chapter 3 of this book.)

Because the poet tends, in a well-ordered city, to adopt the stance of the sovereign, any serious recognition of the philosopher's superiority to the poet does seem, in effect, to banish the poet from the city. It is salutary to notice, in any event, that Plato, even though he may be regarded by some as an enemy of the poets, does teach us how to read their words, as well as his own, with the care that they require and deserve.

It is such care that I attempt to bring to my reading of the artists surveyed in this book, beginning with Homer. He and his characters are repeatedly drawn upon by the authors of the Greek world, as will become evident in the chapters that follow. It should also become evident that it is difficult, if not impossible, to discuss ancient authors without taking seriously what they say about the divine, which can be thought of as the Idea of the Good in an "official" or exalted form. The difficulties that we moderns have in reading carefully have to be reckoned with here. The effects of modern social science upon serious thought may be seen in the epilogue, where we consider how Giambattista Vico read Homer. Particularly in need of rediscovery is the thinking, especially the thinking that is aware of Nature and receptive to the Idea of the Good, which can be so much a part of the equipment of the greatest artists.

I. Homer

PART ONE. On the *Iliad*

> *It is hard for gods to be shown in their true shape.*
> —Hera

i

IT IS INSTRUCTIVE THAT WE, who are at last more or less at peace, first consider the Homeric gods as they appear primarily in the context of war. It was a familiar, however questionable, saying among us during the Second World War that "there are no atheists in foxholes." Is there anyone in the *Iliad*, we may well wonder, who denies the existence of the gods? Most people we encounter there are at least wary of them.

Unless otherwise indicated, the citations in this part of this chapter are to Homer's *Iliad* or to Homer's *Odyssey*. See, for additional discussion by me of Homer, as well as of the other authors discussed in this book, the indexes to my earlier books.

The epigraph is taken from Homer, *Iliad* 20.131. I endorse, for this book, Mark Van Doren's justification for his uses of translations (of Homer, Virgil, Dante, and others): "I am content with the certainty that by most readers half of these poems will be read in translation. That is how I have read them myself, and that is how I have quoted them. It is an interesting fact that Homer wrote in Greek, but what anybody may find in him is vastly more interesting. Nobody fails to find in him, below the level of sound and style, the things that prove him a great poet" (*The Noble Voice*, p. xiv). See, on the folly of some wars, Anastaplo, "Did Anyone 'In Charge' Know What He Was Doing? The Thirty Years War of the Twentieth Century," in *A Weekend with the Great War*, edited by Steven Weingartner (Columbia, Md.: White Mane Publishing Co., 1997).

The divinity of those gods may sometimes be difficult for us to appreciate. That difficulty is anticipated by such comments as these by St. Augustine in *The City of God* (pp. 75–76):

> First, then, why was Troy or Ilium, the cradle of the Roman people . . . conquered, taken, and destroyed by the Greeks, though it esteemed and worshiped the same gods as they? Priam, some answer, paid the penalty of the perjury of his father Laomedon. [Virgil, *Georgics* 1.502, "Laomedontea luimus perjuria Trojae."] Then it is true that Laomedon hired Apollo and Neptune [Poseidon] as his workmen. For the story goes that he promised them wages, and then broke his bargain. I wonder that famous diviner Apollo toiled at so huge a work, and never suspected Laomedon was going to cheat him of his pay. And Neptune too, his uncle, brother of Jupiter [Zeus], king of the sea, it really was not seemly that he should be ignorant of what was to happen. For he is introduced by Homer [*Iliad* 20.295 et seqq.] (who lived and wrote before the building of Rome) as predicting something great of the posterity of Aeneas, who in fact founded Rome. And as Homer says, Neptune also rescued Aeneas in a cloud from the wrath of Achilles, though (according to Virgil) [*Aeneid* 5.810, 811] "All his will was to destroy/His own creation, perjured Troy." Gods, then, so great as Apollo and Neptune, in ignorance of the cheat that was to defraud them of their wages, built the walls of Troy for nothing but thanks and thankless people. [Gratis et ingratis.] There may be some doubt whether it is not a worse crime to believe such persons to be gods, than to cheat such gods. Even Homer himself did not give full credence to the story; for while he represents Neptune, indeed, as hostile to the Trojans, he introduces Apollo as their champion, though the story implies that both were offended by that fraud. If, therefore, they believe their fables, let them blush to worship such gods; if they discredit the fables, let no more be said of the "Trojan perjury"; or let them explain how the gods hated Trojan, but loved Roman perjury.

Similar comments about these gods can be made respecting their jealousy of the counter-wall that the Achaeans built without the aid of any gods. (Ibid., 7.422–63. See Malcolm M. Willcock, *A Companion to the Iliad*, p. 83.)

The Augustinian critique of the Homeric (or Olympian) gods is echoed in our own time by such comments as these by Alain Hus (*Greek and Roman Religion*, p. 33):

The infidelities of Zeus, the rages and the jealousy of Hera, the dishonesty of Hermes, the fickleness of Aphrodite, the violence of Ares, the mockery of Hephaestus, the passions unleashed on Olympus as on earth—all this was eventually too much for the Greeks' respect for their gods. The Olympians long satisfied the piety of simple, rustic folk, and fulfilled the demands of civic cults, but after the archaic age they no longer satisfied the needs of individual citizens or of the educated elite.

Even so, the civic cults were taken seriously enough, long after "the archaic age," to form the basis of the indictment and execution of Socrates in the most sophisticated city in Greece.

What, then, can be seen of and said about the mostly concealed gods in the *Iliad*?

ii

The plot of the *Iliad* can be stated in altogether human terms: An arrogant, even overbearing, leader of a besieging army makes a mistake which leads to a destructive malaise among his followers. His most formidable warrior gets the leader to reverse himself, but not without incurring insulting treatment by that leader, treatment so offensive that the insulted warrior withdraws from action. The suffering that the army then endures includes (in unexpected ways) the most intimate interests of the sulking warrior. That newly aroused warrior is thus driven to return to action, with spectacular results.

This series of responses is keyed to the characters of these actors. (If the characters were not well sketched, the stories would be flat, especially if the actors were seen merely as manipulated by puppeteering divinities. Consider how Poseidon is, and is not, used in Aristotle's summary [in his *Poetics*] of the plot of the *Odyssey* quoted in section iii of part 2 of this chapter.) The strengths and limitations of the various actors are critical, so much so that all or almost all of the human episodes in the *Iliad* may be understood without dependence upon divine interventions. Thus, the disappearance of the somewhat cowardly Paris into the crowd ringing the dangerous duel-site is not difficult to understand; the self-delusion of Hector can be seen to have done him in. (See Willcock, p. 206.) Perhaps even the plague in the first book can be keyed to a thoughtless disregard for an infection introduced into the Achaean camp.

No doubt, the interventions of the gods reinforce all that men do, highlighting aspects of human activity. But the same can be said, in other stories that we know, about various manifestations of poetic talent.

iii

What else do the gods provide in the *Iliad*? Comic relief has been suggested: the doings of the gods may make the work appear less somber than it would otherwise. Perhaps standards or criteria for human action are thereby suggested. Perhaps, also, an effort is made to deal with something we would otherwise call chance. (See Willcock, p. 284.)

Accounts of the gods' doings may permit talking in a coherent manner about cause and effect, assuring us of the overall meaning of the events. Dignity is thereby lent to human actions, especially when men have to be immersed in war with its continuing brutality and its sporadic madness. We recall a familiar question, "What god was it then . . . ?" Is it not repeatedly assumed that something divine must be responsible for anything of the magnitude depicted in the *Iliad*? (See, on what we take for granted about "cause and effect," Anastaplo, "An Introduction to 'Ancient' African Thought," pp. 159–60.)

To introduce the gods is to provide ways of talking about how men are moved, especially in war. (Apollo, Hera, and Athena are seen to spur men on, as are Ares and Poseidon.) Men resort to talk about the gods to explain, if not to excuse, their intermittent folly. (See Willcock, p. 217.) But the gods serve as well to elevate events. (See, for example, Willcock, pp. 188, 190, 244–45.) Even so, one must wonder why the fighting seems fiercest when the gods are directly involved in battle. Is it then that "theological-political" passions are most intense and hence most deadly?

It should be noticed that the ostensible causes of human actions in the *Iliad*, however those actions are keyed to opinions about the gods, are usually if not always sufficient to account for what is happening. The Trojans, for example, understand why the Achaeans are at Troy: they do not depend upon any "real causes" of the war different from what the Achaeans, with their emphasis upon the abduction of Helen, allege.

Thus, aside from the question of whether the Homeric gods ultimately make sense, there is the question of whether the gods are needed to help us understand what is happening among men in the *Iliad*.

iv

Consider, as a case in point, the connections between Athena and Pandaros in books 4 and 5. Her presence or intervention is not known by the warriors at any of the three stages of this episode.

There is first the temptation of Pandaros, who can be labelled a fool by Homer (4.93–103). Athena appears as a comrade talking to Pandaros, who appreciates the blow he can strike for Troy (and the glory he can win for himself) by killing Menalaus, who is vital to the Achaean presence at Troy. Athena is no more needed for such temptation than Apollo is needed for the archer's skill that Pandaros and others are said to have.

Then there is the deflection of the arrow by Athena, saving Menalaus from a mortal wound. Are we not all familiar enough with incompetence to be able to account for it without divine intervention?

Finally, it is not hard to understand that Diomedes should be particularly harsh in the way he kills the truce-breaker (5.290). Of course, for Athena to guide Diomedes in punishing the very man she had tempted to act as he did suggests a certain ruthlessness in the goddess. But does not a rough justice prevail, especially if that man had been unduly receptive to temptation?

That Homer and various of his audience were capable of analyzing episodes as we have just done is suggested again and again in the poem. Consider the exchange between Nestor and Odysseus upon the return of Diomedes and Odysseus with fine horses as booty in book 10. (See part 2 of chapter 6 of this book.) Odysseus is asked by the pious Nestor whether a god had given the horses to them. Odysseus replies that gods can provide even better horses if they should want to (10.544 sq.). That is, this episode can be understood without assuming divine intervention. This does not keep Odysseus, however, from scrupulously fulfilling his vow to dedicate Dolon's armor to Athena upon his safe return from the dangerous mission. Odysseus' public attitude about such matters can be expressed in the observation that he, as a prudent man, merits and receives the protection of Athena on several occasions. (See, e.g., 11.435 sq.)

v

The Homeric gods are not omniscient, a limitation recognized by St. Augustine and perhaps best illustrated by the susceptibility of Zeus to seduction by Hera. Not only can Zeus be unaware of what she is up to but he can be lulled to sleep thereafter. (14.153–351. See Augustine, *The City of God*, p. 620, on Zeus' amours.) On that same occasion, Hera had deceived Aphrodite (in order to secure a useful aphrodisiac) by pretending to be on a peace mission, and all this is done by Hera (it turns out) in order to intensify the fighting. (14.193 sq. Even so, there is a hint that Aphrodite is somehow aware of what Hera is up to. See 14.213. If so, how much "must" Zeus have known after all?)

It should go without saying that if Zeus can be deceived, so can the other gods. Certainly, Zeus can act without the other gods knowing, or knowing fully, what he is up to. But whether or not the gods know what is going on, the action is driven forward. (For one thing, there is the constant influence of Aphrodite in the affairs of men and gods.)

Fate is shown to determine the essential actions, especially the ending of a man's life. Is fate like a divinity, but not a strictly Homeric divinity? (See Augustine, pp. 151–52.) Even Zeus, for example, is bound to permit the death of his son Sarpedon to come when it is ordained. He and other gods talk as if he or they might sometimes postpone or thwart fate—but they are never shown as able to do so. (See, e.g., 16.431 sq. Compare Herodotus, *History* 1.91.)

vi

Although Zeus is not omniscient (and hence not omnipotent), he does seem to know more than the others (gods and mortals alike) most of the time. This is reflected in the repeated references to the accomplishment of "the will of Zeus."

We can again see that this is a way of talking about the order of the whole, about how everything hangs together. For men the will of Zeus is best known from the way that things have in fact turned out. The poets can then tell the overall tale with some effect.

The limitations of men in their efforts to understand what is truly going on are reflected in the fact, several times referred to, that gods and men may have different names for the same things. (See, e.g., 1.403, 2.813, 14.291, 20.74. See, also, Willcock, p. 12.) Certainly, there are indications enough in the *Iliad* that gods and men, or the gods and some men (if not simply all men), see things quite differently. (The importance of having the correct names may be seen in *Genesis*, where Adam's naming of the animals, at God's instigation, can be understood as his characterization, or understanding, and perhaps appropriation of the animals.)

vii

Men speak of the will of Zeus being accomplished. But Achilles may be tempted at times to see it as his own will that is accomplished, with Zeus merely doing what Achilles had arranged with him through Thetis to do.

But does Achilles truly get what he "wants," as outlined in his request to his mother? Neither Thetis nor he appreciates all that they are asking. For example, Achilles is dooming his beloved Patroclus without knowing it.

Zeus is much more in control here than Achilles, if only in that he understands better the implications of what is being sought. (This is not to deny, however, that Zeus works in ways consistent with people's characters and circumstances.) It is not only Achilles who does not fully grasp what is happening in the way that Zeus does. The same can be said, for example, of Hera, who tries to reverse the successes of the Trojans in the absence of Achilles. She does not appreciate that the way to get Hector out in the open, beyond the safety of the city's walls, is to offer the not-altogether-thoughtful Hector an opportunity to run wild for a while. It is this that can get Hector killed, leading almost inevitably thereafter to the destruction of Troy. (See part 2 of chapter 6 of this book, including the comments in section ii thereof about Shakespeare's *Troilus and Cressida*.)

Hera, then, does not grasp the implications of what is happening in the way that Zeus does. (Something of this is indicated to Hera by Zeus after the seduction episode.) Zeus is poet-like in how he organizes matters, just as a great poet can be said to be god-like in how *he* organizes matters. Poetry pushes *chance* into the background, leaving *necessity* to govern. The necessity that poetry favors is tied more obviously to *will* than to *nature*. To be able to notice chance adequately, however, depends upon an awareness of what nature prescribes. (The ancient quarrel between poetry and philosophy may again be noted here.) It is often said that there is no accident or chance in the world of Homer's heroes. (See, e.g., Willcock, pp. 21, 256, 262–64, 283.) It will not do for a story simply to say, for example, that Paris' chin-strap happened to break. Critical events cannot turn (for the Greeks?) on trivial accidents, if there is to be a meaningful account or at least a dramatic one, as distinguished from what may be provided in a philosophical or scientific treatise. And so Aphrodite, looking out for Paris, breaks the strap, permitting Paris to escape.

viii

Hera's lack of sustained power, or knowledge, with respect to Zeus reflects the human situation. Men usually do not know what the gods are up to, but they do have their conjectures. For example, it is rare when men know that a god is visiting them while the god is still there. A god often appears in the form of, or works through, someone the man knows. (Perhaps Achilles sees Athena, at 1.194–202, but this is rare. Perhaps, also, his experience with his mother permits him an occasional glimpse of other divinities. [See, as well, 17.332.] This is not to deny that there may be signs that a god is present, as when the weight of one's companion in a chariot seems far too great for a mortal. See Anastaplo, "An Introduction to Hindu Thought," p. 258.)

The gods make contact with men in various ways, all of which ways we are familiar with and are content to ascribe to natural causes. The gods can take the forms of birds or other animals; they can speak to men through dreams, sometimes through lying dreams. Then there are omens of various kinds. We can see, as in Chapter 12 of Nathaniel Hawthorne's *The Scarlet Letter,* how omens are used even in Christian times: the letter "A" appearing in the New England heavens one night is read in quite different ways by different people, depending upon their character. Similarly, in the *Iliad,* a sign can be read differently by the contending armies. Certainly, men can misread whatever signs the gods vouchsafe them.

Such experiences have made men recognize that they may have problems learning what the gods want or are up to. Are there any divinities who appear to "everyone" at once in the *Iliad*? Only, perhaps, when a poet sings, unless it is when something like thunder or a plague occurs —but even such things have to be interpreted.

ix

Most of what the Olympian gods do or believe or *are* comes to men only through the poets. This means that most of the men at Troy do not know what we learn from Homer about how the gods conduct themselves, including the pulling and tugging among quite divided gods. The account Homer provides comes much later, long after the action. (Odysseus does hear poetic accounts about Troy on his way home. He becomes like us in critical respects.)

Should not Homer be expected to recognize that his audience knows much more than the men at Troy about the gods' roles in that war? Or should we say that those men were able to fight, and to some degree understand, their war without "knowing" what we are led by the poet to "know" about the roles of the gods? For those men almost all of what happened was grasped without benefit of anything like the Homeric accounts of what went on among the gods. If the gods are thus concealed from the principal participants at Troy, does not this suggest that there may be no non-poetic need for them at all? Thus, the poets can be understood to conceal the gods somewhat even as they reveal, or revel in, them. (Some of the diviners at Troy know what the gods are up to. But is this not only on occasion, and for limited purposes?) An underlying question throughout this discussion is what Homer himself understands about how he knows as much as he does about the gods. He does invoke the Muses from time to time—but is it not primarily for help in telling what he has already figured out or somehow knows?

x

Do the gods, as they are depicted in the *Iliad,* care what men know about them or about what causes things to happen as they do or even what men believe about the gods? This bears immediately upon the festivals, sacrifices, and other forms of homage that the gods seem to care for. (In book 1, for example, most of the gods are off in Ethiopia for a nine-day festival. Consider, as discussed in part 1 of chapter 7 of this book, what Aristophanes has to say about these matters.) These gods may need men for far more than the holidays and celebrations dedicated to the gods. Do these gods have anything meaningful to do on their own? Even though Zeus can identify men as "dismal" (17.424), the gods may not have any "life" of their own that makes sense. Nothing can truly happen to immortals, it can be argued, which means that "the only game in town" (or "in the cosmos") may be the one in which human beings play.

Whatever their interests, the gods may sometimes need concealment in order to be effective. (Even [the Homer-like?] Zeus keeps his counsel in organizing the principal action of the *Iliad.*) Furthermore, the gods can be ashamed of some of the things that they do; at least, they want to do them in private, away from the gaze both of other gods and of men. It may be natural enough to keep sexual relations offstage. But what about the cavalier way in which gods can trade cities for destruction? (See Willcock, p. 45.) Does this mean that they care more for their enmities than for their allegiances—or for the welfare of the men or the cities who happen to depend upon them? (We can see this with Aphrodite in part 1 of chapter 6 of this book.)

In addition, gods can "party" while men die. This reveals how heartless they *can* be. But it may also show what an existence devoted to peace is like—that is, for those who are not faced with the imminent prospect of death. (The peacetime alternative for human beings is dramatized in the shield that Hephaestus makes for Achilles [18.478 sq.] Hephaestus is a would-be peacemaker among the gods, even though he is called on for implements of war.) In short, do the gods need to conceal themselves somewhat from men if they are to have the effects they desire among men? On the other hand, do not human beings have means of finding out about the gods, whether or not the gods want them to?

xi

It is Homer who is particularly adept in finding out and displaying men and gods in their differences and relations. We have already glanced at the supposed role of the Muse for Homer. How wise, or sophisticated, is Homer himself about the gods? Homer does know a lot about men, especially in battle. He also knows how much the gods themselves are restricted in their own actions and how different men's views of various of the gods can be. He knows as well how much men do not know at any particular time about the gods' intentions and doings. Although Homer does not identify the gods as human inventions, he does see them as very much dependent upon human interpretations.

The poet's account of human things makes more of the gods than does Hephaestus' account in the Shield of Achilles. (See Willcock, p. 209 f.) But we should not forget that the Hephaestus account, however different it may be from the "Homeric" account of life, is itself an account presented (developed if not invented) by Homer himself.

It is easy for us to assume that Homer "believes" as he does because of his times. May not the Catalogue of Ships (discussed in part 2 of this chapter and in the epilogue of this book) or the account of things presented by Hephaestus on the Shield come out of a time different from that of other things in the *Iliad*? If Homer is thus contrasting two different ages, "where" is he when he does so? (Consider, also, the account of the domestic scene in Hephaestus' dwelling, 18.368 sq.)

It is far from clear what Homer does believe. If Homer is at least as intelligent as we are, which does not seem unlikely, then it is not unthinkable that he himself required substantial evidence to "believe" his own descriptions of the gods. Is it not possible that he may believe much as we do about these gods, whatever he finds it useful to say about them on the surface of his compelling poems?

We must continue to wonder, therefore, what it is that Homer, as a

wise man, wants to say to the more thoughtful members of his audiences. His immunity in what he truly says—an immunity that saves him
from the fate of a Socrates—may depend, at least in part, upon his willingness to tell stories about the gods' doing things, stories that Socrates
can rule out as impossible. Thus, Homer is willing to *present* the gods as
something more than "internal" movements in the souls of men.

xii

What, then, are Homer's gods like? It is often said that they are not
moral, that they do not serve as models of morality, that they do not inculcate moral teachings. (See, e.g., Augustine, pp. 42–43. See, also, Willcock, p. 184. Compare ibid., pp. 228–29.) Is this so? Consider what even
anger or petty-seeming resentment on the part of the gods means. Do
not such responses by the gods draw upon some notion of justice?
(Compare Willcock, pp. 43, 51, 55.) Justice and perhaps even a standard
of excellence may be seen as well in the favoritism shown by gods for
various men and women. Consider, also, what is said many times about
the gods' disapproval of the oath-breaker, and what the gods do to further certain human actions (such as getting Priam into and out of the
Achaean camp with a view to accomplishing Hector's proper burial
[24.305 sq., 677 sq]).

   Besides, it seems to be generally understood that the pious man is
more apt to be good because of his piety. (This appears to be consistent
with the fact that the priest of a god, as seen in book 1, can care more for
his family than for his political allegiance, with Apollo's apparent approval—even though Apollo supports Troy, which the priest is willing to
sacrifice for his daughter's return.) Insofar as the gods do guide events,
an assessment of their morality may be reflected in how things turn out
in the *Iliad*. Do not things work out more or less justly under the auspices of the gods? (Augustine complains that Troy is not saved by the
gods it worshiped [p. 7]. But both sides worshiped those gods, which
suggests that the fate of the city might have been settled on the merits of
their respective cases.)

   Furthermore, do not the various people we come to know well in the
Iliad get what is coming to them? It is evident that piety is not the only

consideration in determining a man's fate, as may be seen in the ineffectiveness of the recourse to Athena that Hector asks of his women. To what extent *is* the way things turn out the gods' doing?

To say that the gods stand more for morality than some modern readers recognize is not to deny that divine morality may be in need of examination. Is there any indication, for example, that the gods disapproved of Achilles' sacrifice of twelve Trojan captives for Patroclus' funeral? (21.27–28. See Willcock, p. 207.) Homer, it seems, disapproves of this. Does not the overall "argument" of the story, in which the gods' opinions can be said to be reflected, also "disapprove" of this barbarity? In any event, there do seem to be places in the *Iliad* where it is assumed that the gods endorse what men generally consider to be moral. (See, e.g., 16.384 sq.)

xiii

Is there at all implicit in the *Iliad,* at least in Homer's underlying position, the kind of assessment of the divine that may be seen in Plato's *Republic*? Socrates does not seem to regard the Homeric account of the gods as either accurate or salutary.

How would Homer respond to these criticisms? What I have said thus far suggests that Homer might agree with respect to the concern about accuracy, so far as the surface of his poem is considered. But he might add that stories, if they are to sustain an audience, have to be told in a way that engages the passions (and through the passions, the mind) of a people.

Homer might respond as well that he had refined considerably the stories of the gods that he had inherited. But he was limited in how much he could refine, especially since poetry does depend upon stories, not upon discourses. Stories make much of particulars, and that means individual gods with names, passions, and even histories. Besides, we recall, a poet tried to warn Socrates that men can dread the sense of chaos that they imagine would become dominant if the gods are not seen as reflecting and yet controlling the passions of men. (Aristophanes' *Clouds* is discussed in part 3 of chapter 7 of this book. The Platonic response to the *Clouds* is discussed in the addendum to part 1 of chapter 7.)

Does Homer truly refine the sensibilities of his audiences, especially audiences guided by a few among them who are induced to reflect upon what happens when and to whom? The great war at Troy is, because of Homer, more to be thought about than it might otherwise have been. Compare the wars before the time of the *Iliad*, such wars as Nestor draws upon in his nostalgic recollections. It is hard for us (as it may have been for Nestor's generation) to see the point of those earlier wars, however grander they may have been for their participants.

Scholars sometimes suggest that the wars Nestor refers to are really Homeric inventions, just as are various other distant events referred to in the *Iliad*, such as the help given once upon a time to Zeus by Thetis and some episodes in Niobe's career. (See Willcock, pp. 10–12, 272. I mention, if only in passing, the question of whether someone who invents great wars might not also invent the divinities assigned to those wars.) My general point would be enhanced by any conclusion that those wars of Nestor's youth are indeed Homeric contrivances. For this would suggest that Homer intends us to notice how different those wars, as presented by Nestor, look from the great war at Troy, about which a true poet was able to speak in his own name. Such a poet can be superior even to Zeus in that he not only organizes the whole as Zeus does but also is free from the passions to which Zeus is shown to be sometimes susceptible. When the action ends at Troy, how many of the gods understand what happened there as well as Homer does? Do they want—are they able—to understand? We can again wonder: Do these gods have anything else to do (or, at least, anything worth recording) once the men of the Trojan War return home and the repercussions of the war (such as those described in Aeschylus' *Oresteia*) are dealt with? What is there to be said about the relations among these gods, except when they act like human beings? (See section viii of the addendum to part 1 of chapter 7 of this book.)

It may be that the full significance of peace, of which philosophic activity is the peak, can be known only by those who have experienced war, that war which poetry may help us experience properly. Does the philosophic somehow depend upon the poetic? Homer *can* be spoken of as the "father of all philosophy." (Rabelais, *The Histories of Gargantua and Pantagruel*, p. 553) We suspect, therefore, that the understanding can be enhanced by access to the poetic way—that is, through stories which use bodies (or particulars).

An account of the general ordering of things which is more philosophic than poetic in tone may be seen in William Blackstone's *Commentaries,* where it is said, "Thus when the supreme being formed the universe, and created matter out of nothing, he impressed certain principles upon that matter, from which it can never depart, and without which it would cease to be" (vol. 1, p. 38). Need it be added that such a supreme being never lusts or sleeps? May not the principles or the laws referred to here by Blackstone, however, be too mechanical for human beings in need of stories? Certainly, such laws are not subject to the kind of will or passions associated with the Homeric gods. Is the poet better able than students of philosophy to give to the variety of human passions their dramatic due, with the gods particularly illuminating those passions?

Even so, may not Homer's underlying understanding of the divine mean that the common opinion about these gods does not welcome, however much it requires, serious examination? In more ways than one, therefore, the gods of the *Iliad* are concealed, even as they are revealed to a remarkable extent for the careful reader.

PART TWO. On the *Odyssey*

> *Some philosophic questions interest only philosophers: they would never occur to the plain man, and if he hears of them he may very well think that those who spend their time on philosophy must be a trifle mad.*
>
> —Phillipa Foot

i

PLUTARCH REPORTS THAT ONE of the lines in the *Odyssey* that was questioned in antiquity comes toward the end of Odysseus' account (to the Phaeacians) of what he observed and did when he visited Hades in

---

Unless otherwise indicated, the citations in this part of this chapter are to Homer's *Odyssey.*

The epigraph is taken from Philippa Foot, "Moral Relativism," in Jack W. Meiland and Michael Krausz, eds., *Relativism, Cognitive and Moral* (Notre Dame: University of Notre Dame Press, 1982), p. 152.

the course of his Great Wanderings. It is where Odysseus reports that he wanted to see even more than he had before he became fearful of Persephone's intervention. Among the inhabitants of Hades whom Odysseus wanted but failed to see he names Theseus and Perithoos, who are identified as "glorious children of gods" (11.631. See Plutarch, *Life of Theseus* 20.2)—and these two names (in the line I have referred to) are taken by one ancient critic to have been added much later than Homer.

My first extended discussion of the *Odyssey* in this book can usefully turn around this disputed line. I believe it fruitful to consider both whether this line was in Homer's original poem and why it should have ever been questioned. (I do not happen to know how this line has been discussed since Plutarch's comment upon it some seventeen hundred years ago.)

This inquiry may seem rather academic, especially to "the plain man." But insofar as it *is* academic, it can be considered "Athenian." Not only was the original academy in Athens, but also academic institutions as we know them have their roots in the Athenian way of life.

ii

But, first, why might this line have been added? It was added at the instance of Pisistratus (an Athenian ruler), said one Hereas (according to Plutarch), in order to make Athens seem important even so early in Greek history. Theseus was recognized as the great founder of a united Athens.

Plutarch tells us that Hereas was a Megarian (*Life of Theseus* 20.2). Athens and Megara, we know were ancient rivals. (The Peloponnesian War broke out, in part, because of that rivalry.) In this way, then, a Megarian critic questioned the claims of Athenians to a distinguished past for their city. The Athenians, on the other hand, were inclined to argue that what "Greece" and "Greekness" always aimed at had come to be realized in what Athens stood for.

In what I am about to say, therefore, I will be providing in more ways than one an "Athenian" interpretation of the *Odyssey*—of that great Homeric epic which had been acclaimed, throughout the Greek world, centuries before Athens became what we celebrate her to have been in the fifth and fourth centuries B.C. (The discussion in chapter 3 of this book returns to the issue of what "Greece" meant. See, on Athens at Troy, Herodotus, *History* 7.161.)

iii

We are particularly concerned here with the Great Wanderings of Odysseus that are recounted in books 9 through 12 of the *Odyssey*. That account has to be put in context, if it is to be understood.

The context is provided by the *Odyssey* as a whole. What is *that* about? We can begin to answer this question by considering the following summary from Aristotle's *Poetics* (1455b17–23):

> The argument of the *Odyssey* is not a long one. A certain man has been abroad many years; Poseidon is ever on the watch for him, and he is all alone. Matters at home too have come to this, that his substance is being wasted and his son's death plotted by suitors to his wife. Then he arrives there himself after his grievous sufferings; reveals himself, and falls on his enemies, and the end is his salvation and their death. This being all that is proper to the *Odyssey*, everything else in it is episode.

The adventures of the Great Wanderings of Odysseus are to be found, if at all in this summary, in the observation that "Poseidon is ever on the watch for him"—that is, on the watch to do him ill whenever possible—and in the reference to his "grievous sufferings."

Even so, the episodes in the Great Wanderings, along with a few in the final books (when Odysseus is home, slaughtering his wife's suitors), are the ones that are apt to be remembered, including episodes having to do with the Lotus-eaters, the Cyclops, Circe, the Sirens, Scylla and Charybdis, the Cattle of the Sun, and Calypso. There are a dozen such episodes during the Wanderings, said to range over a decade. They are preceded by the Trojan War itself (which was drawn upon in the *Iliad*); and they will be followed by the miniature war awaiting Odysseus at home, when he confronts the rapacious suitors (the Homecoming).

It has been argued that the account of the Great Wanderings was probably the first part of the *Odyssey* composed by Homer. Be that as it may, this account is provided by Odysseus himself. That is, *he* tells the story of his decade since Troy; this he does on the eve of his departure from Phaeacia for Ithaca. The Phaeacians are very much caught up by the story, pressing him to tell them everything, as he talks through the night. He is rewarded with rich gifts after his tales.

It is easy to forget, by the way, that half of the *Odyssey* is devoted to the Homecoming of Odysseus: he reaches Ithaca in book 13 of the twenty-four books. This, too, is a tribute to the fascination that the Great Wanderings exercise upon us. Before we learn of the Great Wanderings of Odysseus, we are told (in books 2 through 4) of Telemachus' wanderings in search of Odysseus. His wanderings, however, are far less exciting than his father's. But, then, *his* are told by Homer, whereas Odysseus' are told by Odysseus himself.

iv

Some people, we know, simply cannot tell a story. But that may not be what made Telemachus' wanderings less memorable than Odysseus'. Rather, we must consider whether Odysseus' account has the advantage of not being limited by what we call "facts." For, we again notice, this is the only extensive account in the epic that Homer does not present primarily in his own name but rather in the name of a character.

How reliable *is* Odysseus? We know that he does not hesitate to deceive when the circumstances require it—or, it sometimes seems, whenever the circumstances merely permit it. Even within the account of his wanderings he reports various deceptions he has practiced, the most dramatic perhaps being that practiced upon the Cyclops who, after being misled as to Odysseus' name, is gulled by him into a drunken stupor. Thereupon the Cyclops can be blinded by Odysseus. We then observe Odysseus tell one false, or *supposedly* false, tale after another about who he is and where he has been, deceiving thereby everyone but Athena.

We should not forget that the tales of the Great Wanderings are told by a leader who must account for the loss of all his men and who has much to gain from his Phaeacian hosts. It is evident that the Phaeacians (who are an easygoing, even soft, and certainly not toughminded people) are quite moved by Odysseus' account, even though they are aware of his resourcefulness. (Cannot someone of his resourcefulness be expected to know how they would respond—that is, as they *do* respond, with lavish gifts and a sure trip home?) The Phaeacians hear Odysseus report that he had been advised, by Agamemnon in Hades, not to tell his wife everything when he got home. Agamemnon (to whom we return in chapter 4 of this book) had learned, too late, to be cunning. Does Odysseus follow this advice? Did he need it? And should such care in speech be limited to what one says to one's wife? The Phaeacians do not seem to recognize that this advice might be applied as well in Odysseus' dealings with them. They evidently consider him to be saying everything he knows since he is so frank in saying that he has been advised not to say everything. Is Penelope similarly reassured?

Should the Phaeacians have been taken in by Odysseus' account of the Great Wanderings? Consider how a respected translator sees all this: "In addition to the authentic wanderings of Odysseus recounted by the hero himself or by the poet, there are five false stories told by the hero about himself" (Richmond Lattimore, *The Odyssey of Homer*, p. 11). (They are identified as addressed respectively to Athena [13.256–86], to Eumaios [14.191–359], to the suitors [17.419–44], to Penelope [19.165–202], and to Laertes [24.302–8].) This translator goes on to notice in this passage, "[These false stories] are meant to be plausible, and the supernatural and the marvelous elements of the wanderings find no place here." But why should the account of the wanderings provided to the Phaeacians, which is pervaded by "the supernatural" and by "marvelous elements," be considered "authentic" (if they are so considered) in preference to the more prosaic accounts?

What does Homer mean for us to understand by this arrangement? Few, if any, of the tales Odysseus tells the Phaeacians are referred to by Homer in his own name. No doubt, each of these tales points to something important, if not in the character of Odysseus, then in human life generally. Thus, at the beginning of book 20, Odysseus has occasion (in rough circumstances) to remind himself of his fierce encounter with the Cyclops. How is *this* to be understood? One of us, in rough circumstances, also may be reminded of Odysseus and the Cyclops. We can be heartened thereby, without having to believe that the episode "really" happened. Besides, Odysseus' *personal* recollection of the Cyclops, or of whatever the Cyclops stands for, may not be as spectacular as the account of the Cyclops he provided the Phaeacians. (Zeus, too, we notice, speaks at one place of the Cyclops episode. But what the gods' sayings and doings mean in Homer's poems is a major question [1.64 f.]. Suffice it to say, that here, too, the poet is not speaking in his own name.)

The poet does report in his own name the killing of the Cattle of the Sun and the dire consequences thereof. This may be found, for example, even in the opening lines of the *Odyssey*. But what does this episode consist of and mean? Did Odysseus' men, because of their intemperance, incapacitate themselves for the struggles they had to endure thereafter at sea? What can be said about the Calypso episode, which Homer also ratifies in his own words? It is not the first, or the last, time that a middle-aged man has been attracted by a woman of charm and wealth, especially by a woman whose energetic interest in him makes him feel young again.

We have wondered about the "authentic" and the "real." What can it mean that we distinguish in a work of fiction between the authentic (or real) and the false? Do we mean by the authentic or real that which can happen? In this sense, perhaps, Homer's tales are more nearly authentic than Odysseus'. In saying this, we recall that Homer's tales include accounts of a wily man who is capable of telling for his purposes what we know as "tall tales." His purposes include impressing others, securing gifts, protecting himself, testing others, and generally making life easier for himself. Rarely, if ever, does he do anything just for the fun of it, except perhaps in the company of his wife—and even then one must wonder. We have noticed that Odysseus is dependent upon the Phaeacians. He must make sure of them—his life is completely in their hands. Besides, he does have much to gain from them in the way of gifts and transportation home. He can interrupt his engrossing account of his adventures, in order to give them an opportunity to urge him on.

A tale, whether true or false, can say much about the narrator or about his audience or about both. But whatever it says, does it not say even more when we determine whether the tale itself is indeed true?

Central to the *Odyssey* as a whole, it can be said, is the story-telling by Odysseus in his dealings with the Phaeacians. Central to that story-telling—this account of the Great Wanderings—is the most fanciful tale of all, Odysseus' account of his visit to Hades, which has been percep-tively referred to as the "Raising of the Dead." True, Homer himself has an account, in book 24, of the descent into Hades of the men and women slaughtered by Odysseus and his allies in Ithaca. But no living man is present for this descent: one's understanding of what happens on that later occasion starts with this realization. One also realizes that souls either do or do not survive death. If they do survive, what is re-ported about the suitors can be considered their way of learning what is going on in that realm (that is, among the living) where things are still happening.

We have Odysseus' account of his visit among the dead to reflect upon. We notice that central in the catalogue of those Odysseus reports to have seen in Hades is Ariadne. She is "set off" as no other character is in this catalogue: on either side of her is a pair of names of people who are not otherwise identified here or elsewhere in the epic; there is no other person referred to in this catalogue who is not otherwise identified in the epic. (Patroclus and Antilochus are referred to by name only, in this catalogue, but is it clear, both here and at several other places in the *Odyssey*, that they are intimates of Achilles'.) Thus, Ariadne's centrality in this list is emphasized by the peculiarity of the "silent" pair on either side of her. (The pair preceding Ariadne are Phaedra and Prokris; the pair following her are Maira and Klymene. Phaedra is dealt with at length in part 1 of chapter 6 of this book.)

Here is the passage which includes on either side of Ariadne the "silent" pairs I have referred to (11.321–27):

> I saw Phaedra and Prokris and Ariadne, the beautiful daughter of malig-nant Minos. Theseus at one time was bringing her from Crete to the high ground of sacred Athens, but got no joy of her, since before that Artemis killed her in sea-washed Dia, when Dionysos bore witness against her. I saw Maira, Klymene, and Eriphyle the hateful, who accepted precious gold for the life of her own dear husband.

Many stories about Ariadne and Theseus have come down to us. One of them is drawn upon by Odysseus, about which little more is known than is given here. The various stories have certain features in common: that Theseus took Ariadne from Crete but that he never got back to Athens with her, leaving her instead on one island or another en route (where she either pined away or married Dionysos or was killed). In the various stories, the character of Theseus is a problem: that is, he lies under the suspicion of having deserted the woman who had been of great help to him in Crete. (See, for example, the dedication for this book, which is a revised version of the dedication for *The Artist as Thinker*.)

Ariadne is important because of Theseus (their names are commonly paired). It is useful for us to remind ourselves, by recourse to a conventional encyclopedia entry, of just who he is ("Theseus," *New Century Cyclopedia of Names*):

> *Theseus*: In Greek legend, the chief hero of Attica; son of Aegeus, king of Athens. While Theseus was still an infant, Aegeus hid his sandals and sword under a rock, and told the mother [in Troezen] that when the boy was strong enough to lift the rock, to send him to him at Athens. When he reached the age of sixteen, Theseus lifted the rock, and then set out for Athens, where he was recognized and acknowledged by Aegeus. He captured the Marathonian bull, and when the Athenians sent their tribute of [seven] youths and [seven] maidens to Minos [in Crete], he went with them, and slew the Minotaur with the help of Ariadne, daughter of Minos, who fell in love with him. She gave him a sword, and a clew of thread with which he found his way through the Labyrinth. He sailed away with Ariadne, but abandoned her on the island of Naxos. After this came the incident of the black and white sails, when Theseus forgot to hoist the white sails on the journey home as a sign to his father that he still lived, and Aegeus drowned himself. Theseus thereupon became king of Athens in his father's place. He accompanied Hercules to fight against the Amazons. He was one of the Argonauts, took part in the Calydonian boar hunt, and performed other marvelous exploits. He was slain by Lycomedes, king of Skyros.

Why, then, should the story of Ariadne—Theseus' Ariadne and his relations with her—be so critical to the catalogue of those reported by Odysseus to have been seen by him in Hades? This takes us back to what had happened on Phaeacia—to what Homer himself tells us of what happened on Phaeacia—after Odysseus arrived there storm-battered and naked (some twenty days after he was released by Calypso, who had held him as her lover for seven years). Odysseus encountered down there by the water the daughter of the king of Phaeacia, the only maiden he deals with in the *Odyssey*. This princess, Nausicaa, unlike the other women who have come down to wash their clothes, does not flee at the sight of the rough-looking Odysseus. Indeed, she comes to admire him, once he supplicates her and is permitted to bathe and to be clothed properly. (She has had, for some time, thoughts of marriage; but she has rejected all suitors up to now. It is soon indicated, however, that Odysseus is just the kind of man she would like some day to marry.)

It is Nausicaa—a vibrant, attractive girl—who provides Odysseus the vital entry he needs to the royal court, who guides him to her mother and father, and whom he considers responsible for his salvation. The reader is drawn to the girl as she is described by Homer, so much so that Samuel Butler could suggest that *she* (presumably in her later years) really wrote the epic. She is described by Homer with buoyancy; she comes alive; the portrayal is vivid. (Butler, *The Authoress of the Odyssey*, pp. xiv, 201.) Butler can even call book 6—the one in which Nausicaa comes upon Odysseus—the loveliest in the poem (ibid., p. 145).

I note one more thing about all this, and then I can begin to draw my conclusions. An odd feature of the entire story—which has been remarked upon by various critics over the centuries—is that Nausicaa says farewell to Odysseus in book 8, not in book 13. (See, e.g., Butler, pp. 206–7.) That is, she parts from Odysseus before his long night of storytelling in the royal palace (books 9 through 12) rather than after, which is when he embarks for Ithaca. By book 8 Nausicaa's father had already suggested that Odysseus might well marry his only daughter. (This was even before it was learned who he was; Troy they had heard of and the exploits of the Greek heroes, including Odysseus, but that *this* was Odysseus had not yet been announced by Odysseus.) But it soon became evident to the Phaeacians that this stranger was determined to go home to his wife. Here is the farewell scene, as described directly by Homer, just before the long night of storytelling begins (8.457 sq.):

> Nausicaa, with the gods' loveliness on her, stood beside the pillar that supported the roof with its joinery, and gazed upon Odysseus with all her eyes and admired him, and spoke to him aloud and addressed him in

winged words, saying: "Goodbye, stranger, and think of me sometimes
when you are back at home, how I was the first you owed your life to."
Then resourceful Odysseus spoke in turn and answered her: "Nausicaa,
daughter of great-hearted Alcinous, even so may Zeus, high-thundering
husband of Hera, grant me to reach my house and see my day of homecoming. So even when I am there I will pray to you, as to a goddess, all
the days of my life. For, maiden, my life was your gift." He spoke, and
went to sit on a chair by the king Alcinous.

(Notice the invocation of Zeus in his capacity as the husband of Hera.)
Not long after that, the storytelling begins. Nothing more is said about
Nausicaa. Perhaps she was present throughout (her mother is there), but
Odysseus and she have permanently parted. Does not the relation between Odysseus and the eminently helpful Nausicaa, who is to be left
behind on this island, have in it intriguing echoes of the relation between
Theseus and the eminently helpful Ariadne, who had been useful to him
on one island and left by him on another? There were, I have mentioned,
many stories about just what might have happened between Theseus
and Ariadne. This indicates how complicated and difficult, as well as interesting and challenging, that encounter must have been. But whatever
version one accepts, all versions have Ariadne left on an island while
Theseus returns to his home and a glorious future.

Thus, it seems appropriate (although it is said with discretion, understandable in the circumstances) that Odysseus should place Ariadne
at the center of his central tale about his wanderings. He acknowledges
thereby how he too has "used" and abandoned a woman (perhaps two
women, Nausicaa and her mother, Arete) in order to preserve himself
and to advance his cause. He acknowledges thereby what Homer has
told the reader, that he had deliberated how best to approach and make
use of the maiden he encountered down at the water. (Nausicaa is in
some ways like Penelope: she, too, has been rejecting suitors; she too can
be said to have been awaiting Odysseus.) Should we not be reminded by
all this that Odysseus, more than any of the other heroes in either the
Iliad or the *Odyssey*, not only lives by his wits but does so, in large part,
by relying upon females, whether his mother, Circe, Calypso, Athena,
Nausicaa, Arete, or Penelope?

I have noticed that the only one of the marvelous adventures Odysseus reports which Homer himself substantially ratifies is the experience with the Cattle of the Sun. We can understand that episode to indicate the desires for food and drink that Odysseus' men had gratified to their doom. But Odysseus, too, has desires to overcome, and they are connected with women. This, in turn, can be seen as connected to a desire to know. He must overcome that kind of desire if he is to get home, to *the* woman in his life. If there is not *one* woman in one's life, are there none? (Need that *one* always be the same?) Such overcoming, for a greater good (even for a kind of self-fulfillment), necessitates the abandonment (however heartwrenching and even callous it may seem) of the Ariadnes of one's travels. Ariadne can take various forms: Circe and Calypso and, perhaps most poignantly, Nausicaa.

It is no accident, then, that Ariadne should be at the heart of the account Odysseus gives of the people he conjured up in Hades—for, we must recall, he did control not only who was allowed to talk to him down there but also whom he chose to recall in his account and when. (See, on the specialness of Nausicaa in the *Odyssey,* section iv of chapter 2 of this book. See, on *eros* and the desire to know, the addendum to part 1 of chapter 7 of this book. How much of this did Nausicaa notice?)

vi

The significance of the sequence of the other people Odysseus reports to have seen in Hades should be developed. Much that could once have been said about all this probably cannot be said now, since various of the figures conjured up by Odysseus have become obscure. But, I am confident, the details and how they are ordered would make sense. Concerning Odysseus' account of his trip to Hades, more remains to be said about Theseus and Perithoos.

Still another parallel should be noticed, one which reinforces my suggestion that Odysseus' Catalogue of Personages in Hades must have some principle of order. I refer to the parallel between this Catalogue of Personages in the *Odyssey* and the Catalogue of Ships in the second book of the *Iliad*. There, it will be recalled, is a list (a seemingly chaotic list) of twenty-nine contingents of Achaean (Greek) forces at Troy. In that list,

Odysseus' contingent is central, with the contingents of the fateful competitors Agamemnon and Achilles placed at equal distance on either side
from the prudent, mediating Odysseus. (In the *Odyssey* catalogue,
Agamemnon and Achilles are side by side: their deadly animosity, upon
which the *Iliad* so much depends, no longer seems to matter in Hades.
What matters is epitomized by the Theseus-Ariadne story.)

Just as there are twenty-nine contingents in the Catalogue of Ships in
the *Iliad* (with Odysseus central to that list), I have been encouraged to
discover that there are twenty-nine personages named by Odysseus as
encountered by him during his trip to Hades. (If one includes Persephone, the deity who shepherds the souls around Odysseus, or, if one
does not like to use Persephone, then one can notice that Anticleia, the
mother of Odysseus, emerges twice, once before and once after Tiresias.
However one works it, Ariadne is central, either alone or with Maira.)
This is a rather startling conformity of one catalogue to another, with
the prudent Odysseus who was central to the first catalogue being responsible for the shaping of the second.

I have no reliable suggestions as to why the number *twenty-nine* was
used. It may simply have been dictated by the reports, available to
Homer, about the various contingents that "had" to be acknowledged as
having been at Troy. Homer could have combined or split up contingents as suited his purposes. Still the *twenty-nine* figure means that there
are fourteen on either side of the central figure in the catalogue—or, put
another way, there is on either side of the central figure a pair of *sevens*.
And, as we know from various sources, seven has "always" been a number to be reckoned with.

But these are speculations for another occasion. (Speculation is invited upon noticing such things as the fact that *twenty-nine* is the ninth
prime number, with *nine* itself a number associated with poetry—disregarding *one* here, as the Greeks would, for this purpose. An intensification, or the essence, of poetry may be represented by *eighty-one*.) It
suffices to say at this point that these details do reinforce the impression,
which is otherwise available as well, that all this has been carefully
planned, whether one speaks of the *Iliad* or of the *Odyssey*. What I have
suggested about the Catalogue of Personages in Hades reinforces the
impression that that account, and indeed the account of all of the Great

Wanderings, are to be understood as "constructions" by the resourceful Odysseus. How neatly constructed is further suggested by the fact that the first person "encountered" by Odysseus in Hades is Elpenor, a comrade who had died (and whom Odysseus had not buried); the last person encountered by him is Heracles who, we are told, is not truly there but rather among the gods (only a copy, so to speak, of his soul is in Hades). Thus, neither the first nor the last personage encountered by Odysseus in Hades is fully (or truly) there.

But, it should also be noticed, the last personage (Heracles) is someone who is explicitly likened to Odysseus, in that he too had once gone down to Hades, while still alive, on a mission, and had returned to the land of the living. Odysseus knows where he stands in relation to his most celebrated predecessors—or, at least, where he would like to be seen.

vii

A further suggestion must be ventured. Does not all this point to the conclusion that the two great epics, the *Iliad* and the *Odyssey*, are the work of one poet? (Or alternatively that the *Odyssey* was by a later poet who really knew the *Iliad*, knew it so well that he can be regarded as virtually the same as its poet?) I return to this question, as I do to the Catalogue of Ships, in the epilogue of this book. (See, also, Anastaplo, *The Artist as Thinker*, p. 248.)

Still another, albeit a much more fanciful, suggestion can be ventured. One of the most important characters in the *Odyssey* (perhaps, in a sense, a character second only to Odysseus himself) is barely mentioned at all in the epic, thereby pointing up the remarkable skill and self-restraint of the poet, whoever he or she may be. This barely mentioned, yet vitally important, character—and one who does not appear at all—is, of course, Theseus, Ariadne's Theseus, whom I have described. At the center of the action of the epic (and even physically close to the center, toward the end of book 11) is Ariadne and all that she means for an understanding of Theseus and of the Theseus-like Odysseus.

All this points back to still another great work, something which can be called the *Theseid*. No such work has come down to us. But obviously there must have been a considerable corpus of Theseus, as well as Heracles, stories upon which many generations drew. And, it seems to me, there may well have been a great work on Theseus about which Homer knew. Chance can sometimes be decisive as to what survives and how. The *Theseid*, I suggest, does survive, if only in Homer's covert acknowledgment of his great predecessor in such places as the Catalogue of Personages in Hades. (See, on Socrates' covert acknowledgment, in Plato's *Apology*, of *his* Homeric predecessor for his own descent into Hades, Anastaplo, *Human Being and Citizen*, p. 20 f. See, on *Theseid*s and *Heracleid*s, Aristotle, *Poetics* 1451a20.)

Why should Theseus matter so much for the Odysseus story? Because, we can answer, he too knew how to use women; because he too had many adventures; because he too is heroic in both war and peace; because he too is connected with Athena (in his case, through the city of Athens). What Theseus "meant" can be seen in what classical (fifth-century) Athens did with him. Thus, it has been noticed, "Theseus, more than any other man or demi-god, had become the hero of classical Athens" (A. G. Ward, *The Quest for Theseus*, p. 143). Although Theseus is rarely alluded to in Homer, he assumed (at least for awhile) a greater stature than Odysseus in the fifth and subsequent centuries. His revival, especially in Athens beginning in the sixth century, may suggest that careful Athenian readers of Homer began to realize what the *Odyssey* had "said" about Theseus and why. During this same period—and certainly by the end of the fifth century—Odysseus had become somewhat more dubious. His resourcefulness came to appear as mere craftiness. This, as we shall soon see, has something to do with what Odysseus is interested in.

Odysseus' last encounter in Hades is, we have noticed, with Heracles, whose descent into Hades (while living) Odysseus has duplicated. Similarly, Theseus duplicated Heracles (or, perhaps, the other way around) in his adventures and in *his* descent into Hades while still alive. Thus, Odysseus has drawn upon both of them in what he has done—or at least in what he says he has done—in Hades.

If one sets aside the Heracles manifestation, the conclusions of the two parts of Odysseus' survey of personages encountered in Hades (the

first part devoted to women, the second part, to men)—these two conclusions are with people (men and women alike) whose unjust acts were
known to be punished. Was it important for Odysseus to remind the
Phaeacians of this, lest they take advantage of their helpless guest?

It is bold of Odysseus to invoke the claims of justice in circumstances
where his own conduct might be called into question. We have noticed
that he might be taken to resemble Theseus in some respects—a Theseus
on the verge of abandoning the Ariadne whom he has used to get what
he needs. But, he can be understood to add, he should be distinguished
from Theseus. Is not Odysseus' treatment of *his* Ariadne more humane?
Perhaps he liked women better than had Theseus, getting along with
them better and treating them with more consideration. Also, does he
not treat both his father and his son better than Theseus treated his? We
recall Aegeus' suicide and the fatal cursing of Hippolytus (to which I return in part 1 of chapter 6 of this book).

Theseus is not seen by Odysseus in Hades. Does Odysseus suggest
thereby that Theseus is not "real," that he is legendary, whereas Odysseus
is real? Can this even be taken as a Homeric challenge, somewhat
Odyssean in character, to his distinguished predecessor?

viii

I have suggested that the *Odyssey* points back to another great work, to
something that can be called the *Theseid*. But, as we now know, it also
points ahead in effect to still another great work, the *Republic* of Plato.
We have seen, in the prologue to this book, how Homer was read by
Plato. (I mention in passing that Plato, like Homer, seems to have drawn
upon the *Theseid*—in Plato's case, in what he says in the *Phaedo*. For,
Jacob Klein has argued, there can be seen, in Plato's *Phaedo*, Socrates'
confrontation with the fear of death, which is like Theseus' confrontation with the Minotaur in the Labyrinth [*Lectures and Essays*, p. 375 f.])

Homer was not called "the educator of Greece" for nothing. Of
course, we have also seen, Socrates does talk about suppressing Homer's
bad influence. But Homer may be something of a straw man in that context. Consider, again, what happens at the end of the *Republic*, where (as

related by Er) the long-dead souls return to choose their new lives. Odysseus is presented as the one man who chooses wisely: he seems to choose a private life, a life which (if not that of a philosopher) is at least informed by philosophic inclinations. Is this because of what he had learned the last time around? No doubt that has influenced Odysseus. But, I suspect, this also reflects a Socratic reading of the *Odyssey* which recognizes the predominantly private character of much of what Odysseus does.

This can be seen also in the Great Wanderings. Unlike Heracles and Theseus, Odysseus does not set out to liberate Greece from its monsters and other terrors. Rather, Odysseus looks out primarily for himself, wanting to get home with his life, some booty, and considerable glory (and, in a few instances, as with the Cyclops, with the satisfaction of having secured his revenge, a known revenge). Generally, he does not aim to leave the places he visits better for his having been there. (Consider Socrates' suggestion, in book 6 of the *Republic*, that the philosopher seeks shelter beside a wall.) He is a benefactor of men, if he is, more by the tales he has left behind him than by what he has done.

Socrates and thereafter Plato seem to have recognized this about Odysseus—and so he can be depicted in the last book of the *Republic* as seeking a secure private life. Is this all the more reason—if he is essentially this kind of man—that he should have been portrayed by Homer as someone who could indicate both his kinship with Theseus and yet his profound difference from him?

ix

We are now in a position to answer the scholarly inquiry with which we opened part 2 of this chapter, whether the reference to Theseus and his intimate companion Perithoos belongs in the *Odyssey* (11.631). I suggest, on the basis of what I have said here, that that line was put in either by Homer himself or by someone who understood the poem thoroughly and realized what Homer was drawing upon and indicating. Such a successor to Homer becomes, at least to this extent, a second Homer, whatever his or her name. (I hardly think his name was Pisistratus.)

The reference, at the end of the Catalogue of Personages in Hades, to Perithoos should be noticed, if only briefly. Not only was he the traditional companion of Theseus, but he was the one on whose behalf and with whom Theseus had come down to Hades when *he* came. Perithoos had helped Theseus kidnap the child Helen, and now Theseus was to help Perithoos kidnap out of Hades the goddess Persephone. But they were thwarted in this attempt—that is, they failed in Hades whereas Odysseus succeeded in his primary mission (to secure a prophecy from Tiresias). (Heracles had also succeeded in his primary mission, which has been variously described.) Not only did Theseus fail, but he lost Perithoos in Hades. In this way, too, Odysseus can consider himself superior to Theseus. Even so, he is fearful at the thought of Persephone coming against him.

In a way, Odysseus (who is in his adventures without any intimate companion) is Theseus and Perithoos combined. It is sensible for him to be wary of the fate in Hades attributed to both of them. Of course, this leads us to wonder what it was that Odysseus was *truly* after in Hades. He learns quite early in his "visit" what he had come to learn from Tiresias. Does he not stay on to survey the population and thereby to become master of it, if only in how he organizes thereafter what he sees and hears? Perhaps he senses that Persephone would stand only so much of such usurpation of her rule (even if only in speech?) from a mere mortal. Odysseus always knew when the odds had become too great against him: that is, he (unlike, say, Icarus, who flew too near the sun) could sense when he had gotten out of a situation all that could be gotten without paying an exorbitant price.

This has been a reading of the *Odyssey* which regards as instructive the place of Athens in the story. This seems, at the least, fitting, inasmuch as Athens *was* evidently largely responsible for saving the texts of both the *Iliad* and the *Odyssey*. It was Pisistratus, we recall, who is said to have ordered the oral texts reduced to writing.

This has been an Athenian, or philosophic, reading of the *Odyssey* in still another respect. It is Athenian, that is, to think about what such stories mean, whether "authentic" or "false." Does not Odysseus portray himself as he does ultimately for the sake of those who truly think about what is and is not said? Who, if anyone among the Phaeacians, suspected who their exciting visitor was before he identified himself directly? And how did that affect what happened on that occasion?

In any event, it should be evident that the *Odyssey* is a book which it is profitable to read with the greatest care. It is appropriately "Athenian" to notice further, as I close this chapter on Homer, that many intriguing questions remain about the *Iliad* as well as the *Odyssey*, any one of which (even about the genuineness of a single line) can open up for us unimagined vistas, vistas that even "the plain man" may on occasion enjoy contemplating.

II. Sappho. On the *Poems*

What we cannot speak about we must pass over in silence.
—Ludwig Wittgenstein

i

The words I begin are of air, but yet gratifying. [#1A]

THIS LINE, WHICH HAPPENS to have been preserved for us in an Attic vase-picture of about 430 B.C., is said to have been part of the poem that stood first in Sappho's own collection of her poems. We can detect here both the vulnerability and the appeal of lyric poetry, if not of all poetry. The appeal does tend to be immediate, perhaps without regard to costs, certainly without regard to how enduring either the poem or the sentiments it presents are likely to be. The vase-picture depicts Sappho holding a book entitled *Winged Words*. (See *Lyra Graeca*, 1:181.)

A useful introduction for our purposes to the life and work of Sappho

---

Citations to the lines of Sappho (including those lines found at the head of each section in this chapter) will be to the numbers assigned to poems and fragments in the Loeb Classical Library edition of *Lyra Graeca*. The translations I use, sometimes adapted to my context, are taken either from the *Lyra Graeca* collection or from the Groden collection in the Library of Liberal Arts edition.

The epigraph is taken from Ludwig Wittgenstein, *Tractatus Logico-Philosophicus* (London: Routledge & Kegan Paul Ltd., 1974), p. 4 (concluding sentence of the book).

is provided by an *Encyclopedia Britannica* article about her. Many of the points found in the long passage reproduced here (in three parts) from that article bear upon my discussion. First, there is her biography (Denys L. Page):

> SAPPHO (spelled *Psappho* by herself) (fl. c. 610–c.580 B.C.), the celebrated Greek lyric poetess, was a native of the island Lesbos, off the northwest coast of Asia Minor. Her father's name is most commonly given as Scamandronymus; her mother's name was Cleis. She had three brothers, Charaxus, Larichus, and Erigyus; she is said to have been married to Cercolas, a wealthy man from the island Andros; she had at least one child, a daughter, named Cleis. There is just sufficient evidence to prove that her family belonged to the upper class of society.
>
> Her poetry is composed in the local Lesbian-Aeolic dialect. She had at her disposal a variety of metres (see *Sapphics*), some of which may well be of her own invention. Except for the epithalamiums (which seem to have formed a small and relatively insignificant part of her work) her poems are almost invariably concerned with personal themes. Cult-song and mythological narrative are seldom if at all to be found, and there are only a couple of apparent allusions to the political disturbances of the time which are so frequently reflected in the verse of her contemporary Alcaeus. The tradition that she herself was banished and went to Sicily is likely to be true, but is not confirmed by the extant fragments of her poetry. Alcaeus himself appears to be the person addressed in a stanza which rejects indelicate advances. Her brother Charaxus was the subject of several poems: Sappho prays for him a safe return from Egypt, and release from entanglement with the notorious courtesan Doricha (whom Herodotus calls Rhodopis); in other poems, according to Herodotus, she "taunted him considerably." These, however, are exceptional examples: most of Sappho's poems are concerned with her friendships and enmities with other women.

Then there is an appraisal of her poetry (emphasis added):

> It was the fashion in Lesbos at this period for women of good family to assemble in informal societies and spend their days in idle, graceful pleasures, especially the composition and recitation of poetry. Sappho, the leading spirit of one of these associations, attracted a number of admirers, some from distant places abroad. The principal themes of her poetry are the loves and jealousies and hates which flourished in that sultry at-

mosphere. . . . Ancient writers over a period of time, having a large volume of her work in front of them, allege that Sappho was addicted to Lesbianism. It must be admitted that her poetry shows that she entertained emotions stronger than mere friendship toward other women, but in the extant remains there is not a word to connect herself or her companions with homosexual practices and only half a word—but that decisive enough—to show her awareness of their existence.

The beauty of her writing has been greatly, and justly, admired in all ages. Her vocabulary, like her dialect, is for the most part vernacular, not literary. Her phrasing is concise, direct, and picturesque, sparing of the customary poetic artifices and embellishments, owing little to *that Homeric tradition which is elsewhere almost all-pervasive*. Definite pains are taken to achieve an effect of simplicity and spontaneity. She has the power of standing aloof and critically judging her own ecstasies and pains; but her emotions lose nothing of their force by being recollected in comparative tranquillity. Her simple, candid, and luminous language compels the listener not only to understand but also to participate—to recognize his potential in her actual experience. It is doubtful whether any other poet in the history of Greek literature, except Archilochus and Alcaeus, enters into so close a personal relation with the reader or listener. It is probable that, if the works of Anacreon and Ibycus were extant in much greater volume, it would be found that Sappho influenced them strongly; the only other Greek poet who owes much to her is Theocritus.

Finally, there is her "publishing" history:

It is not known how her poems were published and circulated in her own lifetime and for the following three or four centuries. In the era of Alexandrian scholarship (especially the 3rd and 2nd centuries B.C.), what remained of her work was collected and republished in a standard edition, comprising nine books of lyrical verse and one of elegiac (the latter, so far as the extant specimens permit a judgment, supposititious). The principles of book-division appear to have been purely metrical for the first eight; this is certain enough for the first four and the eighth, probable for the fifth; little or nothing is known of the sixth and seventh. The ninth book was arranged according to subject matter, comprising epithalamian poems, designed for recitation by choirs at weddings, in a variety of metres. The known lengths of books are 1,320 lines for book i, and about 130 (the last digit uncertain) for book viii.

This edition did not survive the early Middle Ages. By the 8th or 9th century A.D. Sappho was represented only by quotations in other authors, comprising one complete poem of 28 lines, the first 16 lines of another, and about 110 short one-line to four-line fragments. Since 1898, the fragments have been greatly increased by papyrus finds, though no complete and unmutilated poem has been recovered, and nothing equal in quality to the two longer pieces preserved in quotations.

The poetess was referred to, again and again in antiquity, as "Sappho the beautiful" (Σαπφώ ἡ καλὴ). (E.g., *Lyra Graeca*, 1:143.) Thus, Maximus commented, "For so Socrates rejoices to call her because of the beauty of her lyric verse, although she was small and dark" (1:161). Antipater can refer to her as "the honey-voiced Sappho" (1:165).

How "winged," and hence fugitive, Sappho's words have been is suggested by their fate. We possess about 600 lines or fragments of lines, which are estimated to be about one-twentieth of her work. Many of these lines have had to be reconstructed, which means that much of what may be seen on the printed page today is highly conjectural. My own count finds that less than 3,000 words survive in lines that are clearly hers, which are about as many words as may be found in two-thirds of the first book of the *Iliad* (with its twenty-four books).

Yet Homer, whose much older work was for centuries evidently transmitted orally, comes down to us in quite good shape. Much is made by scholars of the deliberate destruction by prudish Christians of Sappho's poems. But it is not Sappho alone who has suffered fierce depredations. Of all the lyric poets of Greek antiquity, "we have manuscripts proper only for Theognis and Pindar, and for Pindar all but the victory odes are fragmentary. For other poets, we have only a collection of quotations from subsequent authors and scraps of papyrus from Alexandrian Egypt —mostly fragments, but sometimes poems quoted or preserved in full" (Lattimore, *Greek Lyrics*, p. v). Besides, it has been suggested, Sappho's books disappeared from general knowledge before the Christian era.

We must wonder, therefore, whether there is something intrinsically vulnerable about lyric poetry, especially poetry "concerned with personal themes." After all, there are many dubious features (from the point of view of devout Christians) in the *Iliad* and *Odyssey* as well. Are the epics that preceded Sappho and her fellow lyricists, and the tragedies that followed the great lyricists, much more concerned with public affairs—and hence much more likely than Sapphic lyrics to be protected as public property? (On the other hand, it should be noticed, Aristotle's *Athenian Constitution* seems to have come down to us through only one copy.)

ii

> But I have received true prosperity from the golden Muses,
> and when I die I shall not be forgot. [#11]

How good was (or, should we not say, is) Sappho? It was said of her "flowers" in late antiquity, that they were "few, but roses" (1:165).

In one of her poems this small woman describes herself, not without irony, as "towering . . . over the poets of other lands" (#148). Comparisons to Homer are not inappropriate. Thus, in antiquity, it could be said that Sappho's songs "surpassed the songs of women even as Homer's the songs of men" (1:165). She was known as "the poetess," just as Homer was known as "the poet" (David M. Robinson, *Sappho and Her Influence,* p. 5).

There is more from antiquity *about* Sappho than *by* her. The use of her supposed image on coins, vases and busts is extensive. Much of what comes down to us about her is of a very high order. Thus, Aristotle refers to her three times, evidently with approbation. He seems to quote without reservation "a judgment that placed her in the same rank as Homer and Archilochus" (John A. Symonds, *Studies of the Greek Poets,* 1:293). Aristotle is said to have been the first we know definitely to quote her verses. She is several times referred to by Plutarch. (See *Lyra Graeca,* 1:167–69; Robinson, p. 125.) A reference to her as the Tenth Muse is attributed to Plato (as well as to others). (See *Lyra Graeca,* 1:163, 165, 167. See, also, 1:147, 167.) Consider, also, how she is spoken of in a Platonic dialogue (*Phaedrus* 235B–C):

> *Socrates:* I cannot go so far with you as that. There are wise ancients, both men and women, whose sayings or writings will refute me if I allow you to persuade me of it.
>
> *Phaedrus:* Who may these be? And where have they given you better information in this matter?

Socrates: I cannot say off-hand; but I have certainly got it from one of them, from the beautiful Sappho perhaps, or from the wise Anacreon, or some writer of history.

Solon, the great Athenian leader, could be said to have expressed the wish (not long after Sappho composed her poems) to learn a certain song of hers and then to die (1:141). At the other end (so to speak) of antiquity, there is the Emperor Julian, who drew upon her with approval (1:143). Then there is Strabo's praise of her as a wonder (Θαυμαστόν τι χρῆμα) (1:143). (See, on Julian, Anastaplo, "Rome, Piety, and Law," p. 68.)

In modern times, also, she has been highly praised. Swinburne called her "the very greatest poet that ever lived" (Robinson, p. 11). Certainly, it is said, she is "incomparably the greatest poetess the world has ever seen" (ibid., p. 13). She is spoken of as possessing a "banked and inward-burning fire" (ibid., p. 10). Not that reservations have not been expressed, which draw on what Lesbos came to mean (Henry T. Wharton, *Sappho*, pp. 12–13):

> Nowhere in any age of Greek history, or in any part of Hellas, did the love of physical beauty, the sensibility to radiant scenes of nature, the consuming fervour of personal feeling, assume such grand proportions and receive so illustrious an expression as they did in Lesbos. At first this passion blossomed into the most exquisite lyrical poetry that the world has known: this was the flower-time of the Aeolians, their brief and brilliant spring. But the fruit it bore was bitter and rotten. Lesbos became a by-word for corruption. The passions which for a moment had flamed into the gorgeousness of Art, burnt their envelope of words and images, remained a mere furnace of sensuality, from which no expression of the divine in human life could be expected.

But even this critic could refer to Sappho as "the greatest lyrist of all time" (ibid., p. vi). Consider, also, the following assessment which catches as well the innocence which the highminded can be capable of even in their sensuality (J. W. Mackail, *Lectures on Greek Poetry*, pp. 111–12):

> [H]ere it is that Sappho reaches the absolute summit of the lyric. ἈϊπάρθΕνος ἔσομαι, "Maiden shall I be for ever": just these two words in their liquid beauty, their simple purity, might be the final epitaph on a poetry which with all its swift ardour and flame-like passion is at its inmost heart grave, delicate, almost virginally austere.

Various modern critics have endorsed the assessment made (in the nineteenth century) by a reader who was limited (as we still are) to fragments of her work: "Of all the poets of the world, of all the illustrious artists of all literatures, Sappho is the one whose every word has a peculiar and unmistakable perfume, a seal of absolute perfection and inimitable grace" (Symonds, 1:310). And so it can plausibly be said, "The world has suffered no greater literary loss than the loss of Sappho's poems" (ibid., 1:309). The music of her fragments, it is also said, "is inextricably interwoven with the sadness of a lost past" (Groden, p. xi). But enough does remain, it is evident from the responses of modern readers, to confirm the ancient assessment of Sappho as "the wonder of lyric poetry" (*Lyra Graeca*, 1:163).

We are reminded by all this of what Willa Cather says in likening something to "an old song, incomplete but uncorrupted" (*On Writing*, p. 15).

Certainly, Sappho's poems invite study, not least for her wisdom.

iii

> Evening Star, you bring back
> all that was scattered
> in the shimmer of Dawn.
> You bring the sheep, you bring the goat, and
> you bring her child to the mother. [#149]

How is lyric poetry—and especially Sappho's poetry—different from other poetry, and especially from the grand (particularly Homeric) epics that preceded it?

Two principal ways in which lyric poetry differs can be usefully commented upon here. I refer to differences with respect to forms and differences with respect to subjects. Not that forms and subjects are unrelated. Thus, it has been reported: "Once the fetters of the old [epic] tradition were broken [by Archilochus], the lyric rapidly found its proper forms; it created for itself a versification more melodious, more delicate, more intricate and subtle in its harmonies" (Mackail, p. 87). An earlier critic suggested, at greater length, what is distinctive to the forms that the Greek poet had available (Symonds, 1:289–90):

From the very first commencement of their literature, the Greeks thus determined separate styles and established critical canons, which, though empirically and spontaneously formed, were based on real relations between the moral and aesthetical sides of art, between feeling and expression, substance and form. The hexameter was consecrated to epical narrative; the elegy was confined to songs of lament or meditation; the iambic assumed a satiric character. To have written a narrative in iambics or a satire in hexameters would have been odious to Greek taste; the stately march of the dactylic metre seemed unfit for snarling and invective; the quick flight of the iambic did not carry weight enough or volume to sustain a lengthy narrative. In the same way the infinite divisions of lyrical poetry had all their own peculiar properties. How could a poet have bewailed his loves or losses in the stately structure of the Pindaric ode? Conversely, a hymn to Phoebus required more sonorousness and elaboration than the recurring stanzas of the Sapphic or Alcaic offered. It was the business, therefore, of the Greek poet, after duly considering his subject, to select the special form of poetry consecrated by long usage for his particular purpose; to conform his language to some species of music inseparable from that style, and then, within the prescribed limits both of metre and melody, to exercise his imagination as freely as he could, and to produce novelty. . . . The discrimination shown by the Greeks in all the technicalities of art remained in full vigor till the decline of their literature. It was not until the Alexandrian age that they began to confound these delicate distinctions, and to use the idyllic hexameter for all subjects, whether narrative, descriptive, elegiac, encomiastic, hymeneal.

The technical features of lyric poetry have been further commented upon by various critics.

It is said of Sappho's poetry that it is classed as "melic" or true lyric (Groden, p. xiv):

Such poetry is made up of lines that vary in length but comprise uniformly patterned stanzas . . . ; it was composed to be sung to the accompaniment of instruments and dancing. Melic poetry can exist either as monody, that is, solo lyric, or as choral lyric, as found in some of Sappho's epithalamia, or wedding songs.

It is also observed here that the word μέλος originally meant *member* (or *part*) (ibid., p. xiv). But one can be reminded by this word of *honey* as well. Thus, there is a line—by Alcaeus or by an imitator of Sappho, if not by Sappho herself: "From Sappho pressed is this honey [μέλι] that I bring you" (*Lyra Graeca*, 3:439).

Lyric is related to the lyre, to the accompaniment of which lyrics could be sung (ibid., 3:607–8):

> The instrument of Melic song was originally the lyre. The word μέλος as applied to this sort of song does not occur before Herodotus. In Alcman, who flourished in the latter half of the 7th Century, we find the phrase ἔπη δέ γα καὶ μέλος, meaning "lines and a *tune*." So also Echembrotus speaks of himself early in the 6th Century as μέλε' ἠδ᾽ Ἐλέγους Ἕλλησιν ἄ∈ιδων. And this seemingly older meaning survived along with the other in the 5th and 4th Centuries. [Note 1: μέλος is the "tune" as opposed to the "accompaniment" in Aristotle, *Problems* 9.12.918a.37, 49.922b.28.] It is not unreasonable, then, to suggest that the word μέλος was applied to this sort of poetry at a time when the three others, Epic, Elegiac, and Iambic, had already become mere spoken verse. It meant, in short, *tune-poetry.*

This development, at least as seen in Sappho's poetry, has been summed up thus: "The diction of the poetry is one of its most striking characteristics. It is simple, almost conversational, and repetitive" (Groden, p. xv).

There is achieved in a fine lyric poem a moment of heightened intensity. Even fragments can be indicative of something vital, so much so as to make word-counts misleading. A mood or experience is evoked in language that is peculiarly affecting: something familiar, even ordinary, is touched in us. Does the gifted poet resort to this form because of a belief (divination?) that the world *is* such that the truth about it can best be grasped in this fashion? In any event, this form (it seems to be believed) reflects something about the way things are, how they appear or come into view. Things are best seen, it seems to be said, with the aid of penetrating glimpses or of caressing recollections, not by recourse to the extended descriptions of epics or the shattering arguments of tragedy.

Language is exploited for effect: there is considerable attention to detail. Lyric can never "coast" as epic sometimes seems to. Demetrius noticed that "the pattern of [Sappho's] poetry is inwoven with every beautiful word there is, some of them made by herself" (*Lyra Graeca*, 1:297). Even syllables can matter a great deal: "Sappho makes three syllables of ᾠὸν [egg]"; or she can, to achieve her effect, separate the vowels of the diphthong ει in Μήδ∈ια (Medea) (ibid., 1:227, 305).

A skillful, however simple, use of language may be seen in the Evening Star poem (or, more likely, poem fragment) quoted at the head of this section. It was noticed in antiquity that its "charm" [χάρις] lies in the repetition of the word *bring* [φέρεις] (ibid., 1:287). Sappho's skill inspires skill on the part of her interpreters, as may be seen in a recent comment on this poem by the translator whose version I have used here (the translator works from a two-line Greek text, the first line of which ends with "Dawn"; Groden, p. xx):

> This first line describes the primary gesture, the scattering of all things into the day by the dawn; the second represents the contrapuntal, answering gesture, the gathering back of these things by the evening star. The first line is a masterpiece of effective use of word order. The two forces, Hesperus and Eos, are set against each other as the first and last words. The line breaks into halves, with one verb, "bring," and its subject, the Evening Star, in the first half, and another verb, "scatter," with Dawn, in the second. This division is saved from being overly obvious by the inclusion of the word φαίνολις ("shimmer"), a word which technically modifies Αὔως ("Dawn"), yet can suggest at the same time the light of the star. In the second line, which describes and almost acts out the gathering back, although Sappho does not specifically mention a shepherd, she creates an image of the Evening Star as one by naming the creatures he gathers, a sheep and a goat; and here the repetition of the word φέρεις suggests the physical action of gathering things up, which is usually performed rhythmically, like the repeated gesture of pulling in a length of rope, or stooping and reaching to pick up scattered objects. Although this obviously was not the end of the original poem, the climactic word order of this second line makes the fragment seem somehow complete. After the image of the Evening Star as a shepherd has been established, Sappho again repeats that "gesture-word," φέρεις, and at the end of the line sets the word that is the essential subject of the poem: the child who must be shepherded home to her mother.

Sappho's language itself reflects a reassuring harmony in things both cosmic and mundane. It is as if the star is decisive in continually moving animals and children to their proper places. A regularity in things is suggested, a cyclical sequence of scattering and ingatherings (or disintegrations and restorations)—and all this in a mere sixteen words (in the Greek text). A world in which these things happen with reliability—in which there is a superintending order of this kind—has much to be said for it, as does the poetry which can capture it in a "sweet hymn" (*Lyra Graeca*, 1:177). Or, as a critic observed seventy years ago, "The beauty of [this] fragment needs no emphasizing" (Edwin N. Cox, *The Poems of Sappho*, p. 114).

What does need emphasizing, perhaps, is that such fragments, insofar as they can catch the light of the whole, are somehow much more than fragments. We should be able to divine from them why Sappho could say, "Now I shall sing these delightful songs, beautifully, to my [comrade] girls" (#12).

iv

There are those who say
an array of horsemen,
and others of marching men,
and others of ships, is
the most beautiful thing on the dark earth.

But I say it is whatever one loves.

It is very easy
to show this to all:
for Helen,
by far the most beautiful of mortals,
left her husband
and sailed to Troy
giving no thought at all
to her child nor dear parents,
but was led . . .
[by her love alone.]

Now, far away, Anactoria
comes to my mind.
For I would rather watch her
moving in her lovely way,
and see her face, flashing radiant,
than all the force of Lydian chariots,
and their infantry in full display of arms. [#38]

It has not been possible to speak of the forms of lyric poetry without touching as well upon its subjects. Even so, I can turn now to a more direct discussion of subjects.

One way of putting those subjects is as Demetrius did, "The forms, then, of literary charm are many and various. But charm may also reside in the subject. For instance, it may be the Gardens of the Nymphs, a wedding, a love-affair, in short the entire subject-matter of the poetry of Sappho" (*Lyra Graeca*, 1:173). There is in her poetry, it seems, no extended plot or detailed story. Rather, a sensation, a memory, a mood is conjured up, and in such a way as to make one believe that "every hour of the day comes to Sappho with a fresh surprise" (Robinson, p. 62, quoting Thomas Davidson).

Particularly influential has been her treatment of the sensations of love. Thus Plutarch could say (*Lyra Graeca*, 1:169):

> Sappho fully deserves to be counted among the Muses. The Romans tell how Cacus son of Hephaestus sent forth fire and flames from his mouth; and Sappho utters words really mingled with fire and gives vent through her song to the heat that consumes her heart, thus "healing," in the words of Philoxenus, "the pain of love with the melodies of the Muse."

Is such healing—an exercise in self-awareness and clarification with respect to the passions that most men and women routinely experience—is healing (a species of catharsis?) as much the proper purpose of her love-poetry as the catharsis of pity and fear is of the tragedy Aristotle discusses?

This is not to suggest that love had not been dealt with at all prior to the lyric poets. One has only to recall various passages in the *Odyssey*, for example. But consider how one such passage (discussed in part 2 of chapter 1 of this book), in which the attractive Nausicaa appears, could be commented upon by a critic early in this century (Mackail, p. 35):

> One figure there is in the *Odyssey* never equalled except by the creator of Miranda and Rosalind, the girl-princess of Phaeacia. The poet sketched her in, largely, firmly, beautifully, and then stayed his hand. Perhaps no reader—certainly no modern reader—has not felt a pang of regret when she slips out of the story and out of our sight. Whether the poet felt that he had gone too far, that he had been carried away by the delight of creation beyond what the scheme of the *Odyssey* would bear; whether he

was himself unconscious of the exquisite beauty of what he had created; whether, here as elsewhere, the hard, unromantic Greek temper refused to let the picture be completed, are questions which at once invite and baffle discussion: but Nausicaa disappears, and the sunlight seems to go out with her.

The sunlight radiated by Nausicaa, or by one's memory of her, would have flooded a poem by Sappho on this episode. Such a subject, or rather the mode of treating it, would be distinctive to lyric, however it may have been anticipated by epic or thereafter made use of in tragedy. This mode is diluted (perhaps, sometimes, for the best) in the larger works, whether epic or tragic.

When one works with the proper subject of lyric, it can be added, it is elegance [κομψὸν] (a certain beauty), not grandeur [σέμνου], that one aims at. (See *Lyra Graeca,* 1:179.) Compare the criticism made (by Quintilian) of Alcaeus, that although "his style is concise, lofty, exact, and very like Homer's, . . . he stoops to jesting and love-making though better fitted for higher themes" (ibid., 1:173).

Vital to the concern with love seen in Sappho is an affirmation of life, not an endorsement of virtue or of duty. (I anticipate a question to which I will return, whether a truly disciplined account of love, as is seen in the best poetry, is not already a curbing, or mastery, of love. Is this argued in Plato's *Symposium*?) Related to Sappho's affirmation of life— her savoring of the sweetness of existence—is a turning away from death. Thus, it can be said by a lyric poet, perhaps by Sappho herself, "Alone [of gods, Hades] receives no share of sweet hope" (ibid., 3:439). Love, on the other hand, offers much sweet hope. Indeed, to love *is* to hope, to hope with fervency and perhaps without limit. Is not such hope in need of self-awareness and clarification if what is good in it is to be attained, if men and women are not to be ruined by love (either by indulging in it too much or by being disappointed unduly by it)?

One obvious difference between the subjects of lyric poetry and those of the epics which preceded it may be seen in the Anactoria "letter" quoted at the head of this section. To the lyric poet "the most beautiful thing on the dark earth" is not, it would seem, what a Homer might consider beautiful (or interesting) to dwell upon. Rather, "it is whatever one loves."

But, it should at once be added, the things said about love in Sappho's poems are not the thoughtlessly sentimental things we have become used to at a time when contemporary popular songs work in large part from the proposition that love is *the* solution for all the world's ills. The power of love is evident from the Anactoria letter. But consider what is said about love in other poems as well: it always appears as something special. Thus, a bridegroom can be reassured of something quite unlikely, that "never . . . was there another maiden such as this" (#163). One can be quite moved by one's love: "As for me, love has shaken my heart as a down-rushing whirlwind that falls upon the oaks" (#54). Love can be spoken of by Sappho as Homer speaks of death: "Love the looser of limbs stirs me, that creature irresistible, bitter-sweet . . ." (#81). Aphrodite is understood to be "wile-weaving" (#134). She is also understood to be incapacitating (#135):

> Sweet mother,
> I cannot, I swear, do my weaving!
> I am broken in my desire for the boy,
> by the tender, supple Aphrodite.

Another way of indicating the difference in subjects between lyric poets and the other poets is evident in the following illustration. (This time, the contrast with tragedy is shown.) An ancient critic noted that Aeschylus "says clearly that our object in putting wreaths on our heads is to do honour to Prometheus by a sort of requital of his bonds" (*Lyra Graeca*, 1:265). This is a grander, if not grimmer, view of things than that proposed by Sappho, for "she urges the makers of the sacrifice to wreathe their heads on the plea that that which is the more adorned with flowers is the more pleasing to the gods" (ibid., p. 267; #117).

Which is the sounder opinion? Perhaps this is also to ask which gods are the decisive ones. The emphasis upon love in the poems of Sappho may be seen in her repeated recourse to Aphrodite. She probably speaks of Aphrodite more often than she does of all the other divinities combined. Certainly, no other proper name is used so often. It is Aphrodite who matters most, not the Apollo or the Zeus or the Hera of the *Iliad*, not the Poseidon or the Athena of the *Odyssey*. Hera does figure in Sappho's poems, as the patroness of marriage (e.g., #84). But we gather that even marriage is subordinated to what love offers.

v

Eternal Aphrodite, rainbow-throned,
you cunning, wily child of Zeus, I beg you,
do not break me, Lady,
with the pains and raging ills of love.
But come to me, if ever in the past
you heard my far-off cries
and heeding, came,
leaving the golden home of Zeus
in your bridled chariot.
Beautiful swift sparrows bore you,
eddying through the mid-air, their wings a-whirr,
from heaven to the dark earth,
and there they were. And you, blessed Lady,
smiling your immortal smile,
asked me what ailed me now,
and why I called again,
and what my mad heart most craved:

"Whom, Sappho,
shall I lead to be your love
this time?
Who wrongs you now?
Even if she flees you, soon she'll chase,
and if she scorns your gifts, why, she will offer hers.
And if she does not love you,
soon she'll love, although she does not want to."

Now come to me once again, and free me
from these aching sorrows. Do for my heart
what it desires, and be yourself my help and ally. [#1]

I have suggested that Sappho does more than merely celebrate love. She examines it, recognizing various features (and even limitations) of it. Yet she is willing to appear as the servitor of Aphrodite (#75). Love is longed for by Sappho's women, just as Homer's men long for battle, for killing and for glory (#86).

We, too, should examine love for its significance in lyric poetry (of which Sappho's may be the highest expression). To make much of love is to make much of the personal. One consequence is that it becomes difficult in Sappho's poems, made even more difficult for us by their fragmentary character, to distinguish Sappho from her narrators. Thus, her own name appears in several of her poems (as in the ode to Aphrodite just reproduced here), whereas Homer's name appears nowhere in the *Iliad* or the *Odyssey,* or even in what are said to be his hymns.

The development toward a more personal poetry may be traced through the following quotations from modern critics. First, there is an indication of what preceded lyric poetry (Mackail, pp. 97–98):

> Art could become unrestrainedly personal [among the lyric poets]: for the artist wrote for himself and his own circle. Where an aristocracy make their own poetry, instead of having it made for them by professional poets, the Homeric minstrels or mediaeval jongleurs, they have no temptation to write except about what really interests them. The themes of the epic cycle, the κλέα ανδρῶυ [achievements of men], were what was conventionally supposed to interest them; the professional minstrel, bound alike by his social position and by the inherited tradition of his craft, kept within this limit, or did not venture far beyond it. That kind of poetry was outworn. In the personal note of the lyric, poetry found a new life. Hence the lyric, until in its turn it becomes patterned and conventional, has no defined scope of matter or treatment. Its free drift halts not particularly. Love or adventure or hunger, the beauty of nature, political antagonisms, whatever the lyric poet feels acutely, kindle in him and issue in a lyric note.

Then there is an indication of what happened generally in the Seventh Century (*Lyra Graeca,* 3:630, 632):

> [T]he whole Greek view of life had become more individualistic, more self-conscious, more analytic. Poets now sang more about their own feelings, and addressed themselves to the emotions of individuals as well as to those of collective audiences. . . . [Of Sappho and Alcaeus] more than of any ancient singer it is true to say that we find ourselves dealing with poets rather than poems, with persons rather than books. The curve of individualism reaches its peak in the self-revelations of Sappho.

Of Sappho herself we have this further assessment (Groden, pp. xiii–xiv):

Her poems are personal to an extent that is almost unparalleled in ancient literature. It is not merely a matter of her not being a "metaphysical" or "political" poet. Although she demonstrates a great understanding of human nature, she does not seem to be concerned with extending her observations on the immediate situation to a more general level. . . . In these fragments Sappho appears to wish only to grasp and display the reality of her world, to focus her vision on the minute details of her life and emotions. . . . One detects here the pressure of an immense energy concentrated on the achievement of an accurate expression of the poet's self . . .

That "the poet's self" in this case happens to be female is not, it seems to me, accidental. Is not to make much of love and of Aphrodite, as well as of the personal, to incline toward female interests? Does not the Anactoria letter (set forth at the head of my last section) suggest that women more than men are apt to be deeply, and decisively, moved by love? Sappho's circle seems united by a recollection of the beautiful things they have experienced together—the flowers, the precious unguents, the festivals, the music, their caring for one another. The Aphrodite who is made so much of *is* distinctively feminine (unlike Athena, or even Hera, who can exhibit masculine traits in the ways they conduct themselves). (See Bruno Snell, *Poetry and Society,* p. 44 f.)

Aphrodite, who is seen as the source of many good things, is golden (e.g., #157). Hera, whose throne can be golden in the *Iliad,* is herself silver for Sappho. (See Homer, *Iliad* 1.611; Sappho, #197.) The many references to gold in Sappho's poems have been noticed: "She ranks with Pindar in her special devotion to gold, not for its value but for its fine amber lustre and its permanency" (Robinson, pp. 75–76). The attraction of gold is significant also for what it confirms about the importance of appearance for love (and for art generally), as well as for the fame which Pindar made so much of. Consider Sappho's famous poem, which opens with the word φαίυϵται (appears) (#2):

> He appears to me an equal to the gods,
> the man who, with his face toward yours,
> sits close and listens to the whispers of
> your sweet voice and enticing laugh.
> To watch has made my heart a pounding hammer in my breast.
> For as I look at you, if only for an instant,

my voice no longer comes to me.
My silent tongue is broken,
and a quick and subtle flame
runs up beneath my skin.
I lose my sense of sight, hear only drumming in my ears.
I drip cold sweat,
and a trembling chases all through me.
I am greener than the pale grass
and it seems to me that I am close to death.

Still, I must endure all this

One can be captivated, and deeply moved, by the appearance of one's beloved, an appearance evident to one's ears and eyes, and then to one's heart, tongue and skin. That is, the effect of the beloved upon one can be comprehensive (some would say, devastating).

Catullus, when he came to make a Latin version of this poem, takes a marked departure from "I am greener than the pale grass and it [appears] to me that I am close to death. Still, I must endure all this . . ." This, I suggest, is too much the feminine response for him. He prefers to conclude his version with something like this (Catullus #51):

Catullus, you are all excess,
You surge with hopes, sink in despairs;
The fall of ancient realms and royal heirs
Came through such wantonness.

Here, too, is evident (by way of comparison) Sappho's inclination toward the personal rather than the political. Does not much of Sappho's work turn on the tension between the private and the public (as may be seen in the Anactoria letter)? (See, e.g., #71.)

These are among the considerations that support the suggestion I have made, that lyric poetry may be distinctively female in orientation and interests (just as epic poetry may be distinctively male). Thus, a distinguished American critic once asked, "Does it really constitute a career for a man to do nothing but write lyric poetry?" (Edmund Wilson, as quoted in the *Times Literary Supplement,* May 30, 1980, p. 621.) Alcaeus, we have noticed, was inclined toward rougher subjects than Sappho. Also, he made much of drinking songs, while Sappho evidently did not.

Thus, Sappho can be considered *the* lyric poet (just as Jane Austen, perhaps, is *the* novelist of private life, especially of that marriage-bound courtship which means so much to women).

All this may bear upon one of the many puzzles left us by Plato's *Symposium* where it is said (without protest from the company), "Isn't it awful . . . that hymns and paeans have been made by the poets for other gods, but for Eros, who is so great and important a god, not one of the many poets there have been has ever made even a eulogy?" (*Symposium* 177B. What did Phaedrus, who voiced this complaint, think of the stories then available about Alcestis? Was Alcestis, for example, understood to be moved more by a concern for her children than by love of her husband?) Did these Athenians mean that love had not been properly eulogized by *mortals,* since Sappho was to be ranked among the Muses? Or did they mean that the love-divinity made so much of by Sappho and others had been *female*? Or did they merely mean (again thinking of Sappho) that no *male* had properly praised love? In any event, we are led to notice that whatever *was* said about love on the occasion described in the *Symposium,* something essential about love was somehow missed that evening by Socrates' companions—something intimately tender (verging toward the romantic) and yet physically as well as spiritually consuming—which may be seen in Sappho's poems. Is there not something essential about love, that bitter-sweet passion for generation, that only a woman is apt to appreciate fully? And so Diotima (but not Sappho) is conjured up by Socrates.

Not that Sappho is a mere enthusiast of love. Still, its importance in her scheme of things can at times seem overwhelming. Love promises permanency (see, e.g., #14, #45) even as one recognizes how fickle it can be. The changeableness of love, even of a love which seems for the moment to be unique and eternal, is evident in the ode to Aphrodite quoted at the head of this section. The central lines in the Greek text we have display Aphrodite smiling and twice asking, in effect, "What is it this time?" (That these lines should be central supports the proposition that this poem is complete or virtually complete as we have it, whatever some scholars might believe.) The narrator is aware, even in her present passion, that she has been this desperate on more than one occasion. To be thus self-conscious about one's desperate love—even to mock oneself—is not to be fully or truly "in love"? Also evident here is the notion that love is not altogether a good thing. It can even be an affliction: the lover asks that the unresponsive beloved also be punished by unrequited love.

To go in this way beyond love, to be this self-conscious, is perhaps to go beyond the male-female distinction. It is to look down on such matters from a superior position, almost like an unmoved (and unmovable?) divinity. Does not the mastery aimed at by poetry with its highly disciplined language, testify to, and usually serve, a moderation that is superior to the desires love makes so much of from time to time? (A grimmer form of the influence of Aphrodite, with moderation abandoned, may be seen in the discussion of Euripides' *Hippolytus* in chapter 6 of this book.)

vi

... Hector and his fellows
are bringing home a girl with darting eyes
from holy Thebe and Placia ...
—graceful Andromache—
with a fleet of ships, on a salt sea.
They're bringing, too, a mass of golden bracelets and
of purple robes,
a rainbow of trinkets,
and unnumbered silver cups with ivory work.

The messenger told his tale, and Hector's
dear father jumped right up
and word spread to friends
through the wide city ...

... The young girls sang a sacred song, and
their mighty clamor rose to the skies with sounds
of laughter.

All the road long
they carried bowls and vessels filled
with myrrh, with cinnamon and frankincense.
The older women chorused shouts,
and all the men, as one, gave out

a lovely, high-pitched chant
as they called on far-shooting Paean of the beautiful lyre

and as if to gods they sang a hymn
to Hector and Andromache. [#66]

To go beyond love, as well as beyond male-female differences, is to look
to that upon which love depends and to those things (including a sense
of moderation) by which love is to be guided. (See, on Plato's *Symposium,* the addendum to part 1 of chapter 7 of this book.)

This transcendence of love may be seen in the poem about Hector
and Andromache quoted (in part) at the head of this section. Much can
be made of *this* love-match in large part because of who Hector is. It is
important that Hector is Priam's son, and that he himself is a great warrior. Also, this poem is not without an awareness of another son of
Priam who later brings home a woman for himself as well, with disastrous consequences for Troy, Priam, Hector, and Andromache.

We can, if we but look, see again and again the dependence of the
things that lyric poetry celebrates upon political associations and events.
(This is despite Sappho's indications elsewhere that the public things are
not the beautiful things. See, e.g., #92.) Thus, publicly-sanctioned marriage is made much of, not only for Hector and Andromache but for
men and women generally. (See, e.g., #155, #161.) This is despite the "lesbian" interests of Sappho. See seems, in this respect, sounder than some
of her disciples today who tend to be unfairly condemned (by genetic
quirks or by chance influences, if not by sterile arguments) to what
seems to many an unnatural childhood all their lives. (May the same be
said about the expansion of childhood associated with both the "youth
movements" and the emphasis upon cosmetics and plastic surgery of recent decades?)

There are still other indications in the poems of Sappho's awareness
that the things she cherishes most, including love relations, depend
upon conventional arrangements. Thus, there is her respect for the uses
of money in securing happiness. (See #100. See, also, chapter 12 of this
book.) Thus, also, there is her respect for established opinions regulat-
ing dress, sexual relations and the appropriate ages of marriage partners.
(See, e.g., #98, #35, #36, #37, #99.) She is sensitive about blood relations
and about family status. Love for her does not put everyone on the same

level; it does not make all social and other distinctions negligible. Honor does remain for her a repeated concern. (See, e.g., #10, #71.)

Something, then, has to shape or define (or discover) the whole within which, or against which, gifted men and women work to develop themselves (as, we would say, "individuals"). That "something" seems to be the male-run (or, at least, male-organized) "world." Thus, the political community is vital to the life of the poet, as may be true also of the discipline imposed by poetic forms. Sappho senses this, even when she does not choose explicitly to recognize it. That she may have publicly acknowledged it to some extent is reflected in the tradition that she was important enough politically to be exiled for a period early in her life. (See #40, #82.)

To be interested in political things is to be interested in, among other things, justice. (See #13; also, #36, #37.) Moderation tends to be encouraged by such an interest, as may be seen in Sappho's advice for restraining one's anger: "When wrath runs rampage in your heart, you must hold still that rambunctious tongue!" (#137) That is, self-expression—giving one's passions full rein—is not all there is to life.

Sappho's dependence upon the male-oriented world may be seen in the fact that, again and again, she takes Homer's world for granted, a world of people, gods, and their episodes. She may modify some episodes or put the emphasis elsewhere—but her reliance upon what Homer has described is fundamental. Thus, one can hear in the invocation of Aphrodite (in the poem quoted at the head of section iv of this chapter) echoes of the conversation between Achilles and Thetis in book 1 of the *Iliad*. One can also hear in the Hector and Andromache wedding celebration, in the poem quoted from at the head of this section, the preparations for battle in the *Iliad*. (The Aphrodite poem can be seen as a female *Iliad*, with the wrath-inclined narrator expressing the desire to be a comrade-in-arms, or rather a comrade-in-wiles, with the goddess. The three uses in the poem of *thumos* [spiritedness] may be significant.)

To regard political life as somehow fundamental to lyric poetry is to recognize, if only tacitly, the importance in these matters of political philosophy. Opinions about right and wrong, and about what a good life consists of, if not about the character of truth itself, are accepted by the lyric poet for the most part from her community, that community which (in the best circumstances) political philosophy has helped confirm and refine. In many ways, then, an artist is dependent upon the political—for her existence, for the condition and interests of her audience, for the opportunity to develop her talents.

Of course, cities do rise and fall. (See Herodotus, *History* 1.7; chapter 8 of this book.) This usually affects what survives from a poet, as well as what a poet has to work with. Political, including political-religious, developments have affected what has survived from Sappho. Even so, the transitory and vulnerable character of love itself may be reflected in the mangled and elusive pieces that Sappho has left behind. One can wonder whether this is poetic justice of sorts.

vii

> I have a beautiful child
> whose body is like golden petals.
> She is my darling Cleis
> and I would not have for her
> all Lydia,
> nor even lovely ... [#130]

We have noticed that chance political developments can affect the forms art can take or which forms prosper, can affect the subjects the artist deals with, and can help determine which pieces of art are preserved. Thus, the artist who is dedicated to a conquest of chance is nevertheless somewhat beholden to chance. I say "somewhat" since not all *is* determined by chance in these matters. I have indicated, for example, that there may be good reason why Homer, Pindar, and the great tragedians have survived as well as they have, while the finest lyric poets of a public-spirited antiquity have led such a precarious existence.

One manifestation of chance in Sappho's career, we have seen, is in the extent to which her survival has depended upon grammarians and lexicographers. These more or less conventional people (representatives of what we now call the academic establishment) have made use of, and thereby have made available to us, a poet who is so unconventional that she can plausibly be regarded as "the first liberated woman in history" (Nikos Kazantzakis, *Serpent and Lily,* p. 90). Poetry has been said to have as one important, perhaps even as its primary, purpose that of helping to keep a language and hence "culture" vital. It is appropriate, then, that more or less mundane servants of culture, as grammarians and lexicographers tend to be, should have contributed (if only haphazardly) to the preservation of a great poet.

I have emphasized the extent to which art is dependent upon political life—and hence upon that sound political thought which political philosophy encourages. Even so, is not political order itself ultimately for the sake of the things that poetry, and not least lyric poetry, cherishes and nourishes? Thus, Sappho seems to be interested in the flourishing of civilization and of human beings, and to this end love seems indispensable to her. She is somewhat independent of political regimes and of the concerns, including wars, of politically-minded people.

Consider, in the lines quoted at the head of this section, what a woman (it could well be Sappho herself) says about her daughter Cleis, "whose body is like golden petals." Cleis matters more than an entire country, more even than "lovely . . ." Is it not fitting that the fragment should break off here, as if nothing could be imagined which would be preferred to Cleis? I am reminded of the statue of Mitys referred to in Aristotle's *Poetics,* that statue which fell upon and killed the man who had been the cause of Mitys' death. What, indeed, does Providence mean? (We return to these matters in section ix of this chapter.)

The gold of Lydia is not as desirable as one's child, although gold *can* be useful in helping one to describe what a child means to one. Even so, is not what one's child means likely to be dependent in part upon the institution of marriage which some political order establishes and protects? A child is precious. Is not a man more apt than a woman to make more of honor than of love? But, then, men are more apt to devote themselves to that association which is political in character, while women are more apt to look for their fulfillment to that association which is erotic in character (whether in marriage or otherwise). (See, e.g., #111.) Does not love contribute to the illusion that chance would be conquered in the erotic arrangements one longs for? Yet "whatever one loves" (to recall the Anactoria letter)—and even who one's child is, or what one's child is like (genetically and otherwise)—can be very much affected by chance. Is it not, after all, often very much a matter of chance what attracts or satisfies one?

What lyric poetry says about love—about the appearance of the conquest of chance and perhaps even of death—contributes to its enduring appeal. "Do you not see," it was asked in antiquity, "what a charm the songs of Sappho have to enchant and bewitch the listener?" (*Lyra Graeca*, 1:167. This is quoted by Plutarch.) Indeed, one can say that the city exists not only for the sake of the things celebrated by songs such as Sappho's. It exists also in order that human beings might have poetry and the beauty (and truth) and related pleasures which art, and only art, offers to most men, even though (as we have seen) chance can help shape what form beauty and pleasure take from time to time.

Was it more than a matter of chance that Alcaeus and, evidently, Sappho found themselves in political opposition to Pittacus, the ruler for many years of Lesbos? He is remembered as a man of considerable common sense and self-restraint, so much so that he comes down to us as one of the Seven Sages of Greece. Did he and the political philosophy that he anticipated stand more for duty and prudence, less for nobility and the joys of personal fulfillment, than the lyric poets who opposed him? What should be made of this, in addition to what has been said in the prologue to this book? (See, on the noble and the just, part 2 of chapter 7 of this book. See, on the dependence of the family upon the city, the addendum to part 2 of chapter 7.)

viii

> It is not right for there to be
> the sound of weeping
> in a poet's home.
> Such things do not become us [#108]

I have suggested that art helps one understand how things are. Or, at least, it can foster the impression that one understands things better than one would without it. Art is like love in this respect, for love assures one that one knows: it is a delightful way of learning, it also seems to say. (See *Genesis* 4:1. See, on love letters, Anastaplo, *The Constitutionalist*, p. 546.)

Love, like the poetry to which it has a marked affinity, works through particulars: the universal is detected by love in particular instances. Love may be as close as most human beings, most of the time, can get to that grasp of the whole which intelligence instinctively yearns for. Does love appeal to human beings partly by leading them to believe that they thus have reliable access to the highest things?

This line of inquiry brings to the fore a question that has been with us, at least implicitly, from the outset of this chapter. What *is* the relation of philosophy (not just political philosophy) to lyric poetry (if not to art itself)? We have seen that the interests of philosophy and art are similar: each is moved, ultimately, by a vision of the highest good. (See, on the Idea of the Good, part 2 of chapter 11 of this book.) Even so, it can be said that lyric poetry does concern itself more than does political philosophy with the good in itself, at least in particular cases. That is, political philosophy (or that political discourse rooted in political philosophy) takes a longer view of things, so much so as to make it sometimes seem that it does not care for the here and now, for the aspirations, pleasures, and troubles of this man or that woman.

Comparisons of political philosophy and lyric poetry are not new. Consider this ancient coupling of Socrates and Sappho (*Lyra Graeca*, 1:155):

> The love of the fair Lesbian, if it is right to argue from one age to another, was surely the same as the art of love pursued by Socrates. They both appear to me [Maximus of Tyre] to have practised the same sort of friendship, he of males, she of females, both declaring that their beloved were many in number and that they were captivated by all beautiful persons. What Alcibiades, Charmides, and Phaedrus were to him, Gyrinna, Atthis, and Anactoria were to her, and what his rival craftsmen, Prodicus, Gorgias, Thrasymachus and Protagoras were to Socrates, that Gorgo and Andromeda were to Sappho, who sometimes takes them to task and at others refutes them and dissembles with them exactly like Socrates.

Further similarities are evident: both had aristocratic disciples; both used questions and answers to advance their arguments; neither was physically attractive; both made use of irony in their discourse; and both used homely examples to illustrate their arguments. In addition, an ancient commentator wrote, Socrates and Sappho were obliged to restrain the grief of relatives, he by chiding his wife for weeping when he was about to die, she by chiding her daughter in similar circumstances with the lines quoted at the head of this section. (See *Lyra Graeca*, 1:259.)

Both Socrates and Sappho made much of love. But critical differences can be noticed here. Whereas Socrates could call love (presumably love, as ordinarily understood) "sophistical," Sappho called it a "weaver of tales." (See *Lyra Graeca*, 1:201.) This difference can be seen to have political implications: Meletus ("he who cares"), one of the accusers of Socrates, was linked in antiquity with Sappho as a writer of love songs. (See ibid., 3:243.) Did Meletus develop his fatal dislike for Socrates at least in part because they differed as to what love means and as to how the people are to be courted (and cared for)? Is Sappho too, or what she stands for, somehow in fundamental opposition to what Socrates (as well as Pittacus?) stands for in these matters?

Perhaps the basis of such an opposition may be discerned by reconsidering what both Socrates and Sappho had to say to relatives who wept in the face of impending death. Sappho could say what she did to her daughter, and "mean it." But, unlike Socrates, she had had to rely upon a different view of death throughout her career in order to make her poetry "meaningful" for most people. That is, she, unlike Socrates, generally regarded death as something to be lamented. (See, e.g., #25, #71, #103, #144.) Her deeply-felt attitude is aptly summarized in these lines of hers saved for us by Aristotle (#91):

> Death is an ill; the gods at least think so,
> Or else themselves had perished long ago.

To celebrate love as Sappho does *is*, I have suggested, to struggle (sometimes desperately) against death.

Poetry exploits (and thereby legitimates?) passions that could become the undoing of human beings if such passions should escape from the discipline of poetry. The poet can, by marshaling such passions, move the people at large. Socrates, on the other hand, cannot move the people—he cannot, or will not, bring himself to do that.

Another way of putting this is to repeat that poetry (and especially lyric poetry, with its intense effects) depends upon illusion. "He appears to me an equal to the gods . . ." (#2). Nor does the poet mind contradicting herself. She can make us lament one death after another, even as she counsels against lamentations for her own death. (Is *weeping*, as distinguished from other forms of mourning, a special problem for Sappho, in that it is *undisciplined* sound?) Also, she can celebrate a love of the moment as if there had been nothing like it before, as if there will never be anything like it hereafter. Indeed, she can even extol the beloved of the moment as another Helen. (See #44. See also #72.)

Of course, love does not seem to care if it is inconsistent: it cares primarily to express and enjoy itself on the occasion at hand. An unconcern about consistency—on the part of either love or the art which serves it and is in turn served by it—is what comes from making so much of particulars. But, I have suggested, such dwelling upon particulars may reflect an opinion as to what is "real" or, at least, what is important in the world available to human beings.

All this is not to deny that the intense pleasure that can be generated by love and by poetry can make one feel very much alive and can even give one the sense of immortality. On the other hand, pain and deprivation, as well as stumbling over words, make one very much aware of one's mortality.

Still another way of suggesting the differences between philosophy and poetry touched upon in this section is to recall that Theanon, "a famous woman-philosopher variously described as the wife and the disciple of Pythagoras," could be associated in antiquity with "greatness of mind" (τὸ μεγαλόνουν), whereas Sappho could be associated with "refinement of character" (τὸ γλαφυρὸν τῆς προαιρέσ∈ως)—that is to say, that beauty of deportment known as nobility (τὸ καλόν). (See *Lyra Graeca*, 1:458; 1:171; 1:161.)

ix

> To have beauty [κάλος] is to have only that,
> but to have goodness [ἀγαθος]
> is to be beautiful [κάλος] too. [#58]

Poetry and philosophy may differ, at root, about the relation of appearance to "reality," that is, being. (This, too, bears upon our discussion of the noble and the just in part 2 of chapter 7.)

One *can*, from the perspective of philosophy, begin to study this relation (of appearance to being) by examining art carefully. Martin Heidegger has suggested that certain verses, including some of Sappho's (e.g., #3), "provide a suitable basis for reflection on being and appearance" (*An Introduction to Metaphysics,* p. 85). Does one, in so studying poems, approach them otherwise than as their makers understood them, so much so as to lose sight of what the poems manifestly seem to say?

A related problem is whether poets can be depended upon to understand what they have made. (See, e.g., Plato, *Apology* 22B. See also Anastaplo, *Human Being and Citizen,* p. 11; section ix of part 1 of chapter 3 of this book.) Can a reader properly approach poems without being concerned about the intentions or the understanding of their makers only if poems are like the things found in nature, which we can also study without being concerned about the inscrutable intentions or understanding of *their* Maker? Is art, then, an imitation of nature? Where *is* nature to be seen in the poems of Sappho? Certainly, it is to be seen and enjoyed in simple things such as the orchard scenes Sappho sketches (#1); perhaps, also, in the Evening Star scene (#149); or even in accounts of complex movements of the human soul, as in the ode to Aphrodite (#1).

Sappho can imitate nature in an engaging manner without ever using the word *nature.* It is almost as if she does not want to think, or at least to think out loud, about nature; rather, she wants "merely" to describe how it impinges on human beings. This may be the preference of most poets. (Consider the single, curious use of *nature* in Homer: "So spoke Argeiphontes, and he gave me the medicine, which he picked out of the ground, and he explained the nature of it to me. It was black at the root, but with a milky flower. The gods call it moly. It is hard for mortal man to dig it up, but the gods have power to do all things" [*Odyssey* 10.302–6].) To speak seriously (and hence systematically?) of nature is to begin to move beyond the particularistic realm of art. Sappho's reluctance to speak of nature is pointed up, by way of contrast, in various scholars in antiquity who use her work. They will use the term *nature* as they draw upon her in discussing what *they* are interested in. (See, e.g., #1, #2, #53, #107.)

We have noticed, among the differences between philosophy and poetry, what is suggested by the different ways that Socrates and Sappho regard love. She is more concerned than he about what "everyday" love offers or claims or seems to be, even though she is aware of the changeableness of the objects of one's passions. The appearances of things are vital to her, and this bears upon how she regards the relation of appearance to being. Being, I have suggested, seems to take the form for her primarily of particular things, thereby reinforcing for her the importance of appearances. One consequence of this may be that poetry will care more than does philosophy for the noble, as ordinarily understood. (See #118, #119.)

How do poets know what they say, especially about fundamental matters? How, for instance, do they know about the divine? Poets differ in the stories they tell about the gods or about the episodes connected with the gods. Poets report information about the gods that no one else (except perhaps oracles) evidently has access to—and do not even the oracles depend, in practice, upon poets to help define and establish their jurisdictions, doctrines, and reputations?

Sappho and Socrates can be taken to agree, for the most part, as to whether and how gods intervene in the affairs of men. They seem to agree as well as to what we know about whether particular souls survive death. Socrates could endorse also the emphasis Sappho places upon Aphrodite insofar as this conforms to his opinion about the contribution of the erotic to philosophy. Compare Homer, with his emphasis, at least in the *Iliad* (and in the closing books of the *Odyssey*), upon wrath, war, and oracles. The gentleness of the sometimes waspish Sappho (as well as of Aesop and of Hesiod) can be expected to appeal to a Socrates.

Consider, also, the implications of the Sappho poem in which she celebrates the godlikeness of the lover who is with the beloved (#2). Are the gods seen as somehow related to, if not even dependent upon, men? Is there in Sappho anything of the one god (*the* divine) to which Socrates (as one result perhaps of his study of nature) points? Does poetry naturally tend toward polytheism?

The answers to these, and similar, questions may well depend upon what one considers Sappho to have said about the relation of appearance to being. (Does this in turn depend upon what one believes about female interests and the possibility of philosophy for women?) Consider the lines quoted at the head of this section: the good is truly beautiful. (One is reminded of what Alcibiades says in Plato's *Symposium* about the seemingly ugly but eminently virtuous Socrates.) But what the good is does not seem to be considered explicitly in Sappho's poems, except that it is said to be this and this and this. Is the general understanding, of what the good things are, accepted by the poet, however she may *play* with it? Is that, too, ultimately rooted in, and dependent upon, an established political order and hence (in the better regimes) upon political philosophy?

Both artist and philosopher, it can be said, believe that there is a lively relation between beauty and goodness. (See, for the Idea of the Good, part 2 of chapter 8 of this book.) But art may make more than philosophy does of the goodness of the beautiful appearance. Does the artist try, thereby, to draw the many to an inner beauty (that is, to the truth about things)?

Lyric poetry, it can be said, looks ultimately to love or to the pleasure that love is moved by. It usually needs a healthy community if it is to prosper. Political philosophy, on the other hand, looks ultimately to the community or to the justice that a proper community is dedicated to. So long as men have bodies, the community needs love to help shape most of its desires, those desires among which just allocations are to be made. (See Anastaplo, *Human Being and Citizen,* p. 87 f.)

Still, the question remains, Which is ultimately to rule, and in what way? Much more needs to be said about lyric poetry and about political philosophy, but in order to do that, a further investigation is needed into what appearance and being mean, not only "in" political philosophy or "for" the lyric poet but also in themselves. It is perhaps indicative of the intrinsic worth of Sappho—not least because of the beauty of her language (which points to a certain goodness, to being itself?)—that we have been moved to venture the preliminary inquiry into the considerations and questions touched upon in this chapter. Certainly her intrinsic worth is such that she can be expected to survive abuse at the hands of misdirected scholars who stray off the proper path toward an understanding of art. (See the epilogue of this book.) Or as the beautiful Sappho herself is said to have put it, "Like the hyacinth which the shepherd tramples underfoot on the mountain, and it still blooms purple on the ground" (#151).

III. Pindar

PART ONE. On the *Odes*

> *Leave America divided into thirteen or, if you please, into three or four independent governments—what armies could they raise and pay—what fleets could they ever hope to have? If one was attacked, would the others fly to its succor and spend their blood and money in its defense? Would there be no danger of their being flattered into neutrality by specious promises, or seduced by a too great fondness for peace to decline hazarding their tranquillity and present safety for the sake of neighbors, of whom perhaps they have been jealous, and whose importance they are content to see diminished? Although such conduct would not be wise, it would, nevertheless, be natural. The history of the states of Greece, and of other countries, abounds with such instances, and it is not improbable that what has so often happened would, under similar circumstances, happen again.*
>
> —Publius

Citations to the odes of Pindar in this chapter use the numbers assigned to them in the Loeb Classical Library and the Library of Liberal Arts editions of the odes.

The epigraph is taken from *The Federalist Papers*, No. 4. Notice the possible disjunction here between the *wise* and the *natural*. See, on Publius and the *Federalist Papers*, Anastaplo, *The Constitutionalist*, p. 819; "The Constitution at Two Hundred: Explorations," *Texas Tech Law Review* 22 (1991): 967, 1042–53. See, on the lyric possession of an epic past, Gregory Nagy, *Pindar's Homer* (Baltimore: Johns Hopkins University Press, 1990).

i

IN ANY CONTEST AMONG THE Greek lyric poets of antiquity, Pindar (who was born about 520 B.C.) would be a leading contender. Thus, Lucian could call one of Pindar's odes, *Olympian* 1, "the most splendid of all songs" (Mullen, *Choreia*, p. 164). And so it has been said (Wormell):

> The tradition of Greek choral lyric culminated [during the 5th century
> B.C.] with the odes of Pindar. These are not easy to evaluate and appre-
> ciate, but it is still more difficult to comprehend and assess the poet who
> composed them. Even to his contemporaries, Pindar must have seemed
> an aloof and somewhat enigmatic figure. As an aristocrat he would more
> naturally have been a patron of poetry than himself a poet; he came from
> a part of central Greece that had made a relatively small contribution to
> literature and the arts. . . . A modern reader needs a sympathetic insight
> into the nature and traditions of Greek aristocratic society before he can
> begin to understand how Pindar's subject matter—victory in an athletic
> contest or in a chariot race—could inspire poetry characterized by high
> seriousness and deep feeling. Pindar cannot, indeed, speak across the
> centuries with the directness of Homeric epic poetry or Sophoclean
> tragedy, but he does create, with disciplined mastery of a sophisticated
> and complex art form, a choral lyric of unsurpassed splendor and sus-
> tained nobility.

I hope to begin to supply the "modern reader" the "sympathetic insight" needed to read Pindar properly, a poet who exploited the differences among the Greek cities in order to advance Panhellenic standards and interests.

It has been said of Pindar that "he was not the creator of any new kind [of choral lyric], as Simonides of the *epinikian* [victory odes]; nor again, was he the first who gave a new artistic value to any old form of song, as Simonides gave it to the dirge. What Pindar did was to set the stamp of an original and strongly individual genius on every lyric form in which he composed" (Richard C. Jebb, in Bacchylides, *Poems and Fragments,* p. 41). And it has also been said that the "all-pervading, self-conscious, Greek individualism is no more evident than in Pindar, who likens himself to the eagle, the divine bird of Zeus . . ." (John A. Scott, *The Unity of Homer,* p. 248).

Perhaps, indeed, Pindar may be the most self-conscious of the Greek poets, very much aware of his great gifts and not shy about asserting his superiority. It has been suggested that his aspiration was to be preeminent among poets as the athletic victors he celebrates were preeminent among their rivals (Mullen, p. 165). It seems particularly fitting, then, that a poet who made so much of his own preeminence should have devoted so much of his poetry to celebrating the victories (the momentary superiority?) of others in the great Games of his time. Perhaps it should be considered for him an apt, if not even a divinely ordained, fate that he survives primarily in the poetry that celebrates the athletic feats of others.

The victory odes were dedicated to the winners of the great Games of Greece. Such odes, usually commissioned by the city or family of the winner, were evidently performed with the aid of dance and music. The odes were only a part, but they were a particularly spectacular part, of the rewards showered upon the most spectacular athletes of the day. Among the rewards for these winners might be free meals for life bestowed upon them by their proud and grateful cities.

Such lavish recognition of winners is called into question, as are perhaps the poets and citizens who make much of them, by what Socrates said when the time came for him to discuss an appropriate punishment upon conviction at his trial (Plato, *Apology* 36D–37A):

> What, then, is fitting for a poor man, a benefactor, who needs to have leisure to exhort you? There is nothing more fitting, men of Athens, than for such a man to be given his meals in the Prytaneum, much more so than if any of you has won a victory at Olympia with a horse or a two- or four-horse chariot. For he makes you seem to be happy, while I make you to be so; and he is not in need of sustenance, while I am in need of it. So if I must propose what I am worthy of in accordance with the just, I propose this: to be given my meals in the Prytaneum.

I notice in passing that these winners compete against the world—that is, against all comers, just as did Socrates in the question put about him by Chaerephon at Delphi. To this I will return, just as I visit Delphi in the second part of this chapter.

ii

It is the kind of winner Socrates speaks so slightingly of that Pindar celebrates in his victory odes. We might well wonder what Pindar would think of Socrates' comparison of himself to those winners, a comparison which reflects Socrates' opinions both as to what is worthwhile for its own sake and as to what is helpful to the city. (It is the latter consideration Socrates emphasizes before his judges.)

It has been noticed that "no Greek poet says so much as Pindar about his art" (Bowra, *Pindar,* p. 1). This may be related, I have already suggested, to the self-consciousness and self-confidence of athletes who display their powers. But would not Pindar regard his poetry as superior to the athletes and contests that he celebrates, and superior because of attributes that should win the respect of a Socrates? Thus, he might have been inclined to agree with Socrates if he (Pindar) had seen the winners merely as athletes. But he moves beyond the surface of the victories, examining what is really being exhibited (or at least celebrated by him) in such winning.

In the foreground of Pindar's odes are indeed the Games and their winners—and these the typical Greek citizen and Greek city would probably have been immediately most interested in. In the background of Pindar's odes, however, are the doings of gods and demigods and heroes, especially as founders and saviors of cities. The depiction of this background takes up most of the lines of the odes. In the "deep" background of the odes are the opinions Pindar himself may have had about the games, gods, and cities. For example, can the gods (if omniscient and omnipotent) be as most people evidently believed them to be? Are the Games as important as people generally took them to be? These underlying opinions furnish the most critical subject Pindar deals with, even though he rarely makes that subject explicit.

Whatever reservations Pindar may have about the Games, or for that matter about the gods (as the gods were generally regarded), the odes do provide him opportunities to discourse on the greatest and deepest things. Of course, Pindar writes the things he does for money. The question remains, What are the things he is willing to write for money? The simplest answer to this question is that he is hired to write about win-

ners. We should consider, therefore, what this kind of winning requires
and means.

It seems, especially when the competition is "world-class," that winning usually requires determination, discipline, various physical (or
natural) attributes (which may even be hereditary in some cases), and
(for some events, such as chariot racing) considerable resources. Thus, it
must have taken a certain kind of city, and training not available everywhere, to produce the very best. (I consider in chapter 12 of this book the
role of *equipment* in Aristotle's account of the moral virtues. See, also,
the opening speeches of Plato's *Meno* and my discussion of those
speeches, and of Augustine's *De Magistro*, in "The Teacher," an article
scheduled for publication in the 1997 volume of *The Great Ideas Today*.)

Winning *means* various kinds of excellence. Pindar in one of his
odes passes on the "true saying," "Trial is the true test of mortal men"
(*Olympian* 4). (One may wonder whether Pindar himself is not also
being tested by all this.) Thucydides complains in his *Peloponnesian War*
(1.21) that poets unduly glorify events, thereby distorting them. But Pindar records in one of his odes a saying, "Do not bury high success in
silence" (*Nemean* 9). Elsewhere he observes (in one of the fragments)
that the minds of men are blind without poetry. "To me," he says, "have
[the Muses] handed on this immortal task," the task of enlightening
mankind (Loeb Classical Library edition, p. 545). In still another fragment he says something which can stand as a rationale for his career,
"'Tis meet for the good to be hymned with fairest songs. . . . For this is
the only tribute that vergeth on the honours due to the immortals; but
every noble deed dieth, if suppressed in silence" (ibid., p. 581). Thus, an
excellence, or image of the good, is displayed when the winner of a
Game is celebrated in a poem. It is such celebration that permits Pindar
to go on to bigger things, to talk about the parallels to gods and heroes
suggested by one winner after another. This is not only because the gods
and heroes originally founded the Games and remain their patrons. The
winners themselves display something godlike in their issuing forth victorious. (The spirit of such celebrations does seem healthier than that of
more "realistic" moderns. Thus, Ivan Albright observed, "It matters little
whether I paint a squash, a striped herring, or a man. The space, the
light, the motion, the position have one thing in common—decay.")

iii

Very little is said in Pindar's victory odes either about the athletes and their families or about the condition of the athletes' cities. Nor is there much said even about the contests themselves. Pindar's odes are quite different, in this respect, from the modern sports page. They are different as well from the victory odes prepared by many of his contemporaries, who did so much more than he did with the athletes and the contests in which the athletes had triumphed. One learns very little from Pindar's odes about just how the various contests were conducted. This may be compared to the plays (a generation later) of Sophocles and of Euripides in which there are detailed and graphic accounts of a chariot race in which Orestes is "killed." Those accounts, which so far as Orestes is himself concerned are simply not true, may be accurate enough about what can happen in such a race. (See, also, Homer, *Iliad* 23.) In Pindar's own times, his older and younger contemporaries, Simonides and Bacchylides respectively, provided detailed descriptions of the contests that had led to victory odes. (See Bacchylides, pp. 38, 56. See, also, toward the end of Euripides' *Hippolytus,* the account of the hero's death when his horses panic.)

There can be little doubt about what Pindar regarded as important, as he devotes himself much more to retelling old stories (about gods and heroes) than to developing new ones about the most recent heroics. In Sophocles and Euripides, on the other hand, the accounts of Orestes' supposed chariot race are as detailed as they are in order to show how those who dreaded Orestes' return were persuaded to let down their guard. It usually suffices for Pindar to say that a certain athlete won such and such a contest at this or that place. In a sense, for his purposes, all winning athletes can be taken to have done much the same (the exceptions include such achievements as a son following a parent as a victor or an athlete winning several contests in the same year). To say much about the event itself is, for Pindar, to waste a precious opportunity.

It is likely, however, that those who commissioned victory odes must often have wanted to hear much more about the particular event. Pindar appeals to this kind of desire by recognizing "that words are necessary if deeds are to be properly rewarded by being long remembered"

(Mullen, p. 41). So it came to be believed that one of the greatest rewards for victors was to have poems, such as Pindar's, prepared for them, poems that would be remembered as having been elicited by the thus-honored victors. (It should again be noticed that the best poets of Pindar's age were evidently available for such commissions.) These would be poems in which something beyond one's victories would be looked to, just as the games themselves could be considered as looking beyond mere physical activity.

Were the people who commissioned the poems aware of what was likely to happen at the hands of a Pindar? Were they reconciled, for instance, to the fact that the poem commissioned would say little about the athlete personally, however much it would draw upon gods and heroes and legendary episodes somehow appropriate to the city of the athlete? It does seem, at times, that patrons were primarily interested in getting the best artistic "caterer" for their event—and Pindar had come to be recognized as one of the best, if not the very best. Did this recognition depend upon an informed awareness of his qualities as a poet, aside from the personal portraits he provided (or failed to provide)? To commission Pindar, then, might have been somewhat like persuading Pablo Picasso to do one's portrait: the subject of the portrait may not be recognizable, but one could expect that the resulting picture would be noticed and that having one's name attached to the picture would somehow redound to one's fame. Or, this is like commissioning a museum in which to house works of art—only to find that the architecture of the museum itself is more imposing and of more enduring artistic significance than any of the pictures housed therein.

Pindar did say (or, some might say, advertise), "In payment for praiseworthy deeds, we ought to celebrate the noble man in poetry, extolling him with grace" (*Isthmian* 3). Still, it is hard to believe that Pindar himself did not recognize that his poetry would outlast the athletic deeds he praised. So little were the contests themselves his concern that few of the losers, or the winner's opponents, are identified by him. If the contests themselves had been critical, the achievements of the winners could have been pointed up by describing the prowess of the challengers they had overcome, which *is* to be seen in Pindar's accounts of the achievements of gods and heroes. (*Nemean* 5 is an exception.)

It can be said, therefore, that we owe these poems in part to the pride if not even the vanity of those who commissioned them. Not only were the odes originally brought into existence because of a desire to see oneself thus celebrated but they may have been preserved, by families and cities, for that reason. "Seventeen volumes of Pindar's poetry, comprising almost every genre of choral lyric, were known in antiquity. Only four books of [victory odes] have survived complete . . ." (Wormell). This is attributed to the fact that they chanced to be selected by a teacher as a school book in the second century A.D. But, we must wonder, what permitted them to be available so long for such selection?

Those who commissioned the poems did get their money's worth from Pindar. His vivid accounts of gods and heroes ennobled the athletic deeds that had inspired those accounts. Few would have wondered, as we might well do, whether those accounts somehow showed up the athletic events as petty by comparison. Nor would many have wondered whether Pindar's art did not display itself as higher in its class than even the winners in the great Games were in their respective classes. It probably sufficed for them, winners and patrons alike, to be told by Pindar that "it is those that are prosperous [victorious?] who are deemed wise, even by their fellow citizens" (*Olympian* 5). The winners must have seemed eminently worthy, the honor they received assuring them of their virtue. (See Aristotle, *Nicomachean Ethics* 1.1095b21 sq.) Pindar could tell them that "poets sing the happy man as one who wins by excellence of hands or feet . . . and who, before he dies, sees his young son [win as well]" (*Pythian* 10). One cannot do what the gods do—but one should go as far as men can, recognizing all the while one's limitations and thereby avoiding presumptuousness (or *hubris*). (In some ways, Pindar identifies his own poetic achievements as "athletic." See *Nemean* 5.)

All in all, then, Pindar presents the athletic contest, and especially victory, in the best light possible. He can speak, as in *Olympian* 10, of "the joy of winning, the light in life that compensates for all exertion." Or, as put in a different translation, "Few indeed have won, without trial, the joy that is a light of life above all labours." This would seem a salutary teaching, especially since the winners and their cities are repeatedly reminded by the odes of the gods and heroes who throw the best light upon their momentary achievements.

iv

Critical to Pindar's victory odes is the proposition that the winner "shares the marvelous munificence of deity" (*Nemean* 9). He can add that "a mortal who achieves the praise of fame and great possessions" has reached the peak. It has been noticed that in the time of Simonides, Pindar's great predecessor and evident originator of the victory ode, "the man to whom a hymn was addressed would feel that he was receiving a distinction which had hitherto been reserved for gods and heroes" (Bacchylides, p. 34).

It is not said in the odes that these winners *can* do what the gods had done. Thus, Pindar insists, "I think that nothing done by deity exceeds belief or merits puzzled awe" (*Pythian* 10). The gods are presented by him and by others as pervading everything, certainly manifesting themselves in achievements. The gods "lay out all paths to human excellence, on which the wise, the strong, the eloquent will walk" (*Pythian* 1). By the gift of a god alone does a man flourish forever (*Olympian* 11). It is evident that it is Pindar's opinion that the gods, or at least stories about the gods, are needed for the founding and perpetuation of cities. The great Games, then, are the visible manifestations of the gods and heroes who established not only those Games but the cities as well. Even so, the gods are *not* presented in the victory odes as involving themselves in the affairs of men in Pindar's day. That is, they do not "intervene," in the ordinary sense of that word, however much victory is seen as reflecting the favor of the tutelary god of this or that Game. (Compare the three games in which the gods intervene, in a way, in book 12 of the *Iliad.*)

The gods and heroes *are* presented as being themselves reflections of something which continues to be influential among men in Pindar's time, something which may be more fundamental than the gods as ordinarily conceived. Standards and ends are affirmed thereby, promoting in this way both virtue and the common good. (That the stories about the gods should be reconsidered seems to be quietly suggested by Pindar here and there. Consider, for example, what is implied about what Zeus did to his father, especially in an ode in which filial piety is advocated, *Pythian* 6. See, on Plato's *Euthyphro,* Anastaplo, "On Trial," p. 873.)

Pindar considers it the obligation of the poet to praise excellence (*Nemean* 3.291). The notion of *the best* is again and again pointed up by him (perhaps most famously in the opening lines of *Olympian* 1). In this way, the contemporary winner is both exalted and put in his place. One eminently successful man is advised, "Don't try to be a Zeus; if you get a share of these advantages, then you have everything" (*Isthmian* 5). This may be a useful corrective of what has been called the "selfish individualism" summed up in a famous line of Homer, that one should strive "ever to excel and to surpass other men" (Wormell).

The limits of human achievement are suggested, of course, by the mortality of man. At times, indeed, victory in the games is extolled as somehow a conquest of Hades, of death. It can be said, "You know that the grave is forgotten by him who has won befitting fame" (*Olympian* 8). Still, it seems that winning can do no more than make death more endurable (*Olympian* 10). Does this apply also to those who "identify" themselves with winners? It can be said as well that the dead will welcome news of their survivor's victories (*Olympian* 14). Elsewhere, however, it is indicated that the dead should be left to praise the dead, that one cannot reach across the barrier between life and death (*Nemean* 4). On another occasion, Pindar refuses to supply a poem for a ruler to whom he cannot send a remedy for what seems to be his fatal illness. It is on that occasion that he instructs this man (and us) that there are two ills accompanying each good for mankind (*Pythian* 3).

With these observations we can again be reminded of Socrates' suggestion that the Olympic winners merely seem to make the people of Athens happy. Do they do this, in part, by offering the appearance of the conquest of death? We are reminded also of Thucydides' criticism (1.21) of the pleasantness of hearing Herodotus. Are people easily beguiled from facing up to the way things truly are?

v

How things truly are, especially in the great contests in which one may be engaged, is suggested by the Churchillian observation that one can, in war, deserve victory, but one cannot guarantee it. (See Jaffa, p. 1. See, also, chapter 8, part 2, section viii, end.) One is obliged, that is, to do all that one should do to achieve the best; but one should recognize that providence (or chance?) may have much to say about whether one does indeed achieve what one is entitled to. It is prudent thus to recognize the limits of even prudence. (See, on the kind of prudence exhibited by Pindar on various occasions, Strauss, *Persecution and the Art of Writing*.)

This means that one should do certain things ultimately for their own sake, that the consequences are beyond one's complete control. How much is Pindar aware of this? That is, what does Pindar really believe about the gods and about what makes things happen as they do? Is there something about art itself which not only places the emphasis upon the concrete or particular but also sees all things as decisively subject to an overall order? The sovereignty of art is thereby asserted, a sovereignty which insists that there is an intimate relation between one's character and one's fate. (See Aristotle, *Poetics* 1450a1 sq.)

Even so, victory (however much it is due to providence) is not enough in itself. Or so Pindar is obliged to say, as when he reports, "But when a man works hard and wins, he needs the melody of praise, in prelude, and a pledge in honor of his excellence" (*Olympian* 11). He gives a more poetic account of this sentiment in the same ode: "My words are wont to herd the sheep of glory, and god makes poems blossom in the meadow of the heart." The victor, then, is dependent upon the poet. So, perhaps, is the conscientious loser, who can have explained to him that, indeed, one cannot guarantee victory but only deserve it.

In any event, Pindar's victory does routinely exhibit a competitiveness (vis-à-vis other poets) that may be more intense than that evident in any other great poet we know. In this way he can be said to have very much gotten into the spirit of the Games he took as his point of departure in telling the world how things truly are.

vi

It may be in what Pindar did *not* say, however, that he most dramatically revealed how things are. His great silence, a virtually complete silence, is about the Persian Wars, which were fought while he was in his prime. (See, for allusions to these wars, *Pythian* 1, 9, 10, *Nemean* 8.)

The Persian Wars were, of course, far more glorious for the Greeks than anything performed in any of the Games that Pindar wrote about. Pindar must have recognized this. His use of ancient wars and heroic feats testifies to his opinion that war provides a better test of virtue (whether of men or of cities) than do games. After all, games are but images of greater contests. Simonides, we know, wrote some of his most famous poems about the Persian Wars; Herodotus wrote about them in his famous history. It is obvious that subsequent ages have been far more interested in the exploits of those Wars than in the exploits of any Games mounted during Pindar's time.

But, alas, circumstances were against Pindar here. The Theban city to which he owed allegiance by birth had considered itself obliged, because of its geographical location, to collaborate with the Persian enemy against its fellow Greeks, thereby depriving itself of the great renown won by cities such as Athens and Sparta. (The names of Thermopylae, Marathon, Salamis, and Platea still come readily to mind, more than two thousand years later.)

We observe here the limits even of art. For Pindar could not, as a citizen of Thebes, sing the praises of the Greeks in the Persian Wars. Even to notice the specialness of Athens, in cultural matters, earned him the rebuke of his fellow citizens. (See *Pythian* 9, *Isthmian* 7; Loeb Classical Library edition, p. 557.) We see here, in a particularly difficult situation, the political judgment that the makers of victory odes had to exercise. Thus, it has been noticed, "The choice of the myth for an *epinikian* was a good test of political tact. In some cases, the task was a simple one— namely, when the traditions of the victor's city or family supplied a suitable legend . . ." (Bacchylides, p. 57).

In some ways, then, Pindar was in the position of German writers after the Second World War. And, drawing upon an example closer to home, we can usefully think of Pindar as the Greek William Faulkner, an artist who must make the best of a lost cause as he tries to affirm the humanity of his people and restore their self-respect and their confidence, working all the while for a general reconciliation.

It is possible, of course, that something even deeper is responsible for Pindar's virtually complete silence about the Persian Wars, a silence that found him saying so much by saying so little. Perhaps, that is, there were profound differences between Pindar and, say, Simonides, who did deal both with the actual Games in some detail and with the Persian Wars. These would be differences as to how seriously the modernity of their day should be taken. For one reason or another, Pindar does find his

most instructive stories in antiquity. He is certainly freer to say what he
wishes by staying away from modernity.

Whatever the reputation of Thebes among the Greeks, however, that
of Pindar was most elevated. Thus, a century or so after Pindar's death,
Alexander the Great could order the Theban house of Pindar's family
spared in the general destruction of that city by the Macedonians in 335
B.C. This despite Pindar's acknowledgment, "Verily, as no stranger, nor
as ignorant of the Muses, was I reared by famous Thebes" (Loeb Classical Library edition, p. 609). He may allude to the nightmare of the Persian Wars in these lines: "Now the darkness of the wintry months is past
and on the colored land red roses bloom again" (*Isthmian* 4). But it may
not have been tactful, or kind, of him to say much more than this
openly.

vii

Pindar is often taken by readers today to avow the belief that all human
excellence comes by divine dispensation. (See *Olympian* 14.) Thus, in
Olympian 8, he says, "Some blessings are wont to come to one man,
some to another; and, with the favour of the gods, there are many paths
of prosperity." Elsewhere he observes that men become good and wise
by fate divine (*Olympian* 9). And yet Pindar can, in still other odes,
make much of fortune (as at the outset of *Olympian* 12). Sure tokens of
the future, he can warn, do not exist; reversals can be sudden and unexpected.

What, then, should be understood to be responsible for what happened to Thebes during the Persian Wars? Did its geographical location,
which may have been favorable to its development for centuries, happen
to become a liability when the Persians appeared as enemies of the
Greeks? That is, was it chance that determined what happened to
Thebes? If chance is so critical, how important is the fact that one's
achievements (whether in war or in games) happen to be recognized?
What does all this say, that is, about the claims of art?

Is it possible to conquer chance? And if so, what is the best way to do
so? Does art offer the best hope? Or statesmanship (a special form of
art)? Or philosophy (which makes explicit the concern with nature that

is implicit in art)? Or religion (which shares, in critical respects, the resources and interests of art)?

The use of victory odes as an important, if not the principal, vehicle of one's poetry means, among other things, that one thereby enlists cities and families in an effort to preserve one's poems despite the ravages of chance. On the other hand, we can see, in our attempts to read Pindar, how much depends upon what we happen to know about the things he refers to. Each ode, it seems, was intended to stand alone (although there do seem to be references in some to others). This induces us to wonder, once again, how much of what Pindar says and wants depends upon the accidental—and what this says about (if not even against) what he seems to say about the role of providence and art in ordering human affairs.

viii

Our own circumstances may happen to be such that we do not appreciate as we should certain influences upon Pindar's poetry. Two influences should be noticed here. The first is the Theban character itself. We have wondered whether it was due to chance that Thebes found itself "obliged" to collaborate with the Persian enemy. Or was it the character of Thebes that was more responsible? Perhaps the greatest Theban stories were devoted to Oedipus and his family, who would be understood by many as born losers (however splendid Oedipus' apotheosis at his death, and however noble Antigone's sacrifice). One does get the impression, at least from the surface of those stories, that it was believed that an inexorable divine will was at work. The beleaguered Oedipus is finally driven to say, "It was Apollo, friends, Apollo, that brought this bitter bitterness, my sorrows to completion" (Sophocles, *Oedipus Tyrannus* 1329–30). I deal at greater length with Oedipus in chapter 5 of this book and with Antigone in the addendum to part 2 of chapter 7.)

What the desperate Oedipus says about Apollo brings us to the second major influence upon Pindar that we should notice, the importance for him of Delphi and its oracle. Pindar says in one of the fragments we have, "Muse! be thou mine oracle, and I shall be thine interpreter" (Loeb Classical Library edition, p. 601). And to a Syracusan ruler he could indicate that the god's favor comes somehow through the poet, who becomes a kind of priest (*Olympian* 1). It does seem, sometimes, that Pindar believes himself to speak, even among the poets, from a superior position—and there are hints, here and there, that it is the influence of Delphi, and all that Delphi stands for, which had put him in a privileged state of mind. And so he can speak "with a voice as of Delphi." (See Bacchylides, pp. 15, 41.)

Although Pindar recognizes that poets are often mistaken, he himself proposes to tell the truth. In the process, he reshapes (as Socrates does later) some of the old stories about the gods, denying in effect that they can do the questionable things sometimes imputed to them. His retelling of old stories, which the victory odes license him to do, is from the perspective of one who sounds as if he has access to special revelation himself.

A truly thoughtful winner, whether man or city, would know that a victory ode from a Pindar is more important than the victory itself. The ode is a challenge, somewhat artificial and accidental to be sure, just as the athletic contests celebrated in the odes themselves are. One's mettle as a poet is tested; an opportunity is given to show what one can do, especially if one is working against a deadline; and acclaim can be earned. But it seems obvious that Pindar, in the final analysis, does not really care for the acclaim, except as it contributes to something greater, a Panhellenic reconciliation. In this, too, Pindar can be seen to reflect the Delphic influence. That the securing of peace among the Greeks is to be prized is evident even as Pindar celebrates the victory of one city over all the others in a Game. Thus, Pindar can be recorded as saying, "To the inexperienced, war is pleasant, but he that has had experience of it sorely fears in his heart its approach" (Loeb Classical Library edition, p. 577).

Pindar makes much, whenever he can (it seems), of heroes who can be connected with Thebes (directly, or indirectly through Aegina), people such as Aeacus, Telamon, Ajax, Peleus, Achilles, and even Heracles. No doubt this is partly in order to cater to local interests. But is it not also partly because of Pindar's interest in reintegrating Thebes into the Greek world, something which can be advanced by noticing how much the great Greek heroes are connected with Thebes (or, at least, how much they can be *said* to be connected with Thebes)? (See, e.g., *Isthmian* 8.) The further Pindar can move from contemporary events—whether at the Games or in the Persian Wars—the better he can show the Greeks what they share. In this way, the partisan passions and politics which lead to commissions for Pindar can be employed by him in inducing the Greek cities to rise above their differences in acknowledging their deep, if not even eternal, affinities. (Consider how Thebes and Athens are brought together in Sophocles' *Oedipus at Colonus* and how Argos and Athens are brought together in Aeschylus' *The Eumenides*. Even so, Arrian reports [1.9; p. 61] that when Alexander destroyed Thebes a century after Pindar's death, "people felt that Thebes, at long last, had been punished for her treachery—she had paid the penalty for her betrayal of Greece in the Persian war [etc.]")

ix

To speak of Pindar as I have is to return to the Socrates of Plato and to the Platonic use of Pindar, whatever Socrates found it prudent to say about the treatment afforded in Athens to Olympic victors. Certainly, Pindar can be taken to caution us not to allow athletic contests to become ends in themselves, so much so that they can be made too much of as particular events, promoting and legitimizing in us the lust for victory, if not even for blood. Here, too, there can be seen something Socratic. Something Socratic may be seen as well, especially when we recall the philosopher-king, in the sovereignty Pindar asserts again and again, as he organizes all the elements that he enlists in his service: the gods and heroes of antiquity and the winners of the Games in his day. And so Pindar can ask that "war and all battle remain far from the immortals" (*Olympian* 9).

It is consistent with the theme of reconciliation I have attributed to Pindar that I should say more about the differences between philosophy and poetry, differences rooted perhaps in opinions about the relation between bodies and the ideas. It is salutary, in these circumstances, to place an emphasis instead upon affinities between philosophy and poetry, including their ability if not their duty to say different things (about both divine and human affairs) to different kinds of people (depending upon how attentive and thoughtful one is). (See *Nemean* 5.)

In what is regarded as Pindar's last ode—that is, the last ode we have and can date—the concluding passage recognizes that human beings are but "things of a day" (*Pythian* 8). Pindar thereby acknowledges most emphatically the limitations of human beings and hence of his art. He indicates this elsewhere as well, such as when he says, "Beyond this neither the wise nor fools must go. I'll go no farther. I'd be a fool" (*Olympian* 3).

We are once again reminded of Socrates, with his lively awareness of his limitations. But it was also Socrates who could, like Pindar, recognize his true worth. If Socrates is correct in the *Apology,* he deserves, better than do the winners of the Olympic Games, the largesse that the city is prepared to lavish upon them. Would this largesse not include victory odes of the kind Pindar provided *his* winners? Should we not say that the dialogues of Plato and the recollections of Xenophon are, in effect, Socrates' victory odes? (These are reinforced by the treatises of Aristotle.)

Socrates, we also remember, was spoken of in the highest (human) terms for his wisdom by the oracle of Delphi, the very oracle with which Pindar allied himself. Thus Pindar could say, "Me too hath the Muse raised up for Hellas as a chosen herald of wise words . . ." (Loeb Classical Library edition, p. 561). A Socratic approach may also be noticed in another saying by Pindar: "Yet measure due is meet in all things, and the fitting moment [*kairos*] is the best aim of knowledge." (*Olympian* 13. See, also, Bacchylides, p. 59.)

Still, we should not forget that there *are* differences between the poet and the philosopher, and, with perhaps profound implications, between Pindar and Socrates. Not the least of these differences is related to the fact that Socrates is remembered (along with Sappho?) for talking in the most down-to-earth fashion, employing everyday speech even for the most exalted things. Pindar, on the other hand, was entitled to say of himself, "My voice is sweeter than the bee-wrought honeycombs" (Loeb Classical Library edition, p. 601).

Would Socrates have been entitled to say about Pindar what he said about poets generally, that "they do not make what they make by wisdom, but by some sort of nature and while inspired, like the diviners and those who deliver oracles"? For, Socrates added, "they too say many noble things, but they know nothing of what they speak." (Plato, *Apology* 22B–C. See, also, section ix of chapter 2 of this book.) Does the considerable self-consciousness of Pindar, which some can mistake for mere arrogance, suggest a thoughtfulness that anticipates, if it does not even help instruct, both the dramatists and the philosophers who succeeded him?

PART TWO. On Delphi

Delphi is the sound of bells
Beaten copper, twisted thin
Folded nailed with copper pegs,
Brilliant sparks from metal shells
Struck by fur and skeleton
In rhythms moved by legs.

The mountain's thrust, the birds' wild wings
Scarce touch the air that bears their stress.
This world declares that gentleness
Is strength and bell-like sings.

—Sara Prince Anastaplo

i

IN PART 1 of this chapter I suggest that the great athletic contests of the Greeks contributed to Panhellenic standards of beauty and virtue. The Games, especially as celebrated by poets such as Pindar, provided a cohesive element for the Greeks. Much the same can be said of the great oracular shrines of Greece. The most sacred shrines, like the Games, pointed to a political union of the Greek cities, however long (indeed two millennia) that union was in coming. These shrines can also be understood to have anticipated, in their thoughtful artistry, the philosophers of the ancient world.

Although Apollo's oracle at Delphi (near Pindar's Thebes) was not the only one in Greece, it eventually came to be respected as the preeminent oracular site among the many available. This may be seen in Plato's dialogues, where reliance upon Delphi (for guidance with respect

---

A useful collection of Delphic responses may be found in Joseph Fontenrose, ed., *The Delphic Oracle: Its Responses and Operations* (Berkeley: University of California Press, 1978).

The epigraph, "Delphi," works from the sounds and sight of the goats, donkeys, and birds in and around Delphi. See, for other poems by this poet, the dedication to this book and section vi of chapter 6. See, also, Murley, Stone, and Braithwaite, eds., *Law and Philosophy*, 2:1033.

to shrines and rituals to be established in a well-ordered city) is taken for granted. (See, e.g., *Republic* 427B–C, *Laws* 738C, 759C, 792D, 828A.) It seems to have been recognized that such matters have to be decided by someone, in an authoritative manner—or, at least, in an apparently authoritative manner (which may be, at least in this context, the same thing)—and that Delphi was much the most plausible among the choices available to the Greeks in Plato's time (as it was to be for several centuries after Plato).

Not only do such things have to be decided by someone, somewhat "arbitrarily" if necessary, but also old allegiances and old ways of doing things are difficult to uproot—and why uproot them if what replaces them is not likely to be intrinsically and obviously superior? Besides, may not the priests at Delphi—however obscure, irrational, or unbelievable all that may now seem to us—may not those priests have drawn upon something like natural law, a natural law which, in its deference to an authority guided by revelation, is to be distinguished from natural right, which is more likely to be guided by reason simply? Is it not reasonable to take due account of the revelation and attendant rituals that a people has come to rely upon, especially over a very long time? In any event, whether it is natural right or natural law that the priests at Delphi were receptive to, something enduring must have been looked to for guidance—or so I suggest in what follows from a consideration of what went on at Delphi and how it was received in the ancient Greek world. Delphi is particularly important in several of the plays discussed in the next three chapters of this book. Herodotus and Plato, among others, also made use of Delphi. (See, on natural law, Anastaplo, "Natural Law or Natural Right?" See, on the relation between prophecy and political science, Anastaplo, "Lessons for the Student of Law," p. 112 n. 256. See, also, Strauss, *On Plato's Banquet,* p. 34.)

ii

What did happen at Delphi? Delphi had both its marvelous and its prosaic aspects. (The same can be said of the regime in the United States, with its great men of the founding period and of the period leading up to and through the Civil War, on the one hand, and its various generations since of successful merchants and the like, on the other hand.)

Which was fundamental to the regime at Delphi, the marvelous or the prosaic?

Did the marvelous, which comes down to us in the form of accounts of spectacular prophecies originating in Delphi, provide the legitimation for all that Delphi did of a more prosaic character? This kind of combination may be seen when miracles testify to access to divine powers, powers which once legitimated come to bear upon myriads of everyday problems. Or did the years of prosaic responses from the oracle—which are mostly what we now have records of—did these prosaic responses to everyday questions establish the reliability of the oracle, a soundness evident in the light of common-sense notions of good and bad, of proper and improper, of right and wrong?

I suspect that it was generally understood, even without being explicitly formulated this way, that if the Greeks were to be one people, and if any "national" standards were to be reliable, there would have to be an accepted authority (or set of authorities) to which more or less sovereign cities could look, something which all Greeks could invoke with confidence. (Something like this may be seen in the constitutional documents and their authoritative interpretation of which so much is made in the United States.)

iii

Rituals do tend to appear, especially to outsiders, somewhat arbitrary in their forms. Yet people do seem to have a natural appetite for them, as may be seen, for example, in how much even academic people (supposedly among the most liberated from superstition) still make of graduation ceremonies and the paraphernalia associated with them. Such ceremonies testify to a great tradition, reaching across centuries and oceans; they reaffirm the community's faith in something vital in the present and for the future.

Granted that a religion-based authority was needed in ancient Greece, an authority to which various legendary oracles from time to time could be attributed, why should it have been Delphi that became preeminent? Other places were more important for other things—for example, Eleusis (near Athens) was vital for mystery rites that served fertility concerns. But Delphi did gain the greatest repute with respect to oracles, so much so that an Asian king of fabulous wealth, Croesus, could be said to have settled upon Delphi as the most reliable oracle after having conducted, it is reported, a remarkable experiment designed to test the known oracles of his day for their effectiveness. (See Herodotus, *History* 1.46–49.)

Why Delphi, then? Not the least of the factors that may have led to the primacy of Delphi among the ancient oracles is the simple fact of the awesomeness of the temple site at Delphi, placed as it is overlooking a spectacular valley which runs down to the Gulf of Corinth and itself overlooked by the formidable Parnassus mountain range. The visitor can still feel that if Apollo ever speaks to human beings, it must be here. Even the most sophisticated visitor cannot help but be awed, and moved to considerable respect if not reverence, by Delphi under a full moon. I myself have been there more than once with sensitive people who reported fantastic dreams under the influence of the Delphic landscape.

It is not surprising, therefore, that the ancient Greeks could regard Delphi as the center of the earth and could even have exhibited the *omphalos* there as the marker of that center. (Compare the epigraph for chapter 5 of this book.) Constantine Karamanlis told me, when he was in self-imposed exile in Paris, that once (when he was prime minister of Greece) upon being shown the *omphalos* at Delphi he had suggested that it be thrown into the sea—because, he explained, the Greeks already have far too inflated a sense of self-importance. (This could be said of Mr. Karamanlis as well.) On the other hand, it does require considerable self-esteem for any people at "the crossroads of the world" to be, and to remain, a people, not allowing itself to be assimilated into other peoples. Delphi did come to assume in ancient Greece much of the status that the Vatican, or some would say the White House, has today, as a source of legitimacy and leadership for the civilized world.

iv

To the question, "Why Delphi?" there is still another answer which I can do little more than record here. There *is* the possibility of divine influences at work in promoting the ascendancy of this shrine. Certainly, that should not be ruled out in any consideration of the cause and nature of Delphi's influence. Intimately related to this consideration may be a challenging perceptiveness on the part of the priests of Delphi, a perceptiveness seen most dramatically in the judgment said to have been made by the oracle at Delphi that no man was wiser than Socrates. This judgment, which comes down to us from several sources and in different forms, did have the Delphic oracle testify to the supreme, if not even unique, wisdom of Socrates among human beings, a Socrates who later ran afoul of his own people back in Athens. Was this striking judgment about Socrates an instance of manipulation—say, by Socrates' well-wishers who were not averse to using their wealth in what they considered Socrates' interest? Or was it all merely a fiction developed or exploited by Plato and others?

However one regards the judgment about Socrates attributed to Delphi, it was a judgment that was not thought implausible for the oracle to have pronounced. That is, it seems to have been considered consistent with the principles of Delphi—and it seems to have been accepted (or at least not repudiated) by Delphi, so far as we know. This suggests the possibility that Delphi did see in Socrates something consistent with the sort of thing that Delphi at its best was interested in and stood for. There may well have been between Delphi and Socrates an alliance of sorts, at least with respect to the status of prudence, with respect to the desirability of avoiding excess, and with respect to the necessity of knowing oneself.

To have praised Socrates as Delphi was believed to have done was not only to have been rather astute (at least in our eyes) but also perhaps to have recognized in the Athens of the philosophers something which was distinctively Greek, something which should be made available in some form to everyone, then and since, however disturbing (if not even deadly) Athenian foreign policy might be from time to time. (Similar things can be said about the place of the United States in the western world today.)

v

What Delphi truly thought of Socrates may be difficult, if not impossible, ever to determine. But consider how, in turn, people as sophisticated as Socrates and the Socratics dealt with Delphi. Again and again, as I have indicated, they treated Delphi as reliable and useful, whatever they may really have believed about it. (Reservations are implied, as in Plato's *Laws,* where there is cautious criticism of Delphi, or as in the *Apology,* where Socrates is shown deliberately and repeatedly testing the oracle about him from Delphi.) Certainly, Socrates considered it prudent to make use of institutions such as Delphi. Is it not natural that such institutions should tend, over time, to become sensible?

No doubt, the Delphic authority was vulnerable to science and skepticism. But it should be remembered that, despite the stories popularly accepted, there was little if any frenzied activity on the part of the priestesses (who served as mediums) at Delphi. In any event, the oracle seems to have been run by sober and evidently well-informed priests who were not themselves philosophers, of course, but who might well have had some sympathy for what the more responsible philosophers of their day were evidently interested in.

However this may have been, most of the activity of Delphi during its centuries in ascendancy (from, say, the fifth century B.C. on) had little to do with the likes of Socrates and Croesus, even though the considerable offerings at Delphi did testify to the respect that Croesus and others of wealth and power had long had for Delphi. It must have been the prosaic everyday business of the oracle, when dealing either with public affairs or with private matters, that made it generally evident how important Delphi was for the Greek world.

By looking further, however briefly, into that prosaic everyday business, we can better see not only what Delphi was all about but also, and more critical to our immediate purposes, what Delphi can teach us about the relation of law to morality.

vi

The routine public affairs with which Delphi concerned itself included questions put to the oracle about colonization schemes, about the establishment of shrines, and about the inauguration or modification of forms of worship.

Delphi must have been understood as tending to respect established obligations. Thus, it can insist on what we would call international law. Athens, for example, was once told that she could not expect any services from Apollo at Delphi until she paid a fine that she owed to the Eleans.

It seems to have been assumed that no city is simply on its own, that there were standards (known to and respected by all civilized communities or at least by all Greek cities) which were to be considered and applied in dealings among cities. Furthermore, Delphi did tend to reinforce and rely upon long-accepted stories about the gods: it could be depended upon to commend, and to contribute to the legitimation of, any shrine or worship dedicated to the deities familiar to the Greeks.

In short, we again notice, Delphi must have been a convenient way for the Greek cities to remind each other of the ethical dictates that should govern relations among as well as within cities.

vii

The prosaic private matters with which Delphi concerned itself included questions put to the oracle about possible weddings, proposed trips, commercial undertakings, and the like. Most of the responses that have survived to our day have to do with religious arrangements and family decisions, not with morals or even prophecies (enigmatic or otherwise).

Of course, it seems to have been understood that Apollo did endorse the generally-accepted ethical standards. Thus, to deceive either gods or men was considered a dubious practice. Even the testing of gods, as Croesus did, could be considered questionable—for is not such testing a kind of attempted deception of a god?

The Apollo of Delphi (who could often be referred to simply as "the god") tended to regard the old as the good. Is there not something sound in this? Must there not usually be something sensible and otherwise good in any institution or set of beliefs if it can survive a long time? Nature is likely to assert herself in or through long-established institutions. In any event, it seems to have been assumed by Delphi that one is not free to do as one pleases, that standards transcending immediate practices are to be considered and applied by cities as well as by men.

These standards may be attributed to divine sources, but they can also be identified by us as rationally arrived at because of their effects.

Thus, the priests at Delphi must have conducted themselves much as Common Law judges do today, drawing upon everyday notions of morality, of the common good, and even of public policy. (See, on the Common Law, Anastaplo, *The Constitution of 1787*, p. 332.)

How did the popular opinions about the gods upon which the priests relied get their start? Perhaps they began, in their orthodox forms, with Homer and Hesiod. At least, historians such as Herodotus seem to have thought so. Thereafter, thinkers such as Plato refined, and perhaps reformed, what the poets had usefully said about the divine.

viii

To stand, as Delphi did, for the old and the orthodox tends, in a decent community, to be consistent (I have suggested) with the natural. That is, it combines sensibleness with authority. Even if the Delphic oracle was a fraud (whatever that might mean in this context), centuries of priests were able to appear wise and reliable—or, at least, the Greeks who were interested in wisdom and reliability were able to make allies of the priests.

I return to a theme I have already touched upon in this discussion. Does not any civilized people, if it is to endure, develop in its institutions a tacit respect for natural right (even if it does not explicitly recognize nature herself as an authority)? Although we ourselves no longer believe in the specific divine revelations of the ancient Greeks, can we not, when properly informed, still respect what Delphi stood for and accomplished? Should not the freethinker today be able to say the same about well-established Christian institutions among us (including even some of those institutions, dependent upon rather curious revelations, which were founded in the United States as recently as the nineteenth century)? This is to suggest again that nature asserts herself in and through any institution if she is given enough time.

Still, there are apt to be features, including presuppositions, about any venerable institution that may be highly questionable. But these may be so much a part of the thing, if not even vital to it, that it would be dangerous to the survival of that institution simply to rip out such features. It is much more prudent to smooth them out or to work around them, especially since any institution that is likely to replace what a people has long had (considering the limitations of any truly public opinion) is apt to have distortions of its own, but fresh distortions with unpredictable consequences.

It is also prudent, if one is to make the best possible use of established institutions, to be aware of the built-in limitations of any particular set of orthodox opinions. Thus, a thoughtful Greek in antiquity would have had to ask, "What reservations should one have about Delphi?" Did Delphi foster superstitions that led, in effect, to the subversion of even the most advanced Greek cities? Did it cater to flaws that eventually undermined Greece (especially in the face of the Roman threat)? The crippling of the Athenian fleet by an eclipse in Sicily during the Peloponnesian War and the savagery of the Athenians following upon the Battle of Arginusae come to mind. (See section i of part 1 of chapter 11 of this book. See, also, chapter 9 of this book.)

Delphi could also be faulted for having allowed questions about its integrity to develop. No doubt its priests were at times subject to bribery. But one should not take too seriously the fact that such people *are* human. One can expect those who manage their successor institutions, religious as well as secular, to exhibit the same frailties at times.

More serious, of course, were the shortcomings of the theological opinions upon which Delphi rested, sometimes bizarre opinions about the gods, such opinions as those that Socrates (in the second and third books of Plato's *Republic*) wanted to see purged from public discourse. But here, too, one suspects, it must be difficult for any successor institutions, except those limited to a relatively small number of highly disciplined adherents, not to be receptive to similar opinions, opinions which appeal to and are nourished by the poetic fancy of the people at large. (I return to this subject in the epilogue to this book.)

I have already referred to the failings of Delphi which catered to flaws within the Greek cities and in their relations with one another. It might be well now to refer also to failings, if failings they be, that contributed significantly to the eventual displacement of the religion of which Delphi had become an "official" exponent. The religion of the ancient Greeks, it can be said, did not adequately address itself to the problem of the salvation of the individual soul. That is, it did not allow enough for, or offer enough to, those who had come to be very much concerned about personal survival after death. (See, for Moses Maimonides' discussion of resurrection, Hallein and Hartman, p. 211.)

Delphi allowed the Christianity we are familiar with to arise as a result of what it did (or did not) say about the immortality of the soul. Christianity, rather than the even more purified opinions about the divine advocated by Socrates in Plato's *Republic,* seems to have followed upon the popular religion of the ancient Greeks. Did Christianity tend to make more of humanity and self-realization—and hence less of community and law—as a critical means for emergence of the best? Thus, individual conscience became more important; law, and the use of the law to promote morality, became less important, as we can see down to our day. In any event, Delphi (in its closing centuries) seems to have regarded Christianity as a critical competitor. The surviving Delphic responses, genuine or not, seem to recognize this. No doubt, the two faiths were radically different in critical respects, at least at the outset of Christianity, however similar they became (in their respective maturities) over millennia. (See Dante, *Paradiso* 17.31–36; Anastaplo, "Rome, Piety, and Law," p. 68.)

ix

Delphi, I have suggested, served the interest of lawgivers in promoting moral as well as religious standards. Whether the priests at Delphi were themselves aware of how Delphi was being used may be ultimately irrelevant to our concerns here.

It is not enough in political life for a lawgiver to have the truth. He must also have what we today call "credibility": that is, he must have an authority which makes his opinions seem legitimate. Delphi evidently helped provide such support for various lawgivers. It also provided something else which helps make a healthy political life possible: it made available, or ratified, an account of the whole which assured the many that there was order in the cosmos, an order which could even explain such dangerously unsettling catastrophes as earthquakes, plagues, and famines. Without such an assurance, the meaningfulness of life is called into question, and human beings can begin to despair upon suspecting that they are suspended over an abyss.

The need for meaningfulness is something that the lawgiver should reckon with. If he cannot minister to that need, in a responsible way, others will do so in irresponsible ways. Certainly, there seems to be in mankind an appetite for the divine, an appetite which finds expression in so many varied circumstances and yet in such similar ways that one must wonder whether such an appetite is natural. Can there be an enduring appetite without something in nature to satisfy that appetite? Does the appetite itself, if it is not perverted and misunderstood, point to something that exists to satisfy that appetite properly? To ask this may do no more than to allude still another time to the perennial question, "Quid sit deus?" (Strauss, *The City and Man*, p. 241.)

Much of what I have said here could be reconsidered, or at least restated, by addressing ourselves at length to the significance of the Christian term *conscience* in modern moral discourse. All too often, those who make much of conscience are apt to assume that the human being is somehow autonomous, that he has within himself sufficient reliable guidance for the moral decisions he must make. Either an emphasis upon uninstructed conscience or a purely personal reliance only upon reason tends to undermine the role of the law in directing people not only in what they should do but also in what they should want to do.

But, as it is noticed in Plato's *Laws*, the art of politics is "the art whose business it is to care for souls" (650B). It is also noticed "that an upbringing that is correct in every way must manifest the power to make bodies and souls the most beautiful and the best possible" (788C). If these objectives are to be secured, it is further said, the lawgiver must write not only laws but also "things interwoven with the laws, writings that reveal what seems noble and ignoble to him." (823A. See, also, 821A sq. See, on the moderating of the noble by the just, part 2 of chapter 7 of this book.) Delphi and other oracles, as well as the Games celebrated by poets such as Pindar, I have suggested, helped bind together the peoples of ancient Greece, interweaving into the laws of cities enduring standards, aspirations, and restraints that stand for civilization itself.

ADDENDUM

Piety and Statesmanship

THE SEVEN PASSAGES set forth below from Plato and Aristotle suggest how ancient Greek statesmanship depended upon religion (and particularly upon the oracular priestess of Apollo, or the Pythia, at Delphi). See, also, Plato, *Republic* 327A–331D, 461E, 468–69; Plato, *Laws* 686A, 758E–759D, 828A, 856E, 865B, 871C, 914A, 923A, 947D, 950E; Aristotle, *Politics* 1281b17, 1285a6, 1314b38, 1322b18, 1329a27, 1330a8, 1331b16; Anastaplo, "Church and State," pp. 61, 109. (In these passages, the *Apology of Socrates* is translated by Thomas G. West and Grace Starry West; the *Republic,* by Allan Bloom; the *Laws,* by Thomas L. Pangle; and the *Politics,* by Carnes Lord.)

i

[Socrates:] Now please, men of Athens, do not make a disturbance, not even if I seem to you to be boasting somewhat. For "not mine is the story" that I will tell; rather, I will refer it to a speaker trustworthy to you. Of my wisdom, if indeed it is wisdom of any kind, and what sort of thing it is, I will offer for you as witness the god in Delphi. Now you know Chaerephon, no doubt. He was my comrade from youth as well as a comrade of your multitude, and he shared in your recent exile and returned with you. You do know what sort of man Chaerephon was, how vehement he was in whatever he would set out to do. And in particular he once even went to Delphi and dared to consult the oracle about this— now as I say, do not make disturbances, men—and he asked whether there was anyone wiser than I. The Pythia replied that no one was wiser. And concerning these things his brother here will be a witness for you, since he himself has met his end. [Plato, *Apology* 20E–21A]

ii

"Then what," [Adeimantus] said, "might still remain for our legislation?"

And [Socrates] said, "For us, nothing. However for the Apollo at Delphi there remain the greatest, fairest, and first of the laws which are given."

"What are they about?" [Adeimantus] said.

"Founding of temples, sacrifices, and whatever else belongs to the care of gods, daemons, and heroes; and further, burial of the dead and all the services needed to keep those in that other place gracious. For such things as these we neither know ourselves, nor in founding a city shall we be persuaded by any other man, if we are intelligent, nor shall we make use of any interpreter other than the ancestral one. Now this god is doubtless the ancestral interpreter of such things for all humans, and he sits in the middle of the earth at its navel and delivers his interpretations."

"What you say is fine," [Adeimantus] said. "And that's what must be done."

"So then, son of Ariston," [Socrates] said, "your city would now be founded." [Plato, *Republic* 427A–C]

iii

". . . Once they see the good itself, [Socrates said] they must be compelled, each in his turn, to use it as a pattern for ordering city, private men, and themselves for the rest of their lives. For the most part, each one spends his time in philosophy, but when his turn comes, he drudges in politics and rules for the city's sake, not as though he were doing a thing that is fine, but one that is necessary. And thus always educating other like men and leaving them behind in their place as guardians of the city, they go off to the Isles of the Blessed and dwell. The city makes public memorials and sacrifices to them as to daemons, if the Pythia is in accord; if not, as to happy and divine men."

"Just like a sculptor, Socrates," [Glaucon] said, "you have produced ruling men who are wholly fair."

"And ruling women, too, Glaucon," [Socrates] said. "Don't suppose that what I have said applies any more to men than to women, all those who are born among them with adequate natures."

"That's right," [Glaucon] said, "if they are to share everything in common equally with the men, as we described it." [Plato, *Republic* 540A–C]

iv

[The Athenian Stranger:] These matters must be studied at leisure and firmly understood by those who are given this duty by the law; at any rate, this is the way it is, and the person who is going to set up a city should proclaim these things with a view to the following. The same applies whether someone is making a new city from the beginning or refounding an old city that has become corrupted: as regards gods and temples—which things are to be constructed in the city for each of them, and which gods or daemons they are to be named after—no one intelligence will try to change what has been laid down [at the shrines of] Delphi or Dodona or Ammon, or what has been ordained by the ancient sayings, however they may have become manifest—whether they issue from apparitions or from an inspiration said to come from gods. Through such advice men have established sacrifices, mixed with mystery-rites, some of which have local origins and some of which are borrowed from Etruria, or Cyprus, or somewhere else. Such sayings have led them to sanctify oracles, statues, altars, and shrines, and to lay out sanctuaries for each of these things. Now a lawgiver should not change any of these things in the least. He should give to each group a god or daemon or some hero, and before he makes any other land distribution he should set aside choice places for sanctuaries and everything that goes with them. In this way, when the various parts of the population gather together at the regularly established intervals, they'll be amply supplied with whatever they need; they'll become more friendly to one another, at the sacrifices, will feel they belong together, and will get to know one another. There is no greater good for a city than that its inhabitants be well known to one another; for where men's characters are obscured from one another by the dark instead of being visible in the light, no one ever obtains in a correct way the honor he deserves, either in terms of office or justice. Above everything else, every man in every city must strive to avoid deceit on every occasion and to appear always in simple fashion, as he truly is—and, at the same time, to prevent any other such man from deceiving him. [Plato, *Laws* 738B–E]

v

We must also investigate how many things there are without which a city could not exist; what we speak of as being parts of a city would also be among those things which must necessarily be present. We must therefore have a grasp of the number of tasks [the city requires]; it will be clear from these things. First, then, sustenance must be available; next, arts, for living requires many instruments; . . . fifth, and first, the superintendence connected with the divine, which they call priestcraft. . . . One might order these things, then, in this manner. As for the buildings assigned to divine matters and the common messes for the most authoritative official boards, it is fitting for them to be located together in a proper place, at least in the case of those temples which the law or some prophecy of the Delphic oracle does not require to be separate. This would be the sort of place whose position is adequate for the manifestation of virtue and at the same time better fortified in relation to the neighboring parts of the city. Below this place it is proper to institute a market. . . . Since the multitude of the city is divided into priests, officials, [and soldiers, and since common messes have been provided on sacred grounds for officials,] it is proper that there should be an arrangement to have common messes for the priests too in the vicinity of the sacred buildings. [Aristotle, *Politics* 1328b4–12, 1331a23–1331b8]

vi

As regards the quality of body that would be of most benefit to offspring in the process of generation, we must stop to speak of it more at length in the [discourses] concerning management of children; at present it is enough to speak of it in outline. The [bodily] disposition of athletes is not useful either with a view to the good condition required of the citizen or with a view to health and procreation, and neither is one that is overly valetudinarian and ill-suited for exertion, but a middling sort between these. One should have a disposition formed by exertion, but not by violent exertion, and not with a view to one thing only, like the athletes' disposition, but with a view to the actions belonging to liberal persons. And these things should be present in similar fashion in men and women. Even pregnant women ought to take care of their bodies, not remaining idle or taking meager sustenance. This is easy for the legislator to do by mandating that they make a trip every day to worship the goddesses who have been granted the prerogative connected with birth. [Aristotle, *Politics* 1335b2–16]

vii

[Socrates:] Now consider why I say these things: I am going to teach you where the slander against me has come from. When I heard these things, I pondered them like this: "What ever is the god saying [at Delphi], and what riddle is he posing? For I am conscious that I am not at all wise, either much or little. So what ever is he saying when he claims that I am wisest? Surely he is not saying something false, at least; for that is not sanctioned for him." And for a long time I was at a loss about what ever he was saying, but then very reluctantly I turned to something like the following investigation of it. I went to one of those reputed to be wise, on the ground that there, if anywhere, I would refute the divination and show the oracle, "This man is wiser than I, but you declared that I was wisest." [Plato, *Apology* 21B–C]

IV. Aeschylus. On the *Oresteia*

> *Just as the bachelor arms himself and does not speak till the master submits the question—for argument, not for settlement—, so I armed myself with all my reasons while she was speaking, to be ready for such a questioner and for such a profession.*
>
> —Dante

i

ONE OF THE QUESTIONS THAT may be asked about Aeschylus' *Oresteia* is whether it is truly a tragedy. It has been suggested by some critics that Aristotle avoided the difficulties posed by this trilogy with respect to certain elements of his definition of tragedy by simply ignoring the *Oresteia* in the *Poetics*. Other critics, however, refer to the *Oresteia* as the only example of a complete Greek trilogy of tragedies that has come down to us. An examination of the question about whether the *Oresteia* is a tragedy provides us entry into both Greek tragedy and Aristotle's *Poetics*, two of the forms in which thinkers make use of art. This inquiry into the ancient trilogy can also help us see what Greek tragedy was like.

Unless otherwise indicated, the citations in this chapter are to Aeschylus' *Oresteia* (*Agamemnon, The Libation Bearers,* and *The Eumenides*) or to Aristotle's *Poetics.* See, for additional discussion by me of Aeschylus, "On Trial," p. 796. See, on the *Poetics,* Laurence Berns, "Aristotle's *Poetics.*"

The epigraph is taken from Dante, *Paradiso* 24.46–51.

The three parts of the *Oresteia*—*Agamemnon, The Libation Bearers,* and *The Eumenides*—can be considered somewhat independent and autonomous tragedies. Each of the plays tells a story, the first about the killing of Agamemnon by his wife Clytemnestra upon his return home from the Trojan War, the second about the killing of Clytemnestra by her son Orestes to avenge his father's death, the third (in which the Furies attempt to destroy Orestes) about the resolution of an age-old conflict between partial views of justice.

Each of these accounts is important and interesting enough on its own. Enough of the facts are given us in each of the three plays for understanding that play. It is as if the playwright wished to make sure that each of the plays could stand alone, that the audience would not have to draw upon memory to follow the main lines of the action. In the sense, then, that we can more or less comprehend what is happening in each of the plays without reference to the other two, the plays are somewhat independent and autonomous.

Furthermore, the setting of each of the plays is distinctive. The Argos of the first play is not the Argos of the second; and, of course, the action is removed to Delphi and Athens in the third play. Several years separate the action of the second from the first play; a year or so separates the third from the second. The mood, principal characters, and emphasis change markedly from one play to the next.

Additional indications of autonomy can be found. The objective of the principal character in each of the first two plays—the objective stated at the outset—is carried through to the conclusion planned for it. We see preparations made for killings; we see the plans executed; and we then hear justifications for what has been done.

Consider also the lesson taught by each play. In the first, the arrogant leader meets his doom; in the second, an unfaithful wife is brought to justice; in the third, conventional or traditional justice is made to bow before the demands of comprehensive justice. Each of the plays has a problem to consider, a problem which it seems to dispose of.

These are the ways in which the three plays of the trilogy may be said to be somewhat independent and autonomous, a conclusion reinforced by the fact that single plays of the trilogy are routinely presented to modern audiences. In fact, it is now rare to have the entire trilogy presented at one sitting. But the criteria that I have mentioned thus far are not the vital ones. For despite all these factors, the plays are not truly independent and autonomous.

It is instructive to notice, therefore, how the character of each of the plays is altered because it is a part of the trilogy. The nature and degree of alteration that we find points up the interrelations among the plays. But before we come to that discussion, there are other considerations that also militate against a finding of autonomy.

Aristotle, in examining the requirements for tragedy, speaks in the *Poetics* of the forms of plot to be avoided. What he says of defective plots would seem to apply to any serious dramatic work by a responsible artist (*Poetics* 1452b34):

> A good man must not be seen passing from happiness to misery, or a bad man from misery to happiness. The first situation is not fear-inspiring or piteous, but simply odious to us. The second is the most untragic that can be; it has no one of the requisites of tragedy; it does not appeal either to the human feeling in us, or to our pity, or to our fears.

The reasons Aristotle gives suggest why the *Agamemnon* and *The Libation Bearers* cannot really stand alone. There would be something offensive to our moral sensibilities if Clytemnestra were to be left as triumphant as she is at the end of the first play. Similarly, it would be odious if a desperate Orestes should be last seen (as in *The Libation Bearers*) with the Furies in pursuit.

I must restate, therefore, what I have said. The *Agamemnon* is not simply the story of the arrogant leader who meets his doom. It is as much, if not more, the account of the success of a wicked woman. She is not merely the instrument of fate, an instrument that is insignificant compared to the fallen hero. If she were only that, it might not matter what happens to her thereafter. Despite the fact that the failings of Agamemnon are amply recalled, it is a questionable Clytemnestra who dominates the stage and is left triumphant. It is not right that this should be so, however much we may respect (if not admire) how she carries off her daring plot against the most powerful man in Greece.

Nor is *The Libation Bearers* simply the chronicle of the inevitable punishment of a treacherous wife. It is much more the drama of a young man who finds himself on a dreadful mission as the agent of Apollo. He is compelled to act; he acts with the highest motives. That a man executes, and executes in the proper spirit, the divine command would seem to be justification enough for any act. But the matricidal Orestes, despite the protection promised by an insistent Apollo, is endangered by the unrelenting Furies. There is a conflict here that cannot be left unresolved. The play cannot end at this point.

The care Aeschylus takes to establish Orestes' essential innocence is important. (The character of his Orestes is different in critical respects from Sophocles' and Euripides' versions.) It is not Orestes, but the Chorus and his sister, who talk of blood for blood and simple revenge. He is the only one who, after the momentous deed in either play, can make a sober appraisal of his act (*Libation Bearers* 1014 sq.). Electra is much more like her mother, moved by passions which make her terribly single-minded. Orestes can hesitate; he has to be reminded of Apollo's command (*Libation Bearers* 900). He can wish Agamemnon had died at Troy —not only, we suspect, because of the greater honor that would have come to his father from such a death but also because he dreads the duty before him. Not so with Electra: she can only wish that his murderers had been killed first by those they loved (*Libation Bearers* 345–71). It is no accident that nothing is seen of Electra after the meeting with Orestes at the tomb of Agamemnon: she takes no part in the slaying; she does not appear in *The Eumenides.* Clytemnestra's blood, Aeschylus wants to make sure, will be spilt in as guiltless a way as possible. For there is more to come; this is not the end.

Perhaps Clytemnestra has good reasons for killing her husband. Certainly, it cannot be said that his death is altogether unmerited. But here Aeschylus obscures the good and magnifies the bad motives. The sacrifice of Iphigenia is overshadowed in the *Agamemnon* by the adultery of Clytemnestra, by her implacable hatred, and by her ferocious delight in the accomplishment of a breathtaking deed. Besides, there is in her case no explicit divine decree but rather human passion directing events. At most, we have here the right thing being done for the wrong reason. She cannot be left in her prosperity.

We are given indications, as each of the first two plays draws to a close, not only of the fact that things cannot be left as they are but even of the direction from which correction will come. To be sure, these indications do not create the dominant impressions—the immediate action is too strong for that. But they do provide grounds for supposing that accounts are not yet closed. Clytemnestra can, at the end of the *Agamemnon*, defy the horrified people of Argos and exult in her triumph. But there is talk of Orestes, so much so that he can even be regarded as a character in the first play. Aegisthus' poignant remark, "Exiles feed on empty dreams of hope. I know it. I was one," provides some indication of coming events (*Agamemnon* 1668). Orestes is an exile; Orestes hopes. Will that hope bear fruit? This question is left unanswered. But we do know that Aegisthus was an exile whose hopes were not empty.

At the end of *The Libation Bearers,* Orestes seems to be left to his punishment. But we cannot forget the command of Apollo. "[Loxias] declared I could do this and not be charged with wrong" (*Libation Bearers* 1031). Even the bloodthirsty Chorus—of foreign slave-women, it should be noted—can wonder, "Where shall the fury of fate be stilled to sleep, be done with?" (*Libation Bearers* 1075). By indicating in these ways that there is more to come, that the future is already to be glimpsed in the present, Aeschylus closes the first and second plays in this trilogy. But he does not end them. The end, as Aristotle says, is something after which there is nothing (*Poetics* 1450b30).

ii

I have already suggested important respects in which the character of the individual plays is altered by being a part of a trilogy. The plays do not stand alone partly because they need each other to bring out their full meaning.

In both the *Agamemnon* and *The Libation Bearers,* after their respective double killings, there is defiance expressed by those responsible for the bloody deaths. The opposing "factions" are brought together, elevated to the plane of abstract justice, and reconciled in *The Eumenides.* Orestes is acquitted and the Furies make their peace with Athena. Standing alone, the actions of the first two plays are exciting and gripping enough as actions. But when each play is brought together with the other two plays, the principles underlying the actions are highlighted and can be seen for what they fully are. We may even see here, in anticipation of my discussion in part 2 of chapter 7 of this book, a prudential subordination of the noble to the just.

Even *The Eumenides* is given, by its inclusion in a trilogy, a depth it would not otherwise have had. The issues may be adequately presented before the Temple of Athena. We are at least told enough to know what the problems are. But we run the kind of risk that comes in a Common Law jurisdiction from a reliance upon what the lawyers call "black-letter law." The law set forth in the summary of judicial opinions, even by the most competent compiler of decisions, simply may not tell us what the issues are really like until the facts of actual cases are before us. Similarly, in *The Eumenides,* there is not only a conflict of principles, but also of characters. To forget this is to ignore the dramatic element. It is in this way that the last play is illuminated, and in a sense altered, by the actions of the earlier plays, just as the earlier plays are reshaped by the last one.

I shall return to the level of the principles worked through in the plays after I consider other respects in which these plays affect and alter one another. Take, for example, the problem of Clytemnestra's true feelings upon hearing the report of Orestes' death in the second play. Her speech is sorrowful: "She put a sad face on before the servants, . . . to hide the smile inside her eyes," the nurse tells us (*Libation Bearers* 737–38). But we cannot be certain that the nurse's affection for Orestes and hatred for Clytemnestra do not make her unjustly attribute to the mother so unnatural a reaction. Even the divinely-directed Orestes, we see shortly thereafter, is made to hesitate, upon the threshold of another unnatural action, matricide. Cannot Clytemnestra be similarly restrained by natural sentiments? But we have been prepared by the *Agamemnon* to expect the worst from her in matters such as these. Her hypocrisy, we have learned, can be superb.

Consider also the change in how Clytemnestra's motivation is regarded from play to play. In the *Agamemnon*, the best case is presented for her, as the sacrifice of Iphigenia by her father is recounted and referred to several times. Other motives develop, but this seems to be the one that originally pointed Clytemnestra in the direction she has taken. But after the first play, there is no further mention in this connection of the slain daughter; she seems to drop out altogether from an appraisal of the forces that had moved Clytemnestra. Clytemnestra's position becomes more and more difficult to defend the further we are removed from the spell cast by her personality and by the power of her deeds.

The treatment of the Iphigenia episode indicates also a shift in the impression one has of Agamemnon as the trilogy develops. All of his shortcomings are marshaled against him in the first play. In the second, however, the grandeur of his kingly station comes to the fore. Iphigenia is referred to simply as the "pitilessly slaughtered sister" (not "daughter"), without explicit reference to the slaughterer (*Libation Bearers* 242). In *The Eumenides,* the final judgment on Agamemnon rendered by Apollo wrenches the first play out of the setting in which it had been left (*Eumenides* 631): "He had done [in his campaigning] better than worse, in the eyes of a fair judge."

Interpretations of other events and characters have to change as one play throws light upon another. The sending of the child Orestes away from Argos by his mother, the character of Aegisthus, and even the nature of retribution change in their appearances as we proceed from play to play. We learn, furthermore, that the involvement of the gods has been greater than even the claims of their earthly partisans had led us to expect. Finally, in *The Eumenides,* the powers that had previously lurked behind the human action, that had moved and guided it to some extent, meet face to face. When Apollo and the Furies do meet, the clash of principles dominates the stage and all previous action is thrown into a new light.

Before this *The Libation Bearers* had made necessary a reevaluation of the *Agamemnon.* What was the meaning of Clytemnestra's action if it required Orestes'? On the other hand, would the slain Clytemnestra have her avenger in turn? In *The Eumenides* the differences between the first two plays become crucial. We see in the *Agamemnon* the old pattern of blood for blood. To the casual observer the pattern in *The Libation Bearers* is substantially the same. The outrage expressed by Clytemnestra's ghost and by the Furies in *The Eumenides* is not altogether without justification. This is the way things are done, this is the way things are responded to. It is the problem left by *The Libation Bearers,* not that left by the *Agamemnon,* however, that calls for the establishment of a higher standard than that by which Clytemnestra and her partisans had acted. This higher standard, according to which human beings can both judge and act, is arrived at in *The Eumenides.* Only then can we truly see what happened in the first two plays.

The Furies, it is suggested in the *Agamemnon,* are on the side of a rough kind of justice. But, as we proceed, we see that they do not discriminate, that they are somewhat arbitrary, if not even tyrannical. The claims of true justice, of justice approached in the proper spirit, are muffled in the first two plays. Only later do we see that things need not be the way they have long been, however noble certain blows struck in revenge may appear to be.

There is only a hint in *The Libation Bearers* of a clash of "right with right" (*Libation Bearers* 461). Even Apollo has a limited view of what is right. He is far too scornful of the claims of the Furies, with their "age-old distributions of power" (*Eumenides* 172). An impartial and disinterested tribunal must be established for all time. So impartial and fairminded is the Athenian tribunal, in fact, that it divides its vote evenly, recognizing thereby the justice of the fundamental claims on both sides.

Thus we see law and order where once there was either anarchy or tyranny. There are to be sanctions: "What man who fears nothing at all is ever righteous?" (*Eumenides,* 699). But these are to be sanctions regulated by law. Moreover, order is to be brought out of the relations among the gods; the old and new divinities must be reconciled. Just as there is a need for sanctions among men, so is there among the gods and other immortals. Athena must remind the Furies, in order to persuade them to accept their new status, that she has access to Zeus' thunderbolts (*Eumenides* 827). The chaos of what has gone before cannot be fully appreciated until a model of law and order, of reason and justice, is presented in *The Eumenides.* But the necessity for that model is not fully apparent to us without the experience of the *Agamemnon* and *The Libation Bearers.* Only then can we share the satisfaction of the goddess of reason when she proclaims that her "ambition for good wins out in the whole issue" (*Eumenides* 974).

iii

We can now return to the question about whether the *Oresteia* trilogy as a whole is truly a tragedy. There are two simple, but apparently conflicting, observations critical to this inquiry. The first is that since the change in the hero's fortunes is from misery to happiness, rather than from happiness to misery, the trilogy does not conform with what has been often said to be a crucial element of Aristotle's more or less authoritative test for tragedy. The second observation is that since Aeschylus is obviously a tragedian, his masterpiece is likely to be a tragedy. The form, means, and manner of imitation of the *Oresteia* seem to be those described by Aristotle as distinguishing tragedy from the other poetic forms.

The problem of whether a trilogy *can* be a tragedy should not detain us long. The *Oresteia* can be treated as an extended play, or at least as a series of plays with the effect of one long play. The length of such a play would be limited only by the competence of the author. The longer it is, consistent with its comprehensibility as a whole, the better it may be. (See Aristotle, *Poetics* 1451a9.)

In the early days of poetry, we are told, the graver among the poets "would represent noble actions, and those of noble personages; and the meaner sort the actions of the ignoble" (1448b24). Then, as soon as tragedy and comedy appeared in the field, "those naturally drawn to the one line of poetry became writers of comedies instead of iambs, and those naturally drawn to the other, writers of tragedies instead of epics, because these new modes of art were grander and of more esteem than the old" (1449a1). On the basis of this passage, it would seem that what we know about Aeschylus, both with respect to the gravity of his character and the nobility of the actions and personages that he represents— what we know about him justifies considering the *Oresteia* a tragedy.

Aristotle's survey of the historical development of the tragedy reinforces this judgment. Tragedy attained its natural form only after a long series of changes (1449a13). In the course of this development, two of the principal contributions were made by Aeschylus (1449a16). The perfected form, however, seems to have come later (1449a19). Aeschylus' work is probably ignored in the *Poetics* partly because Aristotle preferred to deal with the full natural form, and partly because Aeschylus' writing is so distinctive, both with respect to the other poets and from play to play. Nevertheless, Aeschylean drama has that "tone of dignity," that magnitude, which Aristotle considers to be found at a late point in the progress of the development of the tragic form (1449a19). It is highly likely, therefore, that Aristotle regarded Aeschylus not only as a tragedian but as one of the outstanding tragedians.

The unity of a plot, to continue with a consideration of some of the points about which questions might be raised with respect to the

Oresteia, does not consist in having one man as a subject (1451a16). Rather, the emphasis should be placed upon the unity of action: "a complete whole, with its several incidents so closely connected that the transposal or withdrawal of any one of them will disjoin and dislocate the whole" (1450a32). My discussion and conclusions thus far speak to this point.

There remains to be considered the problem presented by the ending of the *Oresteia.* Aristotle's criterion here is of the same order as that limiting the action represented to one day (1449b12 sq.). That is to say, it is not absolutely essential for a tragedy to have "the hero's fortunes [change] from happiness to misery," but rather it is something that is to be found in "the perfect plot" (1453a12). It is a caution worth emphasizing, considering the disposition of many authors to minister to the sentimentality of the audience (as we have seen with our soap operas). But it is not a caution or difficulty that is appropriate with respect to Aeschylus. My conclusion here is supported by other indications in the *Poetics.* At an earlier point, Aristotle even accepts tacitly the development from misery to happiness as one that is appropriate in tragedy (1451a12). And, in the context in which is found the caution we are examining, he observes that the finest tragedies are always based upon the story of some few houses, that of Orestes being given as one such house (1453a17). He adds, a little further on, that the original stories must be kept as they are (1453b23). It should be noted that although we do not know exactly what version of the Orestes legend Aristotle referred to, it seems that the hero (albeit a matricide) is permitted eventual redemption in all of the legends that have come down to us. (Several other tragedies also exhibit a movement away from misery in their endings.)

Perhaps most important to any assessment of how the *Oresteia* should be regarded, there is in this trilogy the classic "tragic effect," the purgation of certain passions among the spectators. We see here, in fact, tragedy of the highest order, perhaps the greatest parable in the West, at least outside of the Bible (which it perhaps anticipates for Christians), of the human aspiration for law and justice (if not even personal salvation) in changing circumstances.

V. Sophocles. On the *Oedipus Tyrannus*

i

WHAT CAN BE SAID ABOUT the gods speaking to human beings as well as to gods? We look for guidance here to Sophocles' *Oedipus Tyrannus*, perhaps the greatest play ever written in the West. That play, like the *Oresteia* of Aeschylus and the *Hippolytus* of Euripides, draws upon ancient sources. This story addresses the puzzlement that human beings have always had as to how much control they can have over their own lives. It is the story about the responses first of Oedipus' parents and then of Oedipus himself to the prophecy that he would commit patri-

---

See, for additional discussion by me of Sophocles, "On Trial," p. 830; also, section i of part 1 of chapter 11 and the addendum to part 2 of chapter 7 of this book.

The epigraph is taken from Plato, *Critias* 121B–C (concluding lines of the dialogue; A. E. Taylor, translator).

cide and incest, about how these terrible offenses came about despite extraordinary efforts to avoid them, and about how the truth was revealed and with what consequences.

It is presupposed in the play that the divine exists, with direct references to gods and their doings in one-third of the lines and with the divine and its effects evident throughout the play. It is never questioned that the gods exist, but only whether, and if so how, they manifest themselves to human beings.

It is also presupposed that the gods interest themselves in human affairs. The gods, we are told by the Chorus in *Oedipus Tyrannus,* prescribed "the laws [with respect to piety] that live on high, laws begotten in the clear air of heaven, whose only father is Olympus [Zeus?]." (*Oedipus Tyrannus* 865. See also *Antigone* 450 sq.) Teachings and moral standards are furnished by the gods. These are backed up, it seems, by prospects of eternal rewards and punishments as well as by the temporal consequences of one's deeds. But, we can wonder, what does the play say about whether the gods intervene in the everyday life of human beings and, if so, how, why, and when?

ii

How do the gods express interest in particular cases? It seems that they speak in response to efforts by human beings to secure divine guidance. For example, men seek out oracles at shrines. They seek help elsewhere as well. In Rome, we recall, much was made of the examination of such things as the entrails of animals.

Sometimes an oracle is sought by someone for his own sake, as Oedipus did when he went to Apollo's shrine at Delphi to learn about his parentage. The disclosure made there was personal to Oedipus, even though it had public consequences. The same can be said about the disclosure decades before to Oedipus' parents, Laius and Jocasta.

Sometimes an oracle is sought on behalf of the city, as when Creon was sent by Oedipus to Delphi to learn what could be done about the blight that had settled upon Thebes. This disclosure was about public affairs, even though it had profound personal consequences.

iii

The gods can also express interest in particular cases without waiting upon human inquiries. The very passivity of men with respect to key matters may lead the gods to approach them. The blight that settled upon Thebes, which is connected with vital unfinished business in the city, prompts the Thebans to make inquiries of the gods, inquiries that they should perhaps have made decades before about who had presumed to kill the ruler who preceded Oedipus.

The signs sent by the gods to men sometimes provide guidance enough on their face, thereby encouraging or deterring action. Sometimes the signs, such as the Theban blight in this play, serve to encourage inquiry and investigation.

The signs that move human beings to wonder can be connected with birds, fire, altars, dreams, earthquakes, lightning and thunder. (See, e.g., *Oedipus Tyrannus* 981, *Oedipus at Colonus* 995, 1624.) Some people, it seems, are better equipped than others to read these signs.

Oracles, such as those coming from the priests at Delphi or those that come from Tiresias, the blind Theban seer, offer more precise information than signs usually provide. For example, the career of Oedipus can be given in its awful detail to Oedipus' parents before his birth, to Oedipus himself as a young man, and to Oedipus by Tiresias in the play. Nothing is said in *Oedipus Tyrannus* about how the priests or seers secure the information they relay. (Compare *Revelations* 1:1 sq.)

The play opens with the people of Thebes imploring Oedipus for help with the blight. A priest says to him, "Perhaps you'll hear a wise word from some God . . ." (*Oedipus Tyrannus* 43). Everyone remembers that Oedipus had been able to "read signs" effectively when he dealt with an earlier Theban calamity, the presence there of the deadly Sphinx. Oedipus has been able to think of only one thing to do so far this time, to send Creon to Delphi for help from Apollo (*Oedipus Tyrannus* 68).

Jocasta (Oedipus' wife and Creon's sister), has come to discount oracles, remembering the one she and Laius had had which had been "proved" false, since Laius had died by a stranger's hand, not by the hand of the infant that they had disposed of in their terror. She counsels Oedipus not to allow himself to be intimidated by such prophecies. Questions are thus raised in the play as to who, if anyone, speaks reliably for or about the gods or about what we call the supernatural. (Another way of putting this may be to ask, "Whose general understanding of things, or metaphysics, is sound?")

iv

It should be noticed that the speech of the divine is not usually regarded in this play (or in the Greek plays generally?) as the kind of action that speech is sometimes regarded in the Bible or in the Koran to be, where to speak can be to make or to do. Thus a priest can pray, "May Phoebus [Apollo] who gave us the oracle come to our rescue and stay the plague" (*Oedipus Tyrannus* 149). It is one thing for a god to speak; it is another thing for him to act.

Indeed one can wonder whether the gods of the Greeks, as described in this play, ever operate independently of men in human affairs. Do most, if not all, of their meaningful activities depend upon human beings? Does meaningfulness depend upon the fact, including the implications and possibilities, of mortality? To what extent, and in what way, do the things that happen to human beings flow from what mortals have done without immediate divine intervention? This bears upon the question of the relation between revelation and philosophy. Before we return to that perennial question, we should consider further what revelation means by considering, now that we have surveyed how the gods speak to men, why the gods speak at all.

v

The gods speak in order to advise, to condemn, to encourage—and perhaps out of sheer exuberance? The *whyness* depends in part, that is, on the *whatness*. What is there that needs to be said?

We have seen that the gods sometimes speak to men without any deliberate inquiry by men. Signs may be provided which are designed either as immediate guidance or as spurs to inquiry. Sometimes signs from god may not be recognized as such. Thus, the young Oedipus was prompted by a drunkard's slur, in Corinth, to go to Delphi to inquire about his parentage, which led to his learning that he was destined for patricide and incest. Was the drunkard in effect an agent of the divine? Was it not critical for what happened to Oedipus that he learn the Delphic prophecy and that he try to avoid it? (What Oedipus evidently did not recognize, because of his panic after Delphi, was that his original question in Corinth about his parentage had become even more important than it had been.)

Oedipus' parents in Thebes had had to be told his fate also, or they would not have abandoned him as they did—and this, in turn, permitted him to fulfill the prophecy, in its most literal sense, without seeming to be a degenerate monster. Nor would it do, it seems, for Oedipus to have fulfilled the prophecy without his ever learning that he had done so.

Would it have been better if Oedipus had not lived at all? (See *Oedipus Tyrannus* 1348 sq.) No doubt some think so. We venture to hope that the world is better for all this having been exposed, once it had happened. Perhaps it was even fitting and proper that these things happened when and how they did. It sometimes does seem, however, that men are the gods' playthings, and even that the gods are malevolent. (See, e.g., *Oedipus Tyrannus* 829.)

But should we not insist that the gods are, by and large, benevolent, especially as promoters of piety and guarantors of justice? Are they not bound to be so if they are wise, with wisdom intimately related (as we shall see in our Aristotle chapter) to the moral virtues? But if wisdom is critical to the gods' being, might not a wise man be able to figure out what should be done without immediate divine intervention to guide him? Did not Oedipus, who had been celebrated as the reasoner who had liberated Thebes from the Sphinx, long have available to him, without the spur of Delphi, what he needed to make the inquiries he eventually did? (Was he, then, clever but not wise?)

I will say something about this further on. But more should be said now about the intrinsic goodness of life, especially human life—that is, the life of rational beings. Rationality depends upon, and issues in, speech. Is it possible, ultimately, to lie about the divine? No doubt there have been charlatans and impostors, to say nothing of madmen, posing as prophets and diviners. No doubt, also, there have been men who have believed themselves to be lying about the divine. But, we must wonder, is there not likely to be some truth in what "catches on" because of their lies, a truth that they themselves may not be aware of?

All this suggests that why the divine speaks to man has much to do with the dependence of the universe upon rationality. (This is not unrelated to the medieval argument that the very positing of a certain divinity, or being, is itself proof of its existence. The discussion of the Idea of the Good, in part 2 of chapter 11 of this book, bears upon this, as does the discussion of the *Antigone* in the addendum to part 2 of chapter 7.)

vi

When, then, do the gods speak to men? When they speak, we have seen, is determined in part by when men seek guidance, in part by when men need guidance, whether or not they seek it. Thus, it can be said, the divine speaks intermittently to men, especially when there is more than one god.

The signs, miracles, and oracles used may differ from time to time, depending upon the circumstances of human beings. A god, like any other skilled speaker, can be expected to take account of his audience. Thus, if birds or dreams or thunder should become the provinces of scientific inquiry, then it would no longer be persuasive (or dignified?) for the divine to make use of them as signs. Or if an oracular site should happen to lose its reputation, then it might no longer serve as a source for prophetic utterances. Or, perhaps in other circumstances, Oedipus' character and doings would have as their consequences leprosy or paralysis in him personally rather than in a general blight.

These observations remind us that the gods of the Greeks seem more "civic-minded" than "personal" in their interests. They *are* the gods of cities. (This may be seen in the ultimate fate of Oedipus, in *Oedipus at Colonus,* with the partnership forged between Oedipus and King Theseus and hence Athens.) Especially is this so in the more serious plays, where the heroes tend to be men and women of stature whose fates very much affect what happens to their cities. In any event, there may be far less emphasis than we are used to upon personal salvation as the primary concern of religious observances. (See, on the gods existing by legal conventions, Plato, *Laws* 889c.)

vii

If, as we have noticed, the gods speak, however intermittently, then this means that the divine must exist. But if the divine exists, is it not likely to have a continuous effect, whether or not always perceived (or indeed looked for) by human beings?

The variety of gods, as among the Greeks, testifies not only to continuous involvement but to comprehensiveness as well. All facets of life seem to be provided for. The divine seems to pervade everything. (See *Oedipus Tyrannus* 151–215. St. Augustine seems to ridicule this notion of varied jurisdictions in *The City of God*. Do Christian saints, however, reflect a similar diversity in jurisdictions?)

If the divine is seen as significant if not even as comprehensive in its effects, questions must be raised about the status of nature. Nature may not be recognized as such, however much an awareness of it is critical as the background against which divine interventions can be noticed. What we call the natural ordering of things may itself be a vital sign of the divine, if not even a limitation upon the divine.

We may wonder, however, whether the blight on Thebes *came naturally* because of the pollution of an unexamined regicide, or *was sent by the gods* because the Thebans had shirked their pious, as well as their natural, duty with respect to the regicide. In the play itself it is said again and again that the things that come about, and especially the inexorable fate visited upon Oedipus, are due to the gods, with Zeus and Apollo as the leading influences on this occasion. (See *Oedipus Tyrannus* 738, 1329; *Antigone* 1 sq.)

viii

To ask whether the divine or the natural is ultimately in control may be to ask, still another way, whether revelation or philosophy is the better means to human understanding. Natural religion (as in the Declaration of Independence?) may try to combine revelation and philosophy, with philosophy in control, just as certain kinds of theology make use of philosophy. Also, some may see philosophy as still another way that the divine speaks, so much so that the gods need not speak directly to the truly wise man. (Plato's *Laws* may look in that direction. See, on the invocations of the divine in the Declaration of Independence, Anastaplo, *The Constitution of 1787*, pp. 21–22, 308 n.16.)

But, in everyday terms, there is an inevitable tension between a reliance upon revelation and a reliance upon philosophy. Not only are these two approaches to the world likely to be quite different, but the world itself seems quite different from the two viewpoints. The world of the philosophers tends to be impersonally organized. Vice *is* harmful, not because of any particular or divine intervention but rather because of a general or natural system of cause-and-effect.

The prophets, and the poets to whom they are closely allied, insist that everything means something. Jocasta, in attempting to reassure Oedipus, argues that chance is critical in human affairs. (See *Oedipus Tyrannus* 776, 977.) Oedipus can come even to revel in himself as the Child of Fortune (*Oedipus Tyrannus* 1080). These emphases on chance, by Jocasta and then by Oedipus, are designed to minimize reliance upon prophecies, oracles, and the like, leaving human beings free to reason about, and control, their destinies. But we can see in the *Oedipus* how unpredictable things can be. For example, the Messenger from Corinth happens to have deadly information, blithely volunteering it as a remedy. The most fortunate-looking thing can thus become the most devastating. Or, another example: Oedipus' conscientious efforts to escape his fate make matters worse for him. (See *Oedipus Tyrannus* 1003; *Antigone* 620.)

It is difficult for common sense to do much with such unpredictability. But poets, like the prophets, present stories that display what happens to people over many years because of their character. Poets "read" signs the way that priests and seers do; they, too, work by inspiration. Is there not something godlike, then, in the way that poets organize things? Rulers, too, can be regarded as godlike, as Oedipus is at the beginning of the play—not necessarily in how they comprehend the whole but rather in how they take charge of things.

The better (or true?) poets sense that there must be *will* and *choice* if a story is to be significant. Things may appear meaningless, if not even malignant, to an Oedipus—but is there not a significant pattern working its way out in his life? Whatever the diversity of the gods and their doings, is there not a god of gods, or a divine principle, which guides the overall direction of things? The poets seem to think so.

ix

The philosophers may think so also, but in a different way. Would not they suggest, in any event, that it is important to notice the impulse, or ability, in human beings to rely upon, or to turn to, the gods? Is there not something natural about this human openness to the divine?

What does it mean to say that human beings are receptive to divinity? It may reflect a desire to worship, to enter into a proper, or helpful, relation with the greatest power. Or it may reflect the desire to know, to grasp the sense of the whole. Or it may reflect the overall order in things that human beings can and do notice—and that they need and want. (Does not the Chorus in *Oedipus* see the gods doing more than the gods do? See *Oedipus Tyrannus* 1098 sq.)

Are men better off for what they learn from or about the gods? But for signs from the gods, diligently investigated, Oedipus' unnatural deeds might never have come to light. Would this, we again ask, have been better or worse for Oedipus? Are these the questions of a philosopher, not of the pious man? Both might agree that it is generally better to know than not to know. But the pious man might recognize certain things as properly concealed, things not to be said or even known. (See, e.g., *Oedipus Tyrannus* 993 sq., 1304 sq., 1348 sq., 1409 sq., 1421 sq.) And the philosopher would agree that there are things not to be said in some circumstances. (See, e.g., Plato, *Republic* 414D.)

The philosopher advances knowledge because to understand is fully human, the pious man because knowledge may be necessary in order to avoid impiety. The pious man recognizes his dependence upon what the gods say from time to time as well as always. But what about philosophy? *Can* the wise man, who is listened to by fewer people than either the poet or the pious man is likely to be, figure out the divine will? That is, can he discern on his own the ultimate good by which God also is guided? Is there a correspondence between what follows naturally and what the gods ordain? (See *Oedipus at Colonus* 791.)

Creon reported, upon returning to Thebes from Delphi, that Apollo had said that "the clue is in this land" (*Oedipus Tyrannus* 110). This and other clues, relating to the cause of the oppressive blight, had evidently been there all along for the discerning (not-yet-blinded!) eye to notice. Oedipus, we remember from his encounter with the Sphinx, is good at solving mysteries (*Oedipus Tyrannus* 1058). He might have been some-what better than he was if he had not believed himself to be much bet-ter than he was. That is, he is rather presumptuous, as well as at times unduly fearful, and that clouds his talents. (See *Oedipus Tyrannus* 38, 395 sq., 964 sq.)

One vital clue, of which Oedipus should be more aware than he is, is his own temper (like the temper of Laius before him?). (See *Oedipus Tyrannus* 335 sq., 674, 781–82, 806.) Is his temper related to his desire to master things as well as to his deep fears? (See *Oedipus Tyrannus* 1523.) That temper, along with his failure to investigate properly the fate of his predecessor (which, like his temper, is perhaps an undue emphasis upon himself), contributes to his fate. What the gods say and do may be a po-etic way, then, of explaining what human beings should do and say.

In this chapter I have considered, first, *how* the gods speak to human beings—by request or on their own, through signs and in the very orga-nization of the world; second, *why* the gods speak to men—to instruct, chastise, and otherwise guide them; and third, *when* the gods speak to men—continuously or intermittently, as needed. Perhaps another way of putting all this is to say that the divine speaks to human beings in part, if not primarily, through inspired poets who present the world in a cer-tain way, reinforced as this is by the interest generated in us by an account (called prophecy) which dramatizes the remarkable events we encounter. These events may not truly depend upon any prophecy for their signifi-cance. In a sense, that is, the events come first; the prophecy (whether curse or blessing) or poem comes afterwards for the benefit of those who cannot—or will not or perhaps even should not—confront events in themselves. All this, it can be said, Aeschylus anticipates, Sophocles teaches, and Euripides questions and perhaps thereby teaches even more.

VI. Euripides

PART ONE. On the *Hippolytus*

> *Strephon:* . . . You know, my grandmother looks quite as
> young as my mother [Iolanthe]. So do all my aunts.
>
> *Phyllis:* I quite understand. Whenever I see you kissing a
> very young lady, I shall know it's an elderly relative.
>
> *Strephon:* You will? Then, Phyllis, I think we shall be very
> happy! *(Embracing her.)*
>
> *Phyllis:* We won't wait long.
>
> *Strephon:* No. We might change our minds. We'll get married first.
>
> *Phyllis:* And change our minds afterwards?
>
> *Strephon:* That's the usual course.
>
> —Gilbert and Sullivan

i

IT CAN BE ILLUMINATING to see how the artists of antiquity reworked old stories. I touched upon this in both my Aeschylus and my Sophocles chapters and will return to it in the second part of this chapter and in my Herodotus chapter. It can also be illuminating, in studying ancient

---

Unless otherwise indicated, the citations in part 1 of this chapter are to Euripides' *Hippolytus*.

The epigraph is taken from William S. Gilbert and Arthur Sullivan, *Iolanthe*, Act II. See, on Gilbert and Sullivan, Anastaplo, *The Artist as Thinker*, p. 195.

artists, to see what artists thereafter do with stories that had been used in antiquity. Our immediate concern is with what Euripides and then Racine (a millennium later) do with the familiar story of King Theseus, his wife Phaedra, and his son Hippolytus.

This story can be explained (or is it explained away?) by moderns as still another manifestation of the natural appetite of the older for the young—including, if not especially, for the helpless young under their care. This story is reminiscent of the Oedipus story, with Phaedra (as stepmother to Hippolytus) tempted to claim for herself the role that Jocasta did not want to play. That the desired young man is, as in Euripides' *Hippolytus,* an aggressively chaste votary of Artemis may make the anticipated illicit pleasure more intense for the adventurous woman. Artists may also be drawn to this story because of the peculiar relation between stepmother and stepson. If Phaedra had been regarded as the biological mother of Hippolytus, there would have been no possibility of staging this story in ancient Athens. The characters could not have been taken seriously for a tragedy, however apt they may have been for a horror story: no nobility would have been possible, and without that (compromised though such nobility may be) there cannot be a proper tragedy. (Compare what happens, in Sophocles' play, when Jocasta is discovered to be Oedipus' mother.)

This is, in Euripides' version, the story of a stepmother who, in the absence of her husband, is offered to her stepson and is vigorously rejected by him. (Neither the offer nor the initial rejection is shown on stage.) Hippolytus is thereafter falsely accused of rape by Phaedra to Theseus (882–86). The outraged king then calls upon Poseidon (his "father") to grant him a "favor" due to him, calling for and securing the destruction of his son (887–90).

ii

One cannot begin to think properly about the story of Hippolytus and Phaedra, in whatever version one considers it, if one does not recognize at the outset one massive fact: what Phaedra does, or permits to be done, to Hippolytus is simply inexcusable, whatever may be wrong with

Hippolytus himself. She had no right either to want what she did from Hippolytus or to respond as she did to his rejection of her, however immoderate the tone of that rejection may have been.

Phaedra's crippling love for Hippolytus—aside from whether she was willing to have her passion for him revealed to him—is monstrous. If one cannot see this, then one cannot appreciate the ancient story and the plays built upon it. Everyone involved can see that there is something dreadfully wrong in what Phaedra wants—and wants badly enough to tell others about it. In Euripides' version this is obvious even to an Hippolytus-hating Aphrodite, who is somehow responsible for what happens. The nurse, who eventually serves (evidently on her own initiative) as panderer for Phaedra, is shocked upon first learning of what ails her lovelorn mistress, thereupon calling into question the divinity of Aphrodite. (The monstrousness of Phaedra's love is reflected perhaps in the bull conjured up by Poseidon to terrify Hippolytus' horses. Phaedra's mother, in Crete, had once been cursed with an unnatural passion for a bull [337–38, 1210 sq.].)

Is not Phaedra ultimately tiresome in her single-minded desire? Why should she—or any man or woman (though love is supposed to matter more for women than it does for men)—think that her passion entitles her to have her way, to push ahead for whatever she wants, and at all costs? After all, she is not the first to be required to conceal a love or to suffer rejection.

Phaedra knew, or should have known, that such a revelation as she makes to the nurse is likely to shake things mightily. Phaedra, in seeming possibly receptive to the use of a love potion (and hence other means?) to secure Hippolytus for herself, runs risks with his life, considering his temperament, and with the lives and happiness of others— risks that she is neither obliged nor entitled to run.

It is no wonder, then, that an eventually enlightened Theseus, at the end of the Racine version of the story, can consider her cruelty inexcusable. This is so even in an account as favorable to her as Racine's. In Euripides' version, her last words on stage are to the effect that she will teach Hippolytus a lesson, and this she does by leaving behind a lying suicide note. Dante can speak of Phaedra as Hippolytus' "cruel and perfidious stepmother" (*Paradiso* 17.4).

Yet, as we know, there *are* such people as Phaedra around who are otherwise attractive and decent, if not even noble, but who are voracious and ruthless in their pursuit of what they happen to desire. What, if anything, does all this say about divinities such as Aphrodite and Artemis and about their involvement in the affairs of human beings? (See, for another great poet's account of Aphrodite, Plato, *Republic* 329B-C. See, also, the addendum to part 1 of chapter 7 of this book.)

iii

To recognize Phaedra as inexcusable is not to deny that what she does can be accounted for. Dante reports that Beatrice, a "lady of virtue," could be moved by love to intervene on his behalf with Virgil (*Inferno* 2.70–78). Similarly, what Phaedra tries to do can be understood as a consequence of love, or of a certain kind of love. (In Euripides, it is Aphrodite who is using her; Aphrodite says so, and the rival Artemis confirms this. But do not Phaedra's heritage and temperament make her available to be used?) Such love as hers can be all-consuming: it respects no limits; it is an end to itself. She is, as I have indicated, one of those who tend to believe that to want something is almost enough. This kind of self-indulgence is perhaps magnified in Phaedra by her royal origins.

What is at the core of the intensity of Phaedra's desire for intimacy? Perhaps, ultimately, she is moved by the desire to know, that divine desire which can often take so physical a form. In this sense, there is something philosophic in Phaedra—in her desire, at all costs, *to know,* to strip relations of their conventions, and to attempt to look upon things as they truly are, however much she falls short in seeing the ugliness of what she does and perhaps is.

Is Phaedra peculiarly vulnerable to the passion of love because she is becoming no longer a young woman? Is the form that love takes in her peculiarly the affliction of an older woman, especially one for whom love is no longer critically connected with childbearing? (The principal modern successor, in literature, to Phaedra might well be Madame Renal, in Stendhal's *The Red and the Black*—the successor more perhaps to Racine's than to Euripides' Phaedra. Julien Sorel is somewhat as a stepson to her in that he is a younger, trusted member of the household.

Consider, also, the false accusation of him that she makes upon learning of his relations with another woman. What is one to make of their ultimate reconciliation in Stendhal's novel? How are Phaedra and Hippolytus to conduct themselves if they should meet in Hades?)

There *is* a perennial appeal in the story of what happens when an older woman of some passion is drawn to a young man or, for that matter, to an older man, who reminds her of a young man—or, what may be even more to the point, to a young man who reminds her of, or revives in her, the sweet longings and fond expectations of her youth (especially if the young man should naturally remind her of her husband in his prime). Is such a love, whether or not reciprocated, apt to appear pathetic? Besides, if it is illicit, it may really take one back to one's youth, in that the restraints of public opinion and the law can take the place of the constraints once placed by one's parents, constraints which can make one's youthful yearnings even more intense and attractive.

Such are the things that can be said on Phaedra's behalf. That something should be said may be seen even in Artemis, speaking at the end of Euripides' play, who observes that Phaedra was to some extent noble (1300). Her reason fought her passion, we are told (1304). She did struggle with this passion, so much so as to end up killing herself because of it.

Even so, it should be noticed, one is not praiseworthy merely because one feels badly about the desires one has. That is, may there not be something critically wrong when one *has* the wrong kind of strong feelings? Whatever may be said in Phaedra's defense—and however much we may account for and excuse her conduct—are we not to understand that she should neither have the desires she does nor act upon them as she does? (We can see again here the tension between *the noble* and *the just* discussed in part 2 of chapter 7 of this book.)

iv

To recognize that Phaedra is, by and large, inexcusable is not to say that Hippolytus is without fault. His response to the approach to him on Phaedra's behalf, even if it had been done at her request, is not what it should have been.

One is reminded of a physician, passionately dedicated to the preservation of life, who recoils with horror when a healthy patient he cares for—perhaps even a relative, if not even a parent—begs him for a deadly poison with which to end an unhappy life. *Recoils* is the critical term here. It is an almost instinctive response; it can even be said to be a natural response, depending upon one's temperament and aspirations.

And *recoil* is what Hippolytus does, perhaps in part because he had never suspected the power of love, however much he routinely condemns it. Certainly, it can be said, the Greek audience would have been taught that Hippolytus is in the wrong not to show any honor at all to Aphrodite. A servant had even cautioned him about this (88 sq.). Hippolytus is doomed from the start of Euripides' play, as David Grene has said, not for what he does in the play but "for what he is when the play opens" ("The Interpretation of the *Hippolytus* of Euripides," p. 49).

Does not Hippolytus react as strongly as he does because he is greatly threatened? (Modern psychoanalysts suggest that his reactions reveal what he "really" wanted. But this may be a somewhat forced interpretation, one that cannot tell us how we can distinguish between what one rejects vigorously because of what one does not want and what one rejects vigorously because of what one *does* want.) It does seem, at the least, that Hippolytus' asceticism crippled him, in that he could not appreciate how desperately Phaedra thirsted, and so he could not respond in a way appropriate to the circumstances. (These circumstances include his political and personal vulnerability.) Besides, one suspects, Hippolytus may, to some extent, "enjoy" an opportunity to condemn Phaedra. The nurse's approach to him confirms all that he had ever felt about women, at least in Euripides' version of this story.

For Hippolytus to recoil as he does may mean that he is as much a prisoner of passion as Phaedra herself. But whether or not Hippolytus is a celibate votary of Artemis, it is out of the question that Hippolytus should give in to Phaedra (however much his "repressions" prevent him from responding prudently to Phaedra's advances). There is, as well, something intrinsically polluting in Phaedra's avowal, unless one can learn from it and hence rise above it (which few, in such circumstances, may be equipped to do). Thus, as Mr. Grene has noticed, "A man may be quite normally unchaste and refuse to go to bed with his father's wife" (p. 46). He goes on to say, "Can we possibly imagine that any Greek would consider it a reasonable or natural action to consent to such a proposal as Phaedra makes to Hippolytus? . . . I cannot believe he had any choice in the matter" (p. 49).

We can agree that Hippolytus had no choice. His answer to Phaedra had to be a negative one, however phrased. But Hippolytus did have a choice about how his response would be phrased. What he did was to unleash *his* passions, living up to his name, "loosener of horses" (a name commemorating his mother, Hippolyta, an Amazon queen). This name not only anticipates what happens to him at the end, when his horses get fatally out of control, but also suggests the loosening of the horses, or passions, within himself. (One can be reminded of the black horse in Plato's *Phaedrus*.) Hippolytus unlooses the passions of the ascetic, and does so in such a way as further to arouse erotic passions in another. Phaedra's passions are in part, then, responses to Hippolytus', responses both to the passions he has long displayed in his avowed asceticism and to the passions he now displays upon encountering hers.

Each set of passions here does have something to be said for it. Each, in some form, is essential for civilization—but it may be that, in the long run, the set of passions upon which Phaedra (however improperly) draws may be more critical than that upon which Hippolytus draws, even though Hippolytus may be the more or less innocent victim here. That is, sexuality may ultimately be more important for survival of the human race than restraint—even though it is obviously better to have some of both.

Hippolytus' response, then, should have been *measured*. But he does not know what every sensitive, beautiful woman knows, perhaps instinctively, about how to respond to improper advances—how to respond without either compromising herself or making an enemy of (or destroying) the importunate male. (See, on an improper desire to hear base things, Dante, *Inferno* 30.148.)

Besides, does not one have some obligation to act with consideration toward another who happens to love one, even if one cannot reciprocate? Is there not, that is, something sacred about love, even when its source is most dubious? To say this is, I suppose, to recognize that something—at least the formality of respect—is due to Aphrodite even in the most questionable circumstances. Also called for, of course, is recognition of the peril one places oneself in by being oblivious to something so powerful, and so pervasive, as Aphrodite.

Having said all this—having recognized Hippolytus' limitations—it should still be noticed that every informed mortal in our two plays is agreed (aside from Phaedra in Euripides' version) that Hippolytus should not have been condemned for what he did, that he *is* innocent of the charges made with respect to Phaedra.

v

I have suggested that the failings of Hippolytus may be seen in his aggressive and hence vulnerable innocence, an innocence that can leave him so vulnerable to outrage as to be unable to respond prudently (or at least as civilly, and effectively, as a confident gentleman would) to Phaedra's grossly improper approach.

The source of Hippolytus' failing may go even deeper—and for this we rely upon Euripides, perhaps the greatest playwright ever to have interpreted this story. The central speeches in this play include one of the most infamous lines in ancient drama, a line that raised a storm against Euripides himself when he gave it to one of his actors to recite on the Athenian stage. "My tongue swore, but my mind was still unpledged," says Hippolytus, when the nurse, who had relayed to him Phaedra's shocking proposal, reminds him of the oath he had taken not to reveal what he had just been told by her (612). The entire play can be seen to turn around this line. (Another translation is, "My tongue is sworn, but my mind was unsworn." Still another is, "My tongue swore, but my mind is not on oath.")

Something of Hippolytus' innocence may be seen in the fact that he, without taking proper precautions, gave an oath that trapped him. Is his piety thus always without appropriate safeguards? Perhaps even more instructive is that such an oath *can* bind one, even in the face of a massive threat to one's life and reputation. This suggests what piety can mean. Is there not something unnatural and unjust (however noble) about such piety? Even so, do we not see here what can ultimately be said against Hippolytus? For him even to *consider* repudiating his oath—he does not go on to do so—is to compromise, in spirit, the piety in which he is rooted, or so it might seem. It means, in any event, that he is aware of what prudence calls for, and is not oblivious to its allure.

Does he, if only in his language, stray somewhat from his piety just as Phaedra, if only in her language, strays somewhat from her marital vows? Indeed, it has been suggested by one scholar, and certainly our hero leaves himself open to this interpretation, "Hippolytus does not break his oath . . . , but he considers breaking it, and he is only checked by the consideration that he would need witnesses." (Seth Benardete, "Euripides' *Hippolytus*," p. 25. Compare Plato, *Republic* 330D sq., 414B sq.)

In short, it can be said, there is something deadly about Hippolytus' understandable vacillation with respect to his oath—and it costs him his life. Of course, Artemis at the end of the play does praise Hippolytus as stalwart in his oath (1306 sq.). But is *her* judgment reliable on this and related matters? Perhaps no more so than Aphrodite's.

The practical modern would point out that had Hippolytus fully repudiated his oath, he might have saved his life. But would not this have been at the cost of becoming someone critically different from what he had been? Is not this another way of saying it would have cost him his life, in that the repudiation of an oath points beyond reliance upon piety as a guide? Hippolytus, it would seem, was not prepared (or indeed able) to go that far, however sensible it might have been to do so.

Even so, seriously to entertain repudiation of a solemn oath—as is evident in the central speeches of the Euripides play—is to compromise the insistent purity upon which Hippolytus depends. In these matters, halfway measures may be dangerous. However unnatural Hippolytus' piety may be, it can be argued, it is viable (if at all) only if that piety is truly "pure." (Compare Abraham's response to the divine request that he sacrifice Issac. *That* shows us what thoroughgoing piety can look like. See Anastaplo, "On Trial," p. 854. See, also, Strauss, *On Plato's Banquet*, pp. 144–46.)

vi

To question whether Hippolytus is unequivocally pious is to suggest the most (and a considerable "most" at that) that can be said against him (unless one is prepared to argue for prudence as a replacement for piety). Consider, on the other hand, the most that can be said for Phaedra—and for this we go to the center of Racine's play—not to the central speeches (as we have just done in Euripides) but rather to the central scenes, scene divisions being available there.

There are two central scenes, the fourth and fifth scenes of Act III. These are the fifteenth and sixteenth of the thirty scenes in the Racine play. The fifteenth scene is Phaedra and Theseus, the sixteenth is Hippolytus and Theseus—the scenes in which Theseus encounters first his wife and then his son upon returning home. (It is convenient to retain here the transliteration of the Greek names for these three characters in the French play.) Why are there *thirty* scenes? For the classicist, the Thirty Tyrants can come to mind. The modern reader is more apt to recall Judas Iscariot and his reward upon betraying Jesus—a successor of sorts to Artemis? (See the end of chapter 9 of this book. Theseus several times refers to Hippolytus as perfidious and traitorous, after learning of his supposed rape of Phaedra. There *are* perfidy and betrayal throughout the play.)

It is Phaedra's central scene we are concerned with here (III, iv), the scene in which Phaedra first speaks to Theseus upon his return home. It is a short scene. Theseus says, "Fortune, so long against me, now relents, and to your arms, madame, restores . . ." He evidently tries to embrace her, as she interrupts him: "Stop, Theseus. Do not profane the words of such a gentle greeting, due no more to me, unworthy now to hear them. You have been, in your absence, wronged. Jealous fortune has chosen not to spare your wife. Unfit to please—or even to approach you now—I must seek only where to hide myself." Thus she leaves him, troubled. He turns to Hippolytus (in the following scene) to learn what the matter is, only to have Hippolytus seek to leave the country at once. (We will return to the critical invocations in this short scene of *fortune* and *jealousy*.)

Racine presents, in Phaedra's central scene, this noble woman at her most ambiguous. She is torn between two conflicting purposes. She wants to defend herself (if not to insulate herself from Theseus), especially if Hippolytus should accuse her, and yet she does not want to attack Hippolytus if she does not have to. What she says can be taken, of course, as a self-condemnation: Theseus *has* been in his absence wronged; she does not say by whom. It is enough to notice, on her behalf, that she does not accuse anyone here. But to say this—thus to notice how ambiguous she must be—is to suggest how truly questionable she is. Does not such ambiguity characterize her soul, at least as she is presented by the great artist friendliest to her? She will, even in Racine's play, soon be moved to accuse Hippolytus falsely; but she will later be moved to exculpate him as she commits suicide. Thus, she is presented in her most sympathetic form by Racine. (A further complication in these stories, which I set aside in this discussion, is Phaedra's concern about what is to become of her children if Hippolytus prevails with his father.)

We return to Euripides' version. There we see Phaedra in her "purest" form. Not only does Euripides' Phaedra, Lucretia-like, never repent, unlike Racine's; she levels the fatal accusation against Hippolytus in a way (that is, in a suicide letter) that makes it impossible for her to repent. She is so effective thus that Hippolytus is helpless—even, perhaps, if he *had* violated his oath of secrecy, for would not Phaedra's suicide stand as stronger evidence than anything Hippolytus might say in his defense? Could only his own suicide be used to counter her "evidence"? (Is what happens to him, with his own horses, a kind of suicide? See, on Lucretia, Anastaplo, *The Artist as Thinker,* p. 47 sq.)

Thus, the very last act by Euripides' Phaedra is in part that of revenge—revenge for having been spurned by Hippolytus. It is into this form that her illicit passion is perverted; it is thus that she will at last "possess" Hippolytus. There seems little in Phaedra, as Euripides presents her, that redeems her. She is in a steady decline throughout that version of the story, whereas Hippolytus can be said to be in the ascendancy at the end, both in that a goddess does appear on his behalf and in that a perpetual cult is to be established in his memory. Something of his ascendancy is suggested by Sara Prince Anastaplo's poem, "Lament for Hippolytus":

> At least you tried! Oh, hard to be more than human,
> To disdain the love-sick woman
> For a chaste god, a bow,
> Mastered beasts, the father,
> And a vow.
>
> If Phaedra of the Cretan kin
> Should see the mark she can destroy,
> (Not bull or god, but mortal man,)
> With her death, she kills the boy.

She only craved the things you did,
She dared not name your huntress god.
But her lie was safely hid,
While your father cursed his blood.

Beasts that took feed from your hand,
Maddened by Poseidon's Bull,
Dragged your life out on the sand
Rebellious to your reins or skill.

Does Divine revelation
Free a God from bland inaction,
Who abandons you to die?
Is all our salvation
Just a time for meditation?

A glance at still another "comment" upon Hippolytus and Phaedra may be found in Seneca. In the central speeches of the Senecan version of the story, Phaedra declares her love only after Hippolytus first mistakes her sentiments as signs that she burns for her husband. Phaedra is there revealed as so obsessed by desire as to become shamelessly ruthless; Hippolytus is revealed as so innocent as to invite abuse—by seeming, arguably, to encourage Phaedra. In a sense, both are "responsible" for what happens: his innocence attracts her; her shamelessness repels him.

vii

Racine's Phaedra has much more to redeem her than does either Euripides' or Seneca's, as befits a character who, as we saw in the central scene of the Racine play, is much more ambiguous. Not only does she finally confess to her false witness, killing herself in the process, but she had even been moved earlier to try to save Hippolytus from condemnation by his father. What diverts her from that act of justice is not any concern for either her reputation or her life but rather the discovery that the Hippolytus who had spurned her could not be excused as impervious to the attractions of all women. Her jealousy is aroused when she learns that she has a younger rival. That may be peculiarly galling to the older woman in love. In this, and in other ways, the Racine version differs from the ancient alternative with which we are primarily concerned here: it tends to be softer, more sentimental, more open to love. In short, it is much more modern. (Even more modern is the modern-dress film version with the incomparable Melina Mercouri in the Phaedra role: of course, *she* seems to get her young man, at least for a while.)

One consequence of the modern shift is that it is difficult to see why Hippolytus should have been so vulnerable in the Racine version. What fault *did* he have? Certainly, one cannot regard it as a fatal flaw that he did love an unmarried woman (however much that changes the ancient portrait of him). Euripides' Hippolytus *could* be considered to have been much more at fault in that he worshiped Artemis to the total exclusion of Aphrodite, a neglect that a servant did warn him against. But, it would seem, for Racine's audience he could not be portrayed as questionable for his determined celibacy because Christianity had long since legitimated a radical celibacy. To call Hippolytus' form of celibacy into question, as Euripides does, would be to raise serious questions about something fundamental to the religious orthodoxy of Racine's day. And so, Hippolytus is shown to love a woman.

True, the woman he loves has, for political reasons, been forbidden marriage by his father. But it does not seem that Phaedra's response to the news of that love depends upon who precisely her younger rival is. Still, if Hippolytus *had* courted someone approved by his father, the courtship could have been public. Would this have deterred Phaedra from making her improper declaration of love?

Perhaps it should be added that the fact that Hippolytus was in love should have made him better prepared to appreciate what love can do to someone else, thereby guiding him in what he should have done to finesse Phaedra's "embarrassing" declaration of love. He should have been aware, at least, of what may be the crowning illusion of the lover, the illusion that one's beloved *is* unique, an illusion which *can* promote desperation. (See Benardete, "Euripides' *Hippolytus*," p. 27.)

viii

There are other major ways in which Racine's version of our ancient story differs from Euripides'. Only a few more ways can be indicated here, and these only briefly. One difference may be seen in what is said about Theseus' absence: in Euripides' version, although he is "in foreign lands" (282), he is expected to return; in Racine's, he has been gone for years, and there are reports of his death. Does this not tend to make Phaedra's love for Hippolytus somehow more excusable? (She is now closer to the situation of Jocasta after Laius' death.) This reminds us that in Euripides the ultimate concern is *not* with Phaedra's love, its causes and justifications, but rather with Hippolytus and his remarkable austerity and *its* consequences.

By comparing Euripides and Racine, one can detect differences between the ancients and the moderns, differences relating to the status of love, of individuality, perhaps even of piety. Consider, for example, the shift from a constraining oath in Euripides to a concern for his father's honor in Racine in accounting for why Hippolytus remains silent before Theseus about Phaedra's advances. Consider, also, the implications of the "natural" course of discovery in Racine. Human passions can be depended upon to expose themselves, to insure that justice will eventually be done. A dependence upon piety or the gods is not required to bring about order, Racine seems to say. Much that happened was, it would seem in Racine, the result of bad timing. We recall how much is made of fortune (a substitute for divinity?) in the central scene (Phaedra's central scene) in the Racine play. Not only does this central scene make much of fortune, but the central speech in the Racine play also points to fortune: Phaedra has just declared her love for Hippolytus, after long containing herself, only to learn immediately thereafter of Theseus' return.

In effect, there was no necessity for things to happen as they did in the Racine play. It is quite otherwise in the Euripidean version: there is something about the character of Hippolytus and about the character of Phaedra (to say nothing of the character of Theseus)—there is something about these people that makes their troubles highly likely, if not inevitable. This may be pointed up by the emphasis Euripides places upon the gods, including the reliance upon the epiphany of Artemis to explain everything.

Of course, it can be said (and perhaps shown) that both Racine and Euripides depend upon a grasp of nature in their delineations of human passions. But is not Euripides' view of human nature deeper, or more serious, and is this somehow indicated by reliance in his plays upon the implacable, contending, and inexorable gods?

It is more of a challenge to us to consider in Euripides' play what Hippolytus' scornful rejection of Aphrodite means. Does this mean, at the least, a rejection of the family and, consequently, of the city, however much it looks to the brotherhood of man? (See Gisela Berns, "*Nomos* and *Physis*," pp. 176–77.) This rejection of the erotic can (naturally?) lead not only to a father disowning a son but even to a "grandfather" (in the form of Poseidon) killing his grandson. (Did Poseidon believe he was giving to Theseus what he really wanted? Did Poseidon care?) Is this a male reaction? It is difficult to imagine a woman (Medea notwithstanding) acting as Theseus does. Sarah, after all, had nothing to do with the attempted sacrifice of Isaac. (Nor may she ever have had anything to do with Abraham thereafter, once she learned of it.)

ix

Both ancients and moderns can be drawn upon for instruction as to the kinds of responses Hippolytus could (perhaps should) have made to Phaedra, responses which would have saved both her and him. One response is illustrated by a modern, Benjamin Franklin, in his notorious advice (in 1745) to the young man on the advantages of taking an older woman for a mistress. (See Goodman, pp. 683–84.) The other response is illustrated by an ancient, Socrates, in what he had to say in Plato's *Symposium* and elsewhere about love. (See the addendum to part 1 of chapter 7 of this book.)

Franklin's letter may even be seen as a comic version, so to speak, of the Hippolytus story. (Perhaps the same can be said of the Gilbert and Sullivan *Iolanthe*). A good-humored response might have been salutary for Phaedra to have received from Hippolytus, something that allowed her to see what was amusing and hence unworkable in what she had suggested. Mirth and the erotic do not easily go together. I very much doubt that a Franklin would have allowed himself to have been trapped

by Phaedra's advances (ill-timed or otherwise). He would have reminded her that an older woman has other things to be grateful for in
her relations with the young. (Nursing care for the aged and burial rites
might even be alluded to.) And he might otherwise have suggested the
humorous side of erotic passion.

Nor would a Socrates have been trapped. (It is an instructive tradition that has Socrates helping Euripides with his plays—and when I
consider what is at the center of Euripides' *Hippolytus,* I can believe it.
One source for this tradition is Diogenes Laertius, who is not generally
regarded as reliable. I, on the other hand, consider Diogenes Laertius
one of the more underrated writers of antiquity. But we return to
Socrates.) Plato's *Symposium* does suggest how Phaedra could have been
answered by Euripides' Hippolytus. He should have appealed to her nobility, and to the noble aspect of justice, rather than being influenced
unduly by the nurse's vulgarity. (See Gisela Berns, pp. 178–79.) He
should have looked beyond love, as it is generally viewed, reminding her
of what love really aims at. In short, Hippolytus should have tried to reason with Phaedra. To have done this effectively, he may have needed
more respect for "the labyrinth of human nature" than his asceticism
permitted him to have (ibid., p. 181).

I have dealt somewhat with the shifts from one play to another by
dwelling upon what is central to each of our plays. Thus, we see at the
center of the Euripides play the questioning by Hippolytus of the very
piety upon which he so much depended. (We saw at the center of the
Seneca play, however briefly, the "cooperation," so to speak, between
Hippolytus' innocence and Phaedra's shamelessness.) We see at the center of the Racine play the troubled ambiguity of Phaedra, with Hippolytus by this time becoming secondary. Something of this shift is indicated
also in the extremities of our principal plays—in, that is, what is at their
beginnings and at their endings. At the beginnings, of course, are their
titles: *Hippolytus,* for Euripides; *Phèdre* for Racine. The endings of the
plays reflect this shift as well: there is on stage at the end of the Euripides the body of Hippolytus; there is on stage at the end of the Racine the
body of Phaedra. (On stage at the end of the Seneca version are the bodies both of a dismembered Hippolytus, more or less reassembled, and of
Phaedra.)

Thus, we move in our Greek and French plays from an emphasis

upon the questions posed by a hero who will not love, who disparages
erotic love, to an emphasis upon the questions posed by a heroine who
loves more than she should, who makes too much of love. Phaedra is
very much an Euripidean heroine, distinguishable not only from the
Phaedra of Racine but also from the Clytemnestra and Electra of
Aeschylus and from the Jocasta and Antigone of Sophocles. Moving as
we have should enable us, upon returning to the great Greek playwrights, to see them and their philosophic successors (with "a time for
meditation") better than we otherwise might.

PART TWO. On the *Rhesus*

> *I wol biwaille, in manere of tragedie,*
> *The harm of hem that stoode in heigh degree,*
> *And fillen so that ther nas no remedie*
> *To brynge hem out of hir adversitie.*
> *For certein, whan that Fortune list to flee,*
> *Ther may no man the cours of hire withholde.*
> *Let no man truste on blynd prosperitee . . .*
> —A Chaucerian Monk

i

THE AUTHORSHIP OF the *Rhesus* has been disputed for millennia: some
say it is an early play by Euripides; others say it is not really by Euripides,
but is instead the work of an otherwise unknown fourth-century playwright. If this play is not by Euripides, but by a playwright perhaps as
late as a century after him, it suggests that Greek tragedy was even richer
than we had supposed. We should be reminded, in any event, that we
have a very small part of the tragedies produced for the stage in fifth-
century Athens.

Since the *Rhesus* has long been under suspicion, we are not likely to
be unduly deferential toward it because of the stature of its playwright,

---

The epigraph is taken from Geoffrey Chaucer, *The Canterbury Tales*, "The Monk's
Tale" (opening lines).

whether he is the young Euripides or someone in the following century. We might thus be better able to see what the typical ancient Greek playwright worked with. Not that the *Rhesus* itself has failed to win respect.

Gilbert Norwood, writing in 1920, argued for Euripides' authorship of the *Rhesus* (*Greek Tragedy*, p. 292–94), praising the play as an "admirable drama," and adding:

> There is a minimum of psychology; the lyrics are mostly of slight value. But the writer has not aimed at a tragedy of the usual type. Its excellence lies in the vigour and excitement of the action. Almost all the scenes, especially the debate at the opening, and the escape of the Greeks, are written by a master of vivid realism, who is less concerned with character-drawing. The unwearied Hector, the cautious Aeneas, the vaunting, splendid, barbarian prince [Rhesus], the fiercely loyal charioteer—these are all obvious types. The only really fine stroke of psychological insight occurs where Hector, himself reckless at first, is by the absurd presumptuousness of Rhesus forced into discretion.

G. M. A. Grube, writing in 1941, spoke of the play in this fashion in the opening and closing paragraphs of a chapter that he devoted to it in *The Drama of Euripides* (pp. 439, 447):

> *Rhesus* has been declared spurious by some ancient and many modern critics. Yet there is clear evidence that Euripides did write a play of that name and it has come down to us along with the others in the manuscripts of the poet. . . . The criticisms of those who would reject it mainly amount to saying that this is not the kind of play that Euripides could have written. . . . That *Rhesus* is fundamentally different from any other extant tragedy is undeniable. It is a play of action, it is vigorous, direct, spectacular, there are many characters and many changes of situation. It is the work of no mean playwright, but it has little or no tragic depth; it is a series of exciting events rather than a tragedy. . . .
>
> In short, though there is but little trace in this play of those features of his art which made Euripides the "most tragic of all the poets," there is, on the other hand, little in the handling of the story, except its fundamental treatment, which cannot be paralleled from genuine plays. It is a mistake to think that the author of *Rhesus* tried to write a great tragedy and failed. He tried something very different and succeeded. . . .

ii

The *Rhesus* reminds us of the importance of Homer for the Greek playwrights. One-half of the thirty-three tragedies we have from ancient Greece draw on the Homeric stories. In those plays the characters are familiar to us from the *Iliad* and the *Odyssey*, however much they have been modified by the playwrights, especially by Euripides.

Poets of fifth-century Athens had to work with the Homeric legacy, just as playwrights of recent centuries (including Shakespeare) have had to work with, or around, the Biblical legacy. Homer himself refers to other great stories before him, but his stories have swept the field, leaving virtually only Homer standing from that period. Somewhat the same thing happened when, for example, Virgil developed his authoritative account of the Roman past, when Justinian developed his Code, and when Dante developed his *Divine Comedy*.

Shakespeare's own reworking of Homer in *Troilus and Cressida* offers us an account of Hector that may help us see both what is done in the *Iliad* and how that bears upon the relation between the noble (or a leader's glory) and the just (or a city's safety) discussed in part 2 of chapter 7 of this book. John Alvis' account of Shakespeare's play (in *Shakespeare's Understanding of Honor*, p. 7) is instructive:

> [A]lthough little of the grandeur Homer attributed to military ambition survives Shakespeare's reconfiguration of the *Iliad* in *Troilus and Cressida*, what does survive concentrates in Hector, a sympathetically conceived version of warrior heroism who loves glory more than his own safety and more than the safety of his city. To square his conduct with moral obligation Hector first proposes to return Helen to her Greek husband, yet eventually consents to Troy's retaining her because he believes that the Trojan's "several dignities" would incur damage if the "theme of honor" were returned. He comes to acquiesce in Troilus' contention that Helen should not be returned because he judges that yielding under compulsion—even if what he yields is justly owed—destroys every man's credit and with that confidence the prerequisite for accomplishing any future good. Honor appears the enabling condition for individual and public undertakings. But Hector's decision fails to resolve the further question of how to reconcile devotion to honor with observance of what he refers to as the "moral laws of nature."

(See, also, Anastaplo, *The Artist as Thinker*, p. 275.)

Homer, it will be recalled, could be regarded as the educator of Greece, having been decisive for the culture of Greece across half a millennium. Both philosophic men and men of action were "engaged" by Homer. Thus, as we have seen, Socrates could take issue with him in Plato's *Republic;* and Alexander the Great could try to match Achilles' exploits.

It has been noticed since antiquity that playwrights knew better than to attempt to dramatize the episodes that Homer had already presented. The distinctiveness of the *Rhesus* in this respect is noticed by a modern translator (Lattimore, "Euripides' *Rhesus,*" pp. 2–3):

> This is the only extant tragedy which takes its material straight out of the *Iliad.* The regular practice of the tragic poets when they dealt with the heroes and stories of the Trojan War was to choose episodes which fell outside the scope of the *Iliad,* before its opening or, more frequently, after its close.

The considerable dependence of this play upon Homer is described by another classical scholar, William Arrowsmith (in a foreword to Richard Emil Braun's translation of the *Rhesus,* p. xi):

> For obvious reasons [the *Rhesus*] is more likely to be read than performed. A pity, no doubt about it; but, for us at least, it is likely to remain—with Aeschylus' *Suppliants* and Sophocles' *Ajax*—a "poet's play." Not because it is undramatic, but because its theatrical power and accessibility derive in large part from its saturation in Homer's poetry. Indeed, its essential theatricality depends largely upon its elegant and skillful adaptation of the *Iliad* to the stage. The dramatist's purpose and virtuosity reveal themselves only if we possess, as ancient audiences presumably did, something like full control, and full recall, of Homeric poetry. For Euripides has not simply retold Homer, but everywhere shaped his Homeric material to his own individual ends, even while relying upon his audience's ability to respond "Homerically" to the material so reshaped by the dramatist. It is here that the dramatist's hand is, as in the *Iphigeneia at Aulis,* most clearly revealed. We feel the Euripidean drama in the foreground, but always in creative tension, and even rivalry, with the epic material that provides its informing and contrasting background.

It remains to be seen what this playwright's "individual ends" were.

iii

The plot of the *Rhesus,* the shortest of the extant Greek tragedies, is summarized in this fashion by our 1920 critic (Norwood, pp. 291–92):

> The action is founded on the Tenth Book of the *Iliad,* and takes place at night in the Trojan camp. Hector has defeated the Greeks and hopes to destroy them at dawn. The drama opens with a song by the chorus of sentinels, come to warn Hector that the Greeks are astir. He is ordering instant attack when Aeneas urges that a spy be first sent. Dolon volunteers, and sets forth disguised as a wolf, followed by the admiration and prayers of the chorus. A herdsman announces the approach of the Thracian prince, Rhesus, with an army to aid Troy, but Hector is displeased with his tardiness, and, despite the joyful ode of the chorus, greets his ally with reproaches. Rhesus offers excuses, promising to destroy the Greeks without Trojan help, and to invade Greece; Hector takes him away to bivouac. The chorus depart to rouse the Lycians, whose watch comes next. Odysseus and Diomedes steal in, intending to slay Hector. They have met Dolon and learned from him the position of Hector's tent and the watchword, "Phoebus". Athena appears, bidding them slay Rhesus and take his wondrous steeds. They depart, and seeing Paris draw near, she calms his suspicions under the guise of his protectress Aphrodite. Next she recalls [Odysseus and Diomedes], who have slain Rhesus. An exciting scene follows, in which the chorus seize Odysseus, who escapes by using the pass-word. The chorus sing the daring of Odysseus. A wounded charioteer of Rhesus staggers in, proclaiming his master's death, of which he accuses Hector, who sends him away for tendance. As the chorus lament, a Muse appears in the sky, bearing the body of her son Rhesus. She sings a dirge and curses Odysseus and Diomedes. Next she tells of her union with the river-god, father of Rhesus, and upbraids Athena. Hector promises glorious obsequies [for Rhesus], but she declares that her son shall live on in the Thracian mountains as a spirit half-divine. Hector orders an assault upon the Greeks, and the chorus sing a few courageous words.

Several important differences between Homer's and Euripides' versions of this episode—differences of which the ancient Greek audience was apt to be aware—are commented on further along in this discussion. It has been pointed out, by one translator of the *Rhesus* (Lattimore, p. 2):

[The play's] chief events, the sortie of Dolon, the countermission of Odysseus and Diomedes, who kill Dolon, and the death of Rhesus, are all in Homer, though there are changes in emphasis, particularly in the importance of the part played by Athena, the importance of Rhesus for the Trojan cause, and the introduction of the Muse as Rhesus' mother.

Additional changes made by the playwright include Dolon's bargaining for the horses of Achilles, Dolon's going forth disguised as a wolf, the anticipation by both Dolon and Rhesus of killing Odysseus (who, instead, kills them, with the aid of Diomedes), and the introduction of Rhesus' wounded charioteer who accuses Hector of having had Rhesus killed.

Critical to the story in the play may be the contrast between Hector and Odysseus (whereas, as we shall see, Achilles and Rhesus are in critical respects alike). Hector is in effect "asleep" throughout this pre-dawn play: he does not know what "time" it is (he is urged in the opening speech to be responsive to the *kairos* [the time, circumstances]); he cannot *see* what is before him, which contributes to his failure to do what he could to safeguard Rhesus and thereby to save Troy. Odysseus, on the other hand, is alert and ever watchful, moving effectively through the night.

Also, there seems to be a greater emphasis in the *Rhesus* than in the *Iliad* upon Greek-barbarian differences between the combatants at Troy. This may reflect the increased sensitivity in Athenian audiences to this difference as one result of the spectacular Persian Wars. (But see Euripides, *Andromache* 1249 sq., on both Greek and Trojan being needed in the world.)

iv

Perhaps one of the critical differences between Greek and barbarian, especially as reflected in Homer and in the plays derived from him, is the central place of Helen (a mortal daughter of Zeus) in the great war at Troy. Herodotus reports, in his *History,* the surprise of the barbarians when the Greeks made as much as they did of the abduction of Helen after many generations of retaliatory women-stealing by Greeks and barbarians alike. (See, also, Euripides, *Cyclops* 179 sq., 280 sq.) In this respect, at least, these barbarians are like realists, ancient and modern, who believe that there must be other than the declared causes of war, such as economic rivalry and geopolitical maneuvering.

What *does* it mean that armies, or peoples, can go to war for a woman? True, the Trojans also fought in that war, but they could be understood to have defended their sovereignty, not wanting to surrender Helen under compulsion. It is not likely that the Trojans would have equalled the efforts of the Greeks to recover, as distinguished from efforts to retain, a woman. The Greek propensity in these matters is suggested also by the troubles generated among the Greeks when Achilles is deprived of a woman by Agamemnon: it is from this episode, in the first book of the *Iliad,* that the much-consuming wrath of Achilles follows.

I mention in passing that the stature of various women in the Greek plays obliges us to reconsider what is often said about the status of women in the ancient world. The same can be said about the stature of various women in the Hebrew Bible, even without the influence of goddesses such as Athena. These women are very much to be reckoned with.

Just as the story of the people of Israel, so much dependent as it is upon their enslavement in and exodus from Egypt, is very much affected by the passion of a man for a woman (that is, of Jacob for Rachel, the mother of Joseph [about which Leon R. Kass has useful things to say]), so the story of the people of Greece is very much affected by the passion of the Greeks for Helen. She, somehow or other, arouses the deep-rooted desires of the community. What, then, does she stand for?

v

Helen, who chanced to become a "theme of honor" for the Trojans, is surpassingly beautiful. We can see that beauty is not commensurate in her with conventional virtue, and it is this disparity that contributes to the War.

Even so, there is something profoundly good about Helen. However troublesome Helen's morality may be, there is something great and compelling about her. There is a balm, as well as a terribleness, associated with beauty. One can be reminded here of the monstrousness implicit in the great strength employed by Heracles in systematically ridding the earth of its tormentors, a monstrousness that erupts in

Euripides' *Heracles,* where the berserk hero can slaughter his wife and three children.

The limits of beauty, sovereign though it often is or at least appears to be, are suggested by Athena's astonishing ability to imitate Aphrodite effectively, thereby deceiving Paris who presumably knows Aphrodite well. (Does the "appearance" of Aphrodite to Paris mean, in effect, that he was induced to want to get back to Helen?) In Euripides' *Helen,* Helen herself is effectively imitated for years by a replica of Helen: it was, we are told, not Helen, but her replica, who spent the ten years at Troy with Paris.

Athena's imitation of Aphrodite, deceiving one of Aphrodite's most devoted partisans with an eye for beauty, suggests that the wise are somehow beautiful. That is, the wise can appear, as well as be, good. Consider the implication of our expression, "good-looking." (What does this say about either the sensibleness or the legitimacy of the fateful beauty contest which found Paris judging Aphrodite, Athena, and Hera?)

Consider, also, the implications of stories which have gods and goddesses taking visible forms, and doing so to serve "all-too-human" passions, including illicit sexual passions. The observation by Euripides' Heracles on the matter, after recovering his sanity in *Heracles,* can remind us of books 2 and 3 of Plato's *Republic* (*Heracles* 1341–46; this comes from someone reputed to be a son of Zeus):

> I do not believe the gods commit
> adultery, or bind each other in chains.
> I never did believe it; I never shall;
> nor that one god is tyrant of the rest.
> If god is truly god, he is perfect,
> lacking nothing. These are poets' wretched lies.

With such sentiments as these the somewhat rationalistic Euripides (like his friend, Socrates) may call into question many of the stories about the gods that his audiences cherish. The freedom with which Euripides departed from traditional accounts of gods and heroes must have made people wonder what could be sensibly believed of the theology of the day, a theology which seems intimately linked to political considerations.

vi

One major change in the *Rhesus* from the story in the *Iliad* is with respect to the pivotal character of Rhesus' intervention.

Rhesus is the barbarian counterpart to the Greek Achilles. Both come from the north. Both have goddess-mothers who counsel them against going to Troy, where death awaits them. Both mothers are recorded to have grieved profoundly when their sons died. Achilles had been important for the Greek cause during much of the war, although he would not be necessary for the final taking of Troy. Athena announces to Odysseus and Diomedes (in the *Rhesus,* not in the *Iliad*) that if Rhesus survives this night, the Greeks will not take Troy. Are not we, as the audience, invited to approve of the killing of Rhesus, even if by trickery, if we are (as we are likely to be) partisans of the Greeks?

We can be puzzled by the importance assigned to Rhesus by Athena in the play. After all, Rhesus shows up at Troy because of a debt owed by him to Hector, who had years before established Rhesus in his kingdom. This suggests that Rhesus might be weaker than Hector. Of course, Rhesus himself, during his one long scene in the play (upon his arrival at Troy), announces that he can take on the Greek army alone. It is easy to dismiss this as barbarian bravado, but Athena does seem thereafter to confirm what Rhesus had proclaimed.

vii

Why, then, does Rhesus happen to matter as much as he evidently does? (Or is this all a wry comment, if not a grand joke, by the playwright?) No attempt is made in the play to explain what Rhesus could have done or why he was as important as he was. Still, it is Athena, not Rhesus' mother, who elevates him thus. Is Athena telling the truth—or is she lying in order to keep Odysseus and Diomedes away from Hector and Paris, who are destined to meet their deaths at others' hands? We see Athena skillfully lying in dealing with Paris shortly thereafter in this play. The only thing indicated that might begin to explain Rhesus' potency is the size of his army, which seems to have been considerable—

and which may have depended, for its effectiveness in a foreign land, upon its godlike leader. (See, e.g., *Rhesus* 790 sq.)

Perhaps it is critical both that Rhesus should matter as much as Athena says he matters and that we cannot be sure why this is so, "knowing" only that it is so. After all, is not that the way things often are in ancient stories? We have no more basis for understanding the *why* of various other actions that are ordained in one story after another. Are we not reminded thereby that there is much that happens in the world, and not only in antiquity, that we cannot comprehend, leaving us to wonder about such things as whether gods do control human affairs? After all, why were human beings ordained, if they were, to act as they did in, say, Homer's *Iliad* or in Sophocles' *Oedipus Tyrannus*? (We *can* see in Euripides' *Phoenician Women* how Laius' passions contributed to Oedipus' fate.)

Rhesus despises Odyssean craftiness. Does the vulnerability of splendid Rhesus to Odysseus' guile (and later the vulnerability of great Achilles to Paris' "cowardly" arrow) suggest that the Heroic Age is passing? Does the playwright, with his hints about the potency of the barbarian hordes to the north, anticipate the eclipse of Greece in the fourth and third centuries, something that Thucydides may anticipate as well?

viii

A more technical reason can be added in support of Athena's unexpected counsel to Odysseus and Diomedes. If Rhesus survives the night, will not the story in the play be different, perhaps profoundly different, from the story in the *Iliad*? May not the same be said about any other episode in the *Iliad* or in the *Odyssey*?

To change an important episode (if not *any* episode?), departing thereby from what the Muse had told Homer, could be shattering. After all, once critical changes start to be made in the story of the *Iliad,* as in the story of our lives, who knows what the overall effect or result will be? (Virgil's *Aeneid* suggests what can happen when old stories are recast even as they are built upon.)

The "failure" of Homer to record Athena's counsel about Rhesus could mean that the playwright is suggesting that Homer himself did not recognize how critical Rhesus "really" was. Did this mean that the entire Trojan War required reinterpretation? (One can be reminded of the second part of *Don Quixote*, with the adventurous Don having to deal with reports by someone other than Cervantes about his exploits. One can also be reminded of the contests among playwrights that were routine in Athens.)

Any reinterpretation of the Homeric account could well include questions about what guided the Muse who originally inspired Homer. Did she know what Zeus had ordained? Can any human being ever know such things, no matter what the purported source? Is Zeus the master (that is the supreme or sovereign) playwright, with Athena serving as a director who stages his "plays"?

What, in turn, is Zeus himself guided by? Does divine mystery have to be recognized here, assuming that there is something fundamentally purposive in what happens to human beings, not merely chance events which poets and others then try to "make sense of"? Certainly, the Greek stories (from Homer through the Athenian playwrights) are filled with omens, oracles, portents, prayers, rituals, sacrifices, and theophanies, perhaps obsessively so.

ix

How *are* the things known and understood which happen to human beings? Perhaps they cannot begin to be understood if we do not appreciate how much, and in what ways, the good, the true, and the beautiful guide human life, including what we can know.

The *good* is looked to in order that people might be directed in how to act. Revelations can be useful here, at least in the hands of a thoughtful statesman, with Apollo as the most important source of "official" prophecy for both the Trojans and the Greeks. *Phoebus* (or Apollo, the Shining One) was the Trojan password the fateful night that Rhesus was killed. Yet this password (which is not reported by Homer) did not help the Trojans, but rather could be used by Odysseus to his advantage after he extracted it from Dolon. The Trojans were not enlightened; things were in darkness for them from the beginning of the play. The Trojans were not helped enough by Apollo, no matter how much the Chorus prayed to him (that is, shared their fears and hopes with the god) and no matter how much he had helped Troy in the past, as with the building of its walls. (See Grube, p. 444.)

The *beautiful* is looked to in order that people might be directed in how to desire. Poetry can be useful here, with the Muses guiding the poets. The poet presents a whole, which is thereafter *this* way, not any of the many other possible ways that the poet might have chosen. Particularly potent is that form of art which draws upon, and reinforces, the stories provided by divine revelation. Poetry, whether "religious" or "secular," can move a far greater audience, at least in the short run, than deliberate inquiry can do. (Even Rhesus' very existence, the Muse reports, depended upon a contest among artists. Is it art, or a story, that the Muse settles for, since she will never see her ever-living son again, however much he is worshiped as a deity by the Thracians? That is, is the Muse's account "merely" poetic, something that does not "really" happen?)

The *true* is looked to in order that people might be directed in how to understand. Philosophy can be useful here, with the Odyssean spirit providing guidance, with or without the aid of Athena. (We have seen, in part two of chapter 1 of this book, how the Odyssean spirit is recognized for its philosophic inclinations in book 10 of Plato's *Republic*.) Vital to the philosophical enterprise is a reliable sense of what is and is not possible. (Consider what Euripides, perhaps under the influence of Socrates, has Heracles say about what the gods do and do not do. Heracles is quoted in section v, above. See, on the good, the true, and the beautiful, Anastaplo, *The Artist as Thinker,* p. 275. See, on the beautiful, the addendum to part 2 of chapter 11.)

Philosophy, with the natural sciences that it has made possible, has weakened the staying power of poetic accounts of the world, especially those accounts in which the gods figure prominently. But does not the philosopher know that art and revelation may both be needed, that they can be more effective with multitudes than philosophy alone can ever be? How "revelation" can be put to salutary use by the wise may be seen in how Athena, after counseling Odysseus who "hears" her, appears to Paris in the form of an Aphrodite that he "sees." Or as the iconoclastic Mark Twain, a great American poet with somewhat Euripidean inclinations, put it in *A Connecticut Yankee in King Arthur's Court* (chapter 43), "You can't depend on your eyes when your imagination is out of focus."

VII. Aristophanes

PART ONE. On the *Birds*

> *All gods are better than their conduct.*
> —Mark Twain

i

DOES ZEUS EXIST? This question may be, for us, still another way of asking, What is Zeus and why? A related question is, What is the proper response (that is, the appropriate response by human beings) to Zeus? The appropriate response, as we have seen, probably depends upon what one believes Zeus to be.

The question, or questions, addressed in Aristophanes' *Birds* may be, then, about the practical implications of Zeus' existence. What does Zeus do to or for human beings? How can they learn and know what Zeus is? Who or what tells us about Zeus? Can he be deduced from evidence naturally available to us? We move here from the great tragedians to what Aristophanes has to say (and thereafter to what the historians

---

Unless otherwise indicated, the citations in part 1 of this chapter are to Aristophanes' *Birds*.

The epigraph is taken from Paul M. Zall, *Mark Twain Laughing* (Knoxville: University of Tennessee Press, 1955), p. 91. See, on Mark Twain, Anastaplo, *The Artist as Thinker*, p. 179.

and the philosophers have to say) about how and why gods speak to human beings.

The "theoretical" considerations we may pursue about Zeus are not discussed, at least not discussed directly, in the *Birds*. What Zeus is truly like may not matter for some practical purposes, however important it may be for understanding what does and does not happen in this play.

In any event, Zeus is not presented as creator of the universe, either in this play or by the ancient Greeks generally. Insofar as he endures, he stands for the order of the established universe, perhaps an eternal order. Despite the ignobility suggested by the forms that Zeus' eroticism takes, is there still displayed in this god an exalted, if not the highest, blending of the noble and the just? (One can see in Euripides' *Ion* that divine eroticism may have great plans in view, so much so that it may be imprudent to judge divine doings by human standards. Compare the argument by Unjust Speech quoted at length in section v of part 3 of this chapter.)

ii

A prominent classical scholar has observed, "Nobody denies that *The Birds* is a masterpiece, one of the greatest comedies ever written and probably Aristophanes' finest"(Arrowsmith, Introduction to *The Birds*, p. 1).

The play opens with two Athenians on the road, guided by two live birds they have purchased in Athens. They say that they are trying to get away from the constant activity, particularly the political and legal activity, of Athens. They hope to find among the birds a more relaxed life. They are looking for one bird in particular, Tereus, a Hoopoe who, as a bird that had once been a man, should be able to help them in their transition from life among men to life among the birds. Another advantage of dealing with Tereus, it turns out, is that he has been able to teach the Greek language to the birds he now lives among. (These birds provide the Chorus for this comedy.)

The two Athenians do manage to find Tereus, to whom one of them, Peisthetairos, explains the good things they can do for the birds. Tereus is impressed enough to summon the birds for a meeting with the Athenians. (This assembly of birds must have struck the Athenian audience somewhat the way moving into and through the mammoth bird house in the San Diego Zoo can seem to us. How much, or in what way, does Tereus' human career, with its fateful infidelities, influence who he is and what he does here?)

When the birds learn that they have been summoned to deal with human beings, they are upset. Human beings are their natural enemies, they remind Tereus, and they are prepared to attack their visitors at once. But after the two Athenians show that they can defend themselves, the birds calm down and listen to their proposition.

Peisthetairos effectively appeals to the birds' self-interest, proposing to restore them to the rule of the earth they once had. They are informed by him of an ancient preeminence of theirs that they had never heard of before. They are told that it is the gods, not the men whom they fear so much, who have deprived the birds of what they once had.

The way to proceed, Peisthetairos convinces the birds, is to put the gods under pressure by cutting off the traffic between gods and men. This is to be done by building a city in the sky that effectively separates the two sets of beings. For this purpose to be effected, the birds must unite. We wonder, of course, what everyday Athenian project or development served as the model for this city-in-the-sky comic equivalent.

Peisthetairos gets the birds working on the necessary city wall in the sky, a project his companion Euelpides is assigned to help move along. We never see Euelpides again after he leaves to work on the wall. Peisthetairos is not represented, at least at the outset of the play, as either hostile to the gods or out to get rid of his companion. Rather, he seems (like Odysseus) to be a man who sees opportunities develop and simply takes advantage of them.

While the wall is being built there is a series of human visitors, a half-dozen or so, whom Peisthetairos deals with in turn. Then, he is told, the wall is finished, a wall which rivals the massive wall of Babylon. This is not a wall the audience ever sees; it is not clear that Peisthetairos ever sees it either; he can even speak of it as a fantasy.

But evidently the wall is real enough to lead to another series of visitors because of its consequences, culminating in a visit by a deputation of the gods who are affected by the resulting cessation of the commerce between human beings and gods. This deputation is anticipated by the immortal Prometheus who reports how desperate the gods have become upon learning that the savory-smelling sacrifices made by men on earth can no longer reach them in heaven.

Negotiations between the gods and Peisthetairos, who has by now assumed effective rule over the birds, leads to his elevation to a godlike status, with Basileia (or Kingship) as his wife. (Zeus can be referred to in the play as "Ζεῦ βασιλεῦ." [223]) It is on a high note of celebration that the play ends, with an impending wedding feast attended by the by-now hungry gods with whom Peisthetairos had been negotiating. (See, on the gods' dependence upon sacrifices by human beings, the addendum to this part of chapter 7.)

iii

The key to all of these developments is an enterprising Athenian. The name of Peisthetairos seems to be a hybrid of "persuader of his comrade" and "trustworthy comrade." *Persuader* he certainly is. (See Strauss, *Socrates and Aristophanes*, p. 160.)

The comrade he took along on this expedition from Athens was Euelpides, whose name means "Hopeful" or "Son of Hopeful" (ibid., p. 160). But, it seems, the comrade's hopes were not to be realized: the relaxed life he had hoped for was evidently denied him among the birds. (Where *does* he end up?)

How much of all this did Peisthetairos plan from the outset? He is good at improvisation, as we see early on when he organizes the defense by the two Athenians against the angry birds. Peisthetairos is Athenian in his ingenuity, using common everyday things in unexpected ways. An Athenian audience, in enjoying his inventiveness, must have congratulated themselves for their distinctive liveliness. The admiration of Peisthetairos for his effective use of kitchen implements in combat should be compared to the criticism of Socrates elsewhere for his use of homely illustrations in philosophic discourse.

The success of the ingenious Peisthetairos shows what Athens is capable of. His name can remind us of Pisistratus, the great leader of the Athenians a century earlier—the tyrant who is associated with what may have proved to be the fateful decision to have the Homeric oral narratives reduced to writing. (Peisthetairos, who can eventually be referred to as the tyrant of the birds, proves to be a master usurper. See Strauss, ibid., pp. 184, 191, 194.)

Peisthetairos saw that there were opportunities to be exploited—and he did so with a flourish. Everything falls into place. He becomes, in effect, the master playwright of politics.

iv

How does Peisthetairos do it? He both threatens and promises. It is, as we say, a carrot-and-stick approach (but with the stick first). The birds are brought around, first by a show of effective defense against their attacks and then by generous offerings. The gods are brought around, first by being "starved" of their sacrifices and then by promises of how the birds can help the gods to be more effective in keeping track of human beings and in otherwise getting what they want. Poseidon, especially, is interested in thus enhancing the powers of the gods to see justice done; Heracles, on the other hand, is much more interested in food.

Peisthetairos' power does rest, then, on his persuasive ability. He presents a comprehensive view of things, especially in their practical implications. He plans a worldwide dominion by this city. He can be called, at the end of the play, the highest of the gods. What does this say about what the gods are like?

Does Peisthetairos believe what he is saying to the birds? About the past and hence their claims? About what they can do now? Is this the way a Founder operates? In whose interest is Peisthetairos really acting? Does he himself know?

How *does* he pull off his spectacular accomplishments? What special qualities does he have? It is not, we suspect, simply a matter of opportunity or chance, although that may be necessary if he is to be able to use his talents most effectively. His circumstances may be seen in the resistance he had to overcome—first the resistance of the birds, then of the series of human visitors (mostly from Athens), and finally of the gods.

v

Peisthetairos, or at least Aristophanes, depends upon the way things are at this moment in Athens. Comedy does tend to be more topical than tragedy, at least in its explicit references to personalities and events.

The *Birds* is believed to have been first presented in 414 B.C. Athens, during the preceding year, had launched against Sicily the most formidable armada that had ever sailed from a Greek harbor. The precise time of the play may not matter, but rather that it came at a time when Sicily was very much in the air for the enterprising Athenians.

By this time the Peloponnesian War had been going on for almost two decades. Aristophanes had argued against that war from time to time because of its losses and failures and because of the harm it was doing to the soul of his city, if not to all of Greece. Now, with Athens at the height of its power and evidently destined for a great victory, the playwright shows what the consequences of the looked-for success might be.

Athens, they could all see, was aiming by its Sicilian expedition at universal dominion. (See Arrowsmith, Introduction to *The Birds*, pp. 119–20.) This is reflected in the taking of Basileia by Peisthetairos (an Alcibiades-like figure, but an older and hence cagier man than Alcibiades, and perhaps naturally less passionate). Peisthetairos persuades the birds to do what the Greeks should perhaps have done, live all together in one city (171).

Success in Sicily might have meant that Athens would dominate the life of the Mediterranean world for at least the following century—not only the political life, but also those things that political life in turn controls and depends upon. This includes how the gods are talked about and what forms their worship takes. A redefinition of the relation between the mortal and the divine may be involved here (as it is, in another way, in Aristophanes' *Clouds*, which we turn to in part 3 of this chapter, after anticipating it in the addendum to part 1 of this chapter).

Put otherwise, the elevation of the political—say, by the establishment of a worldwide empire—can transform the ambitions, the self-esteem, and the piety of a prosperous people already notorious for restlessness. In such circumstances, the elevation of a leader to godlike status—which may mean, in effect, the dethronement of Zeus—should come as no surprise.

vi

We can see various ways that the gods may indeed be "the gods of the city," those gods whose acknowledgment (or a lack of due acknowledgment) is critical to the indictment of Socrates. We can see this in how the barbarian divinities are exhibited in this play. They are like *their* people in their attributes, much as the Olympian gods are like the Greeks (with perhaps various of the Olympians taking on the attributes of the various cities that they are particularly associated with).

The city depends upon the gods—or at least upon respect for the gods—for law-abidingness, for the sanctity of oaths, and for the guarantee of morality. But in turn, it sometimes seems, the gods depend upon cities for their authority. At one point in the play, the Chorus of Birds addresses the audience as if campaigning for votes that would elect *them* gods. (See Arrowsmith, ibid., p. 115.) Elsewhere, Peisthetairos instructs (gullible?) Heracles that the modes of family relations and of inheritance among the gods depend upon the laws of Athens. Peisthetairos also proposes to make the gods law-abiding (1223).

It is taken for granted in the play that contracts can be entered into between human beings and gods. Everyone in this play, it seems, "believes in" the gods. But belief is one thing; appropriate conduct by men or birds with respect to the gods is quite another.

Ordinarily, the appropriate conduct is simply that which the city prescribes. To acknowledge the gods of the city is to acknowledge the city's supreme authority in ordering what men are and do. Peisthetairos is so much a Greek that he did not know, before talking to the gods about the barbarian divinities, that there were gods "above" (that is, to the north of?) the Olympian gods (1524). One wonders whether there are any divinities independent of the city. (Consider what our doctrine of "the separation of church and state" implies about this.) Is there a divine—an idea of divinity—which is drawn upon in calling some things divine, others not, and which is also drawn upon in determining what the human response should be?

vii

When the opinions of a people, likely to be organized city by city, happen to change, does the very "existence," or at least the authority, of the gods also change? To be gods, it has been suggested, is to be gods for men. (See Strauss, *Socrates and Aristophanes*, p. 179.) Gods, as "gods," do not exist just for themselves. Do they come to view as "gods" primarily because of the non-gods, especially human beings? We again wonder, Would the gods do anything, or at least anything meaningful, without the doings of human beings? For example, does time otherwise mean anything to the gods? Would they do or be anything without death, successes and failures, if not even that morality which is in part keyed to mortality?

One way or another, the gods are replaced when the opinions of a people change. Those opinions, of the people at large, are not apt to be sophisticated. Such opinions are reflected in the sacrifices and other rituals of a people. Thus, to deprive the gods of sacrifices is to express critically different opinions about them. Opinions on these matters tend to be established, or at least encouraged and policed, by the city.

That is why the birds' blockade matters so much. It means, in effect, a repudiation of the gods by men. Of course, the men do try to sacrifice to the gods, but the gods (it seems) are not interested as much in intentions or even efforts as they are in results. To repudiate the gods is, as Peisthetairos says, to starve them to death.

Why did Peisthetairos (of the *Birds*) "succeed" where Socrates (of the *Clouds*) "failed" in replacing or at least displacing the Olympian gods? Peisthetairos' approach was political, whereas Socrates' was philosophical. With respect to these matters Aristophanes as playwright is more civic-minded than Socrates as philosopher.

The political man knows what to offer the city in order either to entice or to threaten it to do what should be done. He tends to be, like Prometheus, more man-loving. The political man knows the people better, or at least he may show (as well as have) more respect for the people's interests and the common good. Also, the political man is more dependent than the philosopher upon rhetoric or poetry. Thus, he can not only deal better with the people, but he also knows better how to protect himself against the people, as Peisthetairos demonstrates in fending off the attack of the birds while Socrates cannot keep his Thinkery from being burned down by an outraged Athenian father.

Still, it should be noticed, the *Frogs* of Aristophanes teaches that there is not an identity of interest between politics and poetry. There the divine Dionysus recognizes that his (as well as an audience's) artistic preferences should be distinguished from, and ultimately subordinated to, the community's interests. In this respect Aristophanes is closer to Socrates' position about art in Plato's *Republic* than he is to that of the typical intellectual today, even though the poet he rules against, Euripides, is sometimes regarded as the most "Socratic" of the great dramatists. The poetry of particular concern here *is* that of the playwright who must routinely "address" audiences resembling those of the politician.

Socrates, on the other hand, displayed himself as "inept" each time he was obliged to deal with congregations of Athenians. (Consider Callicles' warning to Socrates in Plato's *Gorgias*.) We also notice that Socrates did not limit himself to Athenians in the students he dealt with. (This may be seen, for instance, in those who were with Socrates in his prison cell on the day of his death.)

viii

Peisthetairos "succeeds." He is married off in style. He is even acclaimed as divine. We can see that the vitality of Founders is such that they can be regarded as godlike. Centuries later, if the birds' city survives and prevails, Peisthetairos may be recalled as one of its gods.

What, according to Aristophanes, lies ahead? It does not seem that the Sicilian disaster is forecast by the playwright. It evidently was so massive an armada that failure there was inconceivable. Indeed, the disaster was even greater because so much was devoted to the effort that its failure was unthinkable even by someone as imaginative as Aristophanes, which meant that proper precautions were not taken in the event of a massive defeat. So the deeply practical playwright, who had been so long concerned about the effects of the casualties and disasters of the great war upon his city, looks ahead now to what success will mean for the Athenians.

A successful Bird-land would be a Super-Athens. This can mean the end of the Old Athens, just as can defeat in Sicily. The ominous character of what lies ahead, behind all the glitter of Peisthetairos' successes and acclamations, may be seen in two facts that the playwright records but does not have anyone comment on adversely.

First, Peisthetairos' original comrade, Euelpides, the hopeful one, is no longer on the scene, even though he, like Peisthetairos, now has wings. That is, the relaxed and unambitious side of the Athenian soul has no place in this new city. (Euelpides is not disposed of the way Remus was by Romulus, but he *is* gone.) In critical respects, Socrates is more like Euelpides than he is like Peisthetairos. Euelpides remains an alternative to be reckoned with. (It is unlikely that Socrates would have suffered the fate he did if Athens had been successful in Sicily. He certainly would have been safe if Alcibiades had survived to the end of a successful war as one of the conquerors of Syracuse. I suspect he also would have been safe if the Odysseus-like Xenophon had not been absent from Athens at the time of the trial of Socrates.)

Second, Peisthetairos is not adverse to eating his subjects (that is, the birds, even the supposedly deified birds). The unpredictable boldness of this man may be illustrated by that part of the speech where Peisthetairos, in his successful effort to persuade the incensed birds to accept the two Athenians they unexpectedly find in their midst, recognizes that the birds have long been abused by men (with the fault here ultimately charged to the Olympian gods) (524–38):

> Now they treat you as knaves, and as fools, and as slaves;
> Yea they pelt you as though ye were mad.
> No safety for you can the Temples ensure,
> For the bird-catcher sets his nooses and nets,
> And his traps, and his toils, and his bait, and his lure,
> And his lime-covered rods in the shrine of the Gods!
> Then he takes you, and sets you for sale in the lump;
> And the customers, buying, come poking and prying
> And twitching and trying,
> To feel if your bodies are tender and plump.
> And if they decide on your flesh to sup
> They don't just roast you and serve you up,

But over your bodies, as prone ye lie,
They grate their cheese and their silphium too,
And oil and vinegar add,
Then a gravy, luscious and rich, they brew,
And pour it in soft warm streams o'er you,
As though ye were carrion noisome and dry.

Earlier in the play the birds *had* threatened to eat the two men, but this had been when they still regarded human beings as their natural enemies. (See 347, 372.) Now, a thousand lines after Peisthetairos' recital of serious bird-abuse at the hands of voracious human beings, he is using some birds to help him prepare other birds for a feast by non-birds. (1578f. The sauce being prepared even includes ingredients he mentions in the bird-abuse account I have just quoted.) This reversal of positions, which is a tribute of sorts to Peisthetairos's political skills, is as momentous, astonishing, and cynical (albeit in the comic vein) as the pact between Hitler and Stalin in 1939.

Have the gods been recruited by Peisthetairos in his coldblooded mastery over the birds? The negotiating team from the gods evidently joins him in the wedding feast in which birds (supposedly duly-executed traitors) are the main course. This could mean that the Olympian gods no longer place restraints, if they ever did, upon Peisthetairos' ambitions and depredations. Is there not something cannibalistic about this development?

The restraints of the old religion, for good as well as for ill, may be seen in Nicias, the commander-in-chief of the armada sent to Sicily. (His tactical skills are referred to in the play.) They could also be seen in the oaths that men swear, in the name of the Olympian gods, that are repeatedly exhibited in this play. Now, it seems, politicians are to be liberated to say and do the most daring things. Would a Socrates be useful here, Socrates (but not necessarily the Socrates of the *Clouds*) who probably found salutary such sentiments as this one voiced by a royal ghost in a play by the old-fashioned Aeschylus: "Zeus is the chastener of overboastful minds, a grievous corrector" (*The Persians* 828)?

ix

How do things stand with Zeus at the end of this play? We might ask about him, as we have about Euelpides, "Where" is he now?

It is significant that we never see Zeus in this comedy (or indeed in any Greek tragedy) or hear from him directly. We do see a variety of divinities: Iris, Prometheus, Poseidon, Heracles, a Triballian (a barbarian god), Basileia, and the elevated Peisthetairos. (Central to the appearance of these "divinities" as divinities may be Heracles, the manifestation of the power of the gods, but power without much sense.)

Why did not Zeus use his thunderbolts against Peisthetairos and his city? Can the bolts be used only for certain purposes? Or did this city somehow serve Zeus' purposes? Evidently, Peisthetairos makes a deal with Zeus over the heads of the birds, both figuratively and literally speaking. We recall how the action in Homer's *Iliad* looks to the Achaeans and the Trojans, action which is quite different in critical respects from what Zeus himself intends by what is happening.

Is Zeus' overall purpose reflected in Aristophanes' scheme? Do Zeus' powers among men depend upon stories or illusions? Can human cities undermine those powers? Are human beings, and especially poets, the principal source of, or at least authority for, the gods' earthly powers? The power of words may be seen throughout the play. We have already noticed Peisthetairos' power of persuasion. He speaks to one of his visitors about the power of words. The Hoopoe explains that he himself is dressed (that is to say, *is?*) the way Sophocles had described him in one of his plays, the *Tereus* (100).

Peisthetairos, who can be acclaimed as the highest of the gods, comes to his preeminence not by claiming divinity for himself but by describing both the origins of things and the chronology of divinities. He is like Hesiod in this respect. Socrates, on the other hand, has more questions than answers about the origins and nature of things. Zeus, we have noticed, is mute in this play. (See the epigraph for chapter 5 of this book.) Does that mean he is powerless? Thunderbolts, we must conclude, depend upon the mind that can put them to use—and mind depends upon speech.

The gods are denied that vital support by the people which takes the form of sacrifices. The immortal gods, we have seen, can be said by Peisthetairos to be starving to death. That is, they are being deprived of that respect and deference which makes all the difference *in the world* to them. We have also seen that the birds made so much of here are taught speech, and indeed Greek, by Tereus the Hoopoe. They can even be spoken of as immortal, which may be so if one thinks of the birds as species. (They are, except for Tereus and his once-human servant, not individuals. See, on the deathlessness of the birds, Strauss, *Socrates and Aristophanes*, p. 17 f.)

Still, is there not something *mysterious* beyond any divinities that we can see and hear? Is there not something—an idea or principle—in the light of which particular beings are identified as divine? (These are questions prompted by one author after another examined in this book.) Must there not be something that ratifies, if it does not establish, the standards by which all meaningful talk about the most important matters is guided? Thus, the ambitious birds need a basis for their claims. Justice seems to matter to them and to others before they can devote themselves wholeheartedly to their missions. Peisthetairos must take that into account if he is to be persuasive. We even see that the gods themselves care for justice. Peisthetairos appeals to that care in striking his deal.

It simply would not do, therefore, to show Zeus on this stage—or, for that matter, on any stage. Must there not be an unexamined (perhaps even undisplayable) foundation on the basis of which all the things said and done in this play, if not in the world generally, take place? The most thoughtful commentator I know on the Aristophanic plays has noticed, as perhaps a teaching of this play, that "the supreme guarantor of Right can not be simply subject to Right, but must have his hands free." (Strauss, *Socrates and Aristophanes*, p. 184. Compare William James' question, "Can that which is the ground of rationality in all else be itself properly called rational?" [*Writings*, p. 322]. But see section ix of part 1 of chapter 11 of this book.)

Does Zeus remain such an unfettered (but eminently rational?) guarantor of Right? His authority is reflected in the recourse to oaths in this play. A number of gods are invoked in oaths: Heracles, Apollo, Poseidon, Dionysus, and Demeter. But by far the greatest number (perhaps more than all the others combined) are the invocations of Zeus.

Peisthetairos himself repeatedly swears by Zeus, even on an occasion when he insists that the birds are mankind's gods now: "[Men] must slay victims to [the birds], and not, by Zeus, to Zeus" (1236). Is there not supposed to be something cosmically comic (or should we say comically cosmic) about such an "unconscious" reliance upon Zeus? This may be seen also in the fact that the marriage of Peisthetairos to Basileia cannot be properly described except by comparing it to the marriage of Zeus and Hera (1737–43).

The naturalness of invocations of the gods may be seen in another comic twist by the ever-inventive Aristophanes. Poseidon, in order to reinforce a point, swears "by Poseidon" (1513). Earlier, Peisthetairos, when he undertakes to persuade the suspicious birds, "reports" that in the old days men used to swear by the birds, not by the gods. (520. See, also, 1610.)

Poseidon can also be invoked when the incredible report is received of the building of the great wall in the sky. This can remind us of the role, referred to in chapter 1, that Poseidon is said to have had in building the great wall at Troy. (Are we also supposed to remember that the Trojans eventually suffered for not properly recognizing Poseidon's contribution? How does this bear upon the eventual fate of Peisthetairos' city?)

The continuing power of the divine may be seen in the way that the canny Prometheus remains apprehensive of Zeus even while he reports that the gods have been superseded. Since we never see Zeus appear, he should not be taken as having *dis*appeared. Perhaps all that happens is that Zeus "merely" changes his name—or rather, people change the names by which they believe they know him. (Is there more than a change of names in the *Clouds,* where Strepsiades was taught, or at least believed he was taught, that Zeus had been deposed and replaced in power by Convection-Principle?)

Must Zeus, or the truly divine, be considered ultimately unknowable? (The Bible certainly teaches this, and so do the Greek playwrights who could say, one way or another, "Zeus, whoever you may be . . .") We must wonder whether the divine is wondrously reflected in Aristophanes' poetic gifts, gifts which sometimes appear to be (as in the case, say, of Bernard Shaw) more in the service of sophistry than in the service of philosophy.

We must also wonder whether Aristophanes himself truly recognizes this about himself and what that means, or whether it takes a Socratic (such as Xenophon, Plato, or Aristotle) to do that in the most thoughtful way.

ADDENDUM

Aristophanes' Speech in Plato's Symposium

> *Such as she is, in beauty, virtue, birth,*
> *Is the young Dauphin every way complete.*
> *If not complete of, say he is not she,*
> *And she again wants nothing, to name want,*
> *If want it be not that she is not he.*
> *He is the half part of a blessed man,*
> *Left to be finished by such as she,*
> *And she a fair divided excellence,*
> *Whose fullness of perfection lies in him.*
>
> —A Citizen of Angiers

i

WE HAVE BEEN informed, by the wisest student of Classical things I have been privileged to know personally, that "Aristophanes' presentation of Socrates [in his *Clouds*] is the most important document available to us on the ancient disagreement and opposition between poetry and philosophy as such—between the two forms of wisdom, each of which claims supremacy—as this feud appears from the side of poetry" (Strauss, *Socrates and Aristophanes*, p. 311, citing Plato, *Republic* 607B–C and *Laws* 967C–D). Our informant continues by observing that Aristophanes' comedies confirm the view that he "regards himself as superior to his greatest antagonist [Socrates] on account of his self-knowledge and prudence (*phronesis*)" (ibid., p. 311):

> Whereas Socrates [in the *Clouds*] is wholly indifferent to the city that feeds him, Aristophanes is greatly concerned with the city; whereas Socrates does not respect, or comply with, the fundamental requirements of the city, Aristophanes does. The kind of wisdom that exhausts itself in the self-forgotten study of the things aloft and in its corollaries is unable to protect itself against its enemies because it is unable to act on

---

Unless otherwise indicated, the citations in this Addendum are to Plato's *Symposium*. The epigraph is taken from William Shakespeare, *King John*, II, i, 433–41.

the city or to humanize it by counteracting the waspishness of the city, and it is unable to do this because it does not in the first place recognize the necessity of that waspishness; the poet however, whether comic or tragic, can protect himself against persecution.

Furthermore, it can be said, the poets' claims rely upon the insistence that the knowledge of the particulars which poets make so much of in telling their stories is genuine knowledge. The knowledge is incorporated, so to speak, in the bodies that artists work from and through.

Aristophanes' *Clouds* was first performed in Athens in 423 B.C. (The play that has come down to us seems to be a revised version of 418–416 B.C. See *The Concise Oxford Companion to Classical Literature*, p. 134. That play is discussed in chapter 7, part 3, of this book.) The *Symposium*, a Platonic response to that play on behalf of Socrates, was evidently written four decades later (about 384 B.C.); but it is presented by Plato in the form of an evening of talk at a party in about 416 B.C., not long, that is, after the *Clouds* was first staged. The speeches of Aristophanes (189A–193D), Socrates (198A–212C), and Alcibiades (212D–223A) are featured in the dialogue. Aristophanes, in the *Symposium*, reports that human beings once came in three genders, male, female, and androgynous. All humans were then spherical creatures. The Olympian gods, considering themselves at risk from these boisterous human beings, split them in half. *Eros*, according to the playwright, is the passionate search of the thus-divided halves to find each other again. The speech assigned by Plato to Aristophanes is the central one of the seven speeches about *eros* set out at length in the *Symposium*. (Another kind of coupling that human beings attempt, a sometimes desperate coupling, is the effort to combine what one has been heretofore with what one would like to be hereafter. Old home movies can remind one of "what might have been".)

ii

An inquiry into the nature of *eros* bears upon the question of what is required for completion and self-sufficiency in human beings. Two faces of self-sufficiency are glimpsed in this observation by Aristotle: "He who is incapable of entering into community, or on account of self-sufficiency has need of nothing, is no part of a *polis*, so that he is either a beast or a god" (*Politics* 1253a27; Laurence Berns translation). The bestial in human form may be seen in the monstrous Duke who became Shakespeare's Richard III. The Duke, upon killing Henry VI in the Tower of London, spells out an ambition that will require him to get rid as well of a brother and two nephews who now stand between him and the throne (*3 Henry VI*, V, vi, 80–83):

> I have no brother, I am like no brother;
> And this word "love," which graybeards call divine,
> Be resident in men like one another
> And not in me. I am myself alone.

Further on he says, "Counting myself but bad till I be best" (V, vi, 91).

The philosopher, too, may naturally tend toward self-sufficiency, not by becoming the undisputed ruler of his country (and, in that sense, "best") but by becoming as independent as possible of his fellow citizens. Nor does he want to rule over other philosophers but rather to become as they are—to lose himself, so to speak, in philosophy.

Artists, like political men, depend upon others. They, too, work with bodies. This may be epitomized, for the determinedly political man, in the last words we hear from Shakespeare's Richard III: "A horse! A horse! My kingdom for a horse!" (*Richard III*, V, iv, 13). An illusory dependency upon material things may be seen also in Richard's inability, despite the fierceness of his determination, to find and kill his rival on the battlefield: "I think there be six Richmonds in the field; / Five have I slain today instead of him" (V, iv, 11–12). That is, appearances—which is how material things are likely to come to view—appearances can be deceptive, fatally so.

iii

At the end of the *Symposium*, we are told, Socrates is arguing with Agathon and Aristophanes, a tragic playwright and a comic playwright. They are eventually compelled by Socrates to agree that the same man should know how to make both comedy and tragedy, and that he who is *by art* a tragic poet *is* also a comic poet. (See Strauss, *On Plato's Banquet*, p. 237.)

We can see in the *Clouds* how a poet may present, or misrepresent, a philosopher; we can see in the *Symposium* how a philosopher (who *is* himself a great artist) may present poets, both comic and tragic—and do so with a spirit of generosity. It was Aristophanes who made what most readers would consider the most memorable speech during the evening of talk recalled in the *Symposium*. This is appropriate in that he *is* the greatest artist present. Aristophanes' "argument" shows a critical relation between the shape that bodies have and the passions that human beings are driven by. Again and again, that is, the poet argues that bodies do matter—and that philosophers, in being oblivious to the demands as well as the allure of bodies, are not of this world, sometimes irresponsibly so.

iv

Aristophanes' argument is both confirmed and challenged by the hiccoughing attack which keeps him from making his speech when he is supposed to. (185c–d. This could even be thought of by us as a comic anticipation of "A horse! A horse! My kingdom for a horse!") Also, at the end of the *Symposium*, Aristophanes passes out before Agathon does, following hours of wine-drinking with Socrates. Socrates puts them to bed when they do succumb, revealing thereby some caring for his fellows (including the comic poet who had lampooned him in public a few years before). (See Strauss, *On Plato's Banquet*, p. 213.)

We do see in the *Symposium*, therefore, that someone like Aristophanes is very much dependent, in deed as in speech, upon the condition of his body. Which came first, his argument or his physical limitations? Socrates, we are told, can drink wine all night without effect; he can take it or leave it. And at the beginning of the dialogue his own peculiar bodily "affliction," the "seizure" that came upon him as he was walking to the party that evening, did not keep him from doing what he wanted to do—that is, to think—but rather may even have been moved by his desire to do so at length without being disturbed. We can see here suggestions about mysterious connections between body and soul. (The tons of lead on the roof of Lincoln Cathedral, the visitor is told, affect the sound of each note played on the musical instruments on the floor of that building.)

We sense (with Aristophanes) that *eros* is substantially physical, with an emphasis placed, in ordinary discourse, upon bodies coming together with significant intensity. (Consider the Ovid story, echoing Hephaestus's address to the lover in Aristophanes' account, about the lovers who meld together permanently.) Philosophy, too, depends upon the erotic not only for something vital for the "tone" of its activity, but also for that desire to grasp the whole to which philosophy is dedicated. (Is this to be identified with the *eros* of "engendering and bringing to birth on the beautiful" [206E]?)

v

The Aristophanes story shows that what human beings are like depends in large part upon their troubled relations to the divine. (See, on "the mystical tie of art and the divine," Anastaplo, *The Artist as Thinker*, p. xi.) Aristophanes argues in the *Symposium* that *eros* is the result of *hubris;* it is not intrinsic to human beings. There are parallels to this argument in the Garden of Eden story and the Tower of Babel story. Does this suggest that there is something natural to what is depicted in such stories, that this sort of crippling presumptuousness is intrinsic to human life? (Compare Plato, *Phaedo* 60A–C, where Socrates speaks of physically *joining* heads, rather than separating bodies, in order to moderate quarrels.)

Does Aristophanes understand human beings to have any permanent nature? They are represented by him as being what they are now because of what they did once upon a time. They are also presented as vulnerable, now as then. Certainly, neither they nor even the human species are regarded by him as immortal. Nothing is said about the gods' ever having counseled human beings how to act. (Compare, with respect to Adam and Eve, Anastaplo, "On Trial," p. 767.) Yet are human beings not treated as if they should always have known how to act? Is there something intrinsic to human beings, however, which induces them to do things that threaten the gods? Did human beings truly know the gods, before Aristophanes tells this story—did they know them well enough to recognize how dangerous it was to anger the gods? Those gods, we are told by Plato's Aristophanes, care more for sacrifices offered to them than they do for justice (190C). That is, it is primarily their self-interest (a bodily, almost erotic interest?) that determines what is done by them to human beings.

Does not Aristophanes' union of lovers suppose not only that two become one but also that they exclude from their union everything, including third-party observation, that might mar the completeness of that union? That is, "completeness" means that nothing is absent which should be present, nothing is present which is superfluous. That there is something delusory about this frantic striving for perfection in union is implicit in Aristophanes' recognition that (somehow incomplete) human beings were striving against the gods—that is, they were aware of their limitations or imperfection—even before the ancient partition that lovers now try to repair. (See 190B–C. Does love necessarily direct itself, in its yearning for wholeness, to possession of that "infinite variety" which promises to satisfy the many ever-changing desires with which we have always to contend? See Shakespeare, *Antony and Cleopatra*, II, ii, 241.) Thus, one who is aware of all this might better move toward the completion sought, toward perfection, by directing his attention not to the union of love but to that which even united lovers would again contend (that is, aspire) for, to be godlike. But, the poet might again assert, it is possible for mankind to make that move toward perfection only through the body, not by circumventing it—only by making much of the universals implicit in particulars properly conceived, not by neglecting the demands and lessons of the body. (See Aristotle, *Poetics* 1451b5.) Even so, we have noticed that the limits imposed by the body are playfully alluded to in the hiccoughs that Plato ascribes to Aristophanes in the *Symposium*. (See 185C. In the *Phaedo*, Socrates suggests that disciplined thought takes us away from the body, however much most of us put our thinking in the service of the body.)

A more serious critique of the Aristophanic position may be found, of course, in Socrates' contribution to the occasion. Does not Socrates stand for the proposition that only the knowing man fully *is*? Is not the knower alone among mortal men in full communion with eternal *nous* (that is, with the truly divine)? Only he who knows what it is *to be* can fully be, if only temporarily. To lack such knowledge would mean that one is not being something one could be: a complete being. But may the same be said of one who does not rule or of one who does not indulge in the most intense physical pleasures—that one is not something one could be? Still, can one rule (and hence truly be "best") if one does not know? Can one, without knowing, select what is worth ruling? And what, indeed, are the most intense pleasures—those of the body or those of the knowing mind? Who is best able to decide even this? After all, have not the most intense physical pleasures been experienced by all? Neither wealth nor skill is required here: everyone, for instance, knows what it is to relieve a great thirst on a hot day by drinking cool water. (See Plato, *Phaedo* 60B–C; Plato, *Republic* 582A–D. See, also, Aristotle, *Nicomachean Ethics* 1170a25–b19, *Politics* 1278b25–30. Consider, as well, the exchange about the nature of pleasure between Callicles and Socrates in Plato's *Gorgias*.) It should also be noted that in order to have a full account of love, the shamefully intimate must somehow be dealt with as well: lovers, when properly left to themselves, redeem the shameful by converting the *many* of the public into the apparent *one* of the love union. Alcibiades, in order to speak openly of such matters, must be intoxicated; that is, he must be unable or uninclined to distinguish between the public and the private. (See, on Alcibiades' *parresia*, or uninhibited speaking, 222C.) That the guidance provided here by nature needs to be investigated further is suggested by Plato's assigning to Aristophanes's speech in the *Symposium* almost the same (if not exactly the same) number of uses of *nature* as may be found in the *Clouds* (discussed in part 3 of this chapter). (See *Symposium* 214E, 217E, 222C. Compare *Symposium* 176C, 214A–B, 223C–D, *Phaedo* 118A–B. See, also, Anastaplo, *The Constitutionalist*, pp. 546–47. See, on *parresia*, ibid., pp. 275, 781–82. See, on *nature*, Anastaplo, *The American Moralist*, p. 616. See, for a treasure trove of comments on the *Symposium*, Strauss, *On Plato's Banquet*.)

vi

What is there about Aristophanes' character—or is it his talent and experience—that should make him interpret things the way he does? Does he see in Socrates someone who, in his seeming contempt for the demands of the body, calls into question the things that the poet (along with most human beings) holds most dear? The Socratic manipulation of the marriage lots in Plato's *Republic* (460A) should be grist for an Aristophanic mill.

Socrates' approach to these matters is reflected also in his lack of concern about what happens to his body after death. (In life, that contempt had to be corrected, in effect, by the daemonic thing which served to shield Socrates from harm.) The significance of the body, and its relations to the most elevated or spirited, may be seen, for example, in the efforts people make to bury their dead. (See, on Sophocles' *Antigone*, the addendum to part 2 of this chapter. See, also, William Faulkner, *As I Lay Dying*, and Anastaplo, *Human Being and Citizen*, p. 214.)

Thumos (or spiritedness), which can find vivid expression in the sense of honor, does not appear to be a term used in the *Symposium*. *Thumos* and *eros* do not seem to go well together, especially since *eros* can engender shamelessness. Is *thumos* evident, however, in such activities as a determined effort to bury someone despite the decree forbidding it, especially someone with whom there is an erotic connection, directly or indirectly (that is, through one's own family)? (Leo Strauss suggested, albeit tentatively, that Socrates lacked spiritedness, whereas Plato and Xenophon did not. He added, "Differently stated and perhaps more intelligibly, Socrates was more unqualifiedly the philosopher. . . . You might say Plato and Xenophon, too, were not angry but played angry when necessary. Apparently Socrates could not even do that." *On Plato's Banquet,* p. 206. See, also, ibid., pp. 182, 201–2.)

vii

Aristophanes' account of *eros*, with its "materialistic" basis, may be related to the investigations being conducted today into the relation between *consciousness* and *matter*. (See, for example, Josephson, p. 219. This may be a latter-day version of the suggestions of Thomas Hobbes.) Chance may play a role in how matter does affect our "feelings," if only in helping establish for us the physical connections and hence circumstances that make for the most intense private pleasures, or for their recollection. (Consider Marcel Proust's *madeleine*. Consider, also, the pleasures as well as the pains that the recollections of various places can evoke in one. This may be related to my observation about the effects of old home movies.)

On the other hand, there is the Socratic argument (as in the *Phaedo*) that the highest thinking depends upon one's somehow freeing oneself from the demands and impediments of the body. Are philosophers suspect, then, because they try thereby to take the "fun" out of things? (See, on not allowing Aristotle's ethical prescriptions to get in the way of erotic attachments, Shakespeare, *The Taming of the Shrew*, I, i, 17 sq. Shortly thereafter a young man is smitten by the sight of a maiden he at once takes, probably mistakenly, to be his destined other half. Ibid., I, i, 147 sq.)

viii

Still, we can wonder, are not the greatest philosophers likely to be poetic? Do they have to be so in order to be able to grasp fully the things that they investigate? Do they, too, have access to inspiration? To what extent, and in what way, *is* the thinker an artist? On the other hand, what do the poets understand about the fine things they make? That is, are they philosophical? Do they know what they are saying? Is it fair, or useful, to press them with such questions as, for example, what accounts for animal sexuality and what accounts for the shape the Olympian gods in Aristophanes' story have?

These gods, such as Zeus, Apollo, and Hephaestus, are spoken of by Aristophanes in the *Symposium* as if they have the forms that all of his listeners are familiar with from the statues of the Olympian gods that they have seen (190D–191C, 192D–E). It is *not* suggested by Aristophanes that these gods envy human beings for their original globular shapes, shapes which are said by him to have been derived from cosmic divinities such as the sun, the earth, and the moon (190B).

There is no doubt that Aristophanes' account is generally appealing, drawing as it does upon something we are familiar with, the fierce desire that lovers have to possess each other. But should *eros* be seen as the affliction, if not punishment, that Aristophanes takes it to be when it is also said by him to have been devised by the Olympian gods who made human beings look thereafter more like those very gods than they had before? (Compare *Genesis* 2:18, 21–25.) Might it not make more sense, therefore, to suggest that the erotic, even as depicted by Aristophanes, tends to make us godlike, however ineffectively we may proceed again and again in our erotic pursuits and however dubious the forms that eroticism sometimes takes? Or dare it be said that insofar as divinities themselves have erotic yearnings, it is because they too are suffering from an ancient deficiency that they (like human beings) strive to remedy? Socrates has a response to all this that would be relevant for Aristophanes, but a response that he and other poets probably cannot use if their tales about the gods are to continue to be interesting. Socrates' teaching is that it does not make sense to believe that the gods do the things, and especially the erotic things, that the poets report about them. (See Plato, *Republic*, books 2 and 3. Compare Shakespeare, *The Taming of the Shrew*, I, i, 168.)

ix

Still, it should be noticed, Plato is said to have recommended the reading of Aristophanes to the tyrant, Dionysius of Syracuse. It is also said that when Plato died he had a volume of Aristophanes' comedies under his pillow. At the highest levels, we suspect, much is shared by the philosopher and the poet (including the poet who, in the form of a prophet, serves the cause of divine revelation).

Aristophanes, in any event, could not have wanted to see Socrates indicted and condemned to death. But he did warn him about how public-spirited citizens might attack him and why—and this he could do because he, as an inspired poet, had a "feel" for the desperate measures that men can resort to in protecting, and otherwise ministering to, their bodies. Socrates did survive for about a quarter of a century after Aristophanes' public warning—and perhaps would have died a natural death but for the disastrous outcome for Athens of the Peloponnesian War (to which outcome Socrates' "student," Alcibiades, contributed). Perhaps, that is, Socrates did learn something useful from the *Clouds* of Aristophanes, reinforcing thereby the guidance provided him by his daemonic thing. (See Anastaplo, *Human Being and Citizen*, pp. 10–11, 27–28, 325.)

Did Aristophanes, on the other hand, learn anything from Socrates' Diotima speech? (At the least, Socrates' use of Diotima should remind everyone present how vital to *eros* is the female element that had been neglected by the other speaker. Homosexuality, of which so much is made by these speakers, finds it difficult to look beyond pleasure as the proper end of *eros*. Heterosexuals have always had to anticipate and provide for at least the biological consequences of their liaisons, being reminded thereby of the demands and directives of nature. Do we not see in Socrates' speech a fruitful union of male and female?) Aristophanes does try to return to the fray after Socrates has spoken (212C), moved it seems by what reportedly had been said about him by Diotima. But the discipline of the party broke down in the face of ever more revelry. (Bodies thereby take over?) What seems to have provoked Aristophanes is a speech attributed to Diotima by Socrates, a speech to this effect (205D–206A):

> There is a certain account according to which those who seek their own halves are lovers. But my speech denies that eros is of a half or of a whole—unless, comrade, that half or whole can be presumed to be really good; for human beings are willing to have their own feet and hands cut off, if their opinion is that their own are no good. For I suspect that each does not cleave to his own (unless one calls the good one's own and belonging to oneself, and the bad alien to oneself) since there is nothing that human beings love other than the good.

Particularly provocative for the comic poet, as such, may have been the Socratic report (by way of Diotima, long ago) that Aristophanes' account has not been as original on this occasion as it has been advertised by him to be. Comedy, after all, depends upon novelty—as testified to by that standard request made by the professional comedian: "Stop me if you've heard this one before."

Even more important, for Socrates as well as for Diotima, is the argument that true wholeness or the Good (not merely one's "other half") is what ultimately directs the erotic pursuit. Aristophanes' argument had incorporated only part of the truth, albeit an important and challenging part. Aristophanes, we are given to understand, had mistaken the attractive part he had happened upon for the solid and enduring whole. Even so, Socrates and Diotima are not permitted by Plato to have the last word in this memorable colloquium on *eros*: the irrepressible Alcibiades can be depended upon to bring their disciplined high-mindedness back down to earth.

PART TWO.   On the Noble and the Just

> *I am not a bit anxious about my battles. If I am anxious, I
> don't fight them. I wait until I am ready.*
> —Field Marshal Montgomery

i

IT IS APPROPRIATE, as we move (with the help of a great comic poet) from ancient works of art very much concerned with the noble to ancient historical and philosophical works very much concerned with justice, that we consider in a somewhat more systematic way than we already have the tension between the noble and the just. There are, for our purpose, two somewhat related senses of the term *noble:* (1) "possessing outstanding qualities"; (2) "of high birth or exalted rank" *(Webster's Ninth New Collegiate Dictionary)*. When the affairs of a community are well ordered, it can be expected that those of high birth or exalted rank—the "official" nobility or aristocracy—will usually be people who possess outstanding qualities.

Unfortunately, we all know, there can be privileged classes, including a hereditary nobility, who do not display the virtues that are generally esteemed by the community, especially the virtue of justice. The ambiguous character of the term *nobility* is reflected in the constitutional prohibitions in the United States upon the granting in this country of any "Title of Nobility." It was recognized by the Framers of the Constitution that such grants may not be deserved or, at least, that it may not be healthy in a republic to "freeze" future relations among citizens. (The

----

The epigraph is taken from John Bartlett, *Familiar Quotations,* 13th edition (Boston: Little Brown and Co., 1955), p. 940. Compare Chester Wilmot, *The Struggle for Europe* (New York: Harper Colophon Books, 1963), pp. 462–67, 605. See, on the tension between the noble and the just, Anastaplo, *The Artist as Thinker,* pp. 7–8.

restraint in the Treason Clause of the Constitution upon the disability known as "Corruption of Blood" is to the same effect.)

The Constitution of 1787 *is* concerned to provide for "Posterity," however, as may be seen in its Preamble. It is concerned, as well, that justice be established and maintained and that opportunities always be available for citizens to pursue happiness effectively, something to which "the Blessings of Liberty" can contribute.

It is hoped that the inherent powers of a free people will be unleashed and developed if there is no hereditary nobility clogging up the works. There in fact has been in North America, for two centuries now, an unprecedented mobilization of the energies and talents of the people at large. This republic without hereditary classes, as provided for by the Constitution, has long been acclaimed a success, however troubled it is from time to time.

The Framers of the Constitution did not believe that they were drafting the best possible Constitution, but rather the best that was appropriate for American conditions. The best constitution in the world at that time, it was said more than once in the Constitutional Convention of 1787 without apparent contradiction, was the British Constitution. But it was recognized that that form of constitution was not appropriate for the United States, partly because there was not in North America the deeply-rooted hereditary nobility that the British had, a class of citizens critical there for the House of Lords and hence for the proper balance of the British Constitution. (See Winston Churchill's sketch of Lord Rosebery, in his *Great Contemporaries,* for an anticipation of the late-twentieth-century decline of the political influence of the aristocracy in Great Britain.)

ii

It has long been evident, even in Britain, that nobility can be disparaged as "nothing but ancient riches." (John Ray, 1670, in H. L. Mencken, ed., *A New Dictionary of Quotations,* p. 857). But that criticism applies more perhaps to a nobility in decline. Ralph Waldo Emerson, an American republican, suggested, "All nobility in its beginnings was somebody's natural superiority" (Mencken, p. 857). Unfortunately, natural superiority can take questionable forms, noble though it may be in some (if not even in most) respects.

Genuine superiority is something that Americans have always been open to, at least in principle, however important it is to recognize that "all Men are created equal." Thus, Thomas Jefferson wrote to John Adams on October 28, 1813, "I agree with you that there is a natural aristocracy among men. The grounds of this are virtue and talents" (*The Adams-Jefferson Letters*, p. 388). The Declaration of Independence closes with its Signers pledging to each other their "sacred Honor," a pledge which seems to draw upon an aristocratic spirit. Also aristocratic in its implication is the name of the highest decoration bestowed for military valor in the United States: the Congressional Medal of Honor.

The problem remains what it takes to develop, on a regular basis, the finest expressions of the human soul, whether in the realm of action or in the realms of art and thought. Nobility, even true nobility, is in a sense a luxury, but a luxury which people can (when carried along by it) believe to be worth what has to be taken from others in order to develop and sustain the very best—whether it is the Parthenon in Athens or the Symphony Orchestra in Chicago. The most exquisite human flowering can sometimes take many generations, as may be seen among the Brahmins in India. We must wonder, of course, whether such a system (even in its best form) requires foundations grounded in something like an exploited class of untouchables.

iii

When nobility is defined and supported by law or custom, there may be a formalization not only of titles and families, but also of manners and deeds. Sometimes the most frivolous (albeit exciting) exercises can be magnified into grand affairs, as may be seen in such sports as falconry and the fox-hunt. (Such sports, when studied, can be revealing. Thus, "the practice of medieval falconry can be seen as one aspect of the eternal war between the haves and the would-be's . . ." [Robin S. Oggins and Virginia Darrow Oggins, "Falconry and Medieval Social Status," p. 51].)

The extremity to which frivolity can be carried, in the name of nobility, is suggested by an American jurist speaking in 1918 (O. W. Holmes, "Natural Law," p. 44):

It is not enough for the knight of romance that you agree that his lady is a very nice girl—if you do not admit that she is the best that God ever made or will make, you must fight. There is in all men a demand for the superlative, so much so that the poor devil who has no other way of reaching it attains it by getting drunk.

Thus, it is argued, there is a natural yearning for the highest, which is to be reached for one way or another. (It is not clear that our jurist would accept this old-fashioned natural-right implication of his observation. See, on natural right, Strauss, *Natural Right and History*; Anastaplo, "Natural Law or Natural Right?"; on the Idea of the Good, part 2 of chapter 11 of this book.)

That highest—the nobility in word and deed to which we cannot help but aspire—can be thought of as a yearning for the most beautiful. Still, salutary reservations may be encountered to the noble, which reservations may invoke justice or the common good. (See Anastaplo, *The American Moralist*, pp. 481, 561.) This need not be a problem when the noble and the just overlap, as in the case perhaps of Aristides, the Athenian politician. It is more of a problem in the case of Cato, the Roman politician compared by Plutarch to Aristides: one sees in Cato how harsh and unbecoming justice can be—and in some instances may have to be.

Then there are the situations in which heroic efforts are devoted to an unjust cause. After all, there can be praiseworthy warriors on both sides in a war, and yet one side may be clearly superior to the other in the merits of its cause. In a variety of ways, therefore, nobility may be so compromised that it cannot be regarded as an unequivocal good. Aside from this, there still seems to be something troubling about nobility, so much so that it could be said by Arthur Schopenhauer (Mencken, p. 857): "We always think of a very noble character with a touch of quiet sadness."

iv

Sadness is very much in evidence in the career of someone like Cervantes's Don Quixote, especially as that career draws to an end. Here, indeed, we have "the knight of romance" who insists that "his lady ... is the best that God ever made." In the Don's case, we are also given by the author to see, the "lady" thus praised is a rather unattractive villager. Don

Quixote, it can be said, has gotten drunk on tales of chivalrous nobles. The yearning for nobility takes in him an obviously bizarre, or eccentric, form, with all kinds of curious consequences.

Among those consequences are his hurting of good people and the helping of bad—and all in the name of an exalted chivalry. Even when Don Quixote suffers privations, he seems to enjoy himself, which is more than can be said of some of those whom he undertakes to succor. Here, as elsewhere, the noble may be beyond good and evil. (See Anastaplo, *The American Moralist*, p. 431. See, also, Anastaplo, *The Constitutionalist*, pp. 651, 670–71, 798–99.)

Don Quixote may even be considered a practitioner of charity on a grand scale. The way he goes about his business does provide the basis for entertaining stories, stories which can be good for the human spirit. But how far he should be imitated is another matter: he can remind us of the man who, in his heroic charitableness, beggars his family. The grander, or more noble, his charity, the worse he may appear to commonsensical observers.

Charity on so heroic a scale, with little or no regard for worldly consequences, may well have as its precondition a Christian world. Certainly, it is hard to imagine this kind of romance in pagan antiquity, just as it is hard to imagine among the ancients our perhaps unhealthy preoccupation with love—which may be intimately related to such social pathologies as our high divorce rate and our high illegitimacy rate. (Compare Heracles and his labors.)

v

A more serious, or at least a more somber, form of the nobility that Christianity can nourish may be seen in the careers of its martyrs. Religion is here more in the foreground. A case in point is Sir Thomas More, the sympathetic hero of Robert Bolt's *A Man For All Seasons,* who pursued his illustrious career on the other side of Europe from Don Quixote, a century before Cervantes wrote.

A commonsensical critique of Sir Thomas More's deadly duel with King Henry VIII may be found in what More's wife said to him upon visiting him in prison not long before he was condemned and beheaded (Christopher Hollis, *Sir Thomas More,* pp. 252–53):

I marvel that you, that hitherto have been taken for a wise man, will now so play the fool, to lie here in this close, filthy prison and be content thus to be shut up among mice and rats, when you might be abroad at liberty, and with the favour and goodwill both of the King and his Council, if you would but do as all the bishops and best learned men of this realm have done. And seeing you have at Chelsea a right fair house, your library, your gallery and all other necessaries so handsome about you, where you might in the company of me, your wife, your children and household, be merry, I muse what (a God's name) you mean here still thus fondly to tarry.

More answered her by asking whether his cell in prison was not as near heaven as his house. ("Is this [place] not as nigh heaven as mine own?" [Ibid., p. 253.]) His wife was not as impressed as some of us (at a distance) might be by his answer, however, rebuking him with "Twittle, twattle, twittle, twattle" and with "Bone Deus, bone Deus, man, will this gear [nonsense] never be left?"

The primary concern of Thomas More's wife was, naturally enough, with what his noble resistance to the king meant to him personally and to his family. We might want to consider as well, for the sake of the common good, whether piety and religious practices should not be ultimately subordinated to justice and a political order, at least so long as that political order is a decent one. (This question can be considered critical, if not even central, to much of what is investigated in this book.)

It is far from clear, in any event, that Thomas More's insistence upon conforming to the Pope's interpretation of the relevant texts about marriage and divorce made as much sense in the circumstances as More seemed to believe, especially since the Pope could have come down plausibly on either side of the issues that were being contested. It is also far from clear that the pious Roman Catholic today would consider himself bound, or even justified, to accept More's position in what we call church-state relations. (See Anastaplo, "On Trial," p. 950.)

Still, some would say, the nobility of Thomas More consisted not in the position he happened to take but rather in that he took it at the risk of his life. To make this kind of argument, however, without assessing the intrinsic merits of the position taken is to adopt what we now know as an existentialist approach to serious matters. The emphasis seems to be placed by the existentialist upon a man's willingness to stand by the choice or "commitment" he happens to have made. But, then, there *is* something of existentialism in the critical role often played by forms (including rituals and long-established practices) in the identification and conduct of nobility, even that nobility in the service of the Faith which is called sainthood.

Whatever our reservation may be about the noble, it is evident that the ignoble is always, or almost always, to be shunned. (See Anastaplo, "'Racism,' Political Correctness, and Constitutional Law," Epilogue.)

vi

We have examined nobility in the somewhat attractive forms presented by Don Quixote and Sir Thomas More, both of whom seem to be highly regarded today. Our assessment of such nobility attempts to approach these matters from the perspective of the thoughtful citizen. For this purpose, religious opinions and allegiances may have to be set aside, or at least played down.

A critical fact to be remembered here is that justice, but not nobility, is a true virtue. In fact, nobility is better understood when it is recognized that the noble man or woman may, in some situations, be unjust, although that may not be readily apparent. Nobility *is* very much dependent upon the overall looks of things, so much so that the noble may sometimes be equated (as we have seen) with the beautiful. This can mean in turn that the noble tends to be transformed, in democratic times, into the celebrated—and so we now make more of celebrities than we do either of knights of romance or of saints.

The just act tends to be advantageous for the community at large; the noble act need not be, and indeed may even be, on occasion, disastrous for the community. This leads us to be prepared to curb the noble-minded of the future even as we honor the nobility of the past.

It is well, then, to inculcate in privileged classes the motto, *Noblesse oblige:* nobility has obligations. The term *obligations* reminds us of *justice,* which can often be rather prosaic in its prescriptions. (Consider, as well, the prayer by the Chorus, in Sophocles' *Oedipus Tyrannus* [886–891], "that god may never abolish the eager ambition that keeps the city noble.")

vii

How disastrous the noble can be for the community is suggested by the careers of two more of our heroes: one ancient, Sophocles' Antigone; the other modern, Shakespeare's Prince Hamlet. Social disasters may be more obvious (but no more serious) in their careers than they were in those of Don Quixote and Sir Thomas More.

We are intended to find both Antigone and Hamlet attractive. Each of them is very much concerned about serving the dead properly— a brother in Antigone's case, a father in Hamlet's case. By the time Antigone has run her noble course, not only is she dead, but so are her intended husband and her would-be mother-in-law. Even worse, perhaps, the peace of her recently-besieged city is once again in jeopardy, with its presumptuous but possibly well-meaning king crushed. By the time Hamlet has run *his* noble course, not only is he dead, but so are a half dozen others (including his mother, his intended wife, and her father and brother). Even worse, perhaps, his country has been taken over by an ambitious foreigner.

Hamlet had asked, in his famous soliloquy, "whether 'tis *nobler* in the mind to suffer the slings and arrows of outrageous fortune etc." That he had chosen a noble course is suggested by how Horatio eulogized the dead Hamlet: "Now cracks a *noble* heart!" Nothing is said by Horatio, however, about the sad state of affairs in Denmark resulting from Hamlet's noble impulses. (I have italicized *nobler* and *noble* in these two quotations.)

It is easy to lose sight of the fact that, when all is done and said, Antigone's brother and Hamlet's father are still dead. We may even suspect that they are not really better off for all of the carnage dedicated to their service. (See, on the *Antigone,* the headnote and the addendum to this part of chapter 7. See, on *Hamlet,* Anastaplo, *The Artist as Thinker,* p. 18. Indeed, what did Hamlet's father really want?)

Nobility, when it is not institutionalized, may have a tendency toward its own destruction. At the heart of this matter may be the question whether the suicidal, especially among the most gifted, should be particularly guarded against? That is, there can be serious problems, for the community as well as for the individual, with the kind of self-seeking that takes the form of self-sacrifice.

It may sound heretical to say so today, but does not justice dictate that it is not up to the individual, but rather up to the community, when and how someone in good health should surrender his or her life? Even such a noble-sounding announcement as "Women and children first!" may not be in the best interests of the community and a civilized life, however unseemly it may *look* to prefer rescuing some men at the expense of some children and women in various circumstances. (Trained sailors may be needed, for example, to manage lifeboats.)

viii

The noble, we have noticed, tends to be attractive. On the other hand, we have also noticed, the just is often not pretty. Public executions of terrible criminals come to mind, as do the ten plagues visited by the Lord upon the Egyptians who refused to let the Israelites go when ordered to do so.

The just, we have noticed as well, is likely to be closer to the sensible than is the noble. The just is also more likely to be utilitarian and hence prosaic in that it depends much more upon calculation. (Consider the undramatic epigraph I have taken for this discussion from Field Marshal Montgomery.) Justice is, in critical respects, like a free market economy, the highly productive efficiency of which can make matters quite messy and otherwise unbecoming here and there, as when factories long relied upon by a community "have" to be shut down.

The tension between the just and the noble may be further illustrated by the opposition between, say, the team of Abraham Lincoln and Ulysses S. Grant, on the one hand, and that of Jefferson Davis and Robert E. Lee, on the other hand—that is, between the plebeian and the aristocratic. Is the just inherently sturdier than the noble when they do not overlap? (An overlapping may be seen in how Lincoln has come to be regarded in the South as well as in the North.)

Certainly, justice is far more apt than nobility to be guided by prudence, so much so that Aristides the Just was "willing to set bounds to his justice with a view to the public convenience." (Plutarch, *Life of Aristides* 13.2–3. See, also, ibid., 25.1–3: a country's policy "demanded, sometimes, not a little injustice.") Chance affects more what is regarded as noble than it does what is regarded as just. This may be related to why it is that forms matter more for the noble than they do for the just. In fact, the conscientious minister of justice may seek to abolish some of the crippling forms upon which the noble may depend.

ix

However questionable the noble may sometimes be, we can often admire it, support it, even encourage it. On the other hand, we may find justice boring and tiresome, however much good it produces and protects. This being so, we may even look for relief now and then to reckless or otherwise dangerous expressions of the noble.

Better still, perhaps, we may look for relief to *stories about* adventurous nobles who don't count costs or who can't be bothered to worry about consequences. We may be both exalted and instructed by tragedies that show us what can happen when the noble goes astray. It is, for example, good for us to have *Hamlet* but not to imitate the Prince.

Relief may be found also in the way that Mark Twain brought together the sometimes divergent realms of the just and the noble—the realm of doing good and that of appearing to be (and perhaps even being) good—when he wrote: "To do good is noble; to teach others to do good is nobler, and no trouble." (Churchill, *My Early Life,* p. 573. See, also, Anastaplo, *The American Moralist,* p. 573.) Consider, as well, how the realms of the just and the noble are brought together in Hobbes's *Leviathan* (chapter 15): "That which gives to human Actions the relish of Justice is a certain Noblenesse or Gallantnesse of courage, (rarely found,) by which a man scorns to be beholding for the contentment of his life to fraud or breach of promise." (See Anastaplo, "The Ambiguity of Justice in Plato's *Republic,*" p. 199. See, also, Aristotle, *Politics* 1332a10 sq.; Anastaplo, "Lessons for the Student of Law," pp. 69–85.)

ADDENDUM

The Ode to Man in Sophocles' Antigone

> *Death is an ill; the gods at least think so,*
> *Or else themselves had perished long ago.*
>   —Sappho

i

A THEME SONG for liberal education today can be said to be the *Ode to Man,* the first choral ode in Sophocles' *Antigone.* It goes something like this (332–75, in the David Grene translation):

> Many are the wonders, none
> is more wonderful than what is man.
> This it is that crosses the sea
> with the south winds storming and the waves swelling,
> breaking around him in roaring surf.
> He it is again who wears away
> the Earth, oldest of gods, immortal, unwearied,
> as the ploughs wind across her from year to year
> when he works her with the breed that comes from horses.
>
> The tribe of the lighthearted birds he snares
> and takes prisoner the races of savage beasts
> and the brood of the fish of the sea,
> with the close-spun web of nets.
> A cunning fellow is man. His contrivances
> make him master of beasts of the field
> and those that move in the mountains.
> So he brings the horse with the shaggy neck

Unless otherwise indicated, the citations in this addendum are to Sophocles' *Antigone.* See, for additional discussions by me of the *Antigone,* "On Trial," p. 846; Review of Stephen L. Carter, *Integrity, The Great Ideas Today,* vol. 1996, p. 464 (1996); also, section iv of part 1 of chapter 8 and section i of part 1 of chapter 11 of this book.

The epigraph is taken from *Lyra Graeca,* 1:251.

to bend underneath the yoke;
and also the untamed mountain bull;
and speech and windswift thought
and the tempers that go with city living
he has taught himself, and how to avoid
the sharp frost, when lodging is cold
under the open sky
and pelting strokes of the rain.
He has a way against everything,
and he faces nothing that is to come
without contrivance.
Only against [Hades]
can he call on no means of escape;
but escape from hopeless diseases
he has found in the depths of his mind.
With some sort of cunning, inventive
beyond all expectation,
he reaches sometimes evil,
and sometimes good.

If he honors the laws of earth,
and the justice of the gods he has confirmed by oath,
high is his city; no city
has he with whom dwells dishonor
prompted by recklessness.
He who is so, may he never
share my hearth!
may he never think my thoughts!

(The *deinos* in the opening line of this ode, which is translated here as "wonderful," also has, appropriately enough, the connotations of "strange," "formidable," "daring," "terrible," "fearful," and "awesome." See, as well, 1095–98.)

This ode, devoted in large part to celebrating human achievements, is heard just after Creon, the new ruler of Thebes, has threatened the Guard who brought the unwelcome news that someone had defied a decree by ministering to the corpse that had been denied burial by Creon. The Guard is even accused by Creon of having been corrupted by "ill-gotten gains." The next thing we see after the ode is delivered by the Chorus is the same Guard returning with Antigone as a culprit caught, it is now reported, in still another attempt to bury the corpse of her brother.

Some editors and critics have problems with this ode, at least with respect to its placement here. A few are even so bold as to suggest that Sophocles must have had the text "in his desk drawer," inserting it as the first ode in the *Antigone* in order to be able to make some use of it. But this kind of revisionism may reflect a failure to appreciate what is going on here.

ii

It may be instructive to posit two odes here, the forty-four lines I have just quoted, and an expanded "ode" (or complete speech) which includes the lines elicited immediately thereafter by the entrance of Antigone under guard. The Chorus, or at least a member of the Chorus, then says (376–83):

> Is this a portent sent by God?
> I cannot tell.
> I know her. How can I say
> that this is not Antigone?
> Unhappy girl, child of unhappy Oedipus,
> what is this?
> Surely it is not you they bring here
> as disobedient to the royal edict,
> surely not you, taken in such folly.

The additional lines need not have been recited by the Chorus in the same way as the preceding lines.

These eight lines (in the Greek) complete this speech of the Chorus. No one doubts that at least these eight lines belong here, furthering as they do the action of the play. And these lines do seem to be tied to the preceding forty-four lines, the lines of the ode proper. Does not this tend to testify to the relevance of this fifty-two-line "speech" here?

A minor mystery has always been why a second "burial" was attempted by Antigone after what she had done the first time. Perhaps she was detected, if not even captured, her first (and only) time, with the guards being reluctant to denounce her until they could determine how Creon took the news of a burial by someone. However that may be, nothing is ever said by Antigone about having tried *twice* to bury her brother. Perhaps, also, Creon is correct to suspect that something devious is going on here. He does tell the Guard to produce the culprit or suffer the consequences—and shortly thereafter the Guard returns with Antigone. (I venture to offer my readers, in this fashion, one burial instead of two as a counterpoise to my offering them hereafter two versions of the *Ode to Man* instead of one.)

iii

The *Ode to Man* is inspired, we have noticed, by the Guard's original report of the resistance exhibited by someone (as yet unnamed) to Creon's edict. The war-wracked *polis* has just been shaken again, troubling a Chorus that reflects in this ode the apprehensions not only of Creon and the Guard but also of the community at large.

The first response by the Chorus to the Guard's report of the mysterious burial had been to wonder whether a god were responsible. Creon rebuked the Chorus as foolish old men before going on to berate the Guard for bribery and other misconduct that jeopardize the safety of the *polis*.

The Chorus is thus induced to condemn this form of lawbreaking more than it was at first inclined to do. Still, the Chorus seems to recognize that all lawbreaking, even such as has just been reported to Creon, testifies to the workings of the human mind and what we (not they) call *free will.*

Animals, the seas, fish, and other natural things referred to by the Chorus do not break rules; they cannot make choices. The human achievements that are recalled in the *Ode to Man*, reflecting the human capacity for progress, are shown to be intimately related as well to the human capacity for misconduct.

iv

Literally central to the *Ode to Man* is what is said there about the role of speech and reason in human affairs, a role connected with life in the *polis*. Reason permits that mastery of things catalogued in the first half of this ode. Reason also both permits and is nurtured by that political organizing vital to the capacity of human beings to transform the world.

It is thereafter recognized, almost as an afterthought, that a man's capacity to rule is limited by his mortality: "Only against Hades can he call on no means of escape." But this recognition may be regarded as almost incidental for the *Ode to Man* as a whole, especially if it is also recognized that the human race that is being both extolled and instructed may be regarded as immortal—or, at least, that the potential always exists in the universe for the repeated emergence and maintenance of reasoning beings.

Thus, the overall tenor of the *Ode to Man,* even with the implacable power of Hades acknowledged, *is* predominantly that of celebration, tempered by cautions that counsel law-abidingness for the sake of the *polis* that is essential for the progress acclaimed. Implicit here, too, is the age-old tension between the noble and the just.

v

The tenor of my enlarged "ode"—that is, the speech that includes the eight lines uttered by the Chorus upon observing the arrival of Antigone under guard—is grimmer. It is appropriate, therefore, that central to that enlarged "ode" *is* the reminder of the power of Hades, not (as is central to the original ode) the primarily beneficent power of speech, human reason, and the political order.

However enduring the human race itself may be, the prospect of Hades can be acute for individuals. It can matter very much to them, to their families and other associates, and to their communities what becomes of them personally and when. Antigone, in her nobility, had been determined to pay (on behalf of her brother) what is due to Hades, becoming in effect a priestess of Hades. Thus, both her concern (or piety) and her fate (or death) leave Hades in the center of what the Chorus has to say at this stage of the play.

Hades figures as well in the four choral odes that follow the *Ode to Man,* tracing the Chorus's series of responses to the challenges of the play. The next ode (the second, at 582–625) recalls how great families can carry within them the seeds of self-destruction generation after generation, with the gods coming down hard upon them again and again. The third ode (at 781–800) recognizes that power of young love that can divide families as Creon and his son have just been divided. This is the central ode, with the Chorus moderating therein the emphasis upon lawfulness found in the *Ode to Man.* Thereupon the Chorus (Antigone-like?) itself is "borne out of the course of lawfulness" at the mournful sight of Antigone being led in for her execution. (Creon had said earlier, at 777–80, that Hades was the only divinity that Antigone respected.) In its fourth ode (at 944–87), the Chorus returns to the great ones who have suffered disasters. And in its final ode (at 1115–52), the Chorus invokes the powerful local deity, Dionysus, when it is evident that an impasse has been reached that threatens overwhelming disaster for Thebes. (Shortly thereafter, Creon's son and wife, along with Antigone, will be dead and Creon will be crushed.) We are thus reminded of the limits to those human powers celebrated in the opening choral song, the *Ode to Man.*

vi

The original *Ode to Man* (that is, the first forty-four lines) can provide comfort for those troubled by a sense of personal vulnerability, even as warnings are given about the necessity of the *polis* and its gods and about how one should conduct oneself. This is why this ode can so often, if not even usually, be taken as a paean to humanity. To shake the *polis* (even in the name of piety?) is to threaten effective control of human affairs, deepening thereby our sense of vulnerability.

After all, whatever happens to mortal beings here on earth, the human race is (for the foreseeable future) likely to continue. Such continuation is served by the political order as well as by the divine order. One might even argue that personal mortality is necessary if the Good is to be realized, especially if questions are raised about whether the immortal gods (as commonly believed in) truly live. Thus, the Idea of the Good may make mortality not only bearable but also meaningful. Even those who see the Good only in terms of pleasure may recognize that physical enjoyment can depend upon expenditure as well as upon acquisition—that is, upon both ebb and flow. (See, for example, Plato, *Phaedo* 60A–C.)

Leo Strauss had occasion to observe in 1971, at the funeral of a young University of Chicago instructor: "Death is terrible, terrifying, but we cannot live as human beings if this terror grips us to the point of corroding our core." He argued that it is necessary "to come to grips with the corrosives, to face them, to think them through, to understand the ineluctable necessities, and to understand that without them no life, no human life, no good life, is possible." (See Anastaplo, *The Artist as Thinker*, p. 271. Compare Anastaplo, *Human Being and Citizen*, p. 214.) Still another set of responses to the prospect of death is what is said by Socrates at the end of Plato's *Apology* and how he conducts himself at the end of Plato's *Phaedo*.

vii

The *Ode to Man,* I have argued, turns around the efficacy of speech and reason in the life of man. The expanded "ode," colored more than is the original ode by the fate of a quite young Antigone, turns around the power of Hades. We, as audience, should appreciate both aspects of the Chorus's famous response here to "the human condition," aspects that are in necessary tension with each other. Few of us are either equipped or inclined to accept Socrates' characterization of death as possibly a dreamless sleep, even if we should be reminded that we were evidently not troubled by our condition of nonexistence before our birth. Nor are most of us apt to appreciate the argument that the goodness of human life somehow depends upon "the ineluctable necessities" associated with our mortality. (We also find in Socrates a casualness about his own burial [as in *Phaedo* 115C–E, 118A], a casualness which differs significantly from the opinions of both Creon and Antigone, who do seem agreed that proper burial is vital for personal well-being. Here, too, there is implicit the tension between the noble and the just.)

We draw upon, and thereby reaffirm, the sovereignty of reason in human affairs when we notice and reflect upon the tension between the divergent approaches to human aspirations and mortality which lie at the heart of each of the two "odes" presented here. But a general understanding of things, we can also notice, is not emphasized by the Chorus in its *Ode to Man* as among the achievements of human reason. Perhaps that is left for us to develop in response to that great ode, having been reminded once again of "the ancient disagreement and opposition between poetry and philosophy." (See Strauss, *Socrates and Aristophanes*, p. 311.)

PART THREE. On the *Clouds*

> One can easily receive the impression that Plato and Xenophon presented their Socrates in conscious contradiction to Aristophanes' presentation. It is certainly impossible to say whether the Platonic-Xenophonic Socrates owes his being as much to poetry as does the Aristophanean Socrates. . . . It is almost equally difficult to say whether the profound differences between the Aristophanean Socrates and the Platonic-Xenophontic Socrates must not be traced to a profound change in Socrates himself: to his conversion from a youthful contempt for the political or moral things, for the human things or human beings, to a mature concern with them. . . .
>
> —Leo Strauss

i

WE CAN BEGIN our discussion here of Aristophanes' *Clouds* by observing manifestations of intelligence in the things that "work." Such manifestations are evident in political and legal institutions, dramatic and other literature, and various instruments and machinery. We can see, either immediately upon observation or eventually upon reflection, that it makes sense that this or that thing "operates" as it does.

Unless otherwise indicated, the citations in this part of this chapter are to Aristophanes' *Clouds*.

The epigraph is taken from Strauss, *Socrates and Aristophanes*, p. 314 (concluding paragraph of the book).

Such manifestations of intelligence may be discerned as well in living things and in the parts of living things, vegetable as well as animal. Consider, for example, the typical biological analysis of the organs of a body. Consider, further, how the Darwinian evolutionist argues. It is evident, again and again, that the things studied by biology cannot be understood without taking into account their "purposes." To talk about purpose is to recognize the sense in an arrangement—and this is how intelligence can be said to manifest itself.

What does all this suggest about *Nous (Intelligence)* pervading, if not actually governing, the Universe? Intelligence depends upon things fitting together in a predictable manner; it depends upon principles of order and change that can be relied upon. To speak thus is to recognize the workings of either the Creator or Nature (if not both) in the Universe.

ii

Philosophy, as traditionally understood, is a comprehensive effort, by the use of reason alone, to understand the whole. *Nature* is critical to the philosopher's effort to grasp the whole—to learn the unchanging truth about things, including about the ever-changing things.

The philosopher's inquiry can require him to challenge accepted opinions, or conventions, including opinions about the most elementary things such as linguistic usages. This is caricatured in Aristophanes' presentation in the *Clouds* of Socrates' verbal nonsense and of various absurd investigations by Socrates and his associates. The philosophic enterprise can easily be made to seem ridiculous to ordinary people, to those of common sense who make up the bulk of the city and hence of a playwright's audience.

Most, if not all, conventions relied upon by the community rest upon presuppositions about what *is*—presuppositions about the very nature of things. But that nature which the philosopher investigates is complicated, necessarily so considering the complexity of the Universe itself. It can be instructive to notice those aspects of nature drawn upon explicitly in Aristophanes' *Clouds*.

iii

One aspect of nature drawn upon in the *Clouds* is that of nature as the source of matter or "stuff," particularly the human material, to be worked or reworked. This seems to be the aspect that can be said to be emphasized in the alternate uses of a dozen instances of the term *nature* found in the play, beginning with the first: that is, numbers 1, 3, 5, 7, 9 and 11 of the passages appended to this chapter.

Everyone is somewhat aware of limits imposed upon what one can make or do by the materials provided by nature. Special ingredients may be needed, for example, to prepare certain dishes or to construct certain buildings. Or, to use an illustration with human resources, not one-tenth of one percent of our male population could possibly be developed to become a plausible contender for a position as a lineman for any professional football team in this country today.

It is obvious that there is a variety of ways that nature is depended upon, or used, to make or sustain things. It is again and again wondered in the *Clouds* whether a proposed candidate for philosophical or forensic training by Socrates is capable of being shaped in the desired way. (See, on *nature*, Anastaplo, *The American Moralist*, p. 616.)

iv

That aspect of nature which looks to the matter or stuff to be worked or reworked need not require or elicit a moral judgment. It may be no one's credit or fault that one does, or does not, have this or that capacity. Another aspect of nature, also on display in the *Clouds*, is more likely to invite moral judgments: it is the aspect of nature as the source of the forms or character of things. This seems to be the aspect that can also be said to be emphasized in the alternate uses of the term *nature* in the play, beginning with the second: that is, numbers 2, 4, 6, 8, 10 and 12 of the passages appended to this chapter. These groupings, however arbitrary they may be in some respects, can help us organize our inquiry into these matters.

We often judge the uses to which natural endowments or inclinations are put. Art, law, and education generally can be used to shape the material provided by nature, or to overcome somewhat the limits imposed by nature as the source of that material. The material available on any particular occasion may be due, in a sense, to chance.

Wolves, for example, have a predictable nature—and there may be no moral judgment in identifying them as wolves. But when a human being acts like a wolf, he can be disparaged for having a wolfish nature. Socrates' Clouds imitate the shape of a wolf, in order to show such a man for what he is. That is seen in the first of the uses of *nature* (no. 2) in which a moral judgment is implicit. Such judgment may also be discerned in numbers 4, 6, 8, 10, and 12.

v

Nature, I have suggested, has an aspect in the *Clouds* which reveals it as the source of the matter to be shaped. It also has an aspect which reveals it as the source of the forms which are used in describing and passing judgment upon the shaping that has been done. The question remains whether the source of such judgments—the calling of something good or bad, right or wrong—is itself rooted in nature. Are communities, or at least particular human beings, equipped by nature with intimations of enduring standards by which moral judgments can be made? Or are such standards either essentially conventional (and hence ultimately accidental) or divinely revealed (which could also be a form of the conventional, albeit of a very high order)?

The central use or uses of *nature* as source of forms in the *Clouds*, if not also the central use of *nature* in all its aspects, may be seen in the sixth use, reinforced by what may be seen in the eighth use. In that sixth use, Aristophanes, as Leader of the Chorus (a role he takes up briefly here, evidently for the only time in his surviving comedies) extols his own play as moderate by nature (537). Further on, in the eighth use of *nature,* the Leader of the Chorus (whether or not Aristophanes himself) seems to extol the nature of Just Speech as a longstanding promoter of upright habits (960).

Thus, certain kinds of drama and of speeches (or instruction) are looked to for providing guidance in determining how a community should both be and live. The key concerns implicit in the play are as to the condition of art and rhetoric in the community. Aristophanes does not seem to be hopeful about the immediate prospects for Athens.

The state of art is suggested by the replacement of the old-fashioned Simonides and Aeschylus by the iconoclastic Euripides. More immediately at hand, as indicative of how matters stand, is the failure of the *Clouds* to prevail in its contest in Athens with other comedies, a failure that Aristophanes can lament, not least because his is (he says) a particularly wholesome comedy.

The state of rhetoric in Athens is suggested by the defeat of Just Speech by Unjust Speech, or professional sophistry. The deterioration here is reflected in the uses of *nature* in the second half of the play, culminating in the explicit licensing and empowering of licentiousness by Unjust Speech in the blandishments summoned up for a young man (1071–82):

> For consider, lad, all that moderation involves, and how many pleasures you're going to be deprived of: boys, women, cottabus [a banquet game], relishes, drinking, boisterous laughter. Yet what is living worth to you if you're deprived of these things? Well, then. From here I go on to the necessities of nature. You've done wrong, fallen in love, committed some adultery, and then you've been caught. You're ruined, for you're unable to speak. But if you consort with me, then use your nature, leap, laugh, believe that nothing is shameful! For if you happen to be caught as an adulterer, you'll reply to him that you've done him no injustice. Then you'll refer him to Zeus, how "even he was worsted by love and women; yet how could you, a mortal, be greater than a god?"

(Compare section i of part 1 of this chapter.)

It is only natural, when this approach is ratified, that one's own should be acclaimed as the very best, and this by a man (Strepsiades) who was concerned from the outset of the play to avoid paying the debts more or less justly owed by him. Thus, the final use of a term in which *nature* can be heard is by Strepsiades, who celebrates the wisdom, either natural-born or developed, first of himself, then of the son (Pheidippides) who is being ministered to by Socrates (1208). We are reminded by this speech that both nature and nurture are critical to the shaping of virtuous people.

vi

Aristophanes is concerned not only to identify the deterioration he has observed with respect to both art and rhetoric, or generally in the public discourse of Athens. He is concerned also to suggest why public-spirited art and traditional rhetoric have become inadequate in the Athens of his day. This deterioration has something to do with the influence of sophistry. From Aristophanes' point of view, philosophy (or the Socratic enterprise) is, if not sophistry itself, at least sophistry-like in its social consequences. Somewhat comparable among us today is the influence of the advertising industry.

We have noticed that nature is critical to the philosopher's inquiries and effects. In this play, we are shown what happens to the idea of nature in a community where philosophy has had a considerable influence. The first half-dozen uses of *nature* are by the Chorus, Socrates, and Aristophanes personally (as Leader of the Chorus). Those uses can be regarded as old-fashioned and more or less beneficent. But thereafter, except for the (desperate?) use of nature by the Leader of the Chorus in addressing Just Speech (an ineffectual use, which we have noticed), the uses of *nature* become clearly dubious in the hands of Strepsiades, Unjust Speech, and Pheidippides.

Thus, once the non-philosophers, especially those men with dubious motives, "get the hang" of talking about nature, they can manipulate nature-talk to justify themselves by misreading the available evidence, beginning with the shameless enticement of Pheidippides that I have quoted at length from Unjust Speech. It is difficult to make much of nature without, at the same time, depreciating the conventions of the community, conventions whose foundations in nature (such as they may be) are not likely to be always apparent.

Besides, as we have seen, nature *is* in a sense responsible for the baser impulses pandered to and legitimated by Unjust Speech. After all, nature is the source of desires which have always been recognized as being capable of improper (as well as proper) satisfaction.

vii

The natural basis of the desires is as old as life on earth. Why is more made of desires, all desires, at some times (such as ours today) than at others? Why, in the context of the *Clouds,* can Unjust Speech prosper and Aristophanic art (in the service of justice) find itself out of favor in Athens?

The profoundly unsettling effects of a long and uncommonly destructive war (the Peloponnesian War) should be noticed. (By the time the original version of the *Clouds* was prepared, this war was already almost a decade old.) It was a time also when the old-time religion was "wearing out," so to speak, especially as the restless and highly mobile Athenian people (victims of their spectacular successes in the Persian Wars two generations before) were exposed to more and more of the Mediterranean and Asian worlds. Then, of course, there is the unsettling influence, whether or not intended, of philosophy.

Philosophy, we have noticed, challenges the conventional. It can be contemptuous of the ephemeral and hence of everyday or common concerns and relations. In fact, Socrates' first speech in the play, addressed to Strepsiades, is, "Why are you calling me, ephemeral one?" (223). The limitations routinely (if not even naturally) placed by the community upon our satisfaction of desires or upon the advancement of our personal interests can certainly be wished away by the self-centered (if not also by the philosophic?) as ephemeral. (See Strauss, *Socrates and Aristophanes,* p. 15.)

The extent to which all conventions are open to reexamination may be seen in how Pheidippides can argue, once initiated "indoors" by Socrates, that he is entitled to beat his father, an argument that draws upon natural similarities between human beings and the other animals. One result of the sophistic deprecation of conventions and the legitimation of desires is to subvert the restraints placed upon the community by divine commands. The divine, at least for most people most of the time, depends more upon conventions (or the established opinions of the community) than either upon the dictates of nature or upon personal revelations. (See Boethius, pp. xiii–xiv. See, also, Anastaplo, "Lessons for the Student of Law," p. 179.)

I have raised the question whether the source of moral judgment is itself rooted in nature. Did Aristophanes believe that nature does not provide, or does not reliably provide, a guide to action? Or only that art can be better trusted than philosophy to be the midwife here, whatever the ultimate source of morality may be?

Is art (even though it may be an imitation of nature) somehow divinely inspired when it makes its most effective presentations on behalf of morality? Perhaps art (which can include what we know as revelation) is as effective as it can be, in presenting the attractions and the merits of morality, because it draws upon and portrays nature in its complexity rather than subjecting it to the somewhat artificial definitions and categorizations of philosophy. Thus, for example, the two aspects of nature we have reviewed may not be as neatly separable as we have made them out to be. Besides, are not more than those two aspects implicit in nature in its complexity?

viii

We should again be reminded here of "the ancient disagreement and opposition between poetry and philosophy." Aristophanes uses his art to attempt to rein in philosophy and (perhaps even more) its popular imitator, sophistry. He may also want to enlist philosophy on behalf of the social concerns identified and protected by old-fashioned poetry. (Similarly, Socrates, in Plato's *Gorgias,* tries to enlist rhetoric in the cause of philosophy. See, on Socrates' lack of spiritedness, section vi of the addendum to part 1 of chapter 7 of this book.)

Aristophanes' attempt to rein in both philosophy and sophistry requires that he ridicule philosophy in the eyes of the community. Ridicule in turn depends, at least in part, upon the audience's natural instincts, instincts rooted in or shaping their experiences. But Aristophanes may have reservations about any reliance upon nature. He may be asking, in effect, in the *Clouds,* What is nature—and what is the basis of its authority?

A late, if not the final, use of *nature,* or a term intimately related to nature, is Strepsiades' (1208). (See, also, 1414: "And in fact I was born free." See, as well, West and West, p. 173 n. 216.) That use reminds us that the term *nature* has its origins in *birth* and *growth*. (See ibid., p. 135 n. 82, on *tropos*, or *the way*, and its relation to *nature*.) Strepsiades' identification of his own (by birth) with the best (by nature?) is *hubristic*, serving as a prelude to his, and then to Socrates', downfall. *Hubris* points to the gods, or to the role of the divine in human affairs.

ix

We must wonder, of course, what Aristophanes truly understands, as well as what he does not understand, about philosophy. Does the sovereignty of *nature*, however much nature is the province of the philosophers, re-assert itself in what happens to Strepsiades and then to Socrates?

Or is it really Hermes who moves Strepsiades to act as he does against Socrates? That is, should Hermes be taken as having truly spoken—or is it Strepsiades only imagining that he has heard Hermes? But even if the latter, what moved Strepsiades to attack Socrates and his way of life? The texts are not unanimous as to whether Hermes intervenes here; if Hermes does intervene, what should we say moved *him*? That is, is it natural that either Hermes or Strepsiades, or both, should have responded forcefully to what Pheidippides is doing and saying, especially when he ventures (in the mode of Unjust Speech) to "leap, laugh, [and] believe that nothing is shameful," not even mother-beating (or, perhaps by implication, incest)? Even so, the gods of the Greeks, as popularly understood at that time, did not provide the best examples for moral conduct. Perhaps opinions about those gods needed refinement with the aid of a conscientious poet. The Clouds in Aristophanes' play do seem somewhat refined. (Whether or not they are gods, they do not agree with Socrates about the gods. See Strauss, *Socrates and Aristophanes*, p. 24.)

Aristophanes identified the *Clouds* as his wisest comedy. (522. See Strauss, ibid., p. 53.) Did not the philosophic way of life developed in Athens "rub off" on Aristophanes himself? Is there not something deeply philosophical in what he is doing—for example, in how he arranges the uses of terms such as *nature* in this play, thereby once again reminding us of the thinking that is often evident in the greatest art? Similarly, it can be noticed, the philosopher is willing to use art to advance his ends, as may be seen in the Platonic dialogues.

We have noticed how the uses of *nature* in the *Clouds* move from the more traditional to the more modern or self-serving versions. We can further notice that the half-dozen uses of *nature* in the first half of the play are preceded by a "barren" stretch, of some three hundred lines, from the beginning of the play without any use of *nature,* and that the half-dozen uses of *nature* in the second half of the play are followed by a "barren" stretch, again of some three hundred lines, to the very end of the play (1–275, 1029–1512). These two clumps of uses of *nature* are divided, in the middle of the play, by still another "barren" stretch, also of some three hundred lines (538–876).

May we regard this arrangement—an arrangement that does suggest deliberate craftsmanship, not happenstance or "only" inspiration—as Aristophanes' way of addressing the problem of nature? *Nature* is set off in this way so that it can be properly examined—and so that it can be safely placed within the confines provided by art. Thus, it can be said, Aristophanes looks to a rejuvenation of the natural, but a rejuvenation guided by responsible artistry, not by reckless philosophy.

The Aristophanic position seems to be that the philosophic-sophistic attacks in the name of nature upon conventions, if not also upon the divine, have led to a depreciation of nature herself. Thus, according to Aristophanes, the "liberation" promoted by philosophy (or at least by the sophists influenced by philosophy) leads either to misreadings of nature or to an identification of nature with only the base.

The philosopher's response to the Aristophanic critique is anticipated in what we have noticed about the reliance of Aristophanes himself upon what the philosophers have taught us about nature. How thoughtful Aristophanes truly is depends, in part, upon how much (and in what way) he is aware of what we have been inspired to observe about his own uses of *nature.* Leo Strauss has suggested that Aristophanes considers his comedies "the true Just Speech" (*Socrates and Aristophanes,* pp. 311–12). We are reassured, in our inquiries about Aristophanes' uses of *nature,* by the Strauss observation that "while the Just Speech upheld the law by being silent on nature, the Unjust Speech appeals from law to nature" (ibid., p. 32).

A full critique of the Aristophanes of the *Clouds* should include not only what Socrates says about the Ideas in the *Republic* but also what Plato reveals about Aristophanes in the *Symposium.* (The Platonic Ideas are glanced at in part 2 of chapter 11.) The great comic poet is portrayed in the *Symposium* as reducing the high to the low, proceeding thereby in opposition to the "high-minded" Socrates whom he had presented in the *Clouds,* some time before, as being contemptuous of an ephemeral and hence mundane political life. (Do we see here another form of that juxtaposition of the noble and the just which has been discussed in part 2 of this chapter? We have seen, in the addendum to part 1 of this chapter, a discussion of the Platonic response in the *Symposium* to the Aristophanic attack upon Socrates in the *Clouds.*)

ADDENDUM

The Uses of Nature *in Aristophanes'* Clouds

THESE ARE THE passages in Aristophanes' *Clouds* in which terms are used which can properly be translated as *nature* (as found in a translation by Thomas G. West and Grace Starry West):

(1)   line 278 (Chorus):
>   Ever-flowing Clouds, let us arise, clearly apparent in our
>   dewy, shining nature [φύσιν], from deep-resounding
>   father Oceanus up to lofty mountain peaks . . .

(2)   line 352 (Socrates, to Strepsiades, about the shapes that the
         Clouds take):
>   They make his [Simon's] nature [φύσιν] apparent by sud-
>   denly becoming wolves.

(3)   line 486 (Socrates to Strepsiades):
>   Do you have it in your nature [φύσΕι] to be a speaker?

(4)   line 503 (Socrates to Strepsiades):
>   Your nature [φύσιν] won't be any different from
>   Chaerephon's.
>   (Strepsiades' response: Oh me, miserably unhappy. I'll be-
>   come half dead!)

(5)   line 515 (Chorus, about Strepsiades):
>   May there be good fortune for this human being, because,
>   proceeding into the depth of his age, he colors his own
>   nature [φύσιν] with matters fit for those younger than
>   he and toils at wisdom.

(6)   line 537 (Aristophanes, as Leader of the Chorus, about his play,
>   *Clouds*):
>   So consider how moderate she [this play] is by nature
>   [φύσει] . . .

(7)   line 877 (Strepsiades, to Socrates, about Pheidippides):
>   Have no care, teach him. He's wise-spirited by nature
>   [φύσει]. Even when he was a little boy . . .

(8)   line 960 (Leader of the Chorus to Just Speech):
>   But you who crowned the elders with many upright habits,
>   utter forth your voice however you delight, and tell us
>   your own nature [φύσει].

(9)   line 1075 (Unjust Speech to Pheidippides):
>   From here I go on to the necessities of nature [φύσεως].
>   You've done wrong, fallen in love, committed some
>   adultery, and then you've been caught.

(10)   line 1078 (Unjust Speech to Pheidippides, continuing the preced-
>   ing passage):
>   You're ruined, for you're unable to speak. But if you consort
>   with me, then use your nature [φύσει], leap, laugh, be-
>   lieve that nothing is shameful!

(11)   line 1187 (Pheidippides to Strepsiades):
>   Solon of long ago was a friend of the people in his nature
>   [φύσιν] . . .

(12)   line 1208 (Strepsiades' song about himself):
>   O blessed Strepsiades, your own nature [ἔφυς]—how wise!
>   And such a son you are nurturing!

VIII. Herodotus

PART ONE. On the *History*

> *It has been frequently remarked that it seems to have been reserved to the people of this country, by their conduct and example, to decide the important question, whether societies of men are really capable or not of establishing good government from reflection and choice, or whether they are forever destined to depend for their political constitutions on accident and force.*
>
> —Publius

i

NAMES ARE VITAL TO THE ORDERING of the world, we are taught by Herodotus, a story-teller with philosophic interests. Names are most revealing, however misleading they can be for the unwary.

Croesus should have asked, upon being told by an oracle that his proposed campaign would destroy a mighty empire, precisely what empire was being referred to (1.53, 91). Cambyses should have asked which Smerdis he had been warned against: he had his brother of that name killed, not recognizing that the Smerdis of his prophecy was a Magian

---

Unless otherwise indicated, the citations in this part of this chapter are to Herodotus' *History*.

The epigraph is taken from *The Federalist Papers*, No. 1.

(also of that name) who was to usurp his throne (3.65). Cambyses had been similarly misled about the place where he was to die, not anticipating that more than one town might bear the name of the fatal site that had been prophesied (3.64). (This misunderstanding anticipates the misapprehension, in Shakespeare's *Henry IV, Part 2* [IV, iv], of where the Jerusalem is which is fated to be the place of death for King Henry.)

Not only may one name be mistaken for another, so may a proper noun be mistaken for an ordinary noun. "Herodotus says (1.122) that the true parents of [Cyrus], the royal parents, in order for their own ends to make the birth seem even more miraculous, set afoot the rumor that the child, when exposed, had been suckled by a bitch and so had survived. This, he thinks, was suggested to them by the name of the herdsman's wife, the foster mother, to whom the boy [Cyrus] repeatedly referred. Her name was Cyno, which is vaguely like the Greek word for dog (*kuon*)" (David Grene, trans., Herodotus, *History*, p. 6).

In the celebrated debate on the Constitution among the seven Persian conspirators, the names of the types of regimes mentioned, and not mentioned, by them are revealing (3.80–88). Only the advocate of monarchy uses the name of the regime he advocates. The advocate of oligarchy does not mention the word *oligarchy*, although it is used by another in the debate. Nor does the advocate of democracy mention the word *democracy*. But, then, neither does anyone else in the colloquy. Does this suggest that *democracy*, in the full sense employed elsewhere by Herodotus (a Greek), is not something that Persians know well enough to have a name for, however able they may be to refer to the rule of the many and even of the *demos*?

Is it not appropriate that the advocate of monarchy should display knowledge of the name of the regime he advances? Monarchy, more than the other two regimes, has as its primary claim to authority the fact that it is most likely to depend upon knowledge for rule.

One can appreciate how intelligent Herodotus is—how much of a craftsman or artist he is (that is, how much he knows and hence how much he controls what he is doing)—one can better appreciate these things upon noticing the care with which he uses, and describes the uses of, names.

ii

One way of asking how seriously the uses of names in Herodotus are to be taken is to determine whether the debate about the Constitution reported in book 3 "really" did take place among the seven Persian conspirators in Susa. Herodotus reports that the Greeks of his time denied that this conversation ever took place. David Grene has observed that there is here a rare display of vehemence on Herodotus' part, as he insists upon the historicity of the debate, and this is reinforced by Herodotus' later reaffirmation that this did happen as he reports. (See Herodotus, p. 4.)

One twentieth-century commentary, echoing Greek skeptics of Herodotus' time, has this to say about the colloquy (How and Wells, 1:277–78):

> Probably Herodotus is following the account of a Hellenized Persian . . ; the questions actually discussed were—"Should the Persians revert to the natural condition of the old Iranian society, and let all clans live under their immemorial customs?" or "should they continue the centralized monarchy?" i.e., the liberty claimed was simply the rights of the great nobles . . .

(One can be reminded here of the English barons at Runnymede.) This commentary continues (but not correctly about Shakespeare):

> The passage is the beginning of Greek political philosophy. . . . Herodotus here, as always, clothes Persian ideas in the phrases of his own countrymen . . . , as all men of genius do, e.g., Shakespeare's Venetians are Elizabethan Englishmen and Racine's Greeks are courtiers of the Le Grand Monarque. It is against this arbitrary introduction of speeches that Thucydides (by implication) protests in i.22.1; his own speeches he claims were appropriate to what the occasion demanded.

Another twentieth-century commentator has this to say about the debate (Burn, p. 238, n.1):

> The speeches that follow, totally Greek in tone—and interesting as the earliest extant of the many *Greek* arguments on forms of government— are obviously fantastic. Herodotus' contemporary [skeptical] critics were right, and if we wish to pillory him as a liar, this is the strongest ground.

If we wish to believe in his honesty, we must suppose that he had the substance of the speeches from someone whom he trusted. But it is not totally impossible that the Persians, who were not far from tribal life, may have considered abolishing the despotic monarchy as they had seen it under Cambyses.

The skepticism here of the ancient Greeks may reflect their insistence that they are significantly different from the Persians, at least with respect to political things, something which added luster to their victories in the Great War. Herodotus, as a Greek who had known Persia and Persians intimately, may have been interested in displaying similarities as well as differences in his exploration of the truly human.

Obviously, something had to be determined as to what regime should follow Cambyses, considering what had become of the royal house. Herodotus does not show any such debate among Greeks. Does he not imply that deliberations of this kind were routine among the Greeks? What *needs* to be shown is that they occur as well among barbarians. (The Persian nobility, in their receptivity to Greek modes of thought, may resemble the receptivity of the nobility in nineteenth-century Russia to French modes.)

An exhibition of the Persian mind at work might well throw light as well upon Greek thought—that is to say, upon how human beings everywhere think. A recent commentator has noticed, "These three speeches can be thought of as the most theoretical speeches in Herodotus. They present the possible kinds of regimes and their corruptions without any regard to local conditions" (Benardete, *Herodotean Inquiries*, p. 87). I return at the end of part 1 of this chapter to the question of whether such lack of regard for "local conditions" is sensible. This commentator has summarized what the three Persian nobles argue (ibid., pp. 85–86; there are elements here of the tension, discussed in part 2 of chapter 7 of this book, between the noble and the just):

> Each of the Persians, in proposing the establishment of either democracy, oligarchy, or monarchy (and in criticizing the corrupted forms of each), appeals to some considerations that the others neglect (80.2–87). Otanes relies on the "middle" character of democracy, Megabyzus on the beautiful, and Darius on the best. Their language corresponds to their choice. Otanes never says that democracy is best, nor that it makes use of

the best people, but he implies that it is good and pleasant. It is a low but solid good. Its advantages lie in three things. All its deliberations are referred to the public where it would be unlikely that anything except the ordinary and usual would be passed. Its officers are responsible and elected by lot, so that the innate envy and insolence of men can be kept in check. And third it has the "most beautiful name, equality before the law, and does none of those things a monarch does"; but Otanes is silent about what democracy does do (cf. 5.78).

Now Megabyzus appeals to two things in defense of oligarchy, the beautiful and the best; he alone of the three uses a simile (the demos are "like a torrent") and a verb of knowing . . ; but he never refers to the law. He claims that the people do nothing knowingly, who have never been instructed in or seen for themselves anything beautiful or noble of their own. . . .

Darius speaks last in favor of monarchy. He tries to show that it alone is stable because the other two regimes tend to be corrupted into it. Even though some might admit with Darius that "nothing would appear better than the one best man," he further assumes that the inevitability of monarchy coincides with the excellence of the monarch, for he equates the best with the strongest . . .

The Persian constitutional crisis reported in book 3 is, it can be said, working itself out among Herodotus' Greeks as well. The most obvious course of action for the Persians would seem to be the repudiation of monarchy (because of what they have suffered from a series of tyrannical oppressions) and the perpetuation (and hence ratification) of the approach reflected in the Conspiracy of the Seven. (See Dawson W. Turner, *Notes on Herodotus*, p. 183.) This would mean the establishment of an oligarchy—and it is that which is advocated in the central speech of the three made on this occasion. Thus, it can also be said, oligarchy follows naturally from what the conspirators had been doing.

Indeed, it is an oligarchy which does rule here, at least to the extent of settling upon the regime (a monarchy) the Persians are to have, upon the mode of selecting the monarch, and upon who the candidates are to be. It is these nobles, then, who ordain and establish a constitution for the Persian empire, transferring from themselves to a monarch the power they have seized on behalf of the Persian people.

iii

It is not difficult to suppose, then, that arguments of sorts could have been made on this occasion for either oligarchy or monarchy. Oligarchy, I have suggested, was grounded in the recent experience of these nobles; monarchy, in the traditions of the Persians.

But what basis is there for any advocacy here of democracy? The remarkable character of the argument for democracy is attested to by the fact that Herodotus' *History* is said to be the earliest extant text in which the word *democracy* is used. (See Raphael Sealey, *The Athenian Republic*, p. 100.) Some experience in democracy had been acquired by these nobles in the course of their deliberations during the planning and execution of their conspiracy. (Is it not the democratic mode that is apt to be resorted to within an oligarchy, as seen in the vote relied upon at the end of their debate about the form of government to be established? Oligarchs and democrats differ, of course, as to who is entitled to vote.)

Furthermore, we can work our way to what "must" have been advocated by Otanes, the spokesman for democracy, by considering the suppositions and implications of the evidently acknowledged status in Persia thereafter of the House of Otanes. (Some might argue that the status of this house preceded these events. See How and Wells, 1:279. But that cannot be our concern here. Consider how Magna Carta came to be regarded, whatever the original intentions of its parties.) We can see, from what Otanes, the first leader of the conspiracy, asks for and gets, what his advocacy of democracy primarily stood for: the right to be left alone, at least so long as one is law-abiding. This is an aspect of democracy that we, too, are familiar with: the rule of law can be made much of, especially among equals. Otanes, with his speech, puts future rulers on notice and alerts his colleagues as well, making more of outrageous conduct to be guarded against than of social objectives to be secured.

Both Otanes and Darius seek to be special, if not even self-indulgent —for Otanes, in his considerable autonomy, *is* somewhat monarchical. (One can be reminded, by Otanes' status, of the Athenian citizen praised before Croesus by Solon [1.30].) There is about the juxtaposition of Otanes and Darius a beautiful symmetry. The first and last of the conspirators, in the order of their enlistment in the revolutionary cause, are at opposite extremes of the political spectrum. Not only does one advocate the rule of all while the other advocates the rule of one, but also one wants to be left completely alone while the other wants to control every-thing (that is, to leave no one alone). In a curious way, each must depend upon the other if he is to secure what he wants.

Otanes looks at what is to be avoided, while Darius looks at what is to be gained. Otanes showed, by the deal he made, what he considered most attractive about democracy. Alexis de Tocqueville, in his *Democracy in America,* pointed to enlightened self-interest as central to modern democracy. We have carried this even further with our intensification of the right of privacy. Otanes, on the other hand, combined his personal immunity with considerable public service. (See, on enlightened self-interest, Masugi, p. 425.)

Otanes' principles were carried to a reckless extreme, however, by Intaphrenes, who had been Otanes' nominee for inclusion (as "most trusted" by him) in the Conspiracy. He, as the fourth conspirator, is midway between Otanes and Darius. He is the only one of the seven conspirators, besides Darius, whose death we are told about by Herodotus. This happens not long after Darius is installed as ruler (3.117–18).

Intaphrenes wanted the kind of autonomy that Otanes had earned; perhaps he wanted even more. But he had competed for the monarchy and hence was vulnerable. His grandiose (if not ruthless) self-assertion proves too threatening to Darius, who decides he must wipe him out altogether (including his family). The House of Otanes is thereby reminded of the limitations within which even it must work. (See, on *privacy* and *prudence,* Anastaplo, *The American Moralist,* p. 618.)

iv

I have suggested the basis, in the experiences of these Persian nobles, of the advocacy both of democracy and of oligarchy. (I will say more further on about monarchy.) The arguments for these two regimes are not so special that, despite what many Greeks may have believed, intelligent barbarians could not be expected to develop them.

We are further reminded, by the story of the unfortunate Intaphrenes, of what is similar if not even universal among peoples. All of the males in Intaphrenes' family are condemned to death by Darius. But the lamentations of Intaphrenes' wife move Darius to allow her to choose one male to be spared. She chooses her brother. Darius is astonished, and sends her this message: "The King asks you on what grounds you would abandon your husband and sons and choose your brother to survive. Surely he is more distant from you than your children and less dear to you than your husband" (3.119). She answered, "My lord, I can get a husband again, if it is God's pleasure, and other children if I lose these; but my father and mother being dead, in no way can I have another brother. This is why I have spoken as I did." Herodotus concludes this episode thus: "Darius thought that the woman had spoken well, and so he released the brother she had asked for and also her eldest son, he was so pleased with her; but he killed all the others. So one of the Seven died immediately, and I have told how."

The woman's argument is familiar to us as similar to one made by Sophocles' Antigone shortly before her death. Do not Herodotus and Sophocles, in this "collaboration," remind us of significant similarities between Greeks and barbarians? Appropriately enough, Herodotus does this when dealing with the fate of the conspirators who had heard, and presumably understood, the debate about regimes. Differences between East and West are suggested by the fact that Darius is shown as considerably more receptive to this kind of answer by the woman than, as we know, have been either Creon or the many scholars who have tried to get rid of this troublesome passage in Sophocles' *Antigone*. (See Turner, p. 610; Modern Library edition of Herodotus, p. 260 n; How and Wells, 1:294–95.)

It need not matter for our immediate purpose whether this kind of speech originated among the Greeks or among the Persians. (Herodotus, we are told, was a friend of Sophocles. See H. J. Rose, *A Handbook of Greek Literature*, p. 295.) It suffices to notice, with Herodotus, that Greeks and Persians have enough in common to make their enmity significant. But it is not simply a matter of chance that they do have fatal differences. This kind of relation between peoples, as well as the understanding of human nature upon which it is grounded, can be said to have been discovered by Herodotus in Homer with his account of the great war between the Achaeans and the Trojans.

What does the Antigone-like argument mean? The closest natural ties (that is, on both sides of one's family) are ultimately what matter in family relations, relations which do not "feel" to the child to be determined by the law. Is not an argument which is put in terms of irreplaceability an expression, at bottom, of piety with respect to one's parents?

If Greek and Persian can feel, think, and speak alike with respect to the pious, Herodotus can be taken as saying, it should not be astonishing if they can deliberate alike with respect to the ordering of political things.

v

We have seen that Intaphrenes (Otanes' nominee for the Conspiracy) did not know where to draw the line in pushing the Otanian position. I suspect it was he who provided the third vote to the two supplied in the canvass on regimes by Otanes and Megabyzus, the advocates respectively of democracy and oligarchy.

Otanes, evidently an older man, did know how to accommodate himself to Darius' power. He had, therefore, a distinguished career of public service. (His daughter became one of Darius' wives.) Most revealing, as indicative perhaps of the seriousness of Otanes' dedication to democracy, is what he did in suppressing despots and putting in democratic governments in various Greek cities along the Hellespont. (See 6.43; How and Wells, 2:80.) It has also been pointed out: "The refusal of the Samians to accept democracy leads to their continued enslavement and final extermination, and that at the hands of Otanes, who had been the conspirator to suggest democratizing Persia in the debate of the Seven Conspirators." (Henry Wood, *The Histories of Herodotus*, p. 85. See 3.144–47.)

Thus, Herodotus means for us to believe that the advocacy by Otanes of democracy is so deeprooted as to shape his public actions again and again. This is not to deny, however, that the Persians may have always been much better suited for monarchy.

vi

Why, then, did Darius prevail? Perhaps because the argument he made was the best of the three. After all, does not that argument conform to what most of the best political thinkers have believed over the millennia about the best regime?

But aside from the caliber of Darius' argument, his temperament and deeds should also be taken into account. Darius, who seems to have been about thirty years old when he came to the throne (Turner, p. 583), dominates the conspiracy, once he is in it. And, if he is to be believed, he had embarked on an anti-Median course on his own, coming to Susa for that purpose. (Consider the career of Junius Brutus as discussed in part 2 of chapter 13 of this book.)

In addition, Darius dominates the constitutional debate. He has the advantage of the closing argument, which permits him to deal with what the other two have said, without running the risk of being refuted himself. No indication is given of the reason for the order of speaking. We notice that those who spoke did so in the order in which they happened to join the Conspiracy.

Darius dominates as well the way settled upon for choosing a new king: the first neighing of a horse after sunrise. Nothing is indicated about who proposed this way. Scholars suggest the importance, if not even the sacredness, of both sunrise and horses for the Persians (Turner, p. 185). Darius, enticed by a kingship, figures out, with the aid of a servant whom he knows to be clever, a way to advance himself, working from a knowledge of equine sexuality. Does such a role for sexuality in public life suggest a critical difference between Persian and Greek, or between East and West, perhaps down to this day? Another difference may be reflected in the willingness of Herodotus' Darius to celebrate (in a statue and inscription) the trick he had resorted to in gaining the throne, a trick which others in like circumstances might not want to advertise. Or is this something like an exploit of Odysseus, and hence nothing to be ashamed of?

It is odd that the Persian nobles, on settling upon a form of government which made more of knowledge, should have relied upon what could be considered, at least by us, to be chance in choosing their next king. This reliance by the Persians may seem to us much more like the drawing of lots associated with democracy, implicitly impeaching the system they had just settled upon. (See Benardete, *Herodotean Inquiries,* pp. 86–87. See, also, How and Wells, 1:278. See, on the recourse to Divine Providence through the use of lots, the account in the *Book of Acts* [1:23–26] about the choice of a replacement among the twelve apostles for Judas Iscariot.)

The ability of Darius to exploit the mode of selection settled upon can be considered a tribute to his ability to govern. That is, unknown to them, the conspirators had left the way open to competence, a way confirmed thereafter (it is said) by thunder and lightning. Monarchy means that the *will* of one man can be decisive—and the will of Darius is evident throughout the course of this conspiracy, with Darius making (perhaps having to make) one critical decision after another in the course of these episodes. (See Wood, pp. 71–72, 88.)

Darius is permitted, again and again, to have his way—and this may testify to what the others sense in and perhaps even want from him. It should be noticed that he was the only one of the Conspirators to be chosen for the company by all of the others. (See Wood, p. 73.) It should also be noticed that Cyrus had a prophecy suggesting that Darius might take his throne (1.209–11). Did the Conspirators know of this, and defer to it—that is, to the privileged name of Darius?

In any event, the father of Darius, a prominent official in the court of Cyrus and then of Cambyses, undertook (after Cyrus had learned of the prophesy) to check his son, on Cyrus' behalf, but really to protect him from "the cunning of Cyrus" (1.211). This reference to parental concern reminds us of perhaps the most striking and yet the most concealed exercise by Darius of his will: Darius became King of the Persians while his father was still alive and active. (See Modern Library edition, pp. 287 n, 256 n.) What does this say about his piety, in thus taking precedence over his own father, especially when one recalls the deference to the parental that is celebrated in Antigone and in the wife of Intaphrenes? On the other hand, there had been a sort of piety in Darius' advocacy of the way established by their fathers' fathers, especially through the agency of one man who had liberated the Persians from the rule of the Medes. Darius confirms the old way by marrying Cyrus' daughter, by whom he had Xerxes, his unfortunate successor. (See 7.2.)

vii

Darius' name, we are told by Herodotus, means "the Doer." We are further told that the meanings of his name and of those of his successors (Xerxes: "Warrior"; Artaxerxes: "Great Warrior") are what "the Greeks would correctly call these kings in their own tongues" (6.98).

Darius, as Doer, knows what to use in effecting his ends. Perhaps he had decided, long before the Conspiracy moved, that the next king of the Persians should be himself.

Critical to the uses Darius makes of his opportunities is recourse to deception when "needed." In fact, he can, perhaps more than any other Persian, justify lying as readily as he can justify the truth-telling which the Persians make so much of. (See Benardete, *Herodotean Inquiries,* p. 84.) Darius, in his argument for monarchy, had praised the ability of the monarch to clothe in a "well-judging silence" whatever measures he must devise against evil-doers (3.72). His companions probably believed that he was referring to the need to deceive the enemies of Persia—but the first people upon whom he practices his wiles are the Persians themselves, if not even the best of the Persians. That is inevitable in the founding of any enduring regime, Machiavelli teaches us.

We might well wonder what form of government Herodotus himself prefers. He suggests the limitations of the Persians in political discourse by leaving out of the debate at least two major arguments—one *pro*, one *con*—which bear upon the appropriateness of a monarchy for the Persians.

On behalf of monarchy, it can be said (as we have noticed) that the character of the Persian people is such as to require a monarchy, something which may be seen in their history, customs, and traditions. Even the Conspirators had been drifting dangerously until Darius joined them and took charge.

The circumstances of the Persians may be reflected in the common Greek opinion that no such debate as Herodotus reports could have taken place. That there is at least a correspondence between character and circumstances may be seen in a passage in which the triumphant Cyrus responds to those who had urged that the Persians move, now that they could, from their austere land to something better. Herodotus tells us, "When Cyrus heard [their proposal], he was not amazed at their argument but said that they should do as they said; but in that case they should prepare to be no longer those who rule but those who would be ruled. 'From soft countries come soft men. It is not possible that from the same land stems a growth of wondrous fruit and men who are good soldiers.' So the Persians took this to heart and went away, their judgment had been overcome by that of Cyrus, and they chose to rule, living in a wretched land, rather than to sow the level plains and be slaves to others" (9.122). Is not the reader induced by Herodotus' *History* to wonder what had happened, by the time of Marathon and Platea, to the "good soldiers" that Persia had once routinely produced? (See Herodotus, 1.71; Arrian, pp. 112, 121.)

This question brings us to the second major limitation in the arguments made by the three debaters, the failure to address adequately the lack of a proper succession, from which monarchy can suffer more than any other regime. We see throughout the *History* how sons can differ from their fathers, which means that however competent one monarch may be, his successor may well be a disaster. (See, on successions, Wood, pp. 69–70. See, also, the discussion by Socrates and Anytus in Plato's *Meno*.)

These limitations—relating to the character and circumstances of the Persian people and to the problem of succession—remind us of the question of *nature*, something which the Persians are not equipped to attempt to address systematically. (One may well wonder whether any non-Greek in the *History* self-consciously uses a form of the word *nature*.) Does not Herodotus himself, on the other hand, speak to an audience which is capable of appreciating what *nature* means, thereby being able to engage in political discourse which makes it possible to have genuine aristocratic rule year in and year out?

Furthermore, does not Herodotus, in vouching as he does for the authenticity of the account he gives of the great debate, act somewhat in the spirit of the deception that had been going on during the Conspiracy and immediately thereafter? Whatever the truth may be about whether this conversation "actually" took place, it is a Greek "phenomenon" that it should be recorded as it is here. Indeed, Herodotus is very much the artist—the thinker as artist—who can use this story as I suggest he has done, even employing deceptions (as perhaps Darius does) to tell or at least to advance the truth.

We thereby see true governance and the true ruler emerge, that rule which draws upon craftsmanship as both a reliable source for and the best practical evidence of rightful authority. Craftsmanship of the highest order is to be seen in what artists such as Herodotus can do in shaping their people for generations to come. This points up the importance for Herodotus of the uncharacteristic story of Arion, the story of the minstrel miraculously rescued from drowning by a dolphin (1.23–24).

Thus, in telling us what he does about what was said on the occasion of the great debate, Herodotus would certainly have us notice what is left "unsaid," including how he has organized the matters about which I have been inspired to speak as I have here.

PART TWO.　On the Gyges Story

> *The distinction between historian and poet is not in the one writing prose and the other verse—you might put the work of Herodotus into verse, and it would still be a species of history; it consists really in this, that the one describes the thing that has been, and the other a kind of thing that might be. Hence poetry is something more philosophic and of greater import than history, since its statements are of the nature rather of universals, whereas those of history are singulars. By a universal statement I mean one as to what such or such a kind of man will probably or necessarily say or do—which is the aim of poetry, though it affixes proper names to the characters; by a singular statement, one as to what, say, Alcibiades did or had done to him.*
>
> —Aristotle

i

A COMPARISON OF Herodotus' *History* and Plato's *Republic* provides us another opportunity to see how an episode told by one great author is retold by another. (We have seen how the Rhesus incident in Homer was retold by Euripides and how the Hippolytus story told by Euripides was retold by Racine.) This Herodotus-Plato episode is that of Gyges, King of Lydia, who is said to have come to power in the seventh century B.C. It is recounted by Herodotus in his *History,* which was written in the fifth century B.C.; and it is drawn upon by Plato in his *Republic,* which was written in the fourth century B.C.

Unless otherwise indicated, the citations in this part of this chapter are to Herodotus' *History* or to Plato's *Republic.*

The epigraph is taken from Aristotle 1451b1–11.

The Gyges-based account can be considered the first substantial story in each of these two works, the *History* and the *Republic*. In neither work does the author tell the account "for its own sake," not even as entertainment in itself; rather, in each case the author adapts it to his own larger purpose. This means, among other things, that many details are omitted that were probably in the original sources upon which Herodotus and Plato both drew. It also means that we have here another opportunity to see what "inspiration" looks like, how authors of genius can use their materials. It should also be noticed that the Gyges-based account is critical in each work for much of what is said thereafter.

ii

Herodotus tells the story of Gyges in the course of accounting for the fall of Croesus, the royal descendant of Gyges, whose wealth is legendary to this day. (See, e.g., Marcus Aurelius, *Meditations* 10.27.) The fall of Croesus, we are told, is related to the way Gyges, his ancestor, took power in succeeding Candaules whose family had ruled Lydia for twenty-two generations of men, or 505 years (1.7). The story of the last days of Candaules, the ruler of Lydia, begins this way in Herodotus' account (1.8–11):

> This Candaules fell in love with his own wife; and because he was so in love, he thought he had in her far the most beautiful of women. So he thought. Now, he had a bodyguard named Gyges, the son of Dascylus, who was his chief favorite among them. Candaules used to confide all his most serious concerns to this Gyges, and of course he was forever overpraising the beauty of his wife's body to him. Some time thereafter—for it was fated that Candaules should end ill—he spoke to Gyges thus: "Gyges, I do not think that you credit me when I tell you about the beauty of my wife; for indeed men's ears are duller agents of belief than their eyes. Contrive, then, that you see her naked." The other made outcry against him and said, "Master, what a sick word is this you have spoken, in bidding me look upon my mistress naked! With the laying-aside of her clothes, a woman lays aside the respect that is hers! Many are the fine things discovered by men of old, and among them this one, that each should look upon his own, only. Indeed I believe that your wife is the

most beautiful of all women, and I beg of you not to demand of me what is unlawful."

With these words he would have fought him off, being in dread lest some evil should come to himself out of these things; but the other answered him and said: "Be of good heart, Gyges, and fear neither myself, lest I might suggest this as a trial of you, nor yet my wife, that some hurt might befall you from her. For my own part I will contrive it entirely that she will not know she has been seen by you. For I will place you in the room where we sleep, behind the open door. After my coming-in, my wife too will come to her bed. There is a chair that stands near the entrance. On this she will lay her clothes, one by one, as she takes them off and so will give you full leisure to view her. But when she goes from the chair to the bed and you are behind her, let you heed then that she does not see you as you go through the door."

Inasmuch, then, as Gyges was unable to avoid it, he was ready. Candaules, when he judged the hour to retire had come, led Gyges into his bedroom; afterwards his wife, too, came in at once; and, as she came in and laid her clothes aside, Gyges viewed her. When she went to bed and Gyges was behind her, he slipped out—but the woman saw him as he was going through the door. She understood then what had been done by her husband; and though she was so shamed, she raised no outcry nor let on to have understood, having in mind to take punishment on Candaules. For among the Lydians and indeed among the generality of the barbarians, for even a man to be seen naked is an occasion of great shame.

So for that time she showed nothing but held her peace.

Herodotus notices here both the understanding and the self-control of this woman, traits that Candaules had ignored in praising her only for her physical beauty. Herodotus' account of this episode (which has recently been retold in the movie, *The English Patient*) continues (1.11–12):

But when the day dawned, she made ready such of her household servants as she saw were most loyal to her and sent for Gyges. He gave never a thought to her knowing anything of what had happened and came on her summons, since he had been wont before this, also, to come in attendance whenever the queen should call him. As Gyges appeared, the woman said to him: "Gyges, there are two roads before you, and I give you your choice which you will travel. Either you kill Candaules and take me and the kingship of the Lydians, or you must yourself die straightway, as you are, that you may not, in days to come, obey Candaules in everything and look on what you ought not. For either he that contrived this must die or you, who have viewed me naked and done what is not lawful." For a while Gyges was in amazement at her words; but then he besought her not to bind him in the necessity of such a choice. But he did not persuade her—only saw that necessity truly lay before him: either to kill his master or himself be killed by others. So he chose his own survival. Then he spoke to her and asked her further: "Since you force me to kill my master, all unwilling, let me hear from you in what way we shall attack him." She answered and said: "The attack on him shall be made from the self-same place whence he showed me to you naked, and it is when he is sleeping that you shall attack him."

So they prepared their plot, and, as night came on—for there was no going back for Gyges, nor any riddance of the matter but that either himself or Candaules must die—he followed the woman into the bedroom. She gave him a dagger and hid him behind the very door. And after that, as Candaules was taking his rest, Gyges slipped out and killed him, and so it was that he, Gyges, had the wife and the kingship of Lydia. Archilochus of Paros, who lived at the same time, made mention of him in a poem of iambic trimeters.

I will return to the sequel to this passage for what Herodotus reports about the immediate aftermath of Gyges' usurpation. But first, let us recollect how this episode is told in Plato's *Republic*.

iii

Plato (who wrote in the *Republic* about a century after Herodotus wrote his *History*) presents in his dialogue (narrated by Socrates) a story told by Glaucon to illustrate a proposition set forth thus (359B–C):

That even those who practice [justice] do so unwillingly, from an incapacity to do injustice, we would best perceive if we should in thought do something like this: give each, the just man and the unjust, license to do whatever he wants, while we follow and watch where his desire will lead each. We would catch the just man red-handed going the same way as the unjust man out of a desire to get the better: this is what any nature naturally pursues as good, while it is law which by force perverts it to honor equality.

Glaucon then goes on to illustrate this proposition about what would happen if a man (whether just or unjust) had the "license to do whatever he wants" (359c–360c):

> The license of which I speak would best be realized if [the just and the unjust man] should come into possession of the sort of power that it is said the ancestor of Gyges, the Lydian, once got. They say he was a shepherd toiling in the service of the man who was then ruling Lydia. There came to pass a great thunderstorm and an earthquake; the earth cracked and a chasm opened at the place where he was pasturing. He saw it, wondered at it, and went down. He saw, along with other quite wonderful things about which they tell tales, a hollow bronze horse. It had windows; peeping in, he saw there was a corpse inside that looked larger than human size. It had nothing on except a gold ring on its hand; he slipped it off and went out. When there was the usual gathering of the shepherds to make the monthly report to the king about the flocks, he too came, wearing the ring. Now, while he was sitting with the others, he chanced to turn the collet of the ring to himself, toward the inside of his hand; when he did this, he became invisible to those sitting by him, and they discussed him as though he were away. He wondered at this, and, fingering the ring again, he twisted the collet toward the outside; when he had twisted it, he became visible. Thinking this over, he tested whether the ring had this power, and that was exactly his result: when he turned the collet inward, he became invisible, when outward, visible. Aware of this, he immediately contrived to be one of the messengers to the king. When he arrived, he committed adultery with the king's wife and, along with her, set upon the king and killed him. And so he took over the rule.
>
> Now if there were two such rings, and the just man would put one on, and the unjust man the other, no one, as it would seem, would be so adamant as to stick by justice and bring himself to keep away from what belongs to others and not lay hold of it, although he had license to take what he wanted from the market without fear, and to go into houses and have intercourse with whomever he wanted, and to slay or release from bonds whomever he wanted, and to do other things as an equal to a god among humans. . . .

Thus is the story of Gyges the Lydian, which had been given currency in the Greek world by Herodotus ("the father of history"), transformed in Plato's *Republic,* which has been called "the most famous political work of all times" (Strauss, *The City and Man,* p. 62).

iv

That it *is* somehow the same story in the *Republic* is suggested by the obvious similarities. First, of course, there is the *name* of Gyges. Then, there is the name of the country, Lydia. Finally, there is a usurpation in both accounts. The usurpation, in each case, begins with the relations of the "hero" with the queen. And the usurpation concludes with the "hero" joining with the queen to kill the king. Glaucon's account (in the *Republic*) can be broken down into a dozen key elements:

1) the "hero" is "the ancestor of Gyges, the Lydian." Notice that he is not what he is in Herodotus' story, Gyges himself. Why this change is made (if a change was indeed intended and not, as some suggest, a mistaken copying of "Gyges" for "Croesus")—why this and other changes are made, I will consider further along. For the moment I am concerned primarily to indicate where each element in Glaucon's account comes from in Herodotus' account.

2) "he was a shepherd toiling in the service of the man who was then ruling Lydia." Similarly, the subject of Herodotus' account was, although not a shepherd, in the service of the man who was then ruling Lydia.

3) "There came to pass a great thunderstorm and an earthquake; the earth cracked and a chasm opened." Comparable to this, in Herodotus' account, is the shocking proposal that Candaules made to Gyges, that which moved Gyges to an outcry, "Master, what a sick word is this you have spoken. . . ." It was, for Herodotus' Gyges, a shattering event. Glaucon respects his source here by having the chasm his "hero" comes upon not one that had been long formed and hidden away or otherwise a tame discovery.

4) "He saw it, wondered at it, and went down." One can be reminded of what Herodotus' Gyges went through upon being faced by Candaulus' insistence and being led by him into the bedchamber. There is an echo here as well of the opening of the *Republic* itself: Glaucon's "went down" is the same word as in Socrates' first words, "I went down to the Piraeus

yesterday . . ." (327A). Thus, Glaucon's "descent" leads, as does Socrates',
to an exploration of what justice means.

5) "He saw, along with other quite wonderful things about which they
tell tales, a hollow bronze horse. It had windows . . ." Is there about all
this a reflection of how the wondrous bedroom of a king and queen
must look to a subject? Even if he had seen it before, it would look (and
feel) quite amazing on this occasion.

6) "there was a corpse inside [the horse] that looked larger than
human size." One suspects in this corpse something derived from the
queen in Herodotus' story, especially since Gyges dreaded the consequences of gazing upon her.

7) "[The corpse] had nothing on except a gold ring on its hand; he
slipped it off and went out." One's suspicion of the derivation of this
corpse from Herodotus' queen is confirmed: the extraordinary body
turns out to be naked but for the ring. And that which it did "wear" is
carried away by the intruder, just as is the modesty that the queen had
treasured. (The sexual implications of a ring are seen again and again in
literature, as, for example, Shakespeare's *The Merchant of Venice*.)

8) "When there was the usual gathering of the shepherds to make the
monthly report to the king about the flocks, he too came, wearing the
ring." This can remind one of the summons to Gyges in Herodotus'
story from the queen, someone upon whom he was accustomed to wait.
He goes to her "wearing the ring," so to speak—that is, unaware that she
knew what had happened.

9) We then have in Glaucon's account his hero's discovery (as he is sitting with the other shepherds) of the powers of the ring he is wearing.
Perhaps this is Glaucon's equivalent of the revelation with which the
queen confronts Gyges in Herodotus' account of *their* meeting: What
follows from such revelation (or discovery)?

10) "Aware of [the power of the ring], he immediately contrived to be
one of the messengers to the king." Perhaps this is Glaucon's equivalent
of the conspiracy (reinforced by threats and inducements) that the
queen enlists Gyges for in Herodotus' account.

11) "When he arrived, he committed adultery with the king's wife." In
Herodotus's account, the infidelity of the wife may be seen (if not really
earlier) in that she leads Gyges into the bed chamber, provides him a
dagger, and hides him behind the door.

12) "along with [the queen], he set upon the king and killed him." Just

as at the beginning, so at the end of Glaucon's account, the parallels to Herodotus' account are most obvious.

13) "And so he took over the rule." This, too, is how Herodotus has it. And just as in Herodotus, nothing is said thereafter in Glaucon's account about the role of the queen, once the usurper takes possession of her along with the throne.

These similarities between the two accounts reveal what Glaucon was "thinking of" as he reworked the material he had derived from Herodotus. His reworking is similar to what the dreamer does when he transforms everyday events to his purposes.

v

Glaucon is referred to by Socrates as "poetic" (or, as we would say, "artistic"). It should be instructive to consider what Glaucon's transformations and omissions, compared to his Herodotean source, reveal about his way of thinking about these matters.

The most obvious change of consequence—that which provides his "hero" a ring of invisibility—is dictated, it would seem, by the overall purpose of the account as an illustration of how men really regard *justice*. I shall say more about this further on, as well as about the related problem of Glaucon's recourse to a corpse as the carrier of this remarkable ring.

But, first, suggestions may be in order about various of the other transformations conjured up by Glaucon as well as about his omissions. (Some transformations I have already commented upon, in suggesting the parallels between the two accounts.) The following changes made by Glaucon are perhaps instructive:

1) Glaucon's "hero," we have noticed, is an ancestor of Gyges, not Gyges himself. How far back this ancestor may be is not suggested. (Herodotus, we have seen, had Candaules' family ruling for some five centuries when Gyges took over.) Perhaps Glaucon preferred an ancestor, rather than Gyges himself, because of what Herodotus had *recorded* as the fate of Gyges' descendants *because* of his usurpation. That is, Glaucon wants his "hero" to face opportunities for "getting away" with his self-seeking. (I will say more about this, too, further on.)

2) Glaucon's "hero," we have also noticed, is a shepherd, not the

bodyguard in Herodotus' story. The two are not unrelated, inasmuch as the bodyguard protects not the sheep but the life of his master. Why, then, not simply leave the man a bodyguard, since he too could have come upon a chasm, etc.? Perhaps there is here, on Glaucon's part, a reference back to the use made by Socrates of shepherds and shepherding (in book 1 of the *Republic*) in his handling of Thrasymachus. Perhaps, that is, Glaucon would remind us of the problem of just whose interest shepherds (or, for that matter, bodyguards) really serve. After all, one can become (as Machiavelli knew) the virtual prisoner of one's bodyguard.

3) Glaucon transforms Candaules' astonishing proposal to Gyges into the storm which opens up the ground before the shepherd. Perhaps he indicates thereby the natural (albeit unusually violent) powers which can confront a man. That is, his "hero" would not have been fully on his own if he had depended upon someone such as Candaules to launch him on his career; rather, nature herself should provide him his impetus. Even so, Glaucon chooses to invest a *ring*—not something found in nature—with the power of invisibility. Does this suggest a limit to his "thesis"? (I will return to this question, after I consider additional changes made by Glaucon in Herodotus' story. I should add here, however, that Plato—as distinguished from Glaucon—may well have had in mind as well, in using this chasm, the other openings in the earth which figure in the *Republic*—in connection with the noble lies [in book 3], with the Cave [in book 7], and with the Myth of Er [in book 10]. See Cicero, *On the Commonwealth*, p. 211 n. In addition, some have considered caves, as in Homer's *Odyssey,* to be sexually significant.)

4) Glaucon's most critical change in the story he appropriated from Herodotus may have been what he did to the character of his "hero." Indeed, one could wonder what it says about Glaucon's character and opinions that he varies the story as he does. In Herodotus, Gyges must choose between his life and that of the king. Whether he chooses correctly *is* a problem. But Glaucon's man is faced by no such hard choices: he simply sees an opportunity and takes advantage of it. Indeed, one could say, Glaucon's man came out of the cave the kind of man he was when he went in: he is curious, opportunistic, even a graverobber. (See, on plundering corpses, *Republic* 469D. It is a nice question, What does belong to a corpse? How should it be dealt with? See, also, the story of Leontius, the son of Aglaion, and his desire to look at corpses. *Republic* 439E–440A.) Should Glaucon have started with someone who would *not*

rob a corpse—after all, not everyone would, even if it could be done un-detected. Thus, we see at the outset what kind of a man this is: he is in a sense invisible because he is alone and unwatched, and thus he suc-cumbs to temptation. Perhaps it is to Glaucon's credit—a tribute to his instincts—that he makes this man such: after all he could have had him get the ring legitimately, and then find out its powers. Thus, Glaucon's hero is impious from the outset, in that he *is* a graverobber. And, it can be said, he may be shameless as well, in that he openly wears the ring he has taken from a corpse: when he can be seen, the ring can be seen also, it would seem.

5) Still another change in the story is Glaucon's use of the bronze horse in which the corpse is found. Does Glaucon thereby mean to re-mind us of the country where this episode is set? And does he suggest that *his* "hero" is comparable to the man who conjured up the Trojan horse, the clever Odysseus himself, another man who was able to make full use of *his* opportunities? Perhaps Socrates is aware of this stratagem on Glaucon's part, for he makes a point of showing (in book 10 of the *Republic*, when the Myth of Er is set forth) that Odysseus preferred in his next incarnation (on the basis of what he had learned in the life de-scribed by Homer) a private life, not one of conquering and ruling? That is, Socrates can be understood to have rehabilitated Odysseus (and, by implication, Homer?) in the tenth book of the *Republic*. He implies, thereby, that one acts as Glaucon's "hero" does only if one does not know what one is doing—only if one does not recognize what is implied by the choices one is making.

I have spoken thus far of the changes Glaucon made in Herodotus' account by way of transformation. I add now two changes made by way of omission. For this purpose we must notice the immediate aftermath, in Herodotus' account, of Gyges' usurpation. The passage quoted earlier, which concluded with the killing of Candaules, continues (1.13):

> [Gyges] had, indeed, the kingship, and it was strengthened by an oracle from Delphi. For when the Lydians made a great to-do about what had happened to Candaules and were in arms about it, the conspirators who were with Gyges came to an agreement with the rest of the Lydians that if the oracle should proclaim him king of Lydia, he should indeed be king; if it should not, he should hand back the power to the Heraclids. The oracle gave its answer, and so Gyges gained his kingship. But this much the Pythia said: that the Heraclids should yet have vengeance on a

descendant of Gyges in the fifth generation. But of this word neither the Lydians nor their kings made any account until it was fulfilled.

6) The first major omission by Glaucon, we are reminded by Herodotus' account, has to do with the response of the people to a usurpation. Does it matter to a new ruler what the people's response is? Can one be fully a ruler if one does not manifest oneself? That is, is the desire to rule (and to enjoy oneself as a ruler) somewhat in conflict with the ability to remain invisible? (We do encounter, in Herodotus (1.99), a man who rules and yet remains invisible. But he would have needed to have been highly visible to establish a reputation which then would permit him to seclude himself entirely. Besides, that man had not wanted to rule—and so desired a different relation with his people from that of the typical ruler.) Of course, rulers always remain somewhat hidden from view—it is not indicated in Herodotus' account that the people learned immediately just what had happened (after all, neither Candaules nor Gyges comes off well in the story)—rulers always remain somewhat hidden from view, but they usually have less control over their appearances (and disappearances) than Glaucon's "hero" has. We are familiar with the complaint, by public men, that they have no life of their own, so demanding and consuming is public life. Glaucon avoids these problems by putting his man on the throne—and saying no more about *that.*

7) The second major omission by Glaucon, we are reminded by Herodotus' account, has to do with the response of the divine to improper usurpations. Glaucon, it will be recalled, did allude to the divine, when he observed that his "hero" would be able (with his ring of invisibility) to do various things "as an equal to a god among humans." But in this he draws upon the power, not the justice, of the divine, as that power is commonly understood. We have already noticed that the shift by Glaucon from Gyges himself to an ancestor of Gyges avoids, for him, the problem of the recorded consequences (long-term though they were) of the usurpation. That is, Herodotus has retribution visited upon Gyges, through his descendants, five generations later.

Does the divine figure in Glaucon's account in any way? What should we understand to be the source of the power of invisibility? Is it magical? If so, the divine may be suggested. If not magical, but rather natural, then it is not as special (nor is one so invulnerable) as Glaucon suggests.

What does Glaucon believe about the influences of the divine in human affairs? Does he consider the workings of the divine as pictured by Herodotus to be too remote to worry about? Thus, Herodotus reports that Candaules' family had taken the kingdom in accordance with an oracle—but that had been five centuries earlier (1.7.13). Herodotus had introduced the story of Gyges because of what happened to his descendant, Croesus: Herodotus indicates that one's misconduct somehow catches up with one, whereas Glaucon suggests that one's personal vulnerability is all that matters. That is, Glaucon may suggest either that there is no eventual retribution somehow mandated by the gods (say, five generations later) or that no sensible man would care what happens that long after he has enjoyed (however unjustly) the things of this world. (We do have the testimony of Shakespeare's Macbeth that what happens to one's descendants can very much matter to a king.)

Glaucon's view of things excludes a concern for divine retribution—that retribution which is indicated in the way Delphi, on the occasion of Croesus' fall, is said to have characterized Gyges' conduct five generations earlier (according to Herodotus, 1.91):

> Fate that is decreed, no one can escape, not even a god. Croesus has paid for the offense of his ancestor in the fifth generation, who, being a bodyguard of the Heraclidae, following the lead of a treacherous woman, slew his master and took his honor, which in no way befit himself.

Nothing is indicated here—perhaps because Delphi was concerned primarily to justify what had happened to Croesus—about the shortcomings of the master who was slain, that is, Candaules. (I will return soon to the problem of Candaules.) In any event, one can see in the career of Candaules the limits of friendship—the limits of that sharing by which friendship can be characterized.

Glaucon makes the argument for undetected injustice, for the intrinsic preference men have for injustice. (He is prudent enough to insist that he himself does not endorse this argument, but he wants Socrates to face up to it and, if possible, refute it. What Glaucon truly believes here is a nice question.) He speaks of what is natural to men, of their preference for injustice if they can get away with it.

But does not Glaucon, by failing to provide for divine responses to injustice, neglect something else that is natural to men—that is, to most men most of the time—a concern for what, if anything, is to become of them after death? After all, there are—there have always been—stories that suggest that one's misconduct *here* can have serious consequences *there* (however vague "there" might sometimes be). Even more critical—but easily neglected by "practical" men—is what kind of human being one is to be.

It was left to Glaucon's brother, Adeimantus, to round off Glaucon's argument—and thereby to put fully to Socrates the question of whether justice is good in itself—by positing (for the sake of discussion) that the gods can be placated by the unjust man who takes precautions. It is left to still another brother of Glaucon—that is, Plato himself, of course—to suggest the proper assessment of the use that Glaucon makes of the even-then ancient story about Gyges.

vii

The assessment Plato makes is, I suggest, that which the thoughtful reader would arrive at upon considering the available evidence. That evidence, I have argued, includes what emerges when one compares Glaucon's account to the account of Gyges by Herodotus. (A comparison should include a careful study in each case of the language itself, something I do not undertake here. See Benardete, *Herodotean Inquiries,* p. 15 n. 10a.) The more I compare the two accounts, the more likely it seems to me that Plato intended his readers to recall Herodotus' account and to reflect on the uses made of it by Glaucon. I have already suggested various things that can occur to one who does compare the two versions.

But something more should be said about Glaucon's account, just as it stands in the dialogue itself (that is, without regard to Herodotus). What do Socrates and, by implication, Plato say about Glaucon's account? What should the thoughtful reader notice about it? How should he assess it? The things to be noticed include features in Glaucon's story that Glaucon himself may not have noticed—points and adjustments that he "had" to use in order to make his argument plausible, thereby indicating (if only by implication) certain problems with the argument or with the account upon which it depends.

One feature of Glaucon's story does *not* depend upon a knowledge of Herodotus to appreciate, and that is the significance of the fact that an ancestor of Gyges had been a shepherd and then had become ruler of Lydia. It was generally known, evidently aside from Herodotus, that Gyges himself had taken over rule of Lydia. It would seem, therefore, that there had been (according to Glaucon) dramatic downs as well as ups in the fortunes of the family from which Gyges came. In Herodotus, the account of Candaules, Gyges, and Croesus is immediately preceded by the observation, "For of [the cities of mankind] that were great in earlier times most have now become small, and those that were great in my time were small in the time before" (1.5).

Does such variability in the fortunes of cities, as of families, suggest that the advantages to be gained by injustice are illusory? Are the advantages of justice, on the other hand, less dependent upon chance? This would be so if justice should indeed be something good in itself. Perhaps we should settle for the observation, at least for the moment, that it is often difficult to predict just what the *consequences* will be, in one's worldly fortunes, as a result of what one does, whether what one does is just or unjust. (Compare *Job* with Shakespeare's *Pericles*.)

What can be said about the key element in Glaucon's account, the power of invisibility? Invisibility also figures in Herodotus' account in two ways: the queen very much wants to keep her beauty invisible to all but her husband; Gyges was instructed to keep himself invisible to the queen when he slipped out of the bedchamber. We see in both cases (in the Herodotus account) limits to an individual's ability to remain invisible—and perhaps limits also to the uses of invisibility. A half-dozen points can be made about the invisibility Glaucon conjures up:

1) Love, in the final analysis, requires visibility, not invisibility. Even seduction requires some visibility, if it is to be distinguished from rape. One has to be known, at least somewhat, if one is to *be* loved. Or, as Friedrich Nietzsche has someone say, "One may not deceive where one wants to possess" (*Beyond Good and Evil*, sec. 194). Is there not something about the love relation which makes perfect invisibility impossible? Does not the erotic incline toward exposure, toward revelation of oneself before the beloved? (Consider, for example, the story of Samson and the Delilah from whom he does not want to conceal anything.) Those who love, and want to be loved, do not want to be mistaken for someone else. By and large, the disappointed lover is someone who believes that he is not seen by the beloved as he would like to be seen. (The

story of Cyrano de Bergerac poses special problems here.) Similarly, one who wants to *enjoy* being a ruler must show himself to his people. Thus, neither the lover nor the typical ruler can remain invisible all the time. (Glaucon does not make clear just how the power of invisibility helped with the shepherd's seduction of the queen.) But when the lover shows himself, he becomes vulnerable: that is, he no longer has the immunity that Glaucon prizes. Does not Glaucon's account suggest, whether or not he himself is aware of it, that there was a reason why Herodotus' Gyges was detected by the queen as he slipped out of the room? I will say more about this later. It suffices to notice here, about the Herodotus account, that Gyges prevailed with the queen because he was *not* invisible. My first point about invisibility is, then, that the erotic, including the erotic in the form of the political, undermines invisibility. (Is not Glaucon himself an erotic man? See, on philosophy and concealment, Nietzsche, *Beyond Good and Evil*, sec. 289. Consider, also, what Nietzsche says about the exoteric-esoteric distinction.)

2) Another limit to invisibility can now be noticed: it does not help one in the dark! For half of each day (disregarding the effects of artificial illumination) the invisible man has the same standing as the visible man. Whatever may be his powers, it is as a lover that he is particularly vulnerable: he can be grasped by his beloved (though it be pitch dark). But this is only one of the circumstances in which he can be detected and apprehended. Generally, it can be said, the invisible man can be located just as have been the planet Pluto and such other invisible things as black holes—that is, by their effects elsewhere. (Indeed, one might even wonder, how can we come to know of Glaucon's "hero"?)

3) This leads to my next point: how did that corpse come to be in the horse, and naked at that? Had he been taken in a lover's embrace? His lack of clothing is consistent with that possibility. (Should we assume that the ring makes one's clothing invisible also?) Had he been put into the horse, but perhaps by those who were not aware of the power of the ring? Or did they know all too well its power and had come to recognize that it was a delusion? Perhaps, indeed, the ring is like the Trojan Horse (which Glaucon's bronze horse *can* remind one of): it is a problem for those who come upon such a thing, to decide whether it is a dangerous deception or a rare prize.

4) But however the body got into the horse, one critical fact about

this situation reminds us of the limits of the power of invisibility—and that is that this *is* a corpse. Whatever the ring may do for the wearer, it cannot fend off his death indefinitely. (Glaucon's brother, Adeimantus, we recall, never forgot the implications of this.) In fact, invisibility is, for human beings, a sort of death. *Hades*, I have heard, means invisibility. (Perhaps the ring has no power over a corpse: death may be invisibility enough?) Death threatens us with disappearance. Suppose the man was put into the horse alive (and perhaps even invisible). We can imagine why he might have chosen to die visible. For most men death surely would be invisibility enough, as can be seen by how death is usually associated with darkness. *It* is enough of a disappearance. If one is re-membered as other than one really was, is not that, too, a kind of disap-pearance? However attractive the power of Glaucon's ring, few would want to be invisible permanently: it would be as if one were dead or oth-erwise non-existent in certain critical respects. Related to this reminder of the limits of the power of invisibility is what Glaucon says of one who possessed the ring: he would be able to loose others from bonds. But, alas, the man in the horse could not loose himself: one's power of invis-ibility is not likely to help one secure one's release from the horse if those who put one in there know that one is (or can be) invisible. Thus, one who possesses (or is possessed by) this ring might have an illusion of omnipotence: but nature (if only in the form of mortality) sets limits to that power. Is justice (or, at least, the bad effects of injustice) still another limit to that power?

5) We move now from the physical invisibility of which Glaucon spoke to that systematic deception of others which the ring can be taken to represent. This deception is, of course, with respect to justice, the em-inently social virtue. Deception is far less of a problem with the other cardinal virtues. It can fairly easily be made evident to most people that one hurts oneself when one has merely the appearance of courage, tem-perance, or wisdom. The man who conceals his intemperance—whose intemperate activities are invisible—still suffers the principal disadvan-tage of this vice, the suffering that intemperance brings upon oneself. (Invisibility may help him satisfy some of his desires, but this bears on the question of justice, not of temperance.) Similar things can be said about cowardice. Consider, for example, the memoirs of a nineteenth-century adventurer who recalls a perilous episode in the Mexican War:

"If cowards suffer as much from their fears as I did those long two hours, I pity and sympathize with them" (Samuel E. Chamberlain, *My Confession*, p. 181). But, it is all too evident, there *does* seem to be some advantage if one can escape detection for one's injustice. Invisibility means, among other things, that one can ignore public opinion and hence can disregard to some extent the social character of justice.

Is not the best, even though not a foolproof, way to escape injury for one's actions—for, as we have seen, even invisibility has its limits—is not the best way always to act and speak justly? This reminds of the advice Aristotle gives to the tyrant on how to consolidate his rule: always conduct yourself like a just ruler (*Politics* 1314b38). (Or, as it has been noticed, truth-telling is much easier than lying: it requires a very good memory to lie much and well.) Be all this as it may, one's ability to conceal one's injustice for a very long time, even with the help of a ring of invisibility, comes up against the everyday facts of human experience, as related, say, in a discussion recorded about the English law by Fortescue several hundred years ago (*De Laudibus Legum Anglie*, p. 67):

> But witnesses cannot work such evil [as they can under the civil law] when they make their deposition in the presence of twelve trustworthy men of the neighbourhood in which the fact in question occurred, knowing the circumstances and also the habits of the witnesses, especially if they are neighbors and cannot but know if they are worthy of credence. For whatever is done by or among their neighbours cannot be entirely hid from all those twelve jurors. . . . Nor do I think it possible for what is done, near his home, even with some secrecy, to escape the notice of an honest man.

Or, as Marcus Aurelius put it, the good man is all of a piece—and clearly appears so to others with eyes to see. (*Meditations*, 11.15. Compare 11.13.) Critical to all this, however, is not how one appears to others—this is, to many, at the root of the appeal of any ring of invisibility—but, rather, what kind of a human being one is. Thus Sappho observed, "He that is fair is fair to outward show; he that is good will soon be fair also." (*Lyra Graeca*, 1:225. See another translation of these lines in section ix of chapter 2 of this book. See, also, Alcibiades on Socrates in Plato's *Symposium*.) However much one is shrouded from others, one still has to live with the kind of human being one is.

6) Do not people generally recognize this, when they stop to think about it, that the advantages offered by Glaucon's ring of invisibility are illusory? After all, do not people encounter situations everyday in which they are, for most practical purposes, concealed from view—and yet they, by and large, act as they should? It is news, for instance, when parents mistreat children. It is not news, on the other hand, when people give to charities or pay off debts in circumstances where they do not really "have" to.

Invisibility is not as rare as Glaucon suggests, nor as likely to be exploited as he believes it would be. Consider, for example, the considerable invisibility (or, as we call it, anonymity) provided in large cities today. Yet many people do act contrary to their interest, "as interest is vulgarly understood" (to use Adam Smith's language, *The Wealth of Nations*, p. 718). Furthermore, we are dubious about those who seem to "get away with it": something is all too often obviously wrong with such people. The most serious thing wrong with them is that they do not see themselves for what they are. Is there not something shortsighted, and even ugly, about their self-centeredness? Such people are warnings to us all. Is not that what the tyrant looks like, the man who can take whatever he "wants" without concern for public opinion or the law? Do not such people tend to develop either very narrow or quite perverse interests? (Is not Candaules somewhat of a tyrant in his desires—a friendly kind of tyrant, to be sure—with the consequences we have seen? I will return to him shortly.) What about the other "quite wonderful things" in Glaucon's cavern that Gyges' ancestor could well have concerned himself with?

The problem may not be, therefore, whether anyone can be trusted with a ring of invisibility, but rather whether we could be sure who might have it. For all we know, there may be many such rings about: if there can be one, there is no reason why there should not be others. Would only those able to restrain themselves be able to keep secret, and enjoy for long, the possession of such a ring?

7) My final point about the power of invisibility has to do with how one should speak to those who have powers of invisibility, partial though they be. Is not that what ethical training, and exhortation, is about—an effort to guide human beings to do, and to want to do, what they should? Any effort to shape the desires, to make them what they

should be, is in effect to induce people to use properly a considerable power that is hidden from direct view. That is to say, Glaucon did not appreciate what is around us all the time. Of course, what is also around us is how the power of invisibility *is* abused all too often. It is seen, for example, in the ability one has to talk nonsense without being held to account for it: one can conceal one's intellectual atrocities behind one's reputation or one's rhetorical skills, gratifying one's passions by knowing how to play upon the passions and the ignorance of others. Thus, one can be silly or sloppy or just plain prejudiced without having to pay a penalty. But, here too, we recognize that one is not really "getting away with it," even if one is acclaimed and richly rewarded for one's sophistries. That is, one is condemned, if successful, to remain the kind of human being one is.

Precisely what helps one "get away with it"—what the ring of invisibility (at least as Glaucon sees it) consists of—may be noticed by considering two features of the ring. It is made of gold: we all know how wealth can be used to do (or to protect the doing of) injustice. The ring has its effect when its collet is turned inward (that is emphasized by Glaucon, perhaps without recognizing fully the significance of what he is reporting): one is invisible when one's thoughts are turned inwards, when (that is) one's thoughts are concealed. It is this concealment, by the way, which helps give rhetoric a bad name—when, in fact, it is that art which permits a sensible accommodation between wisdom and the general opinion. Something of what responsible rhetoric appeals to may be seen in Glaucon's desire to make it clear that he recognizes that his hero is doing the wrong thing, that there is indeed something questionable about his conduct, and that his listeners can be depended upon to recognize that also. Does not even this say something about the naturalness of justice? A proper inquiry into that question would oblige us to consider at length the reply Socrates makes to Glaucon's challenge. That the challenge *is* a formidable one—that there *is* a problem about justice that there may not be with courage, temperance or wisdom—is suggested by the fact that so lengthy a reply by Socrates (as is seen in the *Republic*) is required to deal properly with Glaucon. But, perhaps, the underlying problem is not with justice but with the passions and ambitions of those who would issue the challenge Glaucon does.

vii

I have suggested some implications of the changes Glaucon makes in the story he takes from Herodotus. I have also examined his use of the power of invisibility and its bearing upon the status of justice. I should now like to consider, however briefly, what Glaucon's account and Plato's understanding of that account indicates about Herodotus' original story about Gyges. One may be equipped by one's study of the *Republic* to reconsider—or perhaps to see properly—what is said by Herodotus about Gyges' conduct, especially since one critical question, not only in the *Republic* but in various other Platonic dialogues as well, is the question of whether it is better to do or to suffer injustice. Also critical to Herodotus' Gyges, upon which Plato can throw useful light, are questions about the nature of pleasure and about the risks of learning and knowing.

Is there not something in Herodotus' account of Gyges which unwary readers might neglect and to which Glaucon's adaptation might call our attention? Glaucon would have us be "realistic" (to use modern terminology) about what Herodotus' Gyges was moved by. And, to be even more modern about it, we should give full weight to what "really moves" men—and for this a passage from Sigmund Freud about suicide may be useful (*Basic Writings*, pp. 124–25):

> Whoever believes in the occurrence of semi-intentional self-inflicted injury—if this awkward expression be permitted—will become prepared to accept through it the fact that aside from conscious intentional suicide, there also exists semi-intentional annihilation—with unconscious intention—which is capable of aptly utilizing a threat against life and masking it as a casual mishap. Such mechanisms are by no means rare. For the tendency to self-destruction exists to a certain degree in many more persons than in those who bring it to completion. Self-inflicted injuries are, as a rule, a compromise between this impulse and the forces working against it, and even when it really comes to suicide, the inclination has existed for a long time with less strength or as an unconscious and repressed tendency.
>
> Even suicide consciously committed chooses its time, means and opportunity; it is quite natural that unconscious suicide should wait for a

motive to take upon itself one part of the causation and thus free it from its oppression by taking up the defensive forces of the person.

These comments about what Freud calls "semi-intentional annihilation" can perhaps help us understand Candaules' motivations in insisting that Gyges spy on his wife, the queen. And what Freud then says here about the intrinsic difficulties that women have in resisting fully a threatened sexual attack should help us understand what Herodotus' Gyges is again and again "compelled" to do. Freud argues (ibid., p. 125 n. 1) that when there is a sexual attack on a woman it often happens that

> the attack of the man cannot be warded off through the full muscular strength of the woman because a portion of the unconscious feelings of the one attacked meets it with ready acceptance. To be sure, it is said that such a situation paralyzes the strength of a woman; we need only add the reasons for this paralysis. Insofar, the clever sentence of Sancho Panza, which he pronounced as governor of his island, is psychologically unjust (*Don Quixote,* vol. ii, chap. xiv). A woman haled before the judge a man who was supposed to have robbed her of her honor by force of violence. Sancho indemnified her with a full purse which he took from the accused, but after the departure of the woman, he gave the accused permission to follow her and snatch the purse from her. Both returned wrestling, the woman priding herself that the villain was unable to possess himself of the purse. Thereupon Sancho spoke: "Had you shown yourself so stout and valiant to defend your body (nay, but half so much) as you have done to defend your purse, the strength of Hercules could not have forced you."

Similarly, Freud (and perhaps Glaucon) would have us ask whether Herodotus' Gyges had indeed been altogether forced to do the things he did. In particular, did he give in too easily to his master, who wanted him to look at his naked mistress? Was he not quite careful enough in managing his departure from the bedchamber? And did he give in too easily to the queen who wanted him to kill the king and take over her and the throne? All this is not to deny that Herodotus' Gyges was much more on the defensive than Glaucon's shepherd. Also, it is not to deny that Gyges is *not* an enterprising man. Thus, Herodotus reports of him, "When Gyges became king, he, like others, invaded the country of Miletus and Smyrna, and he captured the city of Colophon. However, no other great deed was done by him, although he reigned thirty-eight years . . ." (Herodotus adds, "and so we will pass him by with just such mention as we have made" [1.15].) Consider in turn each of the three questions I have just put, which bear upon what Gyges "really wanted":

1) Should Gyges have agreed to spy on the woman? Herodotus does not say that Gyges' life was threatened by Candaules. Should he have resisted until faced by at least as serious a threat as that later voiced by the queen? And did he make the wrong arguments in trying to dissuade Candaules, relying too much on the authority of the ancients and on the law, perhaps not enough on nature and on the likely consequences of Candaules' experiments? Should he have said something about the evil that he was dreading? Instead, he allows himself to be goaded by challenges to his courage, which may have been particularly effective with a bodyguard. Besides, how safe would Gyges have been with Candaules, if he had succeeded in escaping the bedroom undetected? That is, what further experiments—what new thrills—would the king have sought? Should not Gyges have thought of such matters—he did have time to reconsider and resist—before he went through with what Candaules demanded? Why did he run the great risk he ran, if not because he was not unmoved by a desire to see the woman?

2) Why was not Gyges more careful in slipping out of the bedchamber? Did he "want" to be detected by the queen? Or had he been so intrigued by her beauty that after having seen her from one angle, he wanted to see her from another (that is, as she moved away from him)? (Perhaps also he was inhibited, if not paralyzed, somewhat by what he had seen.) On the other hand, had the queen previously distrusted the king? Was she particularly alert this night, perhaps because of something about Candaules' attitude? Is such a man as this king bound to give himself away (just as he had given his queen away)?

3) Although Gyges was forced by the queen to agree to kill the king, should he have made an "outcry" (as he had done earlier, in his argument with Candaules) in order to alert the king? After all, the saving of one's life is not everything, especially if one is the king's confidant and bodyguard. The king is not now threatening Gyges, if he ever did. What if the king had offended the queen without Gyges' help. Would Gyges then have been entitled to help her kill the king in order to save his own life? Ordinarily, we would not think so. Why should it be different here?

Unseemly as the king's experiment had been, what Candaules and Gyges did was not a capital offense—at least, we would not ordinarily think so.

Such are the kinds of considerations to be taken into account in determining what Gyges should have done in response to the queen's proposition and threat. On the other hand, what *would* have happened if Gyges had lied to her, to save his own life, and then betrayed her to Candaules? What would Candaules have done? What would relations have been among the *three* of them thereafter? Should Gyges have even gone so far, if necessary, as to kill her as she led him in to kill the king? And how would Candaules have been expected to understand *that*, especially since he "loved" her so? Is the least risk, after all, simply to kill this perverse king? This kind of consideration suggests that it *is* difficult to sort out the rights and wrongs in Herodotus' account—a difficulty which is reflected in the mixed verdict handed down by the oracle of Delphi (which did allow Gyges to retain the throne, but to lose it in the fifth generation). Such considerations also suggest the tyrannical inclinations of this ruler. Candaules wants special pleasures, pleasures usually denied to most men. Or is it that he wants to be a full friend to Gyges? Indeed, does he harbor an erotic passion toward Gyges himself, which he serves by sharing his wife with him in this way? Or is it that he is uncertain about his own assessment of his wife's beauty? Does he need, in his lack of confidence, independent verification of her beauty? (This is like the men who seek honor to be assured of their virtue. See Aristotle, *Nicomachean Ethics* 1.1095b26.) Or is he like Gyges' descendant, Croesus, eager to show off his wealth to impress others—and thereby to increase his pleasure in his possessions (1.30)? Does one have such possessions fully only when others know just how much one does have? (Is this particularly a problem for an illicit lover?)

It can be argued that Candaules courted ruin by not sharing even more with Gyges, once he did begin to share with him, the beauty of the queen. But, we are told, he did love his wife—and this impaired his judgment. Perhaps this is why he wanted to retain something of her beauty for himself alone. That is, the most beautiful thing about her— that which could be observed after she went to bed with the no doubt aroused king—Gyges was *not* to be there to observe. This meant, among other things, that Gyges was not instructed to remain in the bedroom until the two of them had fallen asleep, at which time he could have easily gotten out undetected. The same considerations apply, of course, to the second fateful night—but with this difference, the queen (it seems) was willing to risk having Gyges see everything including herself undress once again, in order that he would be there after the king had fallen asleep. She knew how persuasive the king could be with Gyges—and so she did not risk an attack while the king was awake. The extent she was willing to go, it can be speculated, confirms what it means when a woman such as this "lays aside the respect that is hers."

To pursue such speculations as these is to assume a remarkable degree of subtlety on Herodotus' part. However this may be, there is no doubt that this woman is special: Candaules did not recognize how beautiful (that is, talented) his queen was. He recognized, of course, that she would not like what he proposed, if she learned of it; but he did not fully appreciate, it seems, that he controlled her (as much as anyone did) because he had seen (and could see) her without disguise. But, when provoked, she shows us that she is capable of still another disguise, a deadly invisibility: she conceals her reaction to the discovery of Gyges' presence; she conceals the plot she "forces" upon Gyges; and she conceals the execution of the plot.

One wonders whether the queen had come to prefer Gyges to Candaules even before this episode. She *had* talked with him before, and this despite the usual seclusion of women in the oriental household. (Glaucon, it will be remembered, had his shepherd seduce the queen *before* he killed the king. Does *he* suspect an earlier seduction by Herodotus' Gyges?) Be that as it may, she does give Gyges, not Candaules, the choice, perhaps because Candaules, as husband, had proved wanting. So, she will try a royal marriage now with Gyges—and will expect this experience to make *him* behave himself. (Do Gyges' thirty-eight years of uneventful rule suggest that he was somehow permanently traumatized by these two fateful nights in the bedroom of Candaules and his queen?) Still another reason for preferring to deal first with Gyges may be that she could fulfill herself more through him: that is, she was able to use herself completely by developing and executing a plot of this magnitude.

We are not given direct quotations from the arguments Gyges made in trying to dissuade the queen from her plans. Does this indicate that these arguments must have been much the same as those Gyges had used in trying to dissuade the king the day before? And does the queen feel about *her* desire (that is, revenge) as the king had about his desire (to share her beauty)? Certainly, she does not intend to be treated as an object, even if it should be as an object of art.

Of course, one can argue, she could simply have had both Gyges and Candaules killed. But, then, who would inherit the throne? (Is she still without children by Candaules? Perhaps he had not wanted to mar her beauty by pregnancies. Evidently Gyges did have children by her. But, then, did he ever consider her as beautiful as Candaules did?) Besides, there *is* a problem in her attempting to kill Candaules. The queen's retinue *could* be used by her against Gyges, it seems. But could it be relied upon against the king himself? Gyges, however, is trusted by the king and controls (as bodyguard) access to him. The queen, in dealing with Gyges, uses among her people those she knew to be the most faithful to her. Thereafter she uses Gyges effectively in dispatching the king. In short, she is a better judge of people than Candaules was.

Perhaps she was not as good a judge of herself, however. That is, did she overreact? She, too, had time to think things over before acting. What *should* she have done? She could have said nothing—and there is often much to be said for that. But would Candaules have been tempted to try something even more bizarre? Was he really out to degrade her, and all in the name of love? Should she have waited to see what more came of all this before taking final action? Among other things, her fierce action led to a revolution in a regime that had endured five centuries—only to be replaced by a regime that could endure only five generations. Although she is shown to be a woman of remarkable restraint and of considerable astuteness, if not nobility, she is not perhaps as just as she should have been. Does this mean that she was not really as astute and as restrained as she seems? We hear nothing further about her once Gyges takes over—except for Delphi's condemnation, five generations later, of "a treacherous woman."

Does Herodotus say there is a system of cause and effect in the moral universe? And does he say quietly about Gyges, and about what really moves him, some of the things that Glaucon says more openly? Is Herodotus more responsible than Glaucon (as distinguished from Plato) in what he says? Whatever reservations Plato has about Glaucon, his brother, can hardly be explicit. But it is evident that Glaucon's account violates the morality-minded rules that are later laid down by

Socrates. Socrates says of himself that he is *not* poetic (*Republic* 393D). See, also, Klein, "Socrates and Aristophanes." Compare Plato, *Phaedo* 60C sq. The poetic does get carried away—and is likely to be interesting. Glaucon's story *is* memorable.

Glaucon's account, I have suggested, *is* useful, in that it presses us to notice what is just beneath the surface of Herodotus' account. Of course, Herodotus did not count on a Glaucon: he himself shows us what his account is about. For one thing, we can be led to wonder whether Gyges was too easily persuaded both by the king and by the queen, especially when we notice that Gyges' illustrious descendant, Croesus, was too easily persuaded to undertake the invasion which cost him his throne. Was Croesus, like Gyges before him, all too willing to take what he really wanted, especially if he could be assured he could get away with it? Such men, Herodotus seems to argue, are not as astute as they seem. Socrates would agree. (Additional Platonic reworkings of Herodotean accounts may be found in the *Timaeus* and the *Critias*. Those dialogues are considered in my chapter on Plato.)

viii

I should not conclude this discussion without adding, in defense of Glaucon, that Socrates *is* aware of the suppressed passions and desires of men that make them want all manner of things they should not have— passions and desires that are most evident in our dreams. This awareness may be seen again and again in the *Republic*. (See, e.g., 391E, 554A–B, 571C–D sq. [on dreams]; 572B, 573, 578E sq., 580B–C, 582C sq., 587A, 587E, 588, 590D sq., 592A–B, 603E sq., 608C sq., 612B sq.) The Myth of Er, in book 10 of the *Republic,* includes a description of the man raised in a good city, who does behave himself, but whose desires are not truly just. This tends to support what Glaucon argues. Moreover, if Glaucon did not have a hold of something, *we* would not be able to imagine how one could one use the power of invisibility to serve one's desires. (After all, many know how liberated they can feel about parking an automobile with out-of-state license plates illegally, so long as it is not in a towaway zone. Few would deny that the penal law is critical to the promotion of justice in a community, designed primarily for those who have to be *watched* and curbed.) But what Glaucon does not seem to appreciate is something else that the Myth of Er indicates, and that is that people do not always truly want what they desire.

Nor should I conclude without adding, in defense of Candaules, that Socrates does argue (in the *Republic*) that friends share everything with each other. It *is* in that dialogue, it will be recalled, that a community of wives and children is advocated. But in these matters, the law is critical —and Candaules went outside the law (or long-established custom) in what he did—perhaps even, we suspect, because that added to his pleasure. Also, men and women exercising together in the nude, as is prescribed in the *Republic,* might seem to support what Candaules did— but it is not, in Candaules' case, a nudity that he wants to subject himself to as well, so far as we are told. Glaucon says nothing about female nudity in *his* account—perhaps reflecting thereby his awareness of Socrates' opinions on that subject. He eliminates thereby almost altogether the role of the queen in his shepherd's adventures. Does he consider her not an equal of the man? In this, too, he seems to depart from the Socrates who, in the *Republic,* advocates a certain equality of treatment for women.

One of the deeper considerations suggested by Herodotus, which I no more than touch upon here, has to do with how much, and in what ways, one should look beyond one's own. Risks are run thereby with respect to established communities, including the customs and teachings upon which communities depend. Certainly, power is not enough to secure one's happiness: one has to learn precisely what one's power is and how best to use it. (Consider, for example, the story of Dr. Jekyll and Mr. Hyde, another account about the danger for oneself of the power of invisibility.) How best to use one's power depends, in large part, upon an understanding of what truly moves things in the moral universe. The cases one confronts are often not clear: the ultimate blame for misdeeds is often hard to place (as may be seen not only in the account of Gyges, Candaules and their queen, but also in the account, as Herodotus presents it, of the series of grievances accumulated over centuries by the Greeks and the barbarians against each other). But to recognize the difficulty of assessing blame is not to deny that "faultlines" do exist— and this affects how reliable one's power is. Thus, descendants who inherit good things from their forebears must take the bad things also: it is like inheriting a productive farm which has on it here and there patches of quicksand. A mixed heritage all too often comes down through the generations, which makes it difficult for any particular generation to determine what is truly happening. It is no wonder, then, that Glaucon's shepherd could be led astray when he found himself possessed of what seemed a wondrous power. (One is reminded of Midas of the golden touch—with whom, by the way, the corpse in the horse is identified by one ancient author. See, on Dr. Jekyll and Mr. Hyde, Anastaplo, *The Artist as Thinker*, p. 215.)

Herodotus teaches us that, for human beings as for nations, one's conduct (including the opinions that one has and acts upon) can have long-term consequences. Does he depend upon the oracles of the gods to identify the connections generations later between, say, the misconduct of Gyges and the fall of Croesus? Or do such oracles merely dramatize what is intrinsic to the nature of things about the moral consequences of our conduct? Certainly, one can see in the Gyges story the intimate relation of the "personal" to the "public" (or political). No name, we have noticed, is given to the queen, not even in Herodotus' story, where the name of the king is given. Earlier stories, it seems, might have given her the name of Tudo (or perhaps Nysia). Is she nameless here because she is not to be understood as *public figure* but rather as *woman,* as the female element, which tends to be much more personal and private than the male element, but which the political order can disregard or abuse only at its peril?

Socrates seems to place less emphasis than does Herodotus (even in so political a work as the *Republic*) on the public consequences, more on the personal consequences, of one's character and conduct. It is what one does to oneself that matters most, Socrates seems to say, especially since public developments can depend too much upon chance for anyone to be able to understand and control. (This means, among other things, that the best political order is virtually impossible to attain and that a political career is to be shunned whenever possible.) Such is the argument that Socrates makes for the sake of his most talented companion, Glaucon, in the *Republic.* It is an argument later developed by Aristotle in this form (as recapitulated by Diogenes Laertius, 1.477): although it is true that virtue is not sufficient in itself to secure happiness, vice "is sufficient in itself to secure misery, even if it be ever so abundantly furnished with corporeal and external goods." Is not this an argument that the Glaucons and Gygeses of the world need to hear—and to have reinforced by dramatic illustrations? (See chapter 3, part 1, section v, beginning.)

ix

One's tentative explorations of the deepest levels of books such as Herodotus' *History* and Plato's *Republic* depend upon, among other things, a thorough study of what lies on the surface. I have suggested beginnings for the mapping of the surfaces of these two books. It is vital to see each work ultimately in its own terms if one is to learn from them and from their relation to one another.

Herodotus and Plato may well have drawn on the same source, or on the same event in Lydian history. In fact, Plato's account may have been closer than Herodotus' to the original Lydian legend about Gyges. Even so, I have argued, Plato probably expected his readers to know Herodotus' even-by-then classic account. If so, he would also expect his readers to see and judge Glaucon's account in the light provided by the earlier account. (See, also, Herodotus, *History* 7.12–18, 45–53.)

Some scholars suggest (we have noticed) that the text of the *Republic* has been distorted in transmission and that the account given by Glaucon should be, like the account given by Herodotus, about Gyges himself, not about an ancestor of Gyges (as our text now has it). Socrates does refer later to "Gyges' ring" (612B). (See, on the Lydian modes, 398D sq.) But if it *is* a distortion, it can be considered providential—so much so that one could well attribute it to the divinely-inspired Plato himself. That is, one is intrigued to notice how things *are* left by the way the texts read now. Glaucon's account is itself a descendant of Herodotus' account; it clearly follows, perhaps even depends upon, Herodotus' account for its full effect. But, at the same time, Glaucon's "hero" is an ancestor of Herodotus' "hero."

Thus, Glaucon's (or, if one prefers, Plato's) account is both before and after Herodotus' account. Such paradoxes should encourage us to devote an imaginative attention to details whenever we delve into the great mysteries which open up before the reader of books of this stature.

IX. Thucydides. On the *Peloponnesian War*

> *In the situation of this Assembly [the Constitutional Convention of 1787], groping as it were in the dark to find political truth, and scarce able to distinguish it when presented to us, how has it happened, Sir, that we have not hitherto once thought of humbly applying to the Father of lights to illuminate our understandings? . . . I have lived, Sir, a long time, and the longer I live, the more convincing proofs I see of this truth—that God Governs in the affairs of men. And if a sparrow cannot fall to the ground without his notice, is it probable that an empire can rise without his aid?*
>
> —Benjamin Franklin

i

THUCYDIDES IS QUITE CLEAR about the divine: that is, he is clear that opinions about the divine can very much matter in human affairs. In certain respects, indeed, "opinions about the divine" may themselves partake of "the divine."

Thucydides provides in his *Peloponnesian War* whatever he can ob-

---

Unless otherwise indicated, the citations in this chapter are to Thucydides' *Peloponnesian War*.

The epigraph is taken from James Madison, *Notes of Debates in the Federal Convention of 1787*, June 28, 1787 (Athens: Ohio University Press, 1966), pp. 209–10. See Anastaplo, "Church and State," p. 114.

serve, or surmise from what he observes, which seems relevant to an instructive account of the War. Among the things he considers relevant are the opinions the belligerents express about the divine, opinions our historians would not be likely to do much with in reporting on a great war in the twentieth century.

One reason why a historian today would have little to say about religious opinions is that he would tend to believe that such opinions have, or at least should have, little to do with political and military developments, however much the troubles in such places as Northern Ireland, the Middle East, Cyprus, the Indian Subcontinent, and Bosnia may make him wonder. We do make much in our time of "the separation of church and state," but that notion would not have made much sense to Thucydides. He would wonder how much a supposed separation operates even among us (except in a most formal sense), to say nothing of the rest of the world. In Athens, on the other hand, even the gold ornaments on a statue of Athena up on the Acropolis were regarded as part of the treasury or resources of the city and hence available for public use, for the sake of self-preservation, provided that every drachma was restored to the goddess once the emergency had passed (2.13).

The religious life of communities figures prominently in Thucydides' account, more so for example than economic considerations. (Economic considerations are recognized by him as sometimes critical, as in competition between cities for markets and in the difficulties that cities can have in financing their wars.) The religious life of cities—it is much more a communal, than a personal, religious life—may be seen in such "phenomena" as purificatory rites, sacred precincts, temples and altars, sacrifices, libations, oaths, supplicants, heralds and sanctuaries, truces, the great athletic Games, trophies, prayers, portents (or omens), oracles, soothsayers, curses, and burial rites. (The great theatrical festivals, religious in their origins, seem to be set aside by Thucydides.)

A thorough study of Thucydides should include a determination of what aspects of religious life are referred to and how—for example, what gods are invoked, by whom, and when. The relation between darkness and panic is noticed by Thucydides (2.3). This is not unrelated to the recourse to religion on various occasions. As the Great War was obviously drawing near, people collected whatever oracles seemed to anticipate what was happening (2.3). One can be reminded today of commodity brokers looking for clues as to what is going on in the market.

Thucydides was aware, as the Greeks generally were, of the misuse of oracles and other religious signs. The recourse by some to bribery, in order to influence oracles and soothsayers, was also known, as were the efforts made from time to time to turn accusations of sacrilege to political advantage. (See, e.g., 2.13.) Thucydides himself takes a careful look at such matters. He accounts for the extent of the armament that Agamemnon was able to gather for the Trojan War by saying that this was because of the superiority in strength (grounded in family wealth) that Agamemnon had, not because of any oaths the suitors of Helen had made to her father (as the poets had it).

Thucydides, in making use of the divine in his account, draws on traditional sources, but even more on his understanding of how things work. He interprets the evidence available to everyone (including, for example, the things said by Homer). We can begin our own investigation of the divine in Thucydides by considering how two quite different peoples, the Spartans and the Athenians, conducted themselves with respect to these matters. Indeed, it can be said, the response to the divine is one critical means for defining a people.

ii

The most pious people in Thucydides' account seem to be the Spartans. I hasten to add that piety is consistent in them with their ruthless treatment of the Helots and of others (such as the Plateans, with whom they had long been associated). They can even be stupid in their ruthlessness. (See, e.g., 2.67.) By and large, the Spartans do not ask what is right or good or decent, but rather what is *prescribed*, especially by some divine ordinance. Because of a disaster at Pylos, Sparta was ready to abandon her allies in order to make a deal with Athens. The Spartans evidently did not consider this a violation of any religious obligations.

The influence upon the Spartans of their piety is evident again and again. Everyone knows that the Spartans are different from others with respect to divine things. In fact, their credulity can be exploited by others. (See, e.g., 8.9.) They are repeatedly hobbled by religious requirements. Thus they can call off an invasion of Argos because the sacrifices were not propitious. (See 5.116.)

On the other hand, their enduring strength is related to their piety: a

certain steadiness results, however self-centered their political concerns
may be. If the Spartans suspect that they have not lived up to their religious obligations, they can be demoralized and hence less effective than
they would otherwise be. This was a disability they labored under during the first part of the War. But in the second part of the War, they were
persuaded that they were acting in full accord with their religious obligations, and they were all the more effective for that reason. (See 7.18. See,
in Plutarch's *Life of Aristides* [17.6 sq.], the account of the conduct of the
Spartans at the Battle of Platea.)

It is plausible, therefore, that Apollo would say, at Delphi, that he
would help the Spartans in the War, whether bidden or unbidden (1.118).
This reflects the obvious fact that the Spartans were pious. This is not to
suggest that the Spartans could never be shrewd and rationalistic, in the
Athenian fashion. Consider, for example, the Spartan captured at Pylos
who, upon being taunted by an Athenian ally about "those [Spartans]
who had fallen [having been] men of honour," replied that that arrow
"would be worth a great deal if it could tell men of honour from the rest,
in allusion to the fact that the killed were those whom the stones and the
arrows happened to hit" (4.40).

iii

We turn now to the Athenians. Even among that free-thinking people
the divine could very much matter. At times, in fact, they could be as
superstitious as the Spartans. But Athenian piety was not as steady as
Spartan piety—and consistency in these matters may be critical, usually
promoting moderation. The Athenians were generally known to be
volatile in all things, including with respect to religious observances.

That the divine could be taken most seriously by the Athenians is
testified to not only by the notorious fate of Socrates (shortly after
Thucydides' death) but also by the accounts of the gods, and of divine
influence, in the plays of the great Athenian tragedians (written during
Thucydides' lifetime). Thucydides tells of various portents, incidents,
and opinions among the Athenians during the Great War which testify
to their religious sentiments. Athenian piety is more evident in one respect than even Spartan piety—in the magnificence of their temples—
and hence in what was likely to survive for future generations to see in

the two cities (1.10). Of course, appearances can be deceiving, whether in the form of ruins or in the course of stories. But the Athenians were willing to devote to the gods considerable resources, as may be seen in the fact that one-tenth of the Lesbian booty was devoted to the gods (3.50).

Even so, the Athenians did tend to be more daring with respect to these matters than the Spartans. They would question things in ways that the Spartans would not; they were more likely to be attracted to challenges on the edge of propriety. (Thus, Pericles can ignore the gods in his great funeral speech, whatever the awareness there of the arts in Athens [2.34–47].) But the limits of even their daring could be seen upon their learning of the wholesale desecration of the Hermae all over Athens on the eve of the Sicilian expedition (6.27–28, 53, 60–61). The Athenian response to that desecration proved disastrous, leading to civic action that deprived the great fleet of proper leadership and thus contributed to the catastrophe in Sicily.

iv

I have surveyed, however briefly, the Spartan and the Athenian stances toward the divine. What, one may well ask, is Thucydides' own position? Perhaps the most significant thing about his position is that it is so guarded. He does not intend his reader clearly (or, rather, easily) to know what he believes and why about such matters.

What does his guarded account suggest? He does not report the gods as having this or that effect. But neither does he want to dismiss or disparage the gods or, perhaps more important, what men can know and do about them. Is this bound to be the response of the thoughtful man who knows that most, if not all, popular opinions about the divine (as about other vital matters) are likely to be in need of refinement? Socrates, too, was guarded in what he had to say about these matters, at least in the accounts left us by Plato and by Xenophon.

Neither Thucydides nor Socrates may have believed in the gods of the city as the city believed in them. But where does Thucydides go from there? Difficulties with the gods of the city are indicated (but not made explicit) by Thucydides' report that a Northern Greek city had established a hero cult for the Spartan Brasidas when he was killed there (5.10–11). Does not Thucydides show us here how the gods and their worship are "made"? An earlier divinity had been replaced thereby (someone who had once been similarly elevated?).

We can sympathize with Thucydides. After all, why should he believe in various of those gods, omens, etc. any more than we do now looking back at them? Responses to such things varied even in Thucydides' day—and it is not implausible that he should be inclined to the more skeptical end of the spectrum of opinions.

Even so, Thucydides is far more restrained in his public response than his would-be partisans are apt to be today. Did he recognize that philosophy and religion (or, at least, certain religions), despite their considerable differences, have much in common, especially when confronting much of the rest of the world? There is, then, in Thucydides' approach such prudence about these matters as is routinely seen in the more thoughtful men with political interests and a sense of civic decency. This is in contrast to the self-indulgence in such matters of an Alcibiades.

It makes sense for Thucydides, therefore, to leave it to his careful readers to figure things out from what he shows—and almost as important perhaps, how he shows it. Readers can thus understand divine things as Thucydides does, having before them both the same kind of evidence Thucydides had and a display of his approach to such evidence. This may be the only kind of reliable evidence ever generally available for the student of the divine to consider.

Since Thucydides is obviously a thoughtful man, should it not be assumed that he knows about the divine what can be known by someone in his circumstances? The evidence available to him (or to anyone else then) is, I have suggested, that which is often if not always available to human beings. Certainly, he does not reconstruct speeches among the gods (of the type seen in the *Iliad*), whereas he is able to reconstruct speeches by Greek leaders during the war. The implications of this difference may be significant. Nor does he indulge in irrelevant conjectures. The "inside story" about what really happened to the Hermae is of little use in understanding what happened in Athens during the Sicilian expedition—and so he leaves the story as it was generally known. (That "inside story," Leo Strauss has argued, may be suggested in Plato's *Symposium*. See, on the *Symposium*, the addendum to part 1 of chapter 7 of this book.)

Indeed, the nature of the subject of the divine may be such as naturally to lead to *mystery*. The sensible man recognizes what he cannot know.

v

Thucydides' opinions about the divine in human affairs are reflected in how he deals with the greatest disasters to strike Athens during the Great War: the plague in the early years of the war; the Sicilian expedition in the final years of the war. (An unrecognized disaster was what the Athenian said and did in Melos, especially when compared to what they had said and done earlier about Mytilene. See 3.36–50, 5.85–116.)

Since the plague came early in the war, Athens was more resilient than when the Sicilian debacle came. (Even so, the Athenians were remarkable in their ability to come back somewhat after Sicily also.) There is no serious public opinion—or, at least, none recorded by Thucydides—that the plague was some kind of divine retribution for Athenian misconduct.

Perhaps Thucydides' clinical account of the plague makes it less likely that his readers would wonder about the role of the gods here. (He is clinical both about the symptoms and effects of the disease and about how it had moved around the Mediterranean.) In a curious way, religion became irrelevant in Athens because of the plague: recourse to religious observances and remedies stopped after it became evident that they were futile, so overwhelming was the plague. The good and honorable died as readily as the others; restrictions upon the use of temples, chapels, and sacred grounds came to be ignored; necessity overpowered all conventional inhibitions; neither the fear of gods nor the laws of men had any effect. (Does all this suggest that the many are not truly pious, that they are observant primarily in order to benefit, and only so long as they do?)

We can see in the account of the plague how so massive an assault upon resources and sensibilities can affect the conduct of people and can lead to the neglect of long-established standards. It is startling, when one recalls what could be made of one unburied corpse in Sophocles' *Antigone*, to notice how corpses came to be treated during the plague:

they could be left unburied for animals to eat; the sacred places could be filled with them; and they could be thrown, in defiance of all propriety, upon fires built for other corpses. (See the conclusion of Lucretius' *On the Nature of Things.*)

We can also see in Thucydides' account how the interpretation of oracles could be tailored to fit the current facts, with his recognition that another disaster (of famine rather than of plague) would find the oracles appropriately adjusted. (See 2.54.) This testifies, one suspects, to the desire of people to make sense of things, thereby reminding us of the common cause that religion and philosophy can make against those who see the universe as meaningless.

vi

The other great Athenian disaster came from the Sicilian expedition (the sort of enterprise Pericles, who had died in the plague, had cautioned against). Particularly revealing is what happened to the Athenian commander-in-chief, Nicias. The Athenians had crippled the expedition when they recalled Alcibiades to stand trial for his alleged part in the desecration of the Hermae. When it thereafter became evident that things were going badly in Sicily, the Athenians were still in a position to salvage the fleet to which they had devoted so many of their men and resources. Nicias was somewhat stubborn and otherwise unimaginative, but at last, and in time, he was persuaded to order a withdrawal. But the last opportunity to save the great fleet was lost when a lunar eclipse was taken by Nicias to require a month's delay in their departure (7.50–51).

Nicias' superstition was evidently shared by enough of his countrymen to permit him to have his way. Thucydides, on the other hand, had mentioned an earlier solar eclipse rather casually, even scientifically. (See 1.28. See, also, 4.52. Compare 1.23.) It is obvious that Thucydides is rather dubious about Nicias' piety here, even though he does not make explicit his reservations. In fact, he can emphasize the decency of Nicias, as well as Nicias' own sense of having been a pious man and what that means (7.86). Nicias evidently believed that the gods help the pious. But Thucydides' eulogy of Nicias says, in effect, that this is not so, that the gods are, at best, incomprehensible. (See also the *Book of Job.*)

However pious and decent Nicias may have been, was he truly good? Would a good—that is, a sensible—man have acted as Nicias did in response to the eclipse? (Was there not something self-centered in much of what Nicias did? In the process he dragged down with him his gifted colleague Demosthenes and almost all of the fleet. As for the Spartans: they, too, might have been intimidated by such an eclipse, but would they have permitted themselves, at least after the debacle at Pylos, to be so vulnerable to one such episode?) Further omens are disheartening for the desperate Athenians, but these celestial phenomena are described by Thucydides as "often happen[ing] towards autumn" (7.79). We are reminded by this that Thucydides did not comment on what *the* eclipse meant. He leaves it to us to figure this out for ourselves.

Nicias, in his last speech, does not see the Athenian regime as responsible for their plight. Instead, he extols Athenian freedom. Is this not related to his failure to notice (his liberty *not* to notice) how his own piety had helped trap his fleet? Certainly, he is not a man who is prone to self-examination. Can a leader safely act as Nicias did only if the entire pattern of a city's action is Spartan-like? To mix approaches can be fatal. That is, it can be good to be enlightened, but not in a haphazard fashion, as many Athenians were. They were enlightened enough to experiment and gamble, but not enlightened enough to do everything necessary to minimize the risks they were running and to adapt to unexpected "supernatural" manifestations.

We notice the anger of the Athenians against the soothsayers back home once they learned of the disaster in Sicily (8.1). Must not the Athenians have believed that the soothsayers, who had encouraged the Sicilian expedition, had really known better? Otherwise, there is not much sense to being angry in these circumstances. On the other hand, would a truly pious man become angry in this fashion? Would not the truly pious be inclined to believe that the gods move in mysterious ways to achieve their purposes? In any event, the Athenian anger does testify to the general opinion that soothsayers are important and that the divine can be advantageously known to men. (Consider the sensible soothsayers among the Plateans, who helped develop an escape plan. Were the useful calculations they resorted to similar to what soothsayers try to do all the time? See 3.20.)

vii

What and how divine things are may be discerned both in what Thucydides does not say and in how he says what he does say, including how he organizes his account.

Consider, first, the Mycallesus episode, in which a schoolhouse of children are wantonly massacred by a barbaric ally of the Athenians (7.29–30). This is what the cause of Athens, the celebrated School of Hellas, can degenerate to.

Consider, also, Thucydides' juxtaposition of the Melian Dialogue (with its arrogant invocation of "power politics" by the Athenians) and the Sicilian expedition (5.85–116, 6.1). The Athenians are shown as blithely moving from one island adventure at Melos to another in Sicily. This arrangement of episodes suggests a cosmic order, which may be a way of talking about nature and hence about the natural consequences of folly. When one does appreciate nature, one is bound to recognize the part that chance can play in human affairs. The pious too, in their dependence upon the divine, are more apt to recognize the limits of their powers to anticipate events. Certainly, the Spartans seem to be more respectful than the Athenians of chance, or of the limits of human control over events. (They counsel the victorious Athenians thus after Pylos, as they ask for an accommodation. The Athenians did not appreciate how much their victory at Pylos had been due to chance, which Thucydides himself is very much aware of. See 4.3 sq.)

Although Thucydides never shows the gods as obviously intervening in human affairs, may not the divine somehow manifest itself in his account? Thus, the Melian Dialogue both reflects and contributes to a deterioration in Athenian sensibilities, principles, and hence effectiveness.

Sparta, as victor in the Great War, is shown in the overall account to be superior to Athens—but to Athens in its deteriorated condition. Is not Athens in its best form—in that which Athens aspires to, if not even in that clear-headedness seen in the Athenian Thucydides himself—is not *that* Athens superior to Sparta, and not least because it can appreciate what Sparta has to offer much better than Sparta can appreciate what Athens has to offer?

In any event, Thucydides does suggest that the world requires much more thoughtfulness than either the Athenians or the Spartans exhibited. Did he divine that these great Greek cities would be swept aside by such powers as those that we now know as Alexander's Macedonia and as Rome? We must wonder, that is, what was responsible for what happened during the Great War and thereafter. Does not one have to determine what the divine is and how it manifests itself in human affairs if one is to be able to understand what "really happened" in Greece at that time? That is, does not one have to figure out what Thucydides says?

Or must we make do only with what he tried to say? For, we are told, his account was never finished. Even so, the last thing to be seen in his account—which is, for all we know, what he always intended to be the last thing—is the trip of a Persian leader to Ephesus to offer sacrifice to the Greek goddess, Artemis. Persian piety can serve to remind us of what Athens and Sparta shared in their worship of the divine, something which the rest of the world has been obliged to come to terms with in one form or another (first as conquerors, then as conquered?) for more than two millennia. (The Christian associations with Ephesus and another Virgin of note may not be irrelevant here. Christianity can be seen to have built upon divine foundations providentially supplied by the Greeks. See *Acts of the Apostles* 19:23 sq. See, also, Anastaplo, "On the Use, Neglect, and Abuse of Veils.")

X. Gorgias. On the *Nature, Helen,* and *Palamedes*

He words me, girls, he words me,
that I should not be noble to myself!
—Cleopatra

i

SOPHISTS, IT HAS BEEN SUGGESTED by Prodicus of Ceos, are "on the borderline between the philosopher and the statesman." Aristotle observes that "dialecticians and sophists assume the same guise as the philosopher, for sophistic is wisdom which exists only in semblance." Philosophy, he adds, "differs from sophistic in respect of the purpose of the philosophic life. . . . Sophistic is what appears to be philosophy but is not." The philosopher, he explains, is one who studies "the nature of all substance" (*Metaphysics* 1004b18–27). Even so, we can appreciate that for many people the philosopher is indistinguishable from the sophist.

Of particular interest to us here is the Sophist who figures prominently in Plato's *Gorgias.* An encyclopedia entry provides this biographical information about the historical Gorgias (Kerford, "Gorgias of Leontini," 374):

> Gorgias of Leontini in Sicily, Greek Sophist and rhetorician, was probably born before 480 B.C. and is known to have been alive in 399 B.C. He

---

The epigraph is taken from William Shakespeare, *Antony and Cleopatra*, V, ii, 191–92.

came to Athens on a diplomatic mission in 427 B.C. to seek help for his native city and subsequently traveled widely, giving public lectures and private instruction in many Greek cities, especially in Thessaly. Among his numerous pupils were Isocrates and perhaps Thucydides.

The encyclopedia entry continues:

> Whether Gorgias should be classed as a Sophist has been much discussed. In Plato's *Gorgias* he is described as a teacher of rhetoric, not as a Sophist, and in *Meno* (95C) we are told he refused to claim that he could teach virtue, as other Sophists claimed. On the other hand, Plato recognized Gorgias, together with Prodicus and Hippias, as a professional educator of men (*Apology* 19E), and he certainly taught the art of persuasion as a means to political success. Whatever was the precise content of his teaching, he must in a general sense be regarded as belonging to the sophistic movement.

Philostratus, who wrote a *Lives of the Sophists* in antiquity, refers to Gorgias as "a man to whom as to a father we think it right to refer the art of the sophists" (1.9.1). He explains (Sprague, *The Older Sophists,* p. 30):

> For if we consider how much Aeschylus contributed to tragedy by adorning it with costume and the high buskin, and types of heroes, and messengers from abroad or from the house, and with the distinction between suitable onstage and offstage action, Gorgias would correspond to this in his contribution to his fellow artists.

Philostratus continues in his account of the originality of Gorgias:

> For he was an example of forcefulness to the sophists and of unexpected expression and of inspiration and of the grand style for great subjects and of detached phrases and transitions, by which speech becomes sweeter than it has been and more impressive, and he also introduced poetic words for ornament and dignity.

ii

It is reported that Gorgias himself, perhaps after reading in his old age the Platonic dialogue that bears his name, said to his friends, "How well Plato knows how to satirize!" (Sprague, p. 37, quoting Athenaeus, 11.505D).

Aristophanes could have made a similar comment if he had lived to read Plato's *Symposium,* which is discussed in the addendum to part 1 of chapter 7.)

The most effective satire draws upon something critical in the person satirized. We must wonder what the historical Gorgias was like.

It is obvious, from the way Gorgias is referred to in Plato's *Meno* and even more from the way he is dealt with personally in Plato's *Gorgias,* that Socrates respected the man. There *is* an affinity between philosophy and sophistry. Something of Gorgias' teachings can be garnered from the way he is spoken of in the Platonic dialogues. Then there are the fragments that have survived of Gorgias' own works, primarily as quoted excerpts in the works of much later authors.

What is likely thus to be saved may well *not* be the principal work of an author. That is, what is likely to be saved in this fashion is what is distinctive in his work (and hence is used to illustrate a point), even if that which is distinctive (as, for example, in the work of an El Greco, a Monet, or a Degas) may be a small part, and perhaps not even a representative part, of the whole.

The conventional parts of Gorgias' work may have been of no interest to those who drew upon him, especially if he should be quoted only to illustrate points for which no one else provides materials. The materials thus drawn upon may even have been used by Gorgias himself to develop points made by others. One of Gorgias' better known speeches, his encomium of Helen, can be described by a scholar as "a test speech," the work of "a pupil of Gorgias, neither very serious nor very intelligent, but acquainted with the current views of rhetoric and with a certain skill in the technique of the probability argument, a young man endowed with wit and a rather unscrupulous and materialistic outlook" (Hawthorne, "Gorgias of Leontini," p. 75). Even so, we must make do with what has happened to come down to us as words from Gorgias' hand.

iii

Chance can especially be seen in the Gorgian fragments that have been salvaged. We do not have the context for many of them. Nor can we be sure how the others were used, even when we happen to know the work in which they originally appeared. Rather, we have the fragments that happen to have been used by authors in works of their own which in turn happen to have survived.

The minor fragments can be conveniently allocated, for our purposes here, among a half-dozen categories. First, there are the indications in Plato's dialogues, especially the *Meno* and the *Gorgias,* of what Gorgias stood for. Thus, he is said in the *Meno* to have limited himself to enumerating the virtues, not attempting either to define or to inculcate them, an approach that is reflected in the way Meno (who had evidently studied with Gorgias) proceeds in talking with Socrates.

Then there are Gorgias' technical prescriptions. He was known in antiquity for his treatise on rhetoric, which seems to have been lost. This was evidently drawn upon by Aristotle in his own *Rhetoric,* when he reported, "Gorgias said that 'the opposition's seriousness is to be demolished by laughter, and laughter by seriousness,' in which statement he was correct" (Sprague, p. 63, quoting Aristotle, *Rhetoric* 1419b31). This leaves open the question of whether there are in our lives things that are intrinsically serious or intrinsically laughable.

Then there are Gorgias' scientific opinions. These include his account of what color is (taken from Empedocles, and drawn upon in the *Meno*); his description of the power of the burning glass; and his opinion, if it was *his* opinion, that the sun is a molten mass. Plutarch draws upon a description of the tomb of Isocrates in reporting, "Near it was a tablet showing poets and his [Isocrates'?] teachers, among whom is Gorgias looking at an astronomical globe and Isocrates himself standing by" (Sprague, p. 317, quoting *Lives of the Ten Orators* 838D).

Critical to Gorgias' reputation as an orator, or as a teacher of orators, was his ability to fashion vivid expressions which took the public fancy. Thus, he was known to have attempted to moderate struggles between the Greek cities with the observation, "Victories over the barbarians require hymns of celebration, over the Greeks lamentations" (Sprague, p. 48, quoting Philostratus, *Lives of the Sophists* 1.9.5). Related to this sentiment is the observation, "A friend will expect his friend to do only just actions in helping him; but he himself will serve his friend with many actions that belong to the category of unjust also" (Kathleen Freeman, *Ancilla to the Pre-Socratic Philosophers,* p. 138). Similarly paradoxical (or is it "human"?) is what Gorgias had to say about tragedy: "Tragedy, by means of legends and emotions, creates a deception in which the deceiver is more honest than the non-deceiver, and the deceived is wiser than the non-deceived" (Freeman, p. 138).

Of course, risks are run when one has recourse to vivid expressions. For one thing, the novelty can wear off and the expressions turn flat. Or particular images can be ill-conceived from their outset, as is argued in an ancient text reviewing the kinds of rhetoric (Sprague, p. 48, quoting Athanasius, *Introduction to Hermogenes, Rh. Gr.*, 14.180, 9 Rahe):

> [I call] the third kind of rhetoric that which is concerned with something ridiculous, awakening the guffaws of the young and being basically a shameless flattery. The circle of Thrasymachus and Gorgias practiced this in style and in their invalid arguments, making use of many equal clauses and failing to understand when this figure is appropriate. Many also have displayed it in figures of thought and tropes, but especially Gorgias, since he was the most affected, during the course of the very narrative in his *Funeral Oration,* not venturing to say "vultures" he spoke of "animate tombs."

It is said that Gorgias was also laughed at for calling Xerxes "the Persians' Zeus" (Sprague, p. 48, quoting Longinus, *On the Sublime* 3.2).

Then there are fragments from Gorgias in which he exhorts his fellow Greeks. We have already noticed his efforts to discourage war among the Greek cities. Plutarch records this comment (Sprague, p. 49, quoting *Advice to Bride and Groom* 144B–C):

> When Gorgias the orator read a speech at Olympia about concord among the Greeks, Melanthius said: "This fellow advises us about concord, though he has not persuaded himself and his wife and his maid, only three in number, to live in private concord." For it seems that Gorgias had a passion for the little maid and his wife was jealous.

Of women generally, Gorgias could say, "Not the looks of a woman, but her good reputation should be known to many" (Freeman, p. 138). His advice to his fellow Greeks included counsel relating to his long life, reputed by some to have been 108 years (Sprague, p. 36, quoting Athenaeus, 12.548C): "And when someone asked him what regimen he observed to live such a great length of life so pleasantly and with perception he said,

'By never doing anything for the sake of pleasure.'" His final lesson for the Greeks came from his deathbed (Sprague, p. 37, quoting Aelian, *Miscellaneous History* 2.35):

> Gorgias of Leontini at the end of his life and in advanced old age, overtaken by a feeling of weakness, lay down and was gradually slipping off into sleep. When one of his friends came over to see him and asked what he was doing, Gorgias answered, "Sleep already begins to hand me over to his brother Death."

Finally, in this inventory of the minor fragments from Gorgias, there is the observation that "existence is not manifest if it does not involve opinion, and opinion is unreliable if it does not involve existence" (Sprague, p. 66, quoting Proclus on Hesiod's *Works and Days,* 764). Another translation of this passage reads, "Being is unrecognizable unless it succeeds in seeming, and seeming is weak unless it succeeds in being" (Freeman, p. 139). Isocrates, perhaps Gorgias' most famous student, assesses his teacher's reflections upon *being* in this way (Sprague, p. 42, quoting Isocrates, 10.3; 15.268):

> For how could one outdo Gorgias who dared to say that of existing things none exists or Zeno who tried to prove the same things to be possible and again impossible? . . . [The] theories of the early sophists [included one which] said that the number of existing things is limitless . . . but Parmenides and Melissus said it is one and Gorgias none at all.

We can turn now, from this inventory of the minor fragments, to the principal remains of Gorgias, beginning with the discourse in which he had dared to say "that of existing things none exists."

iv

The most famous work we have from Gorgias is what was called by one writer in antiquity "an elegant treatise *On Nature,*" written about 441 B.C. (Sprague, p. 42, quoting Olypidorus). This treatise, with the full title of *On the Nonexistent or On Nature,* is summed up by another ancient writer in this fashion (Sprague, p. 42, quoting Sextus, *Against the Schoolmasters* 7.65):

[Gorgias] proposes three successive headings: first and foremost, that nothing exists; second, that even if it exists it is inapprehensible to man; third, that even if it is apprehensible, still it is without a doubt incapable of being expressed or explained to the next man.

A twentieth-century scholar identifies the major divisions of the treatise in these terms: "Nothing is; if it is, it is unknowable; if it is and is knowable, it cannot be communicated to others" (Kerferd, "Gorgias on Nature," p. 5). This scholar observed that Gorgias' treatise had not received much attention in the first half of the twentieth century (ibid., p. 3):

This is probably due mainly to two reasons—the highly technical and indeed to many readers repulsive nature of its content, and the widely held view that it is not meant seriously but is simply a parody or joke against philosophers, or at least a purely rhetorical exercise.

In response to these objections this scholar continues:

The first of these views [that it is a parody or joke] seems so obviously wrong that it is hardly necessary to devote much time to discussing it. The short answer must be that there is nothing humorous about the treatise and no indication that it was ever intended to be so. In this respect it is in exactly the same position as the second part of Plato's dialogue *Parmenides*. Its general thesis might conceivably amuse those to whom all attempts at philosophy are inherently absurd, but such persons could hardly be expected to work through the difficult arguments which make up the contents of the work. The view that it was purely a rhetorical exercise is no more plausible. . . . The final answer to both views must consist in showing just what is the content of the treatise and the serious purposes to which it is directed.

This scholar, like others before him since antiquity, subjected Gorgias' thesis to a searching, somewhat technical examination. It is not necessary to rehearse these arguments here. It is enough to notice that they are available, as are of course the extended arguments that Gorgias makes in support of his thesis.

It does seem to be assumed by Gorgias in his treatise that man is the measure of all things. It also seems that the existence of things depends upon the ability of the human mind to grasp and to communicate that existence, to grasp it by means of demonstration. In this respect, Gorgias stands with the famous Sophist, Protagoras. But he may be more radical than Protagoras, and perhaps in that way something more than a Sophist. (See Alexander P. D. Mourelatos, *The Pre-Socratics*, pp. 83–84; John Burnet, *Greek Philosophy*, p. 97.)

Socrates would recognize the problems in establishing existence, in reaching an understanding of things, and in communicating what one knows to others, even though he would be more likely to work in the order opposite to that of Gorgias: he would begin with the difficulties in a person's attempt to state what he believes himself to know, which could lead in turn to a consideration of what is and can be known. Then, with his more talented interlocutors, he would move to an awareness of what we would call the ineffableness of Being.

In any event, Socrates would not consider it either prudent or simply correct to argue as categorically as Gorgias does against the conventional positions here. Socrates understands those positions to rest upon a general human intuition and upon common sense. (Consider what Socrates does with wordsmiths in Plato's *Cratylus* and elsewhere. See, on the Platonic Ideas, part 2 of chapter 11 of this book.)

It is difficult to escape the suspicion that there is, in Gorgias' performance, much of the *tour de force,* or exhibitionism. (See Mourelatos, p. 70.) It often does seem that Gorgias argues primarily for the sake of argument. When he seems to be doing that, he can be impressive and admired without really being persuasive. Socrates, it is easier to believe, argues primarily for the sake of the truth.

Gorgias, that is, seems to be more interested than Socrates in success in argument. This is the way that he advances himself. However much he may argue against the existence of things, he does not seem to deny the existence of the money that he was so adept in earning during his long and profitable career, even though his reputed capacity in spending it as fast as he made it must have made him wonder sometimes whether money really existed.

v

How seriously *is* Gorgias' treatise on nature to be taken? Perhaps the most useful thing about it has been the array of arguments it has called forth explaining and reinforcing the conventional understandings of mankind threatened by Gorgias. This treatise does more, however, than deny one conventional position after another. It does affirm, if only implicitly, the power of words. Also assumed is the desirability of the ends served by a skillful use of words. Gorgias' argument assumes as well that both his argument and the minds between which it is passing exist. If his argument were taken in full seriousness, human beings would have to be regarded as completely isolated from one another intellectually, so much so that any attempt at communication and persuasion would be futile. Yet Gorgias tries to persuade others to accept something that he understands—that understanding and communication are impossible. (This is his version of the Cretan Paradox.) If one argues, in effect, that human beings do not exist, then anything seems to go; absurd arguments are not to be wondered at. Do they not become, in such circumstances, something to be played with rather than to be taken seriously?

Another way of putting this response is to say, with various of Gorgias' ancient critics (including, it seems, Aristotle), that Gorgias' approach means that "the criterion is destroyed" upon which understanding and discourse depend. "For there would be no criterion if nature neither exists nor can be understood nor conveyed to another" (Sprague, p. 46, quoting Sextus). A modern scholar put it this way (Hawthorne, p. 26): "Such then being the difficulties raised in Gorgias, the criterion of truth is done away with, so far as they are concerned. For there would be no criterion of what does not exist and cannot be known and cannot be naturally passed on to another."

What is presupposed by Gorgias' treatise, its preparation and promulgation (to say nothing of its preservation over millennia)? To what extent, or in what way, do skeptical positions such as Gorgias' depend, for their effectiveness, upon criteria or standards that are generally appreciated, including standards about good and bad, right and wrong? Do not all skeptics, or relativists, work from or assume something stable, knowable, and permanent? All the fancy dancing is possible because of a fairly steady dance floor, as seen for example in the language that is provided them and the reasoning ability that language reflects. The dancer may become the dance—and the dance floor as well—or so it can seem to the self-centered thinker of Gorgias' persuasion.

Perhaps still another way of putting these observations is to say that human beings have an intuitive grasp of things (a *pistis*) which is not susceptible of demonstration in that it provides the starting point or premise of understanding. Gorgias himself seems to believe that words somehow exist independently of things. This permits him to *argue* (as if it mattered) that things do not exist.

There may be a sound intuition at the root of Gorgias' argument here, but an intuition which undermines his argument. His remarkable reliance upon words as independent of things may reflect, without his being aware of it, that state of things which found more plausible expression in the Platonic Doctrine of the Ideas.

The key, then, to Gorgias' position (and to that of someone such as Martin Heidegger, millennia later) is that an attempt is made to reason to, or to establish by reason, Being itself. But must not Being be grasped or intuited—in that sense, it *is* incomprehensible? Its non-existence or our lack of certainty about its existence does not follow from the necessity of having something beyond which no argument can reach. However salutary it can be to call into question much that is conventionally accepted, especially when dubious cults and myths dominate the thought of one's day, it goes too far to insist that nothing that is conventionally accepted has any grounding in a sound intuition. Socratic sobriety is instructive here, which can include noticing the extent to which the argument in each of the three parts of Gorgias' treatise depends upon notions repudiated in the other two parts. (See Anastaplo, *The American Moralist*, pp. 83, 144; "Lessons for the Student of Law," p. 187.)

We must wonder what the condition was of the Greek cities that permitted Gorgias, with his somewhat nihilistic views, to be well received there for so many years among the political elites. Certainly, his ambitious students did not feel they would be discredited by associating with Gorgias, however much his art permitted, if it did not compel, one to challenge conventional opinions in the most comprehensive manner. But then, the eminently political Pericles risked associating with Anaxagoras, a thinker even more challenging in critical respects than Gorgias.

vi

We can see in Gorgias' *Helen* speech what his skepticism can mean when put in the service of a defense argument. We can see there what a facility with words can mean, what it can mean to assume that speech can somehow rearrange everything.

Gorgias knows what everyone knows about Helen, that she ran off to Troy with her lover, and that a great war followed, which brought much destruction and suffering to Greeks and Trojans alike. But, he argues, she is to be excused, since she did what she did either by will of Fate and decisions of the gods and vote of Necessity or by force reduced or by words seduced or by love possessed (Sprague, p. 51).

To argue as Gorgias does on Helen's behalf is to deny ordinary experience, including experience about the workings of love. Does he not challenge what "everyone knows" about Helen and what she did? Is not the Homeric tradition itself called into question, and in a way different from that sometimes employed by Socrates or Euripides? How seriously is such an approach to be taken, whatever the facts happened to be in Helen's own case?

Gorgias' defense of Helen means, in effect, that no one is culpable. When he defends Helen, however, it is useful for him to condemn others, such as the man who either forced or seduced her. Would not the defense of Helen be ineffective, however, if all culpability—all acknowledgment of good and bad—were explicitly denied? It should be obvious that similar defenses could be made by Gorgias, in due course, on behalf of the man who forced or seduced her. Consider, for example, what could be said about how her beauty stripped others of all self-control.

This is not to deny that we are willing to hear Gorgias' defense of Helen herself. Do we not sense that she *is* special—and therefore that ordinary rules may not apply to her? This would be to recognize and exalt *the noble*—but there may be something too utilitarian, if not even prosaic, in Gorgias to leave much room for the noble. The noble does not permit itself to be diverted from its high purposes by mere words.

It is the poet who looks to, and celebrates, the noble. The Socratic approach to the failings of a Helen would be different from both that of Gorgias and that of the poet. Vice, Socrates argues, depends upon ignorance—and this, in turn, presupposes both that there is a Good and that human beings are capable of knowing vital things that bear upon the preference for right over wrong. (See, on the noble and the just, part 2 of chapter 7 of this book. Consider, also, the discussion of the unjust speech in part 3 of chapter 7.)

vii

We see also in the *Palamedes* defense speech by Gorgias an approach
which can lead to the effective denial of the guilt of any particular de-
fendant, however much the defense exploits condemnations of others as
guilty. We can see as well in the *Palamedes* the considerable reliance
upon words alone that we have noticed elsewhere in Gorgias. What
is the "reality" of the situation? Is it not impossible from such a presentation—without an independent access to the facts and without the
counter-arguments—to assess what "really happened"?

Is the audience supposed to know what happened? (See the end of
Plato's *Apology* for the problem of Palamedes.) Or is it that the facts do
not matter for Gorgias' purpose? There *are* telling lines in the speech—
such as, "The accusers cannot know for certain that I committed the
crime, because I know for certain that I did not." (Freeman, p. 134. See,
also, Sprague, p. 55.) But this and many other such lines can, unfortunately be voiced by guilty men as well as by innocent, especially if the
guilty have had access to the counsel of advocates such as Gorgias.

This obliges us to consider, however briefly, why it is that Socrates'
speeches in the *Apology* are persuasive *with us* standing alone. Or do
they really stand alone? Perhaps important in the Socratic speech is a
display of wisdom in a way that reflects a sound character. There are, as
well, the many references by him to well-known episodes that an uninhibited audience could be expected to shout down if not accurately reported. Besides, we are shown the interventions of Socrates' supporters,
the limitations of his accusers (upon cross-examination as well as in the
form of their indictment), and the interventions of the crowd when
stirred up by him. In the *Palamedes* speech, on the other hand, we have
only a display of the power of words to shape all of the world that matters. (See, on the *Apology*, Anastaplo, *Human Being and Citizen*, p. 8.)

Do not all three of the major works we have from Gorgias (*On Nature, Helen,* and *Palamedes*) depend in the final analysis not only upon
his adroitness but perhaps as much, if not even more, upon the appearance of adroitness? It is the advocate that the audience is asked to vote
for, less so for the client or cause of the advocate. The Sophist, with this
approach, is essentially an actor and a teacher of actors. In these activi-

ties, novelty is often mistaken for that genuine originality which can
present things for what they are.

viii

Much, if not all, that Gorgias did was designed to win over multitudes,
not to discourse seriously with those of genuine philosophical interests.
This may help explain why Gorgias' work has survived only in fragments whereas that of Plato and Aristotle has been preserved and transmitted with obviously great care over millennia.

The preservation of the best work reflects an awareness of the good.
Thus, it is Aristotle's *Rhetoric* that comes down to us substantially as it
was written, not Gorgias'. What Aristotle has to say about rhetoric is illuminated by, and must be in the service of, what he has to say elsewhere
about ethics and politics. (See Larry Arnhart, *Aristotle on Political Reasoning.*) We can see among the accusers of Socrates a rhetorician who
went wrong—that is, a rhetorician who was merely a rhetorician and
hence perhaps jealous of the deeper drawing power exercised by
Socrates. Socrates was done in, to some extent, by men who considered
him a political rival of sorts.

Gorgias, of course, would never be an accuser of Socrates. That may
be partly due to his good-naturedness. But it may also be due to his having cut himself off, as a traveling teacher, from serious political life.
Which came first, Gorgias' skepticism or his apolitical existence? He did
begin his career abroad in the service of his city. But he eventually found
himself both apolitical and aphilosophical (that is, professionally skeptical), however much what he had to say resembled at times either political speeches or philosophical discourse.

Gorgias may have come to sense that there was no firm foundation
upon which he rested. His most positive endorsement of conventional
virtues can be seen in the fragment we have of a funeral oration. On
such an occasion, the principles and aspirations, as well as the very existence, of the community must be approached with deadly seriousness.
That is not the occasion for playing games with words—and even if that
is what one "naturally" tries to do, the solemnity of the occasion invests

one's words with all the seriousness which they are capable of reflecting. The community as community is naturally reaffirmed by any funeral oration, especially one for those who have fallen in battle.

ix

What is common to the longer things we have from Gorgias (*Helen, On Nature,* and *Palamedes*) is an exhibition of, not necessarily a belief in, the power of argument. If one took Gorgias' arguments seriously, either one would not be able to condemn (or properly praise?) anyone or one would not be able to know anything—or, at least, to communicate anything.

How seriously can such an approach be taken? Is its principal effect to legitimate self-interest, even as it makes one wonder whether any interest should be taken seriously? Many are likely to be taught by this approach that one can and should look out completely for oneself, perhaps even that "anything goes." (See Anastaplo, "On Crime, Criminal Lawyers, and O. J. Simpson: Plato's *Gorgias* Revisited" and its sequel on the Simpson Case in volume 28 of the *Loyola University of Chicago Law Journal.*)

Gorgias obviously exhibited great skills, which were admired and imitated (and lavishly rewarded) by quite sophisticated audiences and cities. His were skills that Socrates evidently did not have, however useful they might have been for Socrates on occasion. There is an element of shamelessness in such skills as well as a sometimes silly willingness to believe things that may not be quite so. That is, one usually has to persuade oneself before one can persuade others. Another critical difference is that Gorgias would not have had the reservations Socrates exhibits in Plato's *Crito* about fleeing Athens to save his life. Gorgias always knew how to take care of himself, from a conventional point of view.

The potential usefulness of Gorgias for the cause of philosophy is indicated in the Platonic dialogue named after him. After all, he reports, he is capable of persuading patients to undergo necessary but painful treatment which doctors cannot themselves persuade their patients to undergo. We see Gorgias in that dialogue as a man who somehow senses his limitations—and who prudently leaves some of the more question-able implications of, if not departures from, his position to be developed by his less thoughtful imitators, and especially by an Athenian (Calli-cles) who is not as vulnerable as a visiting alien would be.

We also see Gorgias as in need of guidance as to the ends to which his considerable skills are to be directed, ends which are served by the enlistment of the rhetorician in the development of salutary stories about divine judgment. Gorgias could serve well in medicine so long as a competent physician directed him, just as he could serve well in diplomacy so long as a competent city directed him. A proper study of the Platonic dialogues, including the *Gorgias,* should help us discover both what the original Gorgias and the other Sophists were like and what could properly be done with and through them.

XI. Plato

PART ONE. On the *Timaeus*

> *When they saw that Patroclus was slain,*
> *who had been so stalwart, and strong, and young,*
> *the horses of Achilles started to weep;*
> *their immortal nature was indignant*
> *at the sight of this work of death.*
> *They would shake their heads and toss their manes,*
>   *stamp the ground with their feet, and mourn*
> *Patroclus who they realized was lifeless—undone—*
> *worthless flesh now—his spirit lost—*
>   *defenseless—without breath—*
> *returned from life to the great Nothing.*
>
>   —Constantine P. Cavafy

Unless otherwise indicated, the citations in this part of this chapter are to Plato's *Timaeus*. See, for additional discussion by me of Plato, *The Constitutionalist*, p. 278; *Human Being and Citizen*, pp. 8, 74, 203; *The American Moralist*, p. 37; *The Amendments to the Constitution*, p. 108; "Freedom of Speech and the First Amendment," p. 1945; "On Trial," p. 873; "The Ambiguity of Justice in Plato's *Republic*," p. 199, 353; Book Review, *Review of Metaphysics*, vol. 32 (1979), p. 773; "The Teacher," *The Great Ideas Today* (1997); "Beginnings," *The Great Ideas Today* (1998) (includes a review of Stephen Hawking, *A Brief History of Time*); "Thursday Afternoons," in Kameshwer Wali, ed., *S. Chandrasekhar: The Man Behind the Legend* (London: Imperial College Press, 1997). See, also, the addendum to chapter 7, part 1; chapter 7, part 2; and chapter 8, part 2, of this book.

The epigraph is taken from Constantine P. Cavafy, "The Horses of Achilles," in *The Complete Poems*, trans. Rae Dalven (London: Hogarth Press, 1961), p. 24.

i

STUDENTS OF THE CLASSICS are often asked, "What did 'the Greeks' believe about this or that?" The question assumes, among other things, that the Greeks differed less than we do on various important questions that they confronted.

This kind of question may be prompted, for example, by a first reading of Sophocles' *Antigone.* Thus, it is asked, "What did the Greeks believe about the disposition of a corpse and about the consequences of a failure to bury a corpse?"

No doubt the questioner hopes that one can understand what Antigone did, which includes an awareness of what she should have done, by invoking what "the Greeks" thought about this. Once one knows—once one is *told,* presumably by someone who has read the proper scholars—what "the Greeks" thought about the burial of a corpse, one is then well on the way to understanding what Antigone did and why. Without this vital information about Greek opinion, one would have to determine what to make of what she did; one would have to *think* about the meaning and significance of what is said and done. One might even be obliged to conclude that Antigone is noble but imprudent, perhaps even unjust—something one is not apt to conclude if one believes that there was *a* Greek response to the unburied corpse and that Antigone merely expressed that response in its most dramatic form.

What, then, did "the Greeks" believe about these matters? It is difficult to say. After all, even in the *Antigone,* as we have also seen, various positions are taken. Antigone herself seems to identify her compulsion to bury her brother with some kind of divine injunction. But the reader is led to wonder whether it is because of this, or because it is an affront to her pride or for some other reason, that she makes her desperate effort. Creon, on the other hand, insists that a refusal to bury a traitor is salutary, indeed even sanctified if not required by the gods, especially when that traitor would (as he evidently believes) have destroyed the temples of his city. In any event, Creon sees his decree as politically useful. Antigone's sister, Ismene, is somewhere between Antigone and Creon: she considers the denial of burial lamentable; but she (out of fear, at least) is somewhat respectful of the laws of the city. (See part 2 of chapter 7 of this book, and the addendum thereto.)

What could Sophocles expect his original Athenian audience, in fifth-century-B.C. Greece, to think about this? Were not quite varied responses to be found, even on this relatively simple issue, among the Athenians of Sophocles' generation? Consider what happened when the Athenian generals, after the naval Battle of Arginusae in 406 B.C., failed to recover the bodies of the dead from the water. (This was during the Peloponnesian War.) These generals, despite their victory at Arginusae, were condemned to death and executed by the Athenians. (All this was long after the writing of the *Antigone*. The Athenian people's response was almost hysterical on that occasion. Socrates tells us in his *Apology* that he happened to be the presiding officer in the assembly when this case first came up; the best he could do that day, it seems, was to delay proceedings to another day, and this only at grave risk to himself. See, on Arginusae, Cicero, *On the Commonwealth*, p. 237 n. 36. See, also, section viii of part 2 of chapter 3 of this book.)

This Athenian fervor, then, is one response, no doubt a widespread one, to the problem of proper treatment of corpses. It is a response that is reflected in an observation by a character, centuries later, in one of Cicero's dialogues: "[Men do not believe that] their interests end with their lives; hence the sanctity of burial is part of the pontifical law [in Rome]." (Ibid., p. 237. This sentiment is anticipated in Aristotle's *Nicomachean Ethics*. Compare Plutarch, *Life of Marcellus* 30.1–4.) On the other hand, there is the response of Socrates—not necessarily at the trial of the generals, since that could be understood as an insistence by him upon the procedural proprieties, but rather on the day of his death. Plato's *Phaedo* records Socrates' counsel to Crito that no trouble need be taken with his (Socrates') corpse. It is indicated thereby, as we have seen, that Socrates does not seem concerned (so far as his own interests, as distinguished from the sensibilities of his family and other survivors are concerned) about what happens to his body after he dies.

No doubt, the prevailing beliefs with respect to burial (whether those of Antigone or those of Socrates) are likely to be keyed to opinions one has about the gods. In the *Antigone* itself, we see that the blind seer Tiresias supports Antigone's position on the basis of considerations which can be considered more "theological" than are hers. In that play, we also hear Creon argue that the gods like law-abidingness and patriotism. Or, if we go on to a work such as Cicero's *On the Nature of the Gods,* we can see the ancients' diversity of religious sentiment in full bloom. Various opinions are there indicated about the gods. There are no out-and-out atheists among the characters in this work of Cicero's—but then, atheism is very hard to find any time, whatever the form of words may be.

More immediately at hand is what is to be found in Plato himself about the divine and its relation to the lives of human beings. It should be instructive to consider here what is said in his *Timaeus* about these and other matters. (The *Timaeus*, it has been noticed, was the only Platonic dialogue available to the western world for most of its history.)

ii

The divine, in perhaps its most nearly cosmic form, may be seen in the *Timaeus*. The ordering of the *cosmos* by divine power is related there, an ordering which ranges from the shaping of the heavens above and of various divinities to the emergence on earth of human beings and thereafter of the lowest living things. The range of "creation," as recapitulated by Timaeus, is extensive.

Precisely what Timaeus himself does say about these matters *is* a problem. Two responses, one ancient, the other modern, put us on our guard at the beginning of these investigations. An Epicurean, in Cicero's dialogue *On the Nature of the Gods*, opens his account of the divine with this disclaimer (1.8): "You are going to hear from me no fatuous and fanciful doctrines, such, for example, as that of the carpenter-architect god who put together the world, presented by Plato in his *Timaeus* . . ." (He thereafter makes various adverse comments on the *Timaeus*. See, e.g., ibid., 1.8, 10, 12, 24.)

The modern skeptical response is, it can be said, somewhat more respectful. Kenneth Clark has observed (*Another Part of the Wood*, p. 84): "As for the *Timaeus*, Clive Bell used to say that when he thought he understood the *Timaeus* it was a sure sign that he was drunk. I agree."

Our awareness of such diverse responses, along with our realization of the considerable reputation enjoyed by the *Timaeus* during the Middle Ages, puts us on notice that there is no settled opinion about the *Timaeus* and that, consequently, we must think for ourselves. On the other hand, since there *is* such diversity, whatever we dare say about this subject is not without some support in the literature. (This quite considerable literature includes a useful commentary on the *Timaeus* by Seth Benardete, upon which I draw for this discussion. A comment of sorts may be seen in the principal Raphael fresco discussed in chapter 13 of this book.)

iii

What, then, is said in the *Timaeus* about "the carpenter-architect god who put together the world"? This overarching divinity—this demiurge—is seen, in this dialogue, as primarily a maker, not as contemplative. He works with pre-existing matter: the stuff from which everything visible is made is not itself made by the demiurge in the sequence described by Timaeus (whatever may have been the ultimate origin of that stuff). There does seem to have been a chaotic movement of visible bodies before the making (that is, the ordering?) of the cosmos by the demiurge. (See Benardete, "On Plato's *Timaeus*," p. 41 n.)

The stuff, or material, from which everything visible is made seems to be keyed to four elements: earth, fire, air, and water. The proportions among these are critical in any enduring (not necessarily eternal?) combination of these elements (32C). It is again and again indicated that the material from which these four elements were made had an existence and a decisive nature prior to the shaping of the cosmos by the demiurge (53A–C). When Timaeus turns to an account of this stuff, the probable (or tentative) nature of his account is emphasized (48D–E). It is not possible for him to speak here with the kind of certainty he had exhibited with respect to "the operations of reason," and which may be seen, for example, in his mathematics (47E–48A). In any event, one gets the impression that the preexistent nature of this stuff places limits on what the demiurge can do as creator. There are, for him, necessary limits; he is not omnipotent. Indeed, it can be said, there is something "perplexing and baffling" in the receptivity of the stuff which is very (but not infinitely) malleable. (If the stuff of the universe were infinitely malleable, would it not be as if there could be a creation from nothing as well as complete annihilation?)

In the sequence of creation, three stages are of particular interest to us. There is the creation of the cosmos itself; there is the creation of certain unnamed gods who will, pursuant to the will of the demiurge, exist forever once created; and there is the emergence, through the agency in turn of the created gods, of human beings and other mortal things.

First, the cosmos is created, it seems. It is presented as a living creature, patterned on "that intelligible Creature which is fairest of all and in all ways most perfect" (30D). There can be, it is argued, only one such universe patterned on the eternal perfection, "one generated heaven, unique of its kind" (31B). This question is returned to later: an infinite number of "universes" is again ruled out. But the recourse, in the construction of things, to the five regular solids, raises the more plausible question, whether there are *not* an infinite number but rather five universes. Timaeus stands by the conclusion that there is only one, but he concedes the plausibility of the suggestion that there are five (55D). Is this left open? Does fiveness relate as well to the five participants originally scheduled for the conversation recorded in this dialogue? But only four showed up this day: one of the anticipated participants is ill. Are we meant to wonder whether fiveness *is* capable of sustained realization? (There *had* been five of them the day before?)

The dialogue concludes with a reaffirmation of the oneness of the universe (or cosmos): "And now at length we may say that our discourse concerning the Universe has reached its termination. For this our Cosmos has received the living creatures both mortal and immortal and been thereby fulfilled; it being itself a visible Living Creature embracing the visible creatures, a perceptible God made in the image of the Intelligible, most great and good and fair and perfect in its generation—even this one Heaven sole of its kind" (92C). This emphasis upon the one echoes, it can be said, the somewhat ostentatious counting of the others with which Socrates opens this dialogue (17A): "One, two, three—but where, my dear Timaeus, is the fourth of our guests of yesterday, our hosts of today?" Can things be grasped only in their oneness, in their unity? Is diversity essentially unknowable, unless one can bring it all together as a one, as a "fulfilled" one? Otherwise, can one know whether one has an "it" to grasp? That which has thus far escaped one's grasp might radically change one's view of what one has?

We must turn now, in the sequence of creation, to "the creatures both mortal and immortal." The immortal creatures—the gods made by the demiurge—in turn create mortal creatures. These gods are instructed in their creation of mortal creatures by the demiurge; they model themselves in their creation upon what the demiurge has done.

Male human beings come first among mortal creatures. From them "evolve" women and the lower animals. There even seem to be natural laws (as we would call them) in accordance with which the various mortal creatures, because of their misconduct, pass into one another, evidently as a kind of degeneration, once man is created (91–92). This movement is not a matter of choice (unlike what may be seen in the *Republic's* Myth of Er). Nor is it a matter of chance (as is seen to some extent, it can be said, in the Darwinian scheme). Rather, there is a movement in the *Timaeus* from the highest to the lowest, in this effort to present a comprehensive account of the things that are. Yet that account concludes, as we have already seen, with an emphasis upon the one cosmos, "most great and good and fair and perfect in its generation" (92c). The universe, then, with all that is in it, is seen as eminently purposeful —except that that purpose may be difficult for human beings to realize with respect to *the things that always are,* including the stuff out of which all (that is visible?) is made and the perfect being upon which the cosmos is patterned.

iv

We began, it will be remembered, with a realization of the diversity of opinion among "the Greeks" with respect to matters of overriding importance, both practical (the problem of burial) and theoretical or at least theological (the nature of the gods).

We have seen that this diversity of opinion on such subjects may be found within the work of particular authors (such as Sophocles and Plato). One of their characters may hold one opinion, another character a different opinion. We have also seen, from our preliminary survey of the *Timaeus,* that a diversity of sorts may exist even within the opinions of a single character. That is, Timaeus' account presents somewhat diverse divinities.

There is the demiurge. He seems to be the supreme father. (Is "space" the mother? See Benardete, "On Plato's *Timaeus,*" pp. 24, 33.) His powers, we have seen, are not absolute: he does not create from nothing, but rather "must" work with pre-existing stuff (whose origins are not indicated). In addition, his constant willing seems to be necessary if that which has been made by him is to retain its form and do what is intended. (See ibid., pp. 34–35.) The elementary stuff shaped by the demiurge seems to have a "will" of its own: it will not stay put, it seems, without constant supervision. (See Plato, *Meno* 97D–E.)

Then there is the cosmos—that living, intelligent, and permanent being—which is either divine or is modeled on the divine.

Then there are the various subordinate deities who are entrusted with subordinate creating.

These three sets of divinities are required, Timaeus seems to say, if one is to explain *the all*—if one is to be able to account for the existence of things both divine and earthly. No account is possible, he also seems to say, without invoking the divine, but the divine in rather complicated forms.

When one looks to Plato's other "characters," the diversity in the divine becomes even more marked. Consider what is indicated about the divine by others in the *Timaeus*. But, first, we must recall what the others have said. Among the things provided by Socrates is a summary of part of the conversation of the day before, recorded in the *Republic*, which is itself an account of what had taken place in the Piraeus the day before that. (This emphasis placed in this summary of the conversation of the *Republic* is upon the constitution in words of "the best city.") Then there is an anticipation by Critias of what he will relate in the dialogue that we know as the *Critias* about the ancient war between Atlantis and Athens. (That account will deal, he says, with the history of "the best city" as experienced in deed—a regime which was not immune to catastrophic accident? What does *this* suggest about divinity and the governance of the world?)

One critical difference between the *Republic* and the *Critias* is that the named gods (Zeus and his colleagues, for example) figure hardly at all in the *Republic* but very much in the *Critias*: Athena and Hephaestus established Athens; Poseidon established Atlantis, because of his desire for a woman; and Zeus must finally bring Atlantis to its deserved ruin. (Athens is used to accomplish the divine purpose. Is Zeus, in his concern to deal properly with misbehaving Atlantis, curiously oblivious to what happens to Athens, just as, for example, the Aphrodite of Euripides' *Hippolytus* is oblivious to what happens to Phaedra?)

The named gods (including the Thracian goddess of the opening lines) figure so little in the *Republic* that they are not mentioned at all in the summary of that dialogue that Socrates provides in the *Timaeus*. (But, it should be noticed, neither is the philosopher-king mentioned in this summary. Is this partly because he is an image of the divine?) What is emphasized in the summary is that the institutions of "the best city" are arranged in accordance with nature (17C-D). (We see, among other things, a skillful use of "chance" in arrangement of the marriage lots— by those naturally equipped and properly trained to do so? This use of lots is designed to keep the bad-natured in line [18E].)

Not only are the named gods not mentioned in Socrates' summary, but if the teaching by Socrates in the *Republic* is taken seriously, then the conventional (largely poetic?) accounts of the gods are in need of considerable purgation. Thus, the gods must not be understood to change, to lust, etc. But this understanding of the divine would call for drastic reconsideration of what is depended upon in the *Critias*—where, as we have noticed, Poseidon's lust is critical to the founding of Atlantis.

Still, it can be said, the *Republic* can manage to do without the named gods for the most part (except, perhaps, in oaths) because it reports an ascetic gathering devoted to the discussion of that political asceticism which a truly just regime can be said to be. The regime described in the *Republic* is unresponsive to (or unconcerned with) *eros,* as conventionally understood. Since it is a city in words, it can be independent of the gods who minister to, and in various ways discipline, the passions (erotic and otherwise) of human beings.

On the other hand, named, involved, and hence somewhat passionate gods may be inevitable in a "working" city—if it is not to become cruel or even monstrous. Does conventional piety tend to contain excessive pride? Do the involved gods tend to have a gentling, a civilizing, effect? Consider what happens in the *Critias* as the divine influence wears off: misbehavior becomes rampant. (One is reminded of the accounts in the Hebrew Bible of the falling away of the Israelites when they forgot God. Is the God of the Israelites similar, in critical respects, to the named [properly purged] gods of the Platonic dialogues?) Compare Benardete, "On Plato's *Timaeus*," pp. 30–31: "Critias all but says that the love of wis-

dom is due to nature and the love of war to the gods." Does this mean
that the wise should be reluctant to embrace war?

Of course, a concern by the city for its gods can also have deleterious
effects. This is reflected in Plato's *Euthyphro* and *Apology,* where Socrates'
vulnerability is evident because he does not acknowledge the gods that
the city acknowledges. (The city's conventional opinions of the gods—
somewhat fragmentary, if not contradictory, opinions—are indicated in
such dialogues.) Although it is important to keep the condemnation of
Socrates in mind, too much *can* be made of this (as may be seen in the
modern Enlightenment?). In our times it is well to be reminded instead
of the salutary influence of piety, however destructive of the familial and
the natural an excess of piety can be (as may be seen in the *Euthyphro*).
We can see in Plato's *Phaedrus* Socrates' own use of the gods. He shows
there what *he* can do with the named gods. (See, on the saying that "all
things are full of gods," Plato, *Epinomis* 991D. See, on Plato's *Republic,*
part 2 of chapter 8 of this book.)

                    v

These diverse accounts of the divine prompt us to turn now to a question which is implicit in the *Timaeus:* What is the authority for the various opinions about the divine set forth by Timaeus himself? The reader
is induced to wonder thus when he notices that the accounts of things
provided in the dialogue by others (that is, by Socrates and by Critias)
do have their immediate sources indicated. Socrates' account is, we have
noticed, a summary of what he had related to them the day before
(which, in turn, had been the report of a conversation of the day before
that). Critias' account, about Atlantis and events of nine thousand years
before, came (it is said by Critias) from the Egyptian records by way of
Solon. (It is "a strange piece of fortune," Critias says, that Socrates' account of the best city fits in so well with Solon's account of the compo-
sition and activities of an ancient city [25E]. Is this like the fortune of the
marriage lots earlier referred to [18E]? That is, is "fortune" here likewise
contrived?)

Nothing is said, however, about where Timaeus gets *his* account of
the demiurge and of all its doings. Nor is anything said about how long

ago these things happened. (There is, unlike in the Hebrew Bible, no genealogy or other history since the creation.) Timaeus reports, in considerable detail, what no man could have seen. Consider in this respect the opening chapters of *Genesis*. Are we meant to understand that the word of God, there relied upon, came to mankind through the Biblical prophets?

What is the status of such revelation for Timaeus? The named gods, as we know them, may reflect divinities that appear here and there to men: for example, both in Egypt and in Greece, as Critias reports. Men who travel about encounter the same gods, under different names, in various places. Or rather, they encounter the effects or relics of such gods, in the forms of temples, priests, and rituals, as well as in the form of stories. Also, such gods instructed men in all manner of things "down to divination and the art of medicine" (24c). These gods, it is assumed, somehow manifested themselves in an authoritative fashion, usually "long ago."

But however the gods manifested themselves originally, and to whom, reports about them come down to us, it seems, primarily as the "discoveries" of the poets. It is those discoveries, it also seems, that Timaeus incorporates into his account of the emergence of the named or lesser gods. (Does he, in this respect, reconsider what Hesiod—who is mentioned in the dialogue along with Homer—had done in presenting the emergence of the named gods?) Is Timaeus, because of what he knows of *the* divinity behind the named gods, able to present directly what the poets could do no more than speak figuratively about? The poets cannot, or at least do not, explain what they say. The poets make much of particulars and of passions associated with those particulars. They shape thereby the passions and character of the people. But, it has been noticed, the poets in turn are somewhat shaped by the people. It is said in one of Cicero's dialogues, "By their clamorous approval and applause, the people mold the character of the poets according to their will—as if the public were some great and wise master whose praise is all-sufficient." (Cicero, *On the Commonwealth*, p. 238. Compare Aristotle, *Poetics*, on the judgment by the people of Athens on the tragedies.)

All this, then, can be seen to raise a question about the ultimate authority of the poets with respect to the named gods. Timaeus, because of what he has divined about the demiurge, has a model upon which to base these lesser gods. These gods copy the demiurge in their creations. (See Benardete, "On Plato's *Timaeus*," p. 56.) The poets, it appears from this perspective, have at best a dim awareness of the divinities set forth by Timaeus. How does what the poets offer us compare with what the Biblical prophets and Biblical revelation offer us? Does the Bible provide us access to the divine—to the divine in its particular manifestations among men, to the divine in its "historical" significance—that the poets simply do not provide us, or do not provide us in as reliable a form? (See Cicero, *On the Commonwealth,* pp. 201 n, 221, 233–34.) Certainly, ancient Christian partisans rooted in the Bible claimed that their revelation was essentially different from what the pagan poets had provided. In some ways, it can be said, St. Augustine (in the opening chapters of *The City of God*) uses the teachings of the pagan philosophers against the gods of the pagan poets. Does he, while "using" the philosophers as he does, fail to exhibit the deference toward received opinion that philosophy tends to show? Does he, as a born-again rhetorician, take from philosophy only what is useful for him, thereby either undermining the cogency of that (philosophy) which he relies upon or calling into question the general position he is defending? Perhaps an analogy would be useful here. It is sometimes said, in support of a more or less skeptical position, "Words don't have meanings; it is people themselves who put meanings into words." Does not this statement presuppose that at least the words *people, meanings,* and *words* have comprehensible meanings in themselves? Perhaps one should approach Augustine's critique in the same fashion.

vi

Timaeus concerned himself with the "revelations" then available to him. He suggested where the named or lesser gods came from, and how—the gods which the poets report. How has Timaeus learned what he knows, for example, about the demiurge? Does he not rely upon something other than what the poets and prophets, conventionally understood, drew upon? Is he not trying to do more than merely substitute his intuition or insight for theirs? Does he do anything other than propose a "revelation" of his own? How else, then, may the divine be ascertained?

Perhaps by working back from what one experiences: something has made all things, including the generated gods? A "theology" thus derived might be replaced in modernity by physics, evolutionary biology, psychology, and astronomy. Or perhaps the divine can be ascertained by going beyond experience—by figuring out, on the basis of the very nature of things, what the divine must be like. In proceeding thus, does one work from what one observes, as well as from the ideas innate in human beings, or only from the ideas?

How, then, *does* Timaeus know what he reports about the demiurge and its doings? A clue is perhaps found in what Alfred North Whitehead says about Aristotle. (It is appropriate that Whitehead should be drawn upon here, since he, as a mathematician and scientist with philosophical interests, may be considered the modern equivalent of Timaeus.) Whitehead says, in *Science and the Modern World* (p. 173):

> Aristotle found it necessary to complete his metaphysics by the introduction of a Prime Mover—God. This, for two reasons, is an important fact in the history of metaphysics. In the first place if we are to accord to anyone the position of the greatest metaphysician, having regard to genius of insight, to general equipment in knowledge, and to the stimulus of his metaphysical ancestry, we must choose Aristotle. Secondly, in his consideration of this metaphysical question he was entirely dispassionate; and he is the last European metaphysician of first-rate importance for whom this claim can be made. After Aristotle, ethical and religious interests began to influence metaphysical conclusions.

Thus, Whitehead seems to suggest, Aristotle was the last man to think clearly about God, using only nature and reason. I will have more to say later about what Whitehead calls "ethical and religious interests," which are touched upon in a Whitehead passage following upon the one I have just quoted (ibid., pp. 173–74; emphasis added):

> . . . The Greek gods who surrounded Aristotle were subordinate metaphysical entities, well within nature. [This, as we shall soon see, may be a Timaean view of things.] Accordingly on the subject of his Prime Mover, he would have no motive, except to follow his metaphysical train of thought whithersoever it led him. It did not lead him very far towards the production of a God available for religious purposes. *It may be doubted whether any properly general metaphysics can ever, without the il-*

licit introduction of other considerations, get much further than Aristotle.
But his conclusion does represent a first step without which no evidence
on a narrower experiential basis can be of much avail in shaping the conception. For nothing, within any limited type of experience, can give intelligence to shape our ideas of any entity at the base of all actual things,
unless the general character of things requires that there be such an entity.

The phrase, Prime Mover, warns us that Aristotle's thought was en-
meshed in the details of an erroneous physics and an erroneous cosmology. In Aristotle's physics special causes were required to sustain the
motions of material things. These could easily be fitted into his system,
provided that the general cosmic motions could be sustained. For then
in relation to the general working system, each thing could be provided
with its true end. Hence the necessity for a Prime Mover who sustains the
motions of the spheres on which depend the adjustment of things.

I will have more to say further on also about the problem of what *does*
sustain "the general cosmic motions." We need not concern ourselves
here with whether modern physics is sound in its assumption that bodies once in motion need nothing to sustain their motion. Nor need we
concern ourselves here with whether the statement I have just quoted
from Whitehead is an adequate account of Aristotle's scheme of things.
It suffices to notice that Whitehead's account of Aristotle *is* suggestive
about the Timaean derivation of the demiurge. (See Whitehead, *The
Aims of Education*, p. 164. See, also, Cicero, *On the Gods*, bk. 2; Shorey,
1:424. See, on Plato's *Laws* and *Timaeus* and Aristotle's *De Caelo*, Benardete, "On Plato's *Timaeus*," p. 164.)

Timaeus seems to derive much of what he says about the workings of
the demiurge, and of other beings thereafter, from his studies of astronomy, physics, biology, etc.—that is, from his studies of the things we see
around us. His prowess as an astronomer is pointed up early in the dialogue. (27A. Here, as elsewhere in this discussion, Plato's *Epinomis* is useful.) This had been preceded by an account, transmitted on this occasion
by Critias, from an Egyptian priest who had said to Solon, an Athenian
(22 C–D):

> There have been and there will be many and diverse destructions of
> mankind, of which the greatest are by fire and water, and lesser ones by
> countless other means. For in truth the story that is told in your country
> [Athens? Greece?] as well as ours, how once upon a time Phaethon, son

of Helios, yoked his father's chariot, and, because he was unable to drive it along the course taken by his father, burned up all that was upon the earth and himself perished by a thunderbolt,—that story, as it is told, has the fashion of a legend, but the truth of it lies in the occurrence of a shifting of the bodies in the heavens which move round the earth, and a destruction of the things on the earth by fierce fire, which recurs at long intervals.

Thus, as we see here, dramatic stories about divinities, and about the offspring of divinities, can be said to have been derived from astronomical or from other natural movements. It might help, in order to understand such things, to have available to us the extensive records of the Egyptians. (Compare the opening pages of the *Phaedrus*, where Socrates discourages recourse to such an interpretation of legends as is resorted to here by the Egyptians. Consider what has to be known—one has to know much if not everything, at least about oneself—if one is to be able to determine whether such a story dealt with a "meterological," a divine, or a psychic phenomenon. See Benardete, "On Plato's *Timaeus*," p. 30.)

vii

Timaeus, in developing his derivations, must begin by distinguishing between that which is "existent always and has no becoming" and that which is "becoming always and never is existent" (27D). It is upon this fundamental distinction (between being and becoming) that such reasoning as his must rest. Also brought to bear upon his investigations are such things as opinions about the appropriate shapes for various objects, with the sphere being considered the best for the cosmos, which is a living creature (33A sq.). Also critical are his uses of mathematics, with quite elaborate proportions utilized in his speculations about the fabrication of the soul of the cosmos (35B–36E).

Does Timaeus' mathematics lead to what he has to say about the cosmos? Or does what he understands, somehow or other, about the cosmos lead to the mathematics he makes so much of here? Consider, in this connection, an observation made in a review of a memoir by Leopold Infeld, a longtime collaborator in physics of Einstein's (*Science*, April 6, 1979, p. 49):

Einstein's estrangement from the mainstream of physics and his opposition to quantum mechanics are a recurrent theme [in the Infeld book], but the puzzle remains. Perhaps Einstein felt that when he created general relativity he heard the voice of God and that he listened in vain for that voice in the noises of contemporary physics. This is anyway the impression left on this reader [of the Infeld book].

We can see, in Timaeus' account, a shadowing over from the "supernatural" into the "natural." In large parts of the dialogue, it is difficult to distinguish between divine causes and nature. (One is reminded of the phrase in the Declaration of Independence, "the Laws of Nature and of Nature's God.") Thus, some things are said by Timaeus to come into existence through necessity (48A). We have noticed that no dates are provided by Timaeus: the developments seem timeless, as if in the very nature of things. (We have also noticed that this is to be contrasted to Critias' dates, vague though they may be [*Critias* 108D]. Perhaps this also indicates, still another way, the difference between a "practical" man like Critias and a more "theoretical" man like Timaeus. But Critias, it should be noticed, was not so practical that he could avoid the political, and perhaps also personal, unsavoriness of his career as one of the Thirty Tyrants.) Considerable emphasis is placed by Timaeus upon the likelihood, not the certainty, of his account. He alerts his listeners to this at the outset and repeats his disclaimer a dozen times. (See, e.g., 29C–D, 30B, 48C–E, 49E–50A, 55D, 57D, 59C–D, 90E. Compare, e.g., 40E, 47A, 52D, 53B–C; Loeb Classical Library edition, p. 110 n.) Does not this disclaimer reflect an effort to reason from what nature provides, rather than an effort to relate what has been definitively provided by some authority, divine or human? Must not any effort to reason from that which nature provides recognize that an infinite variety in things is possible? (See 57D.) Until one can know all, we again wonder, is only probable reasoning possible with respect to nature? (Is this further testimony to the mutual irrefutability of Reason and Revelation? See the opening and closing notes of Anastaplo, *The Constitutionalist*.)

Is the God of Nature still working, not only to keep things going but also to bring new things into existence? Or are all things, including the new things yet to manifest themselves, essentially there in the beginning? Nature does seem to be at the root of things. Is not what is said by Timaeus (e.g., 39D–E), about how all things mesh together, at the basis of physics, both modern and ancient? Is this not critical to an understanding of nature as authoritative? Nature, then, is at the root of things, just as it was (earlier in this dialogue) in Socrates' summary of the *Republic.* The question remains whether Timaeus' is the cosmology that fits in with Socrates' political thought. Is it consistent with this emphasis upon nature to see man as somehow keyed to the heavens? This keying may be seen in the fashioning of man by the star-like lesser gods (42D sq.). This is a natural view of man's emergence which accounts for the special character of man—which recognizes the godlike qualities, or at least aspirations, in him. Is not this combination of the mundane and the heavenly in man the basis of the openness of mankind to poetry, to that fashioning of the concrete in the light of the eternal?

Why did not Timaeus suggest that the demiurge created directly the human beings of this world? For one thing, this suggestion would directly contradict the poetic tradition and thus would be, in a sense, wasteful if not even dangerous. Rather, Timaeus incorporates in his account that which he considers essential or useful or at least acceptable in whatever the poets have provided. Besides, he senses that living (mortal) things operate differently from the other created things in the universe. A kind of natural order may be seen in the way living things operate. Does life on earth seem to have emerged in a way, somehow natural, that the use of the stories of the lesser gods reflects? (I notice in passing that there is in the account of the movement from the emergence of men to the emergence of the lower animals a "reverse Darwinism," just as Ptolemy is a "reverse Copernicus." But the direction of the movement may be secondary: the essential relations may be suggested, no matter which "direction" one considers things to move.)

Furthermore, Timaeus senses (like a careful scientist?) that the prevalence of the named gods reflects *something* which is available to mankind. Such gods are widely dispersed, although the names they go under differ from place to place. (The descendants of such gods, and the doings of such descendants, can be left to the poets to describe [40D].) Timaeus evidently cannot discount as being completely without significance the worldwide attempts to describe the gods in the terms that the poets have used. Certainly, the impersonal divinity of the metaphysicians does not, typically, inspire worship. Religious interests and instincts find expression in particular forms of divinity, revealed or otherwise tailored with a view to local circumstances. (See, e.g., Whitehead, *Science and the Modern World,* pp. 178–79. See, also, Cicero, *On the Nature of the Gods* 1.12.)

viii

Since one can see in the Platonic corpus a variety of approaches to the divine, one may be moved to wonder:

1) What determines what one believes about the divine? Is not what one believes influenced, at least in part, by one's character? Just as Zeus is, in Plato's *Phaedrus,* refashioned as the leading divinity to suit and minister to Phaedrus' inclinations, so the leading divinity is fashioned in the *Timaeus* to suit and minister to Timaeus' inclinations, if not with a view to Socrates' interests as well. Other views or aspects of divinity, appropriate to Socrates' interlocutors, may be seen in other Platonic dialogues—for example, in the *Euthyphro* and in the *Crito* (with its godlike laws). Consider, also, the *Republic,* where common notions about the gods are questioned. In that dialogue, where the doctrine of the ideas is developed, a kind of abstract divinity is taken for granted. (See part 2 of this chapter.)

2) What are the uses of various beliefs about the divine? That is, what do these beliefs tend toward? Are not they likely to have corresponding effects? The beliefs espoused may depend, in part, upon one's circumstances, upon one's immediate purpose, or upon chance. But it is prudent to keep in mind here Cicero's warning, "Piety, like all the other virtues, cannot live on specious pretense and ostentation . . ." (*On the Nature of the Gods* 1.2).

3) What is the relation between politics and religion? Much is made both of the appropriateness of a story associated with the divinity of one's city and of the appropriateness of telling such a story in the city on the feast day of that divinity (21E, 23C–D, 21A, 26E). Even so, Timaeus' account of the gods is given by a stranger, about whom relatively little is told us. (See Benardete, "On Plato's *Timaeus,*" p. 29.) This is an outsider's, not an Athenian's, view of things: particular cities, or peoples, do not matter in Timaeus' account, whereas they do in Critias'. Timaeus' view of divinity is cosmopolitan, drawing (I have suggested) upon what nature teaches, here and elsewhere, now and always.

And yet, however much one's opinion about the divine is influenced by one's character or by one's immediate purposes or by considerations which transcend the interests of particular cities, it seems suggested by the *Timaeus-Critias* exposition that even the most elevated cosmology is grounded in, or framed by, the city. Consider the frame provided for Timaeus' account: a city in words ("the best city") precedes Timaeus' account; a city in deeds (the best city in action) anticipates and then follows Timaeus' account. (Timaeus himself, although not an Athenian, *is* said to come from a well-ordered city.) Is not the political, or at least political philosophy, the setting in which such things as Timaeus' cosmology can exist? Timaeus' interest in political philosophy is limited. Does this mean that he cannot truly understand what he is doing—he cannot grasp the conditions of who he is and what he is doing—and hence he can have, at best, no more than a provisional account of the whole?

ix

A key question remains: What may God be? Perhaps this is *the* question of all philosophy. Certainly, this question is implicit throughout the Platonic dialogues. Is there not an awareness of the divine which informs and shapes all of the opinions about the divine that we have begun to examine? Is there not some *one thing* which is manifested in the diverse opinions we have touched upon here? Consider, for example, what Socrates draws upon in the third book of the *Republic* and elsewhere in order to argue that certain common stories about the gods cannot be true, however they happened to have been developed once upon a time.

Is not the truly divine something that is one, unchanging, and hence anything but diverse? The diversity reflected in men's opinions about the divine reflects the differences among, and the varying limitations of, human beings rather than anything unsettled and variable in the "nature" of the divine itself. Is the divine—an eminently single thing—incomprehensible? Indeed, are there not for human beings three intrinsically incomprehensible things in the universe? (1) There is the demiurge (or overarching divinity, or divine "force"). (2) There is the model, including the unchanging truths of geometry, to which the demiurge looked in fashioning the world (28B–C, 29A–B). (3) There is

the stuff out of which all (visible?) things are made. We have already noticed that it is said by Timaeus that there is something "perplexing and
baffling" in the receptivity of the stuff which is so malleable (51A). (Do
the demiurge and the model somehow come together? Are they, in a
sense, one?)

Why are these three things—the demiurge, the model, and the stuff
—incomprehensible? Partly because we cannot know *their origins.* So
far as we can tell, these three things have always been. There is no thing
outside or before them, by which we can take our bearings in understanding the origins, or cause of the being, of these three things. Thus, it
can be said by Timaeus, "Now to discover the Maker and Father of this
Universe were a task indeed; and having discovered Him, to declare Him
unto all men were a thing impossible" (28C). Or, as Whitehead says,
"God is the ultimate limitation, and His existence is the ultimate irrationality. For no reason can be given for just that limitation which it
stands in His nature to impose. God is not concrete, but He is the
ground for concrete actuality. No reason can be given for the nature of
God, because that nature is the ground of rationality." (*Science and the
Modern World,* p. 178. Consider, also, the William James observation
quoted in section ix of part 1 of chapter 7 of this book. Even so, I do not
believe it salutary to suggest that "the ground of rationality, when
grasped in certain ways, may be the ultimate irrationality." Consider, for
example, that *pistis* that we may naturally build upon. See Anastaplo,
"Lessons for the Student of Law," p. 179.)

It is no accident that Zeus is not quoted at the end of the *Critias.* The
dialogue breaks off just as Zeus is about to speak. Critias, it seems, believed he knew what Zeus would (or did) say in particular circumstances.
But, then, this Athenian had made early in the *Critias* a bold statement,
that it is easier to speak about gods than about men—because we are
more familiar with men and can criticize more minutely whatever is
said about men (107B–E). Critias presumes to report about Zeus (who
was troubled by the misconduct of the people of Atlantis) that he called
all the gods together, at the middle of the cosmos, to announce (it
seems) what he proposed to do about Atlantis (121C). To place Zeus at
the center of the cosmos may be to have Critias' gods (and especially
Zeus as ruler) usurp the place of Timaeus' god (the demiurge, as creator).

Plato, it can be said, knew better than that—and so he breaks off the dialogue before Zeus can speak. (See the epigraph for chapter 5 of this book.) "Zeus" is *not* permitted such a usurpation as Critias, a future tyrant, was about to "lead" in his name. (We are provided, in Critias' anticipation in the *Timaeus,* the end of the war between Atlantis and Athens. That is, we are told earlier what happens after Zeus speaks.) Besides, what Zeus does say to human beings is what all can hear and see—especially if we consider that what Zeus "says" has to be evident primarily in what happens among men. This means, that there may be, in Plato's opinions, no special revelation of the divine will. It may also mean that the reports of the poets about the conversations among gods, such as may be seen in Homer's *Iliad,* are implicitly called into question, especially if speaking (as well as other actions) requires bodies.

Still, we *are* given the direct discourse (in the *Timaeus*) of the demiurge to the lesser gods (41A–D):

> Gods of gods, those works whereof I am framer and father are indissoluble save by my will. For though all that is bound may be dissolved, yet to will to dissolve that which is fairly joined together and in good case were the deed of a wicked one. Wherefore ye also, seeing that ye were generated, are not wholly immortal or indissoluble, yet in no wise shall ye be dissolved nor incur the doom of death, seeing that in my will ye possess a bond greater and more sovereign than the bonds wherewith at your birth, ye were bound together. Now, therefore, what I manifest and declare unto you do ye learn. Three mortal kinds still remain ungenerated; but if these come not into being the Heaven will be imperfect; for it will not contain within itself the whole sum of the kinds of living creatures, yet contain them it must if it is to be fully perfect. But if by my doing these creatures came into existence and partook of life, they would be made equal unto gods; in order, therefore, that they may be mortal and that this World-all may be truly All, do ye turn yourselves, as Nature directs, to the work of fashioning these living creatures, imitating the power showed by me in my generating of you. Now so much of them as it is proper to designate "immortal," the part we call divine which rules supreme in those who are fain to follow justice always and yourselves, that part I will deliver unto you when I have sown it and given it origin. For the rest, do ye weave together the mortal with the immortal, and thereby fashion and generate living creatures, and give them food that they may grow, and when they waste away receive them to yourselves again.

(See, also, Benardete, "On Plato's *Timaeus*," p. 41.) Is not this kind of discourse, of a general "philosophical" character, radically different from the sort of thing (the battle orders, so to speak) that Zeus was believed by Critias to have said on a special occasion? Has what the demiurge is reported by Timaeus to say always been said or ordained by that nature which images for us the doings and arrangements of the demiurge?

Three things—the demiurge, the model, and the stuff—I have suggested, are in principle incomprehensible. All other things are subject to investigation to a degree or in ways that these three things are not. The origins of other things, for example, *can* be known (at least, in a probable sense). But even the other things we are familiar with are "secondarily" incomprehensible—in that they are made up of or have been modeled upon or have been made by things which are themselves intrinsically incomprehensible. For example, the motives of the demiurge must remain somewhat mysterious. It *is* said of him, by Timaeus, "He was good, and in him that is good no envy ariseth ever concerning anything; and being devoid of envy He desired that all should be, so far as possible, like himself" (29E). This is, we are told, "the supreme originating principle of Becoming and the Cosmos," according to the wise. We are also told, "For God desired that, so far as possible, all things should be good and nothing evil" (30A). These motives, which remind us of the first chapter of *Genesis*, in which God is reported to have regarded various of His creations as "good," *do* remain somewhat mysterious. Did the demiurge need to create, based on an eternal model, in order to *possess* that which He can otherwise do "no more" than contemplate? (See Benardete, "On Plato's *Timaeus*," p. 32.) Indeed, does the demiurge surpass His eternal model, in that the "working" model includes mortal beings (as we saw in the long quotation from 41B) and hence is complete in a way that the eternal model could not be? Such an ambition on the part of the demiurge would be mysterious indeed. (See, on whether things are better for man's disobedience, Maimonides, *Guide for the Perplexed*, pt. 1, chap. 2; John Milton, *Paradise Lost*, 12.469 sq.)

The divine itself is inevitably diverse in the opinions of men (just as justice is), in part because of men's varying talents in quite different circumstances. (See Cicero, *On the Commonwealth*, p. 203 f.) The divine, I have suggested, is so difficult to grasp that only diverse accounts of it can emerge—and we need all of these accounts if we are to be able to have a reliable indication of how divine things and divine doings truly are. (See Benardete, "On Plato's *Timaeus*," p. 50.)

Certainly, not every soul is capable of grasping all that *can* be said about the divine—and so, mythology is made use of (28B–C). But what of Timaeus' account? Socrates gives his preliminary assessment of it at the beginning of the *Critias,* when he refers to it as theatrical (albeit theater on a grand scale?). (This is reminiscent of what Socrates says in the *Meno* about the "tragic" style of Gorgias [70C, 76D–E].) Is Timaeus' account regarded by Socrates as a theatrical—that is, fanciful and dramatic —counterpart to what Socrates had said (two days before) about the Ideas in the *Republic*?

As a fanciful account it is entertaining (however difficult) and otherwise useful. But perhaps it does not suffice. Just as Plato knew better than Critias about what (and whether) Zeus speaks to men, so perhaps Plato knows better than Timaeus about what the divine can be said to be and to do. Why do I say "Plato" and not "Socrates" here? The fifth member of this party is missing, we notice at the outset of the *Timaeus.* And the missing fifth member (who would complete "the hand" that seeks to grasp these matters) is said to be ill. One is reminded of the *Phaedo,* the Platonic dialogue reporting Socrates' death, where it is said that Plato himself is missing because *he* is ill. For this and other reasons, perhaps, it has long been suggested by students of the *Timaeus* that Plato is the missing fifth member of this gathering. (See Loeb Classical Library edition, p. 16 n. 1.) This "Plato" can be considered a Socrates who had had the advantage of being able to reflect upon what Socrates thought and heard and upon what had happened to him. And this observer is artist enough to be able to present these matters effectively in writing.

What would Plato have said when his time to speak came? Hermocrates is not recorded as giving an account either. But perhaps *he* can be understood as the most inarticulate member of this gathering, someone who contributes little in the way of opinions but is still useful almost as "matter"—perhaps like the stuff out of which the universe is made. But back to Plato: what *would* he have said? Do we not have his position in the view presented of all this together (including the doings of the various characters and what is done to them)? Does Plato have a comprehensive view of divinity which incorporates, one way or another, all the opinions men generate about the divine? It is this comprehensive view that Plato provides his readers an opportunity to secure for themselves. They are thus encouraged to aspire to a grasp of the one thing which unites and informs all these diverse opinions of the divine.

I return, then, to the familiar question, "What did 'the Greeks' believe about this or that?" Or, rather, I return to the question of what we should make of such a question. Recourse to such a question ("What did 'the Greeks' believe . . ?") is no substitute for thinking through problems. Are we not obliged to think about the things that the Greeks, including Plato's characters, thought about if we are to begin to understand them—or, at least, to begin to be clear about which questions matter? *To think* means, among other things, that one's city or one's character or other influences or factors cannot be ultimately decisive in determining what one opines. One should be aware of such things and how they affect one's opinions, but one must be able to look beyond—above or beneath—them if one is to understand how things truly are.

One is not thinking, or thinking for oneself, if the Greeks are used as authorities for the opinions one happens to have. But neither should the Greeks be regarded of use only *as* authorities, and therefore to be rejected because we try to reject all authority as such. Rather, we must consider their arguments and assess their evidence, whether with respect to the divine or to the human. That is, we must try to think—and we must hope we can begin to do as well as the best of them did.

PART TWO. On the Doctrine of the Ideas

*Why call ye Me [whom ye see] good; none is good [the
model of good] but God only [whom ye do not see]?*
—Jesus (as expounded by Immanuel Kant)

i

A CONTEMPORARY CLASSICIST, Eva T. H. Brann, in surveying Plato's
Republic, reports that "the greatest Socratic term is *eídos* (plural *eíde*)
and its equivalent *idéa*" (Introduction to the Raymond Larson translation, p. xxx). She goes on to observe (pp. xxx–xxxi):

> The most common translation [of this term] is "form," for the English
> word "idea" has . . . no longer anything to do with the Platonic "Theory
> of Ideas." . . . "Idea" to us means a mental object, something our mind
> contains or grasps or peels off from reality, a dim image or a concept or
> an *abstraction.* The *eide,* in contrast, are emphatically not abstractions.
> Although they are intelligible, that is to say, present to the intellect, they
> are not "in our mind." Nor are they meant to be thin or insubstantial; in-
> deed, it is their very character to be substantial, to be rich. This stable,
> self-subsistent plenitude is precisely what Socrates calls "being."

Leo Strauss, in an essay on Plato, was intrigued by the mysteriousness
of *eidos* (*History of Political Philosophy,* p. 27):

> The doctrine of ideas which Socrates expounds to Glaucon is very hard
> to understand; to begin with it is utterly incredible, not to say that it ap-
> pears to be fantastic. Hitherto we have been given to understand that jus-

---

Unless otherwise indicated, the citations in this part of this chapter are to Plato's *Republic.* See, for my suggestions about the Christian form that the Platonic "doctrine of
ideas" takes in Augustine's *De Magistro,* "The Teacher," *The Great Ideas Today* (1997). See,
for additional discussion by me of the matters touched upon here, the review of Subrah-
manyan Chandrasekhar's *Newton's "Principia" for the Common reader* that I am scheduled
to publish in the 1997 volume of *The Great Ideas Today.* See, also, Thomas K. Simpson,
"Science as Mystery: A Speculative Reading of Newton's *Principia,*" *The Great Ideas Today*
(1992), p. 96.

The epigraph is taken from Immanuel Kant, *Fundamental Principles of the Metaphysics of Morals* (Library of Liberal Arts), p. 26. See, on Kant, Anastaplo, *The American
Moralist,* p. 27.

tice is fundamentally a certain character of the human soul, or of the city, i.e., something which is not self-subsisting. Now we are asked to believe that it is self-subsisting, being at home as it were in an entirely different place than human beings and everything else that participates in justice [509B–510A]. No one has ever succeeded in giving a satisfactory or clear account of this doctrine of ideas.

Even so, Mr. Strauss, in his characteristic insistence upon the knowability of the enduring questions, whatever may be said about the availability of conclusive answers to those questions, continues with his own account of the "doctrine of ideas" (ibid., pp. 27–28):

> It is possible, however, to define rather precisely the central difficulty. "Idea" means primarily the looks or shape of a thing; it means then a kind or class of things which are united by the fact that they all possess the same "looks," i.e., the same character and power, or the same "nature"; therewith it means the class-character or the nature of the things belonging to the class in question: the "idea" of a thing is that which we mean by trying to find out the "what" or the "nature" of a thing or a class of things. . . . The connection between "idea" and "nature" appears in the *Republic* from the facts that "the idea of justice" is called "that which is just by nature," and that the ideas in contradistinction to the things which are not ideas or to the sensibly perceived things are said to be "in nature." [501B, 597B–D] This does not explain, however, why the ideas are presented as "separated" from the things which are what they are by participating in an idea or, in other words, why "dogness" (the class character of dogs) should be "the true dog."

Mr. Strauss suggests "two kinds of phenomena" [which] lend support to Socrates' assertion about the "separateness" of the ideas (ibid., p. 28; emphasis added):

> In the first place the mathematical things as such can never be found among sensible things: no line drawn on sand or paper is a line as meant by the mathematician. Secondly and above all, what we mean by justice and kindred things is not as such, in its purity or perfection, necessarily found in human beings or societies; *it rather seems that what is meant by justice transcends everything which men can ever achieve;* precisely the justest men were and are the ones most aware of the shortcomings of their justice. Socrates seems to say that what is patently true of mathe-

matical things and of the virtues is true universally: there is an idea of the bed or the table just as of the circle and of justice.

Mr. Strauss then adds (ibid., p. 28): "Now while it is obviously reasonable to say that a perfect circle or perfect justice transcends everything which can ever be seen, it is hard to say that the perfect bed is something on which no man can ever rest." Not even the perfect man?

Be this as it may, "Glaukon and Adeimantos accept this doctrine of ideas with relative ease . . ." (ibid., p. 28). Why this is so is suggested in the last passage I take here from the Strauss account (ibid., pp. 28–29):

> Yet while Glaukon and Adeimantos cannot be credited with a genuine understanding of the doctrine of ideas, they have heard, and in a way they know, that there are gods like *Dike* or Right, [536B, 487A] and *Nike* or Victory who is not this or that victory or this or that statue of Nike but a self-subsisting being which is the cause of every victory and which is of unbelievable splendor. More generally, they know that there are gods—self-subsisting beings which are the causes of everything good, which are of unbelievable splendor, and which cannot be apprehended by the senses since they never change their "form." [379A–B, 380D sq.] This is not to deny that there is a profound difference between the gods as understood in the "theology" [379A] of the *Republic* and the ideas, or that in the *Republic* the gods are in a way replaced by the ideas. It is merely to assert that those who accept that theology and draw all conclusions from it are likely to arrive at the doctrine of ideas.

That the "doctrine of ideas" is difficult to explain is also evident upon recalling Aristotle's touching upon it, almost as if in passing, in the sixth chapter of the first book of the *Nicomachean Ethics*. About this, too, it can be said that "no one has ever succeeded in giving a satisfactory or clear account. . . ." One thing may seem to be clear in this *Ethics* chapter, however, and that is that Aristotle seems to separate himself from the Platonic Socrates, if only to permit himself to approach the moral virtues as more or less independent of the philosophic enterprise. It does not seem to suit Aristotle's immediate purpose to have the moral virtues regarded as dependent upon standards "which men can [n]ever achieve."

ii

Still, we must wonder how seriously the supposed separation of Aristotle from Plato should be taken. It is difficult for us to be sure about this, certainly with respect to the "doctrine of ideas," inasmuch as the doctrine itself is so difficult to be sure about. Besides, it should be expected, whatever may be sound in the Platonic argument is likely to have been grasped and accepted by Aristotle.

The special relation between Plato and Aristotle is suggested by the "somewhat apocryphal tradition [which] relates that a large audience assembled to hear Plato lecture on the Good." Gradually, we are told, that audience "melted away as [Plato] plunged deeper and deeper into transcendental mathematics, until Aristotle remained the solitary auditor" (Paul Shorey, *Selected Papers,* 2:28).

I return to Leo Strauss briefly, as still another aid to my own preliminary examination of the Idea of the Good in the *Republic.* One of Mr. Strauss's students, Laurence Berns, has observed (in an unpublished paper on Kenneth H. Green's *Jew and Philosopher)* that his teacher considered as the most plausible alternative that "the whole is fundamentally characterized by Platonic-Aristotelian noetic heterogeneity." An affinity between Plato and Aristotle is taken for granted here as it is in the following report (in the same paper) from Mr. Berns:

> In a question period at one of his weekly classes at St. John's College during his last years, a student asked [Leo Strauss], "If you had a chance now to talk to Plato and Aristotle what would you ask them?" Strauss hesitated for a moment, pursed his lips as he often did when gathering his thoughts, and then said, "I think I would ask them whether the development from Galileo and Newton would cause them to modify in any way their teaching about the forms."

(Another useful question [but only if Plato and Aristotle truly became "personally" available] might be, "Where, pray tell, have you been for the past two thousand years?" This could be to the same effect as the Strauss question, even as other perennial issues were also illuminated thereby.)

Mr. Berns's account, following upon the Strauss question which presupposes that Plato and Aristotle are in substantial agreement here, continues with instructive reflections upon the forms themselves:

The elementary meanings of the word form, Greek *eidos,* are looks and class character. Socrates in the *Meno* (72c) speaks of the *eidos* as that through which things are what they are and that towards which one looks in order to give an account of what they are. It is that which determines the being of the object of knowledge at the same time that it constitutes in the knower the knowledge of the object. The *eidos* is what all the instances of a class point to by defect. In modern mathematical physics we have a new kind of formal cause. It is primarily an explanatory principle, the objects of knowledge in certain ways conform to it, or it applies to them, but it no longer is in them.

Furthermore, we are told, the "new kind of formal cause" of "modern mathematical physics":

is a symbolic representation . . . which describes the quantitative or measurable relations between those factors in its instantiations which can be represented together in mathematical symbols. . . . Quantitative relations between different factors constituting corporeal or physical reality, especially the manipulable aspects of that reality, are discovered and explained with unprecedented precision.

Whether we can be more precise than we have been thus far about the forms, or the ideas, remains to be seen.

iii

The Berns-Strauss question, about "the development from Galileo and Newton," does seem to suggest that the Platonic-Aristotelian "teaching about the forms" (of which I have already noticed three or four tentative accounts) might well be affected by modern mathematical physics. What is there about modern science that could raise concerns about the "doctrine of ideas," but in such a way perhaps as to help us be somewhat more precise about that doctrine? It might be useful to begin here with observations by a Russian physicist which can be said to have implicit in them an awareness of the "doctrine of ideas" (A. M. Polyakov, *Gauge Fields and Strings,* p. 1 [emphasis added]):

We have no better way of describing elementary particles than quantum field theory. A quantum field in general is an assembly of an infinite

number of interacting harmonic oscillators. Excitations of such oscillators are associated with particles. The special importance of the harmonic oscillator follows from the fact that its excitation spectrum is
additive.... It is precisely this property that we expect to be true for a system of elementary particles.... All this has the flavor of the XIX century,
when people tried to construct mechanical models for all phenomena. *I
see nothing wrong with it because any nontrivial idea is in a certain sense
correct. The garbage of the past often becomes the treasure of the present
(and vice versa).* For this reason we shall boldly investigate all possible
analogies together with our main problem.

Does modern science somehow deny the universality of its truths?
Perhaps it does this in the sense that it considers its findings always open
to reconsideration, refinement, and even correction (and, in a way, made
into "garbage"), in a way other than that expected from, say, a study of
Aristotelian physics. This openness may be even more of a problem in
the biological sciences, with moderns no longer able to rely upon fixed
species, so much so that chance may help determine what forms of life
develop and what they look like and for how long. Can the *eidos* be
thought of as "at work" (to use Jacob Klein's Aristotelian expression) if
each species is constantly evolving, in different ways in different places
and along unpredictable lines?

The status of teleology (a related issue here) is also affected by modern science. The Aristotelian general view of things, it has been suggested, very much depends upon the eternity of the visible universe.
·(See Strauss, *Natural Right and History*, pp. 7–8.) Related to this in turn,
at least for the Platonic Socrates (as in the *Republic*), is the status of the
Sun in the overall scheme of things, something to which I will return.

In addition, one would expect a "doctrine of ideas" to be much
affected by natural sciences such as ours, which are widely recognized as
remarkably successful, but which have little if anything to do (at least
explicitly) with formal and final causes. (See Thomas Aquinas, *Summa
Theologiae*, 1A, Q. 5, A. 3, on the four causes.) Still, we have noticed, the
Strauss question for Plato and Aristotle does seem to recognize that
there is enough of a material basis for the Forms to make them perhaps
susceptible to the influences of modern science. To this, too, we shall
return.

iv

Critical to our inquiry here is what the Idea of the Good looks like in the *Republic*. The dominant Platonic use of *eidos/idea* does seem to be in the *Republic*. (Little seems to have been done with this term, at least in a philosophic sense, prior to Plato, except among the Pythagoreans and perhaps in Thucydides. See A. E. Taylor, *Varia Socratica*, 1st series, pp. 178 f., 187 f., 246 f.) And in the *Republic, eidos* first comes to view with respect to the good, but not (curiously enough) in the most elevated form of the good. (This is at 357c.) The most elevated form, in this context, would be the goods desired both for their own sake and for their consequences. These had already been referred to in the context, but the term *eidos* was not used there. Rather, *eidos* is introduced when those goods are referred to which are desired only for their consequences (the other two, it is indicated, are also forms of good, but the term *form* is not made explicit with respect to them). This, then, is how *eidos* is introduced in the dialogue (357c):

> And do you see a third form of good, which includes gymnastic exercise, medical treatment when sick as well as the practice of medicine, and the rest of the activities from which money is made? We would say that they are drudgery but beneficial to us, and we would not choose to have them for themselves but for the sake of the wages and whatever else comes out of them.

This form of the good is adulterated by not-good elements which are tolerated for the sake of the consequences, which can indeed be good (such as health).

The last use of *eidos* in the dialogue (at 618A) reminds us, despite the heights to which the *eide* are raised in this dialogue, that *eidos* can find dubious expression. (At one point Socrates can even speak of the forms of vice. [445c. See, also, 449A and 476A.]) The last use of *eidos*, which is in the Myth of Er passage, goes like this (618A–B):

> There were all sorts [of patterns of lives available on the ground before them]; lives of all animals, and, in particular, all the varieties of human lives. There were tyrannies among them, some lasting to the end, others ruined midway, ending both in poverty and exile and in beggary. And

there were lives of men of repute—some for their forms *[eidesi]* and beauty and for strength in general as well as capacity in contests; others for their birth and the virtues of their ancestors—and there were some for men without repute in these things; and the same was the case for women, too. An ordering of the soul was not in them, due to the necessity that a soul become different according to the life it chooses.

It is evident here, as elsewhere, that critical though the forms may be, appearances can certainly be deceptive. Even so, may not the appearances (or forms) of things testify to the very existence (and hence some goodness) of things? (See Thomas Aquinas upon existence itself as good, even when associated with terrible things. *SummaTheologica,* 1a, Q. 5, A.)

v

However deceptive appearances can be, *eidos/idea* does work, it has long been known, from the appearances, or looks, of things. The physical aspect or material substratum of things is thereby recognized as critical—and perhaps also common sense. (This is one reason why *form* may be a better translation than *idea* for *eidos/idea,* however useful it may be, because of the tradition, to continue to make considerable use of *idea* in our discussions.) Perhaps also implicit here is the role of what we call materialism both for human existence and for human understanding. (We can be reminded here of an old problem: what may a disembodied human soul be and do? [This problem is reflected in the alternative question I proposed for Plato and Aristotle.] Consider the implications of the series of *idein,* or the *seeing* of souls by Er, in book 10 of the *Republic.* That verb is not used, by the way, with respect to Odysseus, the most Socratic of the souls described. See 620A.)

Thomas Aquinas can refer to the Platonists' opinion that matter is non-existent (*SummaTheologica,* 1a, Q. 5, A. 3). But do not the looks of things depend somehow, as the more thoughtful Platonists have always known, upon matter? Among the intriguing looks of the *Republic* itself are its one hundred uses of various forms of *eidos/idea.* (We return to this further on.) The central usage of *form/idea* in the *Republic* is related to what we might call *relativism* (at 479A–B):

["Now," Socrates said, "let us address] that good man who doesn't believe that there is anything fair in itself and an *idea* of the beautiful itself, which always stays the same in all respects, but does hold that there are many fair things, this lover of sights who can in no way endure it if anyone asserts the fair is one and the just is one and so on with the rest. 'Now, of these many fair things, you best of men,' we'll say, 'is there any that won't also look ugly? And of the just, any that won't look unjust? And of the holy, any that won't look unholy?'"

"No," [Glaucon] said, "but it's necessary that they look somehow both fair and ugly, and so it is with all the others you ask about."

Much is made of pairs or doubles in this context, perhaps appropriately so considering that this is at the midpoint of the inventory of *eidos/idea* in this dialogue. But we can see, even here, the limits of relativism. For does not "that good man" who is dealt with here by Socrates want to be considered correct in what he says about the nature of things? (One can be reminded of Thrasymachus before his "conversion.") Socrates would even have him addressed as "you best of men," something which the man aspire to deserve to be called—but which has implicit in it an enduring standard of goodness. The sovereign form, we are taught in the *Republic,* is that related to the Good. This is most dramatic, perhaps, in the ascent of the knower, culminating in the Idea of the Good. It is said to be the cause of the right and fair in everything. (See 517c.)

But, it should not be forgotten, the overall context of this discussion *is* an inquiry into the nature of justice. (A. E. Taylor has argued, p. 164, that the *eidos* of a thing means the same as its *phusis* [nature]. It is *not* a group of sensible things. See ibid., p. 178.) A concern with justice is primarily a concern with the ordering of human relations, including (if not even primarily) with respect to the distribution of the material things that happen to be available in a community. Action seems to be critical here, with even philosophy and poetry (and hence nobility) put in the service of justice. This makes prudence vital to all the virtues, as well as to human activities generally.

We are accustomed to hearing the good, the true, and the beautiful spoken of as somehow aspects of one thing. Even so, it should be noticed that both beauty (or the noble) and truth (or at least truth-telling) seem to be subordinated in the *Republic* to morality (or the good).

vi

The divine, too, is dealt with in the *Republic* from the perspective of the good, not primarily from that of either the beautiful or the truthful. This is reflected in the context of the last uses of *eidos/idea,* the context provided by the Myth of Er. We do not see at work there Aristotle's Unmoved Mover, but rather a divinity who cares about, and who rewards and punishes, human beings (if not other living things as well) with a view to the Idea of the Good.

The divine is presented in the *Republic* as the cause of all, with an emphasis placed upon the Sun as somehow exhibiting (if not exerting the power of) the Idea of the Good. (See, also, Sophocles, *Oedipus Tyrannus* 660, on the Sun as the foremost of the gods.) Thus, the Idea of the Good is used to purge poetic or popular accounts of the gods. (Consider the implications of the distinction made by Leo Strauss "between a profound religious thought and a languishing superstition" *What Is Political Philosophy?* p. 21).

One likely consequence of modern science, with perhaps a critical effect on the Platonic-Aristotelian "teaching about the forms," is that it becomes difficult for enlightened human beings to exalt the Sun as Socrates does in the *Republic.* Not only are the material causes and exertions of our sun studied and even harnessed more and more, but there is also a growing acceptance of the existence in the universe of billions upon billions of grander suns (whatever that may mean).

Of course, our sun is still recognized as essential for human life—but artificial lighting and energy sources are no longer inconceivable to replace a burnt-out sun for the earth as well as emigration by the human species to another habitat if the earth should become uninhabitable because of changes in its sun. These prospects are, of course, virtually impossible to anticipate—but to be able to imagine them, with our experience of many other "impossible" technological accomplishments in recent centuries, does suggest how modern science has challenged, if it has not subverted, the ancient teaching about the forms.

vii

But whatever the effects may be of modern science upon the teaching about the forms, if that teaching is sound it can be expected that the forms would somehow keep exerting themselves. We have already noticed this upon considering how even the "relativist" cannot help but look to an enduring standard of excellence.

In our natural sciences, also, the laws of nature (especially when mathematized) may take somewhat the place of the forms, especially laws about motion and the workings of energy. Do such laws appeal to us in part because they partake of the dignity, if not also the effectiveness, of the forms? Those who are proficient in modern science should be helped to show us how the ancient teaching about the forms somehow informs and directs contemporary scientific formulations. (Similarly, did Aristophanes believe that the new philosophic way, however much it challenged the established gods, was bound to make use of gods in some form or another, with the Clouds as one possibility? Consider, also, what was done with Vladimir Lenin's body for more than a half-century by "atheistic" Marxists.)

Whatever the problems with modern science—including its limited self-awareness with respect to its foundations and presuppositions—it does stand for rationality. However much science may blind us to certain things, it is certainly responsible for many splendid achievements which do affect our understanding not only of the universe but also of understanding itself. (Eva T. H. Brann has spoken of "the reverence-producing splendor of modern science and mathematics." Robert L. Stone, ed., *Essays on "The Closing of the American Mind,"* p. 186. See, also, ibid., pp. 225, 267.)

Even so, it should be noticed, the liberation and empowerment that modern science promises and has already (to some extent) delivered are not without grave risks for the survival, let alone the happiness, of the human species. Our current dependence upon chance may be unprecedented, however much "in control" we may seem to be. The instinctive human awareness of, and deference to, the Idea of the Good may continue to benefit even those who have nominally repudiated such things.

viii

I return to Leo Strauss's instructive question, whether the development from Galileo and Newton would cause Plato and Aristotle to modify in any way their teaching about the forms.

The reverse of this question might also be instructive: What does the teaching about the forms do to the understanding of modern science? It is this which I have just now been touching upon. The presuppositions of modern science do seem to be in need of examination by scientists themselves, however much they are reassured by the remarkable things they have found and done.

Among the presuppositions of these scientists, who alone are likely to be competent enough to grasp what they do, is what is assumed by them about what they are looking for. How will they know they have reached their goal? If there is no ascertainable end-of-the-road, what constitutes progress? (Are we not back in the *Meno* with such questions?) Activity for its own sake may eventually begin to pall—and even the more "success-ful" scientists can become demoralized. (See, on the *ultron*, Anastaplo, *The Artist as Thinker,* pp. 252–53, 355.)

One consequence of all this can be the promotion of disillusionment, which can take the form either of apathy or of desperation. Neither of these is likely to be good either for understanding or for citizenship.

In short, the development of more and more sophisticated methods (very much the instruments of modern science) should not be mistaken for a proper teaching about the forms. Indeed, the forms may continue to have some of their effects, however much they may be systematically concealed by the progressive character of modern science.

ix

I return, however briefly, to Aristotle's discussion of the Platonic Idea of the Good in book 1 of the *Nicomachean Ethics.* He mentions, in the course of that discussion, a column of the goods (1.6; 1096b5).

This Pythagorean list of the principles of the universe is provided by Aristotle in his *Metaphysics* (1.5.6; 986a23–27):

1) ἄπειρον (unlimited)	πέρας (limit)
2) ἄρτιον (even)	περιττὸν (odd)
3) πλῆθος (plurality)	ἕν (unity)
4) ἀριστερόν (left)	δεχιὸν (right)
5) θῆλυ (female)	ἄρρεν (male)
6) κινούμενον (motion)	ἠρεμοῦν (rest)
7) καμπύλον (crooked)	εὐθὺ (straight)
8) σκότος (darkness)	φῶς (light)
9) κακόν (bad, evil)	ἀγαθὸν (good)
10) ἑτερόμηκες (oblong)	τετράγωνον (square)

(Taylor, p. 263, records the tradition that the Pythagoreans made much of *ten* as the sum of the first four natural integers. See, on Aristotle and the Pythagoreans, Klein, *Lectures and Essays,* p. 45 f.)

I must reserve for another occasion a systematic investigation of the Pythagorean ordering of principles, principles which seem to regard the tension of dualism as vital to the world that we can know. But since Aristotle does refer to this list in his consideration of the Platonic teaching about the good, I am encouraged to offer here at least some preliminary speculations about the Pythagorean column of the goods. (Is the dualism seen in this list related to the tension between the noble and the just discussed in part 2 of chapter 7 of this book?)

Perhaps Aristotle tacitly recognizes here the Pythagorean influence upon at least the Platonic vocabulary with respect to the Idea of the Good. (A. E. Taylor talks about the Pythagorean influence on Socrates.) Perhaps more important is the suggestion that the good is somehow dependent upon, or derived from, the other pairs in this list, several of which are more or less "materialistic" in their character.

Should we not be challenged to determine how this Pythagorean list fits together? Why, for example, is not *good* either first or last? Not first, perhaps, because it must be built up to in order to be properly grasped, but not to exist? Then why not last? Perhaps partly because the beginning and end of the list recognize limits as conditions for the existence of everything. The teaching of the *Republic* about the Sun may be anticipated in this list by the placement of *light* immediately before *good,* as if one was needed for the emergence (or at least for the perception) of the other.

The Pythagorean approach to things may be evident in the reliance upon a geometrical figure for the form that the concluding limit of the list would take. But why a square and not, say, a circle? A circle may be harder to imagine as a foundation stone. Besides, we recall the "mystical" tradition associated with the Pythagorean discovery of the irrational character of the square root of certain squares (something that is played with in the *Meno*).

Another tradition has to be reckoned with here: the square was evidently associated by some with the just. But this may make more of the moral orientation, and less of the theoretical, than one expects of the Pythagoreans. Even more intriguing, perhaps, is what might follow if there should indeed be a hundred uses of *eidos/idea* in the *Republic*. This could suggest to the more poetic that Plato decided to "pull a Pythagoras," so to speak, on the Pythagoreans, squaring (or virtually squaring, if my count is off) their table of ten principles. That this might have been done by Plato in the context of a discussion of justice, not in the context of the kind of cosmological discussion that some of the Pythagoreans may have been more prone to, suggests in the ordering of human relations a playful element that is good.

ADDENDUM

The Uses of Eidos and Idea in Plato's Republic

FORMS OF *eidos* (form?) may be found at the following places in Plato's *Republic* (with one or more instances at each place): 357C, 358A, 363E, 376E, 380D, 389B, 392A, 396B–C, 397B–C, 400A, 402C–D, 406C, 413D, 424C, 427A, 432B, 433A, 434B, 434D, 435B–E, 437C–D, 439E, 440E, 445C–D, 449A, 449C, 454A–C, 459D, 475B, 476A, 477C, 477E, 504A, 509D, 510B–D, 511A, 511C, 530C, 532E, 544A, 544C, 559E, 572A, 572C, 580D, 581C, 581E, 584C, 585B, 590A, 590C, 592B, 595A, 596A, 597A–C, 612A, 618A.

Forms of *idea* (idea?) may be found at the following places in Plato's *Republic* (with one or more instances at each place): 369A, 380D–E, 479A, 486D, 505A, 507B, 508A, 508E, 517C, 526E, 534B, 544C, 588C–D, 596B. I have drawn here as elsewhere upon the [duly–corrected] index to the very useful Allan Bloom translation of Plato's *Republic*. See, on *eidos* and the beautiful, Strauss, *On Plato's Banquet,* pp. 25, 145–46, 164 f., 192 f. Consider, also, ibid., pp. 195–96:

> Everthing beautiful is beautiful and something else. The beauty of the *Iliad* is not the beauty of the *Odyssey.* But both poems are beautiful. What is that identical thing which is responsible for any particular thing being beautiful? This is what is traditionally called the concept of beauty, but it is not quite what Plato means. What is the beautiful which we meet in everything beautiful? I will give you a few answers. For example, in Thomas Aquinas the beautiful is that the apprehension of which pleases. This, ultimately, goes back to the Platonic view. In Kant it is that which creates disinterested joy or pleasure. The opposite of that is the view expressed by Stendhal as the promise of happiness; ultimately, this is the Hobbesian view of beauty. The apprehension is not the crucial point. At any rate, we must try to find out what this is which underlies all [that is] beautiful. Plato says that this "universal" alone is truly beautiful—that's the paradox—hence that this "concept" of beauty is the object of eros. For example, let the beautiful be the promise of happiness. Do we not love the promise of happiness as such in every love of a beautiful thing? Is promise of happiness not that beautiful thing which we always love, whereas if we love this particular puppy we do not love another puppy? Is this not the way of understanding what Plato means by the fact that the universally beautiful, the beautiful itself, is the only thing which is truly beautiful?

XII. Aristotle. On the *Nicomachean Ethics*

*They stepped from the strong-benched ship out onto the dry
land [of Ithaca], and first they lifted and carried Odysseus
out of the hollow hull, along with his bed linen and shining
coverlet, and set him down on the sand. He was still bound
fast in sleep. Then they lifted and carried out the possessions, those which the haughty Phaiakians, urged by great-
hearted Athena, had given him, as he set out for home, and
laid them next to the trunk of the olive, all in a pile and
away from the road, lest some wayfarer might come before
Odysseus awoke, and spoil his possessions.*

—Homer

i

HAPPINESS, WE ARE TOLD by Aristotle, is the end of all human activity.
It is that highest good at which all human activity aims. (See 1099a24.) It
is or can be complete, not lacking anything. (See 1176b6.)

Happiness itself can be understood to depend upon a half–dozen
things or conditions. A preliminary survey of the things upon which

---

Unless otherwise indicated, the citations in this chapter are to Aristotle's *Nicomachean Ethics*. See, for additional discussions by me of Aristotle, *The American Moralist*,
p 20; "Slavery and the Constitution," p. 691.

The epigraph is taken from Homer, *Odyssey* 13.116–24. See Plato, *Republic* 620C–D.

happiness depends anticipates my extended discussion here of the last one of them, equipment, before returning in the second half of this chapter to the virtues themselves. (I draw upon all of the *Nicomachean Ethics* in this discussion of problems dealt with by Aristotle primarily in the first half of his treatise. His *Poetics* has been drawn upon in chapter 4 of this book.) Here, first, are the things upon which happiness depends:

1) *Virtues.* This is complicated. Most of the *Ethics* is devoted to an examination of the virtues, moral and intellectual, upon which happiness primarily depends. (See 1099b7.)

2) *Life itself.* The emphasis is upon a "complete life," preferably not a short one. (1098a18. See, also, 1100a3 sq.) Life and pleasure, it seems, are intimately linked (1175a20). Pleasures, as well as pains, can be used as rudders by the artist-in-ethics (or "the architect of the end") to steer the young and thereby to educate them (1152b1, 1172a20).

3) *A city (or community).* This includes the constitution and laws of the city (1179b35 sq.). The city is useful for preserving and training citizens who are, in a sense, among the things that the city uses. (Thus, the citizen cannot properly destroy himself on his own initiative [1138a7 sq.].)

4) *A body—preferably a healthy and beautiful body.* Chance can be important here (1099b4). Self-sufficiency is aimed at, but it can never be complete. (See 1097b8 sq.)

5) *Friends.* This includes the importance of good birth, of family, and of the household. (See 1155a1 sq.) Various kinds of friendship, for various purposes and for different lengths of time, are examined.

6) *Circumstances.* For example, a man who is being tortured is, other things being equal, not as happy as someone who is not being tortured. Virtue alone, we are thereby reminded, is not enough to ensure happiness. (See, e.g., 1100b20 sq., 1153b13 sq.)

7) *Equipment.* This, too, is complicated. It could be understood, for instance, as another way of saying either "body" or "circumstances." We can, by considering equipment at some length, remind ourselves of how "realistic" the "idealistic" ancients could be.

ii

In a sense, various of the half-dozen conditions that I have just listed as things upon which happiness depends could be considered as "equipment," not just the last item—things such as virtue, life itself, friends, and the city. But they, unlike the last item listed, are not *called* equipment by Aristotle. Those things do tend to be desired more for their own sake. (Some parts of the body are called "instrumental" [1110a15]. The body as a whole may be considered instrumental, with a view to certain purposes.) Virtue, life, and friends *can* be considered good in themselves, things to be "pursued even when isolated from others," even as are "intelligence, sight, and certain pleasures and honors" (1096b17). Thus, "life itself is good and pleasant" (1170a25). Thus, also, virtue is called "the greatest of goods" (1169a10). Friends, too, can be desired for themselves, even though friends can be spoken of as "useful people" (1169b24); "no one would choose the whole world on condition of being alone, since man is a political creature" (1169b18).

Consider, on the other hand, how equipment, or certain kinds of external goods, are spoken of. It is indicated at the outset of book 1 that any preparation of equipment takes its bearings from a higher calling. The equipment of horses, for example, is determined by the "art of riding," which in turn is subsumed under strategy (1094a12). Toward the end of book 1 (1101a14), the importance of equipment is summed up in this fashion: "Why then should we not say that he is happy who is active in accordance with complete virtue and is sufficiently equipped with external goods, not for some chance period but throughout a complete life?"

To speak of equipment, then, is to recognize a hierarchy. This means, among other things, that money-making is "undertaken under compulsion"—that it is done not for its own sake but for a higher purpose (1096a5). Again and again, the "final good" is pointed to. (See 1097b8.) This is related to the "function of man." (See 1097b26.) We are also told, "The study of pleasure and pain belongs to the province of the political philosopher; for he is the architect of the end, with a view to which we call one thing bad and another good without qualification" (1152b1).

iii

What is to be done with respect to property considered primarily as equipment? Virtue can direct one how to deal with various kinds of property in various circumstances. The virtue of justice helps to determine, for example, how property is to be acquired and transferred.

Certain virtues can even depend upon property, if one is to exercise them. Liberality determines how property is to be shared with friends and others; magnificence, which can be related to piety in some instances, determines how one's great wealth is to be used. (See, e.g., 1123a6.) The magnificent man knows how to spend large sums tastefully for the enrichment of all (1122a34). We can see here, in the practice of liberality and in the practice of magnificence, uses of property for the sake of a good life. So it can be said that "it is impossible, or not easy, to do noble acts without the proper equipment." (1099b1. We recall the armor evidently required by Achilles for his greatest exploits.)

These uses of property are in addition to the uses of property for survival and for certain pleasures or comforts. (The virtue of temperance can be critical, as well as the virtue of courage, in that one is in a condition to fight.) Thus, property can be seen here as useful for the sake of life itself. Care is needed, of course: "drink or food which is above or below a certain amount destroys the health, while that which is proportionate both produces and increases and preserves it" (1104a18). Care is needed also lest property become a hindrance rather than a help. Thus, one's property can be thrown overboard to save oneself on a ship (1110a10). Certainly, wealth has undone people (1094b19). It is not something good for its own sake. The effects of its presence or absence can depend upon circumstances. For example, some who have nothing may be the best soldiers, because they are ready to face great dangers and sell their life for trifling gains (1117b17). On the other hand, professional soldiers, who are moved only by prospect of gain, can become unreliable when their numbers or weapons are inferior to those of the enemy (1116b17).

iv

The importance of property in helping to determine or shape one's circumstance, as well as the condition of one's body and one's relations with one's friends, is evident throughout the *Ethics*. The importance of circumstances is what helps make prudence critical both for virtue and for happiness. Prudence is related to deliberations about what is good and expedient, especially with respect to the good life in general (1140a27). "Practical wisdom," we are told, "must be a reasoned and true state or capacity to act with regard to human goods" (1140b20). Prudence, we have been told by Edmund Burke, is "the god of this lower world." (See Anastaplo, *The Constitutionalist*, p. 783.)

Prudence does reflect a recognition of the role of bodies and the requirements of (including the taxes collected by) cities which are, to a considerable extent, dedicated to the survival and health of living bodies. The dictates of prudence may even be seen in the management of what we would call "spiritual matters." (See, on how temples should be placed, Aristotle, *Politics* 1331a24–31, 1335b13–17; chapter 3, addendum, sections v–vi. See, also, Anastaplo, "Church and State," pp. 61, 109.)

Furthermore, prudence recognizes (and is required by) the fact that not all can be expected to understand everything that a privileged few can. It recognizes the limited prospects of most people, the limited views of most with respect to happiness, which many do tend to see primarily in terms of pleasure as ordinarily understood.

Even so, the opinions of the many with respect to these matters are not without foundation. If various physical pleasures are added to an otherwise good life, the total effect is usually greater (and better) than it would have been—provided, however, that the more important activities necessary for a truly good life are not impeded by such pleasures. (See 1097b20. See, also, 1172b26 sq.)

v

We have seen that the need for equipment reflects critical human limitations. Several requirements should be met if virtue is to be fully supplemented as a basis for happiness. We have also seen that these limitations, which are due in part to our mortality and hence to our dependence upon the body, are intimately related to the vital role among us of prudence.

Since bodies, the cities that serve them, and the circumstances that affect them all differ as much as they do, it does not make sense to have inflexible rules by which to conduct ourselves. Inflexible rules presuppose fixed quantities or entities (as in mathematics). But bodies are so constituted that no one activity is always pleasant (1154b20). The variety of circumstances is such, for example, that stumbling can be worse than pleurisy on some occasions (1138b2). To deal with bodies is, among other things, to deal with chance to a considerable degree.

Prudence is aware of, and responds to, that infinite variety which material things—whether bodies or cities—exhibit, that variety which again and again requires adjustments in our responses. This means that the subject-matter of ethics does not permit of precise treatment. Aristotle reminds us of this repeatedly. (See, e.g., 1094b11 sq., 1098a26, 1103b34 sq., 1165a13.)

vi

Much more precision is available to the student of the unchanging things which are the concern of scientific inquiry and of metaphysics. (See, e.g., bk. 6, chap. 3.) It is to the grasp of eternal things that the contemplative life is primarily directed, that activity which is best for happiness. This is the most human if not even a divine life—or so it would seem from the following passage in which may be found things we have noticed (1177a11–19):

> If happiness is activity in accordance with virtue, it is reasonable that it should be in accordance with the highest virtue; and this will be that of the best thing in us. Whether it be reason or something else that is this element which is thought to be our natural ruler and guide and to take thought of things noble and divine, whether it be itself also divine or only the most divine element in us, the activity of this in accordance with its proper virtue will be perfect happiness. That this activity is contemplation we have already said.

This emphasis upon the reasonable conforms with the fact that the contemplative life has the least need for equipment or property, that property which is, in a sense, an a-rational element in the fabric of human existence. Thus, it is said that "the excellence of the reason" "would seem . . . to need external equipment but little, or less than moral virtue does" (1178a20–25).

Of course, the contemplative life does require some property, so long as one is concerned with and dependent upon life on earth. (See 1178b32 sq.) Still, the physical needs of such a human being are likely to be moderate. Perhaps these needs are further restrained because he knows that "man is not the best thing in the world" (1141a23). Should not this recognition curtail his bodily as well as his social desires (including that ambition which will be discussed further on in this chapter)?

Yet, it should be remembered, "it is for himself most of all that each man wishes what is good" (1159a12). Existence is good to the virtuous man, so much so that he does not want, in order to gain even the greatest goods, to become someone else (1166a18 sq.). And is not to be oneself (at least as a human being) somehow to be, or at least to have been, associated with a body in need of sustenance and other support?

vii

Much of what I have said thus far in this chapter is summed up by the following quite practical comment by Aristotle in book 7 (1153b13–20):

> The chief good would be some pleasure, though most pleasures might perhaps be bad without qualification. And for this reason all men think that the happy life is pleasant and weave pleasure into their ideal of happiness—and reasonably too; for no activity is perfect when it is impeded, and happiness is a perfect thing; this is why the happy man needs the goods of the body and external goods, i.e., those of fortune, viz. in order that he may not be impeded in these ways. Those who say that the victim on the rack or the man who falls into great misfortunes is happy if he is good, are, whether they mean to or not, talking nonsense.

Thus, it would seem, virtue (including intellectual virtue) is not so self-sufficient, or sufficient enough in making one happy, that it is in no need at all of equipment. So much is external equipment needed in all walks of life that some people mistakenly identify happiness with good fortune. (1099b8. See, also, 1153b20.) This is not unlike those who, in post-classical times, would identify happiness (or salvation) as dependent primarily if not exclusively upon grace.

The Aristotelian approach to these matters, which is in part natural and hence "pragmatic," is to be contrasted with approaches that see virtue—in the form, say, of a determined good will, or in the form of a confession of the true faith—as in itself sufficient for happiness. In either case, prudence is depreciated, if not altogether discarded. We may even be told that it suffices, if one is to be happy (indeed eternally happy) that one believe and act as one should, irrespective of the circumstances and consequences. That one is a "victim on the rack" should not matter—indeed, some have borne witness, it may even enhance one's merit and hence one's reward.

We can see in Aristotle a more prosaic approach than these more "idealistic" alternatives to the virtues, especially the moral virtues to which the happiness of most people is keyed. We turn now, in order to see what the moral virtues do look like, to how they are organized in the *Nicomachean Ethics*. (See, on the "idealistic" alternatives, Anastaplo, *The American Moralist*, p. 27.)

viii

There are discussed, in books 3, 4, and 5 of the *Ethics*, eleven moral virtues distributed among seven categories. The seven categories are (to adopt W. D. Ross's designations) the following (with numbering added here):

1. Courage
2. Temperance
3. The virtues concerned with money
4. The virtues concerned with honor
5. The virtue concerned with anger
6. The virtues of social intercourse
7. Justice

Another categorization could combine, as we shall see, courage and temperance, on the one hand, and the virtues concerned with anger and with social intercourse, on the other hand, resulting in five categories.

The eleven moral virtues surveyed by Aristotle in books 3–5 of the *Ethics* are the following (with the Ross vocabulary set forth first in each case):

1. Courage
2. Temperance (Self-control)
3. Liberality (Generosity)
4. Magnificence
5. Pride (High-mindedness; Magnanimity; Greatsouledness)
6. Ambition and unambitiousness as the extremes of a nameless virtue
7. Good temper (Gentleness)
8. Friendliness
9. Truthfulness
10. Ready wit (Wittiness)
11. Justice

(A quasi-virtue, shame, is considered between ready wit and justice.)

One recognized Aristotelian contribution to moral philosophy has been to encourage us to regard each of these virtues as separate, or at least as separable. (Aristotle thereby refines, perhaps, the approach taken by Gorgias.) This draws upon the general opinion that it is possible for a man to have, or to exhibit, some of these virtues but not others. Still, may there not be something to the Platonic assumption that the virtues are interrelated, however much Aristotle (at least in this context) resists reducing all of the moral virtues to one only (that is, to prudence)?

Even so, an interrelatedness among the virtues is reflected in our expectation that a principle of order may be discerned for the sequence supplied by Aristotle. We are confident that his is not a haphazard arrangement, even though we may be far from sure about what his ordering principle is, except that the virtues may be unified in their contributions to happiness. (Was the number of the moral virtues intended to recall "The Eleven," the administrators, chosen in Athens by lot, who were in charge of the prison and executions? The Eleven were, in effect, the official executors of the moral judgments of the city. See, for example, Plato, *Apology* 37 B–C.)

ix

The array of moral virtues is framed by the two most complex of the eleven virtues, courage and justice.

The complexity of these two virtues is suggested by the particularly extended discussion allocated to each of them. It is suggested as well by the complications in their names. Various things are called courage, which are not quite that; and justice has both a more general and a more specific form, with several branches of the latter.

We sense that courage (along with temperance) is fundamental, as providing a foundation for the development of the moral virtues, and we sense that justice is fundamental, as illuminating for the moral virtues their ultimate objective or end in the city. Both courage and justice are needed if the city is to exist—if it is to be able to preserve itself and if it is truly to be a city and hence worth preserving. The virtues of social intercourse, which are related to friendship, anticipate justice or are somehow related to it. Do we see in justice a social amalgam of what courage and temperance permit, aim at, or are guided by?

When Aristotle discusses the greatsouledness which may be seen in μεγαλοφυχία, the term usually translated as *pride*, the other virtues casually taken for granted are courage and justice. We can see again and again that these two virtues define the limits within which the moral virtues range. They further resemble each other in that both of them, more than the others, can be regarded ultimately as another's good, however much all of the virtues are good for their practitioners.

We move from the framing of the moral virtues by courage and justice to a preliminary suggestion of how the two halves of the Aristotelian array fit together. The first half of the moral virtues are directed, for the most part, toward material things (including one's body) and their management. This kind of concern extends even to glimpses of how the greatsouled man talks and walks in his pride. The orientation in the discussion of the first five virtues seems more "personal," however socially important virtues such as courage, liberality, and magnificence may be.

In the second half of the moral virtues the emphasis is less upon how one is "personally" and more upon how one is "socially," upon how one carries on with others. Thus, although courage (the first of the virtues) does refer to how a man deals with others, he can be seen as standing alone against others; gentleness (the first of the second half of the virtues) very much looks to how he deals with others. This dealing with others culminates for the second half of the array in justice, whereas the standing-alone culminates for the first half of the array in greatsouledness, seen in the man who is of all moral actors the most nearly self-sufficient.

Critical to the greatsouled man is his self-assessment: he is what he is, conducting himself as he should, no matter what others think. Similarly, acts of courage and of temperance may be called for even in circumstances where it cannot be expected that others would ever hear of those acts. Others may benefit from these, as well as they do from one's liberality and magnificence, but the "personal" character of the activity may be more critical here than in the virtues concerned with anger and social intercourse.

x

Central to the array of the specific virtues is a concern with honor: ambition and lack of ambition are listed as extremes of a nameless virtue.

The greatsouled (or highminded) man, although he is worthy of the highest honors, is not primarily concerned with honor or ambition but with doing properly the things that one should be honored for in a well-ordered community. The virtue of pride, or greatsouledness, which is immediately before the central virtue keyed to ambition, includes a lack of concern about either ambition or honor. Yet the proper response to ambition, with its deference to public opinion, lies at the core of the workings of the moral virtues in a city. (Does gentleness, the virtue immediately after the central [nameless] virtue pertaining to ambition, tend to counter the effects of pride, the greatsouledness-inclined virtue that precedes the central virtue in Aristotle's list?)

The brevity of the discussion of this central but nameless virtue—the shortest discussion allotted to any of the moral virtues—invites quotation of the passage in its entirety (1125b1–25):

> There seems to be in the sphere of honour also, as was said in our first remarks on the subject [1123b24–27], a virtue which would appear to be related to pride as liberality is to magnificence. For neither of these has

anything to do with the grand scale, but both dispose us as is right with regard to middling and unimportant objects; as in getting and giving of wealth there is a mean and an excess and defect, so too honour may be desired more than is right, or less, or from the right sources and in the right way. We blame both the ambitious man as aiming at honour more than is right and from wrong sources, and the unambitious man as not willing to be honoured even for noble reasons. But sometimes we praise the ambitious man as being manly and a lover of what is noble, and the unambitious man as being moderate and self-controlled, as we said in our first treatment of the subject [1107b33]. Evidently, since "fond of such and such an object" has more than one meaning, we do not assign the term "ambition" or "love of honour" always to the same thing, but when we praise the quality we think of the man who loves honour more than most people, and when we blame it we think of him who loves it more than is right. The mean being without a name, the extremes seem to dispute for its place as though that were vacant by default. But where there is excess and defect, there is also an intermediate; now men desire honour both more than they should and less; therefore it is possible also to do so as one should; at all events this is the state of character that is praised, being an unnamed mean in respect to honour. Relatively to ambition it seems to be unambitiousness, and relatively to unambitiousness it seems to be ambition, while relatively to both severally it seems in a sense to be both together. This appears to be true of the other virtues also. But in this case the extremes seem to be contradictories because the mean has not received a name.

The reliance upon honor, at the core of the moral virtues, points up the political importance, or orientation, of those virtues. They are not only for one's self-satisfaction, personal fulfillment, or "salvation." A civic perspective informs our grasp of all of the moral virtues. But, as we have noticed, the model of the greatsouled man reminds us that the ultimate justification for honor is that it can encourage self-assessment and self-direction, as one is led to do the things that make one truly worthy of honor. (These observations hearken back to the reservations recorded in the opening pages of the *Ethics* about any pursuit of honor for its own sake.) Moreover, we must ultimately depend upon the citizen who wants to be a certain kind of human being, whether or not anyone is watching.

It is emphasized by Aristotle in the brief discussion of this central virtue that it *is* nameless, the only one of the eleven virtues thus singled out emphatically. Why should he have so arranged matters as to drama-tize this virtue as nameless? Names reflect the settled opinions of the community about things. But, it seems, there is something inherently ambiguous about this virtue, the virtue that may "make things happen." Indeed, we may even be alerted to this kind of problem with all of the moral virtues by a dramatization of namelessness in the presentation of the central virtue. The status, or at least the precision, of the moral virtues may thereby be called into question, especially from the perspec-tive of anyone adept in the intellectual virtues.

Is not a rough general awareness usually relied upon, and perhaps even sufficient, for the typical moral virtue? A strict scientific, or theo-retical, approach should not be expected in such matters, an approach which would require and result in precise namings. (A full discussion of this would have to consider at length what Aristotle has to say in book 1 of the *Ethics* about the Platonic account of the Idea of the Good, some-thing that is touched upon in part two of chapter 11 of this book.) The vying of extremes for possession of this unnamed virtue suggests that assessments of moral activities may all too often depend in part upon "where one is coming from."

The namelessness of the central virtue also reminds us that the moral virtues have developed out of the everyday practice from which they have taken their names. This is not to deny that nature may have been at work in their emergence, but that is possible without a people's being self-conscious. It is only after critical conditions exist, and perhaps have existed for some time—conditions that depend in large part upon es-tablished moral virtues—that a philosophical inquiry into, and refine-ment of, the moral virtues can take place.

Such refinement may be seen in the way that the moral virtues are arranged. The philosopher, in the ordering of his discussion of what the various virtues look like in practice, says more about them than the typ-ical practitioner can appreciate.

xi

We return now to more detail on how Aristotle moves from one virtue to another. The sequence, we have seen, builds upon courage and temperance. We know from everyday experience that these two virtues may be separated in practice, that a man can be courageous without being temperate (consider the brave soldier on a drunken furlough) or that a man can be temperate without being courageous (consider the timid man who watches his weight).

We must wonder, however, whether these two virtues are not the proper foundation for all the other moral virtues. Certainly, these two virtues represent the preliminary shaping of *fear* and *desire* (which can lead, all too often, to cowardice and greed). Courage and temperance are said by Aristotle to be the virtues of the irrational part, however much reason may have to be used in determining what should be done about fear and desire. (See 1117b22.) Children, in particular, it seems, need to have both fear and desire curbed if something noteworthy is to be made of their lives.

If courage and temperance are the foundations, then civic concerns must build on personal traits. We can recognize here the perennial problem of the proper relation between the city and the family, that family which helps prepare human beings for citizenship. We know that Sophocles' *Antigone,* with its defiance of the law for the sake of a brother, addresses this problem one way; Plato's *Republic,* with its community of wives and children, another way.

xii

Aristotle's sequence of the moral virtues continues. The virtues concerned with money follow upon the virtue of temperance. Rather than spending on oneself, one should spend properly on others; rather than be self-indulgent, one should use one's property in a manner reflecting a sound character in oneself.

Then there come the virtues concerned with honor. Greatsouledness follows naturally upon magnificence. Magnificence makes much of grandeur, using money instead of virtue to achieve the desired effect. The greatsouled man is, so to speak, the real thing: he is that which the wealthy man with his tasteful expenditures on a grand scale properly appears to be. These two pairs of virtues (liberality and magnificence, on the one hand; pride and the unnamed response to ambition, on the other) are brought together by Aristotle in a ratio: "There seems to be in the sphere of honor . . . a virtue which would appear to be related to pride as liberality is to magnificence." (See 1125b1. See, also, 1107b24 sq. The typical citizen, even with the Greek term before him, is not apt to appreciate the greatsouled element in μεγαλοψυχία, making *pride* the more comfortable translation for him.)

Just as the virtues concerned with money may be keyed to the virtue of temperance, so the virtues concerned with honor may be keyed to the virtue of courage. One should use one's courage in the service of the community, making oneself worthy of honor. In some people, one suspects, the prospects of honor or of dishonor can counteract to a considerable extent the influence of fear. Just as the virtues concerned with money guide one to a proper paying out to others, so the virtues concerned with honor guide one to a proper gathering in from others (that is, one is paid in the best available "coin of the realm").

Following immediately upon the virtues concerned with honor and hence ambition is the virtue concerned with anger. We have noticed that courage may be at the root of ambition—and anger is easily, if not naturally, provoked by both courage and ambition. Does not the virtue of gentleness help moderate the competition for honors? Anger should not be altogether extinguished, however, since it not only helps one to brave death in battle but it also helps to fuel the proper indignation sometimes needed if justice is to be pursued.

Then there come the virtues concerned with social intercourse. These are related to the friendship made so much of in books 8 and 9 of the *Ethics*. In a way, people care more for these virtues, most of the time, than for the others. Once honor has been put in proper perspective, with anger sufficiently curbed, a satisfying social intercourse can be developed.

Finally, there is the virtue of justice. The other ten virtues have to be developed first because one aspect of justice incorporates all the other virtues, at least in their social dimensions. Then there is justice in the particular sense having to do with transactions of one kind or another. Justice-in-its-general-form and particular justice are related to one another, especially as they both take their bearings by the common good and often by the law. Justice, then, can be seen as the culmination of the moral virtues in their communal manifestations, just as greatsouledness can be seen as the culmination of the moral virtues in their highest human manifestation.

xiii

Whether the moral virtues are themselves the highest form of human excellence depends upon the status among us of the intellectual virtues, the discussion of which Aristotle turns to in book 6. The authority of the intellectual virtues may be seen not only in the way the moral virtues are organized in the *Ethics* but also in what Aristotle indicates about the significance of names.

Consider, for example, what we have noticed about the uses of names in the ordering of the virtues. The first of the moral virtues, courage, has to be distinguished from several other things that look like it and bear the same name in everyday parlance; the central moral virtue is a nameless virtue dependent upon honor, with honor itself being a kind of naming of a man by the community or public opinion; and the final moral virtue, justice, incorporates under one name related but different things vital to the well-being of the community.

It can be important to know what the names of things are. Honor is less determinable, less knowable, than either courage or justice, it would seem. This working with, and continual reworking of, names points beyond the moral virtues to the intellectual virtues.

The human passions may well have a cognitive element at their core, although that may be difficult to discern in some cases. If the opinion underlying a passion is addressed, what happens to the passion? If nothing happens, then we may be dealing with a kind of insanity that cannot be treated except perhaps by physical (including chemical) means.

This brings us to major questions which can be little more than mentioned here: How critical, in Aristotle, is the understanding for virtue? To what extent, or in what way, are the moral virtues grounded in nature? (These are questions that may be important for the *Rhetoric* as well as for the *Ethics*.) These questions are illuminated by what Aristotle says in the *Ethics* about shame in book 4 and about continence in book 7. What does it mean, for example, that a man can appear to recognize something as wrong and yet still do it? Can he, in these circumstances, truly know either what is wrong or what he is doing?

The cognitive element in the virtues may best be seen in Aristotle's discussion of justice, which sometimes requires sustained and intricate calculations. It may be seen as well in the confident self-knowledge of the greatsouled man. Further indicative of the cognitive element in the virtues may be how Aristotle arranges the moral virtues, something that we have just begun to examine.

This is related to the effort I have made throughout this book to examine the intimate relation between the thinker and the artist, including the artist who devotes himself to the creation and maintenance of a moral community and the thinker who draws upon the intellectual virtues in ordering, relying on, and describing the moral virtues. (See Anastaplo, "Lessons for the Student of Law," p. 179. See, also, my article in volume 28 of the *Loyola University of Chicago Law Journal*, "Individualism, Professional Ethics, and the Sense of Community: From Runnymede to a London Telephone Booth." This includes a discussion of Milton's *Paradise Lost*.)

XIII. Raphael

PART ONE. On *The School of Athens*

O Sancte Socrate ora pro nobis!
—Erasmus

i

ANY CAREFUL READING OF Raffaello Sanzio's *The School of Athens* should remind us how little we usually see in most pictures, even in those pictures we are quite familiar with. A study of *The School of Athens*, with its attendant pictures, permits us to review several of the artists, thinkers, and subjects touched upon in this book, subjects touched upon in our consideration of the movement from Homer to Plato/Aristotle. (It is convenient, if not even providential, for us that the *Timaeus* and the *Ethics* are prominent in *The School of Athens*.)

The general context of Raphael's work is the period, or movement (especially in Italy), we know as the Renaissance. That period was accompanied elsewhere in Europe by what we know as the Reformation.

The reader is urged to consult a photograph of Raphael's *The School of Athens* while reading this chapter.

The epigraph ("Saint Socrates, pray for us") is taken from Erasmus, *The Colloquies* (Chicago: University of Chicago Press, 1965), p. 68.

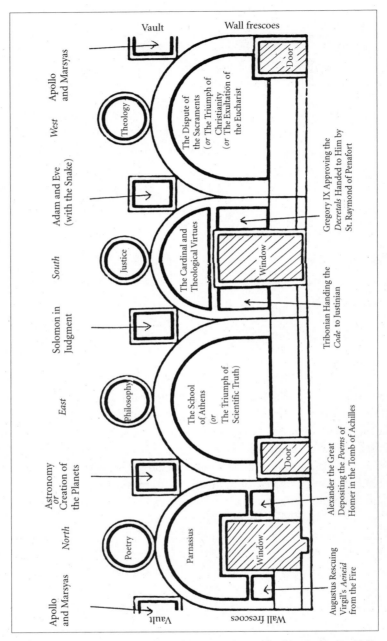

The scheme of various of the representations by Raphael in the *Stanza della Segnatura*, The Vatican

In fact, Raphael and Martin Luther, who can be considered leaders of their respective movements, were born in the same year, 1483. (It is believed that both were once in Rome at the same time, 1511, while Raphael was working in the Vatican room which I will be visiting here.) It is useful to remember as well that Tomás de Torquemada, the most celebrated of the Grand Inquisitors of Spain, practiced his own art during the lifetime of Luther and Raphael.

The esteem in which Raphael was held by his contemporaries—he even had for many of them the aura of sanctity, it seems—may be indicated by the willingness of people to believe that the day of his death in 1520, just like the day of his birth in 1483, was Good Friday. (See, e.g., Vasari, pp. 232–33.)

ii

The immediate context of *The School of Athens* and the related pictures is the papal apartment on the second floor of the Vatican Palace. Julius II, a learned, strong-minded and cosmopolitan pope, set in motion the decoration of four rooms under the supervision of Raphael, who was then a young man newly arrived in Rome from the town of Urbino, where his father too had been a painter. Raphael brought with him (as a protege of his fellow townsman and eminent architect, Donato Bramante) the reputation of an artistic genius. The work he did in the Vatican rooms—either directly himself (beginning in 1509) or through his disciples working from his designs—included pictures generally regarded as the culmination of his art. The four rooms are known as the *Stanze* of Raphael, with the *Stanza della Segnatura* (the one in which *The School of Athens* is to be found) perhaps the finest of them all. It has been said that with the *Stanze* of Raphael we reach the culmination of monumental painting in Italy. It has also been said that the *Stanza della Segnatura* of Raphael and the Sistine Chapel of Michelangelo, which are a short walk from each other in the Vatican, are the two most famous decorated rooms in the world. (The *Stanza della Segnatura* evidently takes its name from the fact that this room came to be used as a place for the signing of papal documents of state. There is remarkable work by Raphael in the *Heliodorus* room as well. "Centuries later another genius,

Goethe, said that no one who had not seen the Sistine Chapel can have a complete conception of what a single man can accomplish." Masson, p. 470.)

Among the differences between Raphael and Michelangelo is that Raphael appeared much more a conduit, so to speak, for the thought of others. It was true of Raphael, as it seems to be of every great artist, that he could execute whatever he conceived of. But it also seems true that the critical selection of subjects for the *Stanza della Segnatura* was done by someone else—to some extent by the pope himself, to some extent by learned cardinals associated with the pope. This is not to suggest that Raphael did not make vital adjustments as he went along, especially as he got into the spirit of the subjects of this room. It is well to keep in mind that although Raphael is believed to have been hardly literate himself, "he remained forever receptive to the inspirations from learned humanists, Neo-Platonists, cultivated churchmen, and art-loving popes" (Karl Joachim Weintraub, p. 3). Thus, one is left with such questions as whether the thought of the *Stanza della Segnatura*, and especially of *The School of Athens*, is consistent with the sentiments suggested by the piety evident in, say, the famous paintings of the Madonna by Raphael. To what extent, and in what ways, may the artist be moved to say more than he himself may explicitly understand? It has been said of Raphael that although he was "very much his own man," he was "yet the eclectic who subsumed other valuable stimulations in his own style" (ibid., p. 4).

Illustrative of Raphael's remarkable power of assimilation is the array of subjects to be seen in the *Stanza della Segnatura,* subjects developed on large frescoes after having been anticipated in the vault above. Those four subjects have been described in this fashion by Mr. Weintraub (p. 5):

> The rich allegorical-historical representations of the ceiling decoration center on Philosophy, Justice, Poetry and Theology, while the main wall frescoes move from the pictorial summation of human wisdom in the School of Athens, past the panel on the cardinal virtues . . . to the Parnassus panel in which Apollo and the Muses are being approached by the great poets, and the whole ends with the great vision of the Disputa over the Sacrament on the altar, centered between the great popes, bishops and theologians, over whom preside God, Christ, and the Dove, amid a semicircle of apostles and saints. It is almost a pictorial Summa in which the Church, as the great mediator, brings into one view the human truth

of Philosophy, Olympian Beauty, the Good of Virtue and Law, and the exaltation of the Sacrament and Christian Faith.

We should at once add that Philosophy and Theology are opposite one another in this room, with Philosophy on the east wall and Theology on the west wall. That leaves the north and south walls of the room for Poetry and Justice, respectively. These placements, one suspects, are not simply arbitrary—and hence they bear thinking about. (A sketch is provided, with this chapter, of the scheme of the representations by Raphael in the *Stanza della Segnatura*.)

Also instructive is the disposition of Raphael's body after his death. He was buried in the Pantheon, a great pagan monument from the Roman empire, which had been converted into a Christian church. Not only that, but his body was placed in an ancient Roman sarcophagus, on top of which a cross was added. Thus, we can see, Raphael's remarkable power of assimilation extended even to his final resting place. Someone knew what he was doing when he considered it fitting to adapt a pagan tomb for the burial place of "the divine Raphael." (See, for Raphael's appellation, George Bernard Shaw, 2:932.)

iii

We proceed now to an examination of the *Stanza della Segnatura*, especially of how its parts are related to one another. At the very top of the room is a group of angels or children dancing around the escutcheon of an earlier pope. This ensemble seems to have preceded the other things now visible in the room; it does not seem to have anything to do with the themes suggested on the four sides of the room, except perhaps that it may remind the visitor of the ecclesiastical auspices of the entire enterprise evident in the palace in which this room is located.

Various scholars speak of the subjects illustrated in this room as representations of the Good, the True, and the Beautiful. This is related to the Neo-Platonic orientation of the day that they also speak of, with Theology and Philosophy both serving the Truth. (One is reminded also of Dante, with his portrayals of the Good, the True, and the Beautiful— but, it seems, with a more "Aristotelian" cast in Dante's case—with the result perhaps of his regarding Theology as serving the Good more than the True, however congruent these three—the Good, the True, and the Beautiful—may be at the highest level. I myself am not confident either as to what distinguishes Aristotle from Plato here or as to how lesser mortals can reasonably choose between them whenever they do seem to differ.)

There is in the vault (or ceiling) of this room, over each of the four walls, a circular fresco which presents, in a somewhat abstract form, the subject that is "spelled out" in a much more concrete way on the wall below. The circular frescoes in the vault were evidently already there, at least in part, when Raphael began working below—and thus certain fundamental relations were for him among the "givens" he had to work with. But then, as I have already indicated, much of his career can be seen as an adaptation to pre-established conditions.

The two larger walls and hence the dominant sides of the room are those where Theology and Philosophy are to be found. (The Theology fresco, it seems, was the first one of the four walls painted by Raphael.) One can see the artist facing a critical question posed by this room: What is the relation of Philosophy to Theology? The things portrayed in the other two, considerably smaller, wall frescoes—Poetry and Justice (or Law)—can be seen to connect Philosophy and Theology. Religion may be seen (especially perhaps by the Neo-Platonists) as an artistic adaptation of the truth of philosophy to the interests, passions, and limitations of ordinary people; and justice may be seen to be required to help keep Philosophy and Theology in the proper relation to one another in practice.

In accordance with these suggestions is the observation that the principal Poetry and Justice frescoes do not take up all of the wall available to them. The lower part of the Poetry wall is devoted to depictions of the Emperor Augustus and of Alexander the Great, and the lower part (an even greater part) of the Justice wall is devoted to depictions of the Emperor Justinian and of Pope Gregory IX. The Augustus-Alexander scenes remind us of the political order upon which art depends and of the political uses to which art may be put. The Justinian-Gregory scenes remind us of the implementations by leaders, whether emperor or pope, of the principles of justice which should govern both the empire and the church. The political underpinnings of the harmonizing enterprises, Poetry and Justice, which make it possible for Philosophy and Theology to "co-exist," are thereby quietly indicated.

Let us now return to the vault. I have mentioned the circular frescoes associated with each wall. Each of them displays a woman, attended either by small angels or, in the case of Philosophy, by two small children *and* by two small statues of the many-breasted goddess of fertility, Diana of Ephesus. More can be said about each of these circular frescoes when we turn to the major frescoes below them. Something should be said now, instead, about the rectangular scenes which so lie in the curves of the vault as to connect the major frescoes below. (There are at least eight other little scenes in the vault which I have disregarded in this chapter. I must disregard as well most of the scenes under *The School of Athens* and *The Disputa*.) We now move around the vault, noticing the rectangular connecting scenes.

Philosophy is connected with Justice through *Solomon in Judgment* and with Poetry through *Astronomy* (or *Creation of the Planets*). The Solomon scene shows the ruler having to decide which woman is to get the disputed baby; the Astronomy scene shows a woman (or a female divinity) either studying the planets or setting them in motion. Thus, it seems, the just ruler needs philosophy in order to be able to do right. Thus, it also seems, the artist needs philosophy if he is to secure a reliable understanding of the natural order. Conversely, philosophy may depend upon the political order for its effective existence, and it may depend upon poetry in its descriptions of things, and especially of the origins of things.

Poetry is connected with Philosophy, as we have just seen, through the planetary depiction and with Theology through *Apollo and Marsyas*. (Marsyas is the mortal who dared to challenge Apollo to a musical contest. He is portrayed here as bound to the stake in preparation for the flaying he earned for his presumptuousness. [See Herodotus, *History* 7.26.] Apollo appears three times in this room, probably more than any other major figure. He may be seen in the *Marsyas* scene in the vault, in the *Parnassus* fresco, and as a statue in the *School of Athens* fresco.) Not only does Poetry depend upon Philosophy for the grander schemes depicted in art, but also it depends upon Theology for restraints upon art. Or, put another way, the artist needs to be reminded of the limits of his adventuresomeness.

Justice is connected with Philosophy, as we have seen, through the Solomon depiction and with Theology through *Adam and Eve*. Adam and Eve are shown with the snake. Thus, on the one hand, the judgment required by justice turns out to be a happy one (with the true mother identified and the baby restored to her); on the other hand, the fall of man is to be reckoned with. The happy judgment is in the panel connected with Philosophy—and seems to have been made possible by Solomonic wisdom. The unhappy judgment (that is, the condemnation of mankind) is in the panel connected with Theology—and hence can be seen to have been influenced by a given theological view of the world, a view which provides at the same time means for the eventual redemption of mankind.

Theology, then, has the grimmest flanking in the depictions set forth above. On one side is the fall of man, on the other is the flaying of Marsyas. Is it because of the teachings of theology that things look grim? Or is it because things are "naturally" grim that theology must provide as it does? (One can be reminded here of Plato's *Euthyphro*.) But, then, there is theology and theology: the Christian version sees all men as doomed since Adam and Eve unless there is an extraordinary divine intervention, while the pagan version assumes that if one acts as one should (avoiding, for example, the presumptuousness of a Marsyas) one may be more or less invulnerable and even happy (at least so long as one's natural powers remain). (The discussion of *equipment* in chapter 12 of this book recalls the Aristotelian recognition of the dependence of even the virtuous human being upon circumstances.)

iv

A Christian version of theology is offered in the *Disputa* fresco. It is appropriate to start our detailed analysis in this room with *The Disputa,* for it assumes the ecclesiastical authority that made all this possible. (A better name for the fresco may be *The Triumph of Christianity*—but it is now more convenient to use the misnomer.)

The juxtaposition (or as some would say today, the confrontation) of the *Disputa* and the *School of Athens* frescoes heightens the challenge of this room. Not only are these the two largest frescoes in the room, but there are several indications of affinities between them. Thus, they depict roughly, perhaps even exactly, the same number of people; they both have marble floors underfoot, with rectangular patterns in the foreground; they have stairs leading down—four steps in *The School of Athens* (related to the Four Causes or to the Four Cardinal Virtues, or to both), three steps in *The Disputa* (related to the Three Theological Virtues or to the Trinity, with three and a half at one point: a comment perhaps upon the status of Mary?); the bottom half of the fresco in each case is devoted to earthly activity, while the upper half is devoted to divine matters; and they each have a man with one arm pointing upward—and these arms "happen" to be directly across from each other in the room. Indeed, the similarities are such that if the one fresco is usefully called *The School of Athens,* the other could well be called *The School of Jerusalem* (even though it is Jerusalem mediated by Rome). (Perhaps the misnomer, *The Disputa,* is clung to because it reflects a modern view of the nature of religious discourse. Is "disputa" more appropriate for the activities depicted in *The School of Athens*?)

The Disputa is said to exhibit still early artistic influences upon Raphael. But it is hardly prudent to make much of the temporal *sequence* of paintings executed by an artist, for he may have planned his works long in advance of their execution. Is it not safer for us to assume that *The Disputa* was painted with the subsequently painted *The School of Athens* in mind? And if so, the artist (or his principal guide) can be considered to have wanted to say something about such things as the character of the unity to be found in the "world-view" drawn upon in each of these two frescoes.

A line dropped from the clearly marked center of the arch in *The Disputa* falls across the overarching God, the enthroned Jesus, the Dove and, further down, the Monstrance on the altar. (In *The School of Athens* a comparable line falls between Plato and Aristotle, touching nothing at all.) Somehow, in *The Disputa,* everything in the heavens above or on the earth below turns around the Persons and Objects along its central line. The people in the heavenly array (drawing for the most part upon figures in the Old and New Testaments) present a fixed, perhaps even static unity (with Saint Peter and Saint Paul herding them all in, so to speak). The people in the earthly array—the church figures in everyday life—seem almost a disorganized rabble by comparison, with no one providing unity to the community. (See, on how *The Disputa* "works" and the importance of the Monstrance on the altar, Camesasca, *All the Frescoes of Raphael,* 1:13–14.)

At first glance, *The Disputa* may be more "impressive" than *The School of Athens,* and may appear more unified. But the unity I have noticed, along the middle vertically, does not conceal—in fact, it may be intended to accentuate—the naturally unbridgeable gulf between earth and heaven. (Does this, perhaps even more than the stage of development of Raphael's style, have something to do with the lack of depth, or the flatness, of this picture?) One can almost conclude that if one is not left with duality one way, one will get it another way. Might there not be in *The School of Athens* a more natural unity, rooted in an explicit recognition of an inevitable duality?

In *The Disputa* that which is below (the everyday life of mankind) pales in significance in the light of what is above. Is this related to the fact that what is presented below has the immediate appearance of being "inside," even as it is set "outside"? There is a considerable amount of stone piled up in the background, which has been said to be for the rebuilding of St. Peter's. (See Masson, pp. 437–38.) The man next to the altar pointing up deals with people and with circumstances which make what *is* above to be authoritative. (The comparable pointing-up in *The School of Athens* does not have the same significance: what is above there simply does not seem as critical to what is below. In neither picture, it seems, does anyone below look up; nor does anyone above look down.) The relations among the people below in *The Disputa* seem more tense, even "emotional," than do the relations in *The School of Athens.* Earthly activity is subordinated to the overall religious purpose or meaning. (A contemporary artist has spoken to me of "a creepy religious feeling" about *The Disputa.*) All of the figures that matter in *The Disputa* rest on a solid cloud which comes just about at the level of the top line of heads in *The School of Athens.* This, too, would indicate that the "world-view" of *The Disputa,* or of Christianity, depends upon something that is pictorially, and literally, supernatural. There is about the heavenly array, thus superimposed, something dreamlike, or like an apparition. That array is to be found where the statues of the gods of mythology are placed in *The School of Athens.*

Both *The Disputa* and *The School of Athens* display a considerable use of intellectual aids, such as books. But in *The Disputa* most of those books are to be seen scattered about underfoot. Does the subordination of everything to what is envisioned above tend to disparage the works of the human mind? Certainly, the Renaissance, with its revival of classical learning, made much more of works of the mind as things to be treasured. Perhaps all this has something to do with someone's decision to place the Theological panels on the west wall (the wall of the setting sun), while the Philosophical panels are placed on the east wall. It may be no accident either that the part of the philosophical enterprise nearest to the viewer in *The School of Athens* is that which has to do with mathematics and the physical sciences. This observation in turn depends upon the fact that there is no clear, unobstructed path between the viewer and the central figures in *The School of Athens*. (About this, too, I will have to say much more further on.) In *The Disputa*, on the other hand, there is a wide-open path for all viewers to the altar here on earth below, whatever barriers there may be to an ascent to the realm of the exalted above. (The placing of the Philosophy and Theology frescoes could be explained, if need be, by observing that Athens is to the east and Rome to the west. On the other hand, would not the altar of a Christian Church ordinarily have been at the east end of the building?)

v

The *Parnassus* fresco, with its portrayal of the arts and especially the art of poetry, suggests how art can be used to help move mankind from the most lowly to the most exalted things. (The *Justice* fresco, on the opposite wall, may also do this, in its way, but in a far less impressive, or obvious, manner.) After all, it is the artist (including the artist in the form of the prophet) who can depict for mankind the splendid things hidden from normal human vision here on earth.

The *Parnassus* fresco is the only one among the four major frescoes in this room freely to combine historical figures and mythological characters (aside from statues). Apollo with his lyre is central to the scene, but the others (except for the Muses immediately around Apollo) operate pretty much on their own. Homer seems the dominant figure among the mortals; Dante is quite noticeable next to him. (There seems to me an affinity between the way this Apollo is presented and the traditional depiction of Dionysus. It may be significant that both gods have been long associated with Delphi. Also Dionysian is the way that females can be made so much of in this scene. See, on Delphi, part 2 of chapter 3 of this book.)

The figures in the *Parnassus* fresco seem closer to us physically than those in either *The Disputa* or *The School of Athens*. Does not art tend to project more of a sense of immediacy? Certainly, the figures in *Parnassus* seem larger, if only in that the space there is much more filled with bodies. Yet there are only one-half of the number of bodies in *Parnassus* compared to either *The Disputa* or *The School of Athens*. Why should there be one-half? Does art, with its reliance upon imitation, somehow duplicate things?

In any event, the *Parnassus* fresco is the only one of the four which shows the figures flowing continuously from low to high and back again. Artists use mundane images to describe the most elevated things in order to permit us to see the most mundane things fully.

Also, this is the only one of the four principal frescoes in this room to be set on the earth itself, without any man-made things underfoot. The artist does depend upon nature. He is a minister of nature. Nature, in its most obvious sense, may be seen in the *Parnassus* fresco—that is, in the form of rocks, grass, and trees.

A different kind of nature, evident in the workings of the mind, may be seen in *The School of Athens* fresco, where the study of nature is pointed up, primarily with a view to understanding nature, but perhaps also with a view to permitting us both to be guided in our conduct by nature and to use it to better the material life of mankind (as may be seen in the magnificent building in which the philosophic activity is housed). It is to this fresco that we can at last turn in order to begin its proper examination, having been brought to it by the artist. One must wonder, of course, whether any artist's understanding of philosophy is bound to be limited, if only by the artist's natural reliance upon the concrete or the particular.

vi

The intimate relation between philosophy and nature—for without an explicit awareness of nature, philosophy is unlikely if not impossible— this intimate relation is testified to in the Philosophy depictions in this room. Thus, in the circular presentation of Philosophy in the vault, there is the motto, "Causarum Cognitio" (Knowledge of Causes). In that scene Philosophy holds two books, whose titles are *Moralis* and *Naturalis*, with *Moralis* held vertically over the horizontal *Naturalis*. Below, in *The School of Athens*, Plato's book (his *Timaeus*) is held vertically, while Aristotle's book (his *Ethica*) is held more or less horizontally. There is a circularity evident here: above, it is indicated that morality depends upon (stands upon) nature; below, it is indicated that that study of nature (including of the planets and the origins of things) found in the *Timaeus* somehow stands upon an ethical foundation. Indeed, there may be something natural about such circularity or interdependence.

The following account of *The School of Athens* should be useful as an introduction to our examination of various features of this fresco (*The Vatican: Spirit and Art of Christian Rome*, p. 114):

> [It] shows an imagined meeting of the most famous philosophers of ancient times, with Plato and Aristotle, the leaders of Greek thought, presiding, under the arches and vaults of a vast basilica designed by Bramante and prefiguring his design for Saint Peter's. In the short space of time that had elapsed between the painting of the previous fresco [*The Disputa*] and the present one [*The School of Athens*], Raphael had gained complete mastery of the technique. His style has lost all trace of uncertainty and is fully sixteenth-century. Here again are a number of portraits: Plato is Leonardo da Vinci; Euclid is Bramante, measuring with a pair of compasses a geometrical design drawn on a slate; beside him, in the right-hand corner, stand Raphael himself, wearing a black cap, and, it is thought, Sodoma in a white cloak. Meditating alone in the foreground is Heraclitus, the pessimist, a powerful idealized portrait of Michelangelo, inspired by the prophets of the Sistine Chapel and especially by the Isaiah. . . .
>
> It is interesting to compare this fresco with *The Disputa*. The unfinished church in which the meeting of the theologians is taking place is complemented by the vision of Paradise, as natural theology is completed by divine revelation; in *The School of Athens* the hall is indeed finished but the sky is empty, because philosophy alone cannot lead to the understanding of revealed mysteries.

Even so, one need not get the impression from *The School of Athens* that there is anything particularly troublesome about the relative bareness of the upper half of this picture. The men conversing in the lower half of the picture do not seem concerned that they are limited to their own resources. (I will say more further on about the one possible exception to this.) There *are* gods portrayed in the upper half of *The School of Athens,* in the form of statues of Apollo and Athena—but they seem more or less honorary, perhaps reminders of the excellence toward which human beings can aspire. There is, of course, a duality in the divine, with one divinity male and nude, the other female and clothed. (No sovereign deity is to be seen.) It can well be added here that the *Stanza della Segnatura* does show philosophy as quite compatible with theology, with each enjoying an honored place in this room.

I have already noticed that the number of persons in *The Disputa* (excluding the angels) may be exactly the same as the number of persons in *The School of Athens* (excluding the statues of Apollo, Athena, and others). But there are additional, perhaps even more startling, numerical relations between the two frescoes. There are, in the heavenly array in *The Disputa,* seventeen persons, if the Holy Spirit, in the form of a Dove, is included. And in the top level of men in *The School of Athens,* there are thirty-four persons depicted, with Plato and Aristotle the central figures. (It could be said that there are only thirty-three on that level, since one man *is* moving down from the top step; but he could he thought related to the ambiguous status of the Dove as a person in *The Disputa.* Besides, one man may also be seen moving up.) It can therefore be said to be suggested by the heavenly array in *The Disputa* that *seventeen* is the key to extraordinary (if not supernatural) understanding. (There may be other indications of this as well.) If so, the thirty-four (or twice-seventeen) in the top level in *The School of Athens* indicates that there may be for philosophy, at least at first glance or from the conventional point of view, two principal ways of presenting the *natural* understanding, the Platonic and the Aristotelian. (It can also be noticed that the *fifty-seven* so important in both frescoes is the seventeenth prime number, if [like the ancient Greeks] we do not regard *one* as a number. Why fifty-seven and not fifty-eight? By not counting the cherub-like figure in the left-hand margin of *The School of Athens,* and by not counting, for this purpose, the Dove in *The Disputa.* A relaxed playfulness may be implicit in all this.)

It should be instructive to notice the kind of people lined up on each side of the picture, in its entirety. They are divided almost equally: there are twenty-nine (or thirty, depending on the status of the cherub) on Plato's side of the picture, twenty-eight on Aristotle's side (with the more poetic Apollo on Plato's side and the more prudent Athena on Aristotle's side). Plato does hold the place of honor, on Aristotle's right. Among the people on Plato's side of the picture is someone who is probably Socrates, who is shown talking to a small group which includes the only man in a military helmet. (This warrior has been identified variously as Alcibiades, Xenophon, and Alexander. I am inclined to consider him Alcibiades, with Xenophon the young man in blue. Whoever he is, his body's oddly twisted stance shows him as torn between listening to Socrates and getting on with his adventures elsewhere.)

Whatever the division between Plato and Aristotle, there is a comfortable unity in this picture, exhibiting that marvelous harmonizing effect of which Raphael was capable. The beginning of an explanation of how this unity is achieved is suggested by Michael Levey (*From Giotto to Cézanne*, p. 112):

> The philosophers in the *School of Athens* are Michelangelesque in stature but serene in mood; and serenity comes partly from the intervals between the groups of figures, partly from the spacious vaulting which curves high above them, framing without constricting, and conceived as grandly as they are.

Or, as a sculptor (Phyllis Kresnoff) remarked to me in recalling this fresco, the figures have a sculpted quality (again Michelangelo was referred to), seeming to walk right out of the wall. This sculptor also remembered the richness of the colors—which is a revealing recollection since I am always surprised, upon seeing this painting in the Vatican, by how subdued (even faded) its colors appear. (I have not seen the *Stanza della Segnatura* since it has been rehabilitated.) Perhaps the way the colors are put together do make them seem more vivid in retrospect than they physically are. In addition, Raphael's use of whites not only brings the colors out but also helps tie together the parts of the picture, and especially the two levels. The whites suggest a flow from the lower left-hand corner to the upper middle and then back across to the lower right-hand corner. One way or another, the figures are presented in a relaxed opened-up circle.

Who these men are supposed to be does leave room for speculation. The name, *The School of Athens* (not Raphael's title), has been associated with it over the centuries—but not because it was believed that all of these people had ever been in Athens. Rather, what these men represent—the various kinds of inquiry related to philosophy—comes down to us primarily through, or because of, Athens. This *is* an urban setting—and Athens is *the* city associated with philosophy. We are again reminded also of what Thucydides' Pericles said about Athens as the School of Hellas. (Only in this fresco is space more or less enclosed. Even so, architects tell me that a building could not be arranged as this one is, that it is an illusion that Raphael has created. These and other illusions, such as the sense of being both inside and outside, remind us of the painter's ability to suggest *being* by the use of *appearances*.)

The civilizing effect of the city seems to be recognized by the artist. We have already noticed the political underpinnings for both the Poetry and the Justice frescoes. In *The School of Athens* we are reminded of the human aggressiveness which must be held in check—for we see there the only violence portrayed in the four major frescoes. Behind the helmeted figure, and immediately under Apollo, there are bas reliefs of young nude men fighting and of a centaur (or satyr?) seizing a struggling woman. (There is also the head of Medusa on the shield of Athena. And, we recall, Apollo is shown, in the vault, as responsible for the violence done to Marsyas.)

Why should violence be thus portrayed here? Is it that only philosophy, through any city which it may guide, can properly curb violence? Or is it that violence is something that philosophy (outside a limited circle) can do no more than contain at times, that it takes something else (perhaps the means available to Poetry and Christian Theology, itself grounded in a kind of poetry) to master, if not even to eliminate, the darker passions? Is violence somehow intrinsic to the pagan (if not the human) way of life outside of the academy? (On the other hand, is it not argued in Plato's *Laws* that the good tend to be safe and happy? May not this also be said to be the teaching, or at least the hope, of the Declaration of Independence? In both cases, *goodness* includes *prudence*.)

vii

The limitations of philosophy may be further suggested by the way that the viewer of *The School of Athens* (who is taken to be a Christian?) is obstructed from direct access to the central figures, Plato and Aristotle. Sprawled on the steps, immediately impeding Aristotle's movement down and forward, is Diogenes; and, further on, brooding at a marble block "desk," is the Heraclitus said to have been modeled on Michelangelo (and supposedly employing the sculpture-like style picked up by Raphael from what he had seen of work-in-progress in the Sistine Chapel). Diogenes is half-naked, shoeless, while Heraclitus, fully clothed, is one of only two men in the picture with boots on (the other being the warrior).

The people obstructing the paths of Plato and Aristotle are, respectively, Aristotle-like in appearance (but with something of the dress of Plato), and Plato-like in appearance (but with something of the dress of Aristotle). That is, they can be considered the extremes (if not even caricatures) of Aristotle and of Plato. Plato and Aristotle together can move in harmony, and progress (or learn and teach effectively), even as they differ. (Their differences are suggested by the gestures employed by each, Plato pointing upwards and Aristotle's horizontal motion suggesting a more sober approach, if not even an earthly one.) But, an aspect of Plato (or Socrates), radicalized (in Diogenes), can prove obstructive for Aristotle, and an aspect of Aristotle, radicalized (in Heraclitus), can prove obstructive for Plato. The barefoot, half-naked Diogenes can even be considered a Socrates gone mad, while Socrates himself (if that is who it is) is shown as completely clothed (with *his* feet not in view). (Diogenes Laertius' account of Diogenes is instructive.)

Furthermore, Diogenes can be seen as an extreme in moralism (and in this he can prove troublesome for an Aristotle who made so much of ethics), while Heraclitus can be seen as an extreme in materialism (and in this he can prove troublesome for a Plato who made so much of cosmology, as in the *Timaeus*). It is appropriate, then, that the Heraclitus figure should be placed as the central figure down on the level of the mathematicians and physical scientists. One must wonder, further, whether there is something about what Michelangelo has seen or done (for it is Michelangelo, we again notice, who seems to have provided the inspiration for Raphael here)—one must wonder whether there is something about Michelangelo (and hence Heraclitus), with the glorification of the body, which suggests problems for the Platonic approach. (It is fitting, considering the Socratic strictures against art in Plato's *Republic,* that an artist should provide *the* challenge to Plato. Is it not irrelevant to our inquiry that Heraclitus may have been something of an afterthought? Was not the Heraclitean challenge likely to suggest itself as Raphael developed what he was painting? I suspect that Raphael mulled over things and learned much during the years that he worked on these frescoes.)

Michelangelo's glorification of the body would not be enough, of course, to account for the brooding, if not even menacing, character of the Heraclitus figure. For the Christianity in which Michelangelo's then-current work was steeped made much as well of the vulnerability of the body. This may have contributed to the temperamental difficulties for which Michelangelo was notorious (especially as distinguished from Raphael, who was known for good temper and graciousness).

Indeed, one must wonder, had Christianity made more (than does philosophy) of the passions exhibited by the iconoclastic Diogenes and by the pessimistic Heraclitus? Consider, for example, the affinity in the three major frescoes between the three prominent figures who are only half-clothed: Diogenes in *The School of Athens,* Jesus in *The Disputa,* and Apollo in *Parnassus* (as well as his completely nude statue in *The School of Athens*). (In each of these three frescoes, there is also a secondary figure, to the viewer's left, who is under-clothed.) What affinity is thus suggested among these three prominent figures and about the passions they respond to and make use of?

In any event, it should also be noticed that the half-clothed figure in *The School of Athens is* something of an aberration there and hence an obstruction to the smooth flow of the philosophic movement, unlike the more exalted place of such a figure in both *The Disputa* and *Parnassus.* It should be noticed as well that the Apollo and Marsyas panel in the vault can be said to show the hero of *Parnassus* overcoming the hero of *The Disputa,* with Marsyas bound in a Christ-like attitude to something like a cross awaiting his execution. Again we see exhibited the passions, and the Passion, which philosophy may not be able to cope with for the generality of mankind, however adept the "idealistic" philosophers (with their respect for duality) were in mediating between the highest and the lowest, occupying the middle ground between the heavens above and the earth below. The space above, empty of human beings, *is* reserved for the gods, or rather for their statues; but it does happen to be space that is defined in *The School of Athens* by a building made by men obviously skilled in mathematics and the manual arts.

viii

When I refer to the idealistic philosophers, I mean Aristotle as well as Plato, for (as I have indicated both in this chapter and throughout this book) what they, as Socratics, shared was much more important than what separated them. They are shown as moving together here. It also seems that they are moving down and out, which happens in no other fresco in this room. (In the other major frescoes, the figures are much more fixed in place.) And it is *down* that they must come in *The School of Athens,* is it not, down to the level of the mathematicians and physical scientists? The discursive, peripatetic activity is to be seen only on the top level. Is this the higher activity? Only one man on the upper level is writing (he "sits" against a wall to do so); no one on the upper level is reading. (Are the readers studying what has been done higher up?)

The men below in *The School of Athens* seem more divided than the men on the upper level; it is below that most of the instruments of research are to be seen. The two most abstracted "loners" are to be found beneath the upper level. (There is also the mysterious figure in scarlet at the right side of the upper level. He does point down, as if there is where he belongs?) And it is on the lower level that Raphael places himself, the second head from the right. This suggests the relation between art and mathematics. I once heard a Vatican Museum guide say, as she pointed out the shifting perspective in a tapestry based on a Raphael drawing, "All the artists were great mathematicians." Geometry was evidently being referred to there by the guide. (This was said in connection with a *Supper of Emmaus,* from Raphael's *Scuola Nuova.* See, on artists as students of anatomy, M. A. Lavin and S. M. Anastaplo, "Heart and Soul and the Pulmonary Tree . . ." See, on artists as teachers of political science,

William H. Honan, "Scholar [Roger D. Masters] Sees Leonardo's Influence on Machiavelli," *New York Times,* Dec. 8, 1996, p. 18-Y.)

I have suggested that it is not accidental that the mathematicians and physical scientists should be closest to us—that is, to the modern world. One must wonder whether modernity has required both a dependence upon philosophy and a descent from it. What does the "below" I have been referring to mean? Is it that the sciences are subservient to, as well as derived from, philosophy (that is, the metaphysics and the ethics represented by Plato and Aristotle)? Or is it that the mathematical and physical sciences, especially if one includes the organization of elementary perceptions, provide the foundations for philosophy?

In any event, the men below seem more diverse than those above, perhaps more specialized (as we would say). Things can be said to be more complicated here than in *The Disputa,* as may be indicated by the more intricate floor pattern here.

Still, are not the human beings in *The School of Athens* more "sympathetic"? All are active, working on something and evidently enjoying their birthright as rational beings who are more concerned for their understanding than for their salvation (insofar as these can be distinguished).

ix

These observations about the higher and the lower should remind us again of that excellence which the Apollo and Athena statues in *The School of Athens* can be said to stand for. And with this remark we can turn to our remaining major fresco, *The Cardinal and Theological Virtues,* on the Justice wall. This, too, it will be remembered, provides a bridge between Philosophy and Theology.

The four cardinal virtues are more obviously connected with philosophy, the three theological virtues with theology. (A half dozen figures suffice as the principal representations here.) In *The School of Athens,* the earthly activity is worth undertaking for its own sake, with divergent people working there on somewhat independent inquiries. In *The Disputa,* the earthly activity is worth doing primarily in light of that which is believed to be above.

We see on the Justice wall the smallest of the four major frescoes: this fresco is even more dependent than is its Poetry counterpart on *its* political underpinnings. The modesty of this presentation of the virtues may be appropriate. Is there not something simple, if not even austere, about the virtues? They perhaps should not be complicated if they are to have the most salutary effect for most people. Besides, the virtues are being presented throughout the room. Thus, we can be brief in our look at the *Virtues* fresco, taking our cue here from Raphael's allocation of space directly to this subject.

This is not to suggest, however, that Raphael is not properly acclaimed for the execution of several of the figures on this wall. Nor is it to suggest that the virtues may never be examined in considerable detail, especially for those willing to submit to the discipline of careful study. When one does, the richness of the subject becomes evident, as may be seen in Aristotle's *Nicomachean Ethics*. Thus, it has been suggested, the virtue of prudence in the *Virtues* fresco has in front the face of a fair young woman and in back a second face (indicated by the shape of the hair-style), the face of a worn old man of experience. (See Redig de Campos, p. 21.) Is it not essential for the continued effectiveness of prudence that it should appear fair? Indeed, this can be said to be a concern of Raphael's art generally, that by and large the fairer side of things should be shown, thereby contributing to a harmonizing effect among men and institutions otherwise prone to difficulties with one another. (In this, and certain other respects, he may be Xenophon-like.)

x

The relatively sparse direct treatment of the virtues induces us to wonder what may be missing in this room. One can think of critical Biblical scenes that are referred to only indirectly, such as the bringing down by Moses of the Ten Commandments and the raising up of Jesus on the Cross (to say nothing of the Resurrection itself). Moses, with his Tablets, is to be seen seated in the heavenly array in *The Disputa* (but a more active presentation might have been expected somewhere on the Justice wall). The nearest we come to the dramatic Cross is what is given us of Marsyas' execution at the hands of a vengeful pagan divinity, something which can perhaps be seen as an anthropological commentary on the Crucifixion. (The Cross may also be hinted at in the figures in *The Disputa,* with the heavenly array providing the transverse beam.)

One may wonder as well which of the major frescoes Raphael himself preferred. It is remarkable how he was able to "switch gears" in going from one picture to the other. He seems to have done so effortlessly, making each picture seem somehow self-contained, self-sufficient, perhaps even sovereign.

Should Raphael's preference be said to have been for the fresco he did best? If that should be the criterion—and why should he not be taken, like us, to prefer the best?—then his ultimate sympathy with *The School of Athens* must be suspected. This celebration of excellence, perhaps for its own sake, may be reflected as well in the love of beautiful women that Raphael is known for.

But if he did prefer *The School of Athens* and what it stands for, it is a preference expressed delicately and with prudence. Perhaps we should leave it at that, noticing only that he may have come to learn more and more about the subjects assigned him by his patron as he worked on the frescoes and thus thought about what each stood for. In a sense, then, the primary student of *The School of Athens* was Raphael himself.

xi

Whatever may be missing in the *Stanza della Segnatura,* there is even more missing in this, my preliminary examination of the room. It will be noticed, for example, that I have done relatively little with the colors and lines used in the pictures. I have also done little with the variety of opinions from and about other artists drawn upon by Raphael.

That artists do draw upon one another we all know—and have seen illustrated in several chapters in this book. These uses point up the particulars upon which art relies, and hence the accidental character of the materials available to the artist. The limits to our understanding here are set in part by our inability to know all the models used by Raphael and all the people alluded to in his paintings. (One may wonder, indeed, how these paintings would seem, simply as "works of art," to someone who comes to them without *any* outside information.)

I have referred to Raphael's reputed debt to Michelangelo for the Heraclitus figure, drawing thereby on the Sistine Chapel ceiling. This is a kind of tribute to Michelangelo, just as is the way Raphael places Euclid as lower then Heraclitus. That is, even Raphael's teacher and sponsor Bramante, who is said to be the model for Euclid, must bow to the superior genius of Raphael's friendly rival, Michelangelo.

It would also be interesting to consider various artistic "commentaries" on Raphael's *The School of Athens*. Particularly instructive is what I call *The School of Rome*, which will be glanced at in part 2 of this chapter.

An even more dramatic artistic commentary on *The School of Athens* may be found in *The Last Judgment*, which was painted by Michelangelo after Raphael had finished his own work. I venture to suggest that the portrait of "The Desperate One" in *The Last Judgment*—the squatting figure, with his face partially covered by his hand and with one eye looking out in horror at what is happening around and to him as he is being dragged down to everlasting damnation—that portrait may well be Michelangelo's "commentary" on Raphael's Heraclitus figure and indeed on *The School of Athens* (if not even on the entire argument in the *Stanza della Segnatura*).

The difficult Michelangelo, I have suggested, was more deeply touched by a tumultuous (and perhaps now challenged) Christianity and the Bible than the gentle Raphael. Can we see in the portrait of "The Desperate One" an indication by Michelangelo of the horror of a world viewed (as in *The School of Athens*) by the light of reason alone, light which may no longer suffice for him in his agony as it seems to suffice in *The School of Athens*? (One can be reminded of the frantic, even desperate, efforts by the elderly Pablo Picasso to hang on to, by expressing, his animal vitality. I find intriguing the Stars of David that I have noticed in Raphael's work. Consider, also, how Niccolò Machiavelli draws upon what we call the Old Testament, rather than upon the New Testament, for explicit illustrations in *The Prince*.)

I venture to suggest one more possible connection between the Heraclitus of Raphael and "the Desperate One" of Michelangelo. The historical Heraclitus made much of fire; and the desperate man in *The Last Judgment* contemplates being subjected eternally to fire. (See, for Diogenes Laertius' comment on Heraclitus, Anastaplo, *The Artist as Thinker*, pp. 317–18.)

xii

Far less controversial is the suggestion that artists are bound to differ from one another, if only because they do depend so much upon the particulars that they happen to be influenced by and to work with and through.

Another indication of the dependence of artists upon particulars may be seen in the very fact of the use by Raphael of contemporary models for the ancient philosophers and scientists he portrays. Do not artists tend to believe that the inner truth of things lies in the surface, as well as in the heart, of particulars?

Raphael does seem to do more with this belief in the *School of Athens* fresco than in the others. Does he not recognize thereby that thoughtful men across the ages are more like one another than are poets? (Are theologians somewhere in between the two kinds?) Does his use of contemporary models suggest that there *is* something perennial which keeps reappearing in one's own time from ancient times?

Perhaps it is particularly significant that Raphael uses so many contemporary artists to portray ancient philosophers. (Thus, as we have seen, the portrait of Plato is said to have been modeled on Leonardo da Vinci.) All this may suggest, among other things, that the men who once would have appeared as philosophers now appear as artists, just as in the centuries before the Renaissance they would have appeared as theologians. Thus, it may also be suggested, artists are better able than scholars, in the circumstances of Raphael's day, to delve into philosophic subjects. (See Anastaplo, *Brief on the Merits,* p. 78 n. 56. Still, we should not forget the "ancient disagreement and opposition between poetry [or art] and philosophy." See the beginning of the addendum to part 1 of chapter 7 and the ending of the addendum to part 2 of chapter 7 of this book. This may be related to the tension between the noble [or beautiful] and the just [or prudential].)

Did Raphael anticipate as well that a day was coming when philosophers could once again approach their subjects more directly than it may have been prudent to do in Raphael's own day? But the answer to this question depends in part upon whether Raphael was indeed obliged to depend ultimately upon particulars and the concrete, something which would limit anyone's understanding of the philosophical enterprise.

xiii

But this is an inquiry not limited to Raphael alone—and so we can let it rest for the moment. (See Anastaplo, *The Artist as Thinker,* p. 10.) Our final set of questions at this stage of our inquiry can be directed, if only briefly, to what more we can learn from *The School of Athens* and its companion paintings. I hope that I have said things that suggest how one might begin to answer this question.

These paintings may be a useful way for getting a sense of what the much-referred-to Neo-Platonism of the Renaissance was like—its strengths and weaknesses. It *is* somewhat different from the original Platonism, if only in that it is a response to a massive Christian challenge. We too are all Neo-Platonists, in a sense. We may not be able to accept (that is, understand) Plato as he understood himself; we are, for example, unable to grasp or to appreciate the moral-political order, including perhaps the Idea of the Good, upon which Plato's thought evidently rested.

Perhaps too much is made, in the Neo-Platonism of Raphael's (and, as I have several times suggested, of our) day, of the differences between Plato and Aristotle. This may have been in part due to an accidental cause, the fact that one faction in the Church drew more on Aristotle and another drew more on Plato. Yet Raphael himself shows the two philosophers as civil, and evidently productive, collaborators. However diverse the philosophers seem in print, or in the contentions of rival schools, there is a sense in *The School of Athens* of an overall compatibility among the philosophers (at least as an artist sees, and understands, the relations among philosophers). Some may wonder, of course, whether philosophy is somewhat diluted, if not distorted, in this presentation.

The Greek world, as seen in *The School of Athens,* may be considered by Raphael a critical source for what leads, by way of Parnassus, into Christianity. Athens, it may be indicated in this room, may not have sufficed, in that it was not "popular" enough. The lack of any human figures in the upper part of *The School of Athens* reminds us that philosophy does not require, or posit with determination, an afterlife, even though it must be difficult for much of mankind to regard life here as good enough to be satisfied with.

Even so, one can see that philosophy is presented as more lively than its "competitors" (if competitors they be). It is only in *The School of Athens* that figures are seen to be moving in and out (coming in, it "happens," from Plato's side and leaving from Aristotle's), as well as to be moving up and down. (We can surmise from *The Disputa* that some human beings, now settled into the heavenly array, moved up "once upon a time.")

We can also learn from the *Stanza della Segnatura* how an artist accommodated himself to an established and still demanding Christianity. (One is reminded of the then-recent Torquemada.) Indeed, Raphael can be said to have recognized that *some* religion is needed for a people, and better a long-established religion than either a new or no religion.

Of course, someone might protest that there is in principle nothing indispensable to learn from a painting if one can put its teachings into words. But for every reader who would pay attention to my kind of words, there are thousands who will go to see, to enjoy, and somehow to learn from Raphael's work. At the very least, then, a Raphael can say things about and on behalf of philosophy to the many who themselves cannot really be expected to understand philosophy. (Perhaps *The School of Athens* did for philosophy in Raphael's time what the *Crito* did for it in Plato's time.) The many who are in need of guidance and edification, if not of education, can include those in privileged positions in the Church of Raphael's day, those who (for all their learning and culture) were still very much the products of their more or less single-minded spiritual upbringing.

The question remains, then, Who is the master here? That is, we again wonder, Who did think out what is suggested by the work on exhibit in the *Stanza della Segnatura*? And who were *his* teachers? It is significant that whoever did plan all this was safely, if not most comfortably, lodged in the Church in a time of transition. The movements since in both philosophical and artistic discourse have been downward and even outward, even as more and more has been made of introspection. Should the same be said about modern theological discourse? Certainly, one cannot easily think of any prominent artist in the twentieth century with the sophistication and restraint, and perhaps the genuine thoughtfulness, to be discerned in Raphael's work.

In any event, one can see in the *Stanza della Segnatura* a most gifted representation of alternative ways of life, similar in many respects and yet so different, which are shown as living in apparently fruitful collaboration. That is, one can see here, as elsewhere in the work and time of Raphael, a particularly persuasive artistic recognition of that productive tension between Reason and Revelation which has made possible for the West its distinctive vitality. (See, for Laurence Berns on Leo Strauss with respect to "the secret of the vitality of Western Civilization," L. P. de Alvarez, p. 164 n. 61. See also, Anastaplo, "Shadia Drury on 'Leo Strauss.'")

PART TWO. On *The School of Rome*

> *O, you and I have heard our fathers say*
> *There was a Brutus once that would have brooked*
> *Th' eternal devil to keep his state in Rome*
> *As easily as a king.*

> —Cassius to Marcus Brutus

i

TOMASSO LAURETI, a Sicilian, was born ten years after Raphael died. He is responsible for the *Sala dei Capitani* frescoes in the Conservatore Palace on the Capitoline Hill (in the building which serves as the city hall of Rome). The room is dominated by large pictures of memorable events in the early years of the Roman Republic, frescoes which remind viewers of the sombre events that helped shape the character of the Republic. (See Pietrangeli, pp. 641, 644; "Hall of the Captains," pp. 64–66.)

We are particularly interested here in the presentation, on one of the walls, of the condemnation by Lucius Junius Brutus of his sons. The background for this episode is included in the entry on Brutus, *New Century Cyclopedia of Names:*

References to lcoations of photographs of the Laureti fresco discussed here are collected at the end of this chapter.

The epigraph is taken from William Shakespeare's *Julius Caesar,* I, ii, 158–61. See, on this play, Anastaplo, *The Artist as Thinker,* pp. 22–23.

Roman consul in 509 B.C. According to unhistorical legend, he feigned
idiocy (whence the name *Brutus*, stupid; probably an erroneous etymol-
ogy) to avoid exciting the fear of his uncle Tarquin the Proud [Tarquinus
Superbus], who had put to death the elder brother of Brutus to possess
himself of their wealth. Tarquin, alarmed at the prodigy of a serpent appearing in the royal palace, sent his sons Titus and Aruns to consult the
oracle at Delphi. They took with them for amusement Brutus, who pro-
pitiated the priestess with a hollow staff filled with gold. When the oracle, in response to an inquiry of Titus and Aruns as to who should
succeed to the throne, replied, "He who first kisses his mother," Brutus
stumbled to the ground and kissed mother earth. After the outrage on
Lucretia, Brutus threw off his pretence of idiocy, expelled the Tarquins,
and established (c510 B.C.) the republic. While consul he condemned his
own sons Titus and Tiberius to death for having conspired to restore
Tarquin. He led (c507) an army against Tarquin, who was returning to
Rome. Brutus and [Tarquin's son] Aruns fell in the battle, pierced by
each other's spears.

(See, on the outrage of Lucretia and its political consequences, Anastaplo, *The Artist as Thinker*, p. 46 f.)

The Laureti depiction of the condemnation ·of the sons of Brutus,
Bruto Che Condanna A Morete I Figli (also known as *The Justice of Brutus*), is very much influenced by Raphael's *The School of Athens*. Here,
too, there are two central figures (one of them Junius Brutus) framed by
an arch, with people arrayed at different levels on either side, and with
three lone figures in the central foreground. Our attention is attracted
both to these figures and to the central standing figures in the arch. Brutus is firm in his determination to destroy those who have attempted to
restore the monarchy. His sons are among those destined to be executed
on this occasion for that offense. The lone figures in front include Junius
Brutus' wife and the two sons for whom she has been pleading. One of
her sons has just been decapitated, the other is about to be. It should be
useful to insert here an extended technical description of the Laureti
frescoes which I found after having prepared the discussion in this chapter (Aikin, pp. 102–3):

> Clearly Laureti based the composition of his *Brutus* wall on Raphael's
> *The School of Athens*, and also quoted many of the stanze figures as well
> as the architectural setting. He insisted on the measured space and invi-

olate picture plane of the High Renaissance, and in fact created a setting even deeper than Raphael's; but he also crowded his setting with a great many figures, mostly passive observers of the main action. In the *Brutus* scene and in the other three frescoes as well, this multitude serves as a rhetorical emphasis on the magnitude of the threats to Rome and on the importance of the incidents on universal history. . . . [Laureti] uses the arrangement, gestures, and sheer numbers of his figures to draw attention to the principal action and to underscore its significance.

The compelling symmetry and strict organization of the Brutus scene serve the propaganda function of the fresco by enhancing clarity and readability. This strict, bilateral symmetry might also be a manifestation of the steady evolution of a greater symmetry and simplicity in late-sixteenth-century painting as a whole. . . . And perhaps Raphael's seriousness and symmetry attracted Laureti. The high moral values implicit in the attitudes and actions of the central figures in *The School of Athens* are highly compatible with the moral intent of the *Capitani* frescoes. Laureti's adaptation of the monumental arch also serves the ideal of moral virtue and self-sacrifice in the interests of Rome. Visually, the arch under which Laureti placed his Brutus resembles the triumphal Arch of Constantine. Metaphorically, it can stand for the victory over Tarquinius, the victory of justice and morality over injustice and conspiracy, or the historic victory of Rome over all her adversaries.

Laureti's depiction, which I find instructive to refer to as *The School of Rome,* may be usefully compared with *The School of Athens.* Each of these frescoes occupies a wall in a room: *Athens* is in a building at the Vatican; *Rome* is in a building on the Capitoline Hill. *Rome* is a "busier," far less serene, picture, not only because of its grim subject but also because of the way its figures are arranged. In *Athens,* the two central figures (of Plato and Aristotle) are in the lower half of the picture, with all of the upper half of the scene empty of living human beings. In *Rome,* the two critical figures (of Brutus and his consular colleague) are in the upper half of the scene, which is filled with people and buildings. In *Athens,* the vertical dimension of the fresco is more than four times the height of the central figures; in *Rome,* the vertical dimensions in the two frescoes are less than three times the height of the central figures. (The horizonal dimension in the two frescoes are the same in terms of the size of the central figures.)

There are roughly the same number of people in the *Rome* scene as in the *Athens* scene, but those in *Rome* are crowded into less space and consequently seem many more. In both frescoes, the dozens of figures fan out right and left as well as up and down. In *Rome,* the central figures are on a platform or rostrum, from which they issue orders, to which various people below (some with *fasces*) will respond; in *Athens,* no orders are being issued. In *Rome,* the arms of the central figures point downward, with Brutus signaling the executions, while in *Athens,* we have noticed, Plato points upward and Aristotle horizontally. In the *Rome* foreground, where the two sons of Brutus are being executed despite their mother's pleas, the three of them occupy the places in *Athens* of Diogenes, Heraclitus, and an ascending figure who points to them.

Few visitors to Rome notice, or even have their attention called to, *The School of Rome* (under whatever name). The fresco is interesting enough, but not so interesting to moderns ignorant of Roman history as to make up for its inferiority to the great art available elsewhere in the city from Raphael and others.

ii

Major statuary is evident in both frescoes—one statue on either side of the central figures, above them (but closer to the men in *Rome* than in *Athens*). The one on the viewer's right in both pictures is clothed in armor; the one on the left is virtually nude. But in *Rome* that figure is also armed, while in *Athens* he (Apollo) holds a lyre. This difference between *Athens* and *Rome* points up as well the movement from *philosophy* to *politics* as the dominant mode.

Most of the figures in *Athens* are pretty much on their own, more or less unconcerned about the central figures and engaging either in personal conversations or in private study. Not so in *Rome,* where an act of overriding political import is in progress, with several more prisoners slated for execution. So much is the orientation political in *Rome* that Brutus prefers the Republic to his own family. There is no indication that Brutus laments what is happening to his sons. (Compare David's lament upon the death of the rebellious Absalom.) Critical to the Roman response, at least in the most robust days of the Republic, seems to have been the desire for glory.

All this, we are taught, is what the Republic needs: a radical subordination of the personal to the public. Philosophy is not political (or public), but neither is it simply the fulfillment (or perfection) of the personal. However much the political may be needed to produce and preserve conditions for philosophy, there may be an inevitable tension between the moral virtues (or politics in the service of the virtues) and philosophy. (This may be related to, although it is not the same as, the tension between the noble and the just that is discussed in part 2 of chapter 7 of this book.)

iii

Laureti, who seems to invite comparisons to Raphael's work, dramatizes an aspect of life left out of the *Stanza della Segnatura,* a room that encompasses justice, art, theology, and philosophy. Laureti (as a Sicilian?) shows the tough, even ugly, underpinning upon which the enduring order presupposed by *The School of Athens,* and provided by the Roman Republic, rested. We can be reminded again of the tension between nobility and justice.

Was "the divine Raphael" too civilized (like Sappho and unlike Michelangelo), too serene to portray this element fully? Indeed, does Laureti provide in his *Rome* a "realistic" (even Homeric) comment on Raphael's *Athens*? (Perhaps he would remind Raphael of the sometimes ruthless Theseus, later celebrated by Machiavelli for having laid the foundations for the flowering that became Athens.)

One Greek counterpart to what Junius Brutus did to his sons may be seen in Agamemnon's sacrifice of his daughter. But the daughter was not guilty of any misconduct; if anyone, Agamemnon himself was. Nor is he celebrated (but, at most, commiserated with) for what he did—and he comes to be hated, and killed, by his wife. (We are not told of any such development in Junius Brutus' family.) What Agamemnon did may have been somewhat more personal, if not less political, than what Junius Brutus did, even though it served the Greek campaign against Troy. Clytemnestra, at least, took it that way. (See chapter 4 of this book.)

A similar distinction can be drawn between Raphael's *Athens* and Laureti's *Rome.* In *Athens,* there is relatively little physical movement, with all of the activity depicted contained by an arcade which is generously decorated by sculpture and bas-reliefs. In *Rome,* there is much movement, most of it directed to the executions in the foreground, with a heavily built-up city all around (two streets with horses are in evidence), with relatively little art on display.

In *Rome,* human beings occupy the lower three-fourths of the picture, with Junius Brutus and his colleague dominating the action. Behind them, soaring above the human beings in the picture, are the standards of the city, the most prominent of which is the Eagle.

In *Athens,* we have noticed, there are no living human beings in the upper half of the picture. Although Plato and Aristotle are prominent, they do not control (however much they might inspire) the others. Of the others, two-thirds are on the same level as Plato and Aristotle; the remaining third are mostly in clumps to the right and left below. The lower ones seem to be more concerned with studies that make use of drawings.

The sky behind Plato and Aristotle has no standards or banners. The upper half of *Athens,* devoid of living human beings but not of statues of divinities (in human form) and other art, suggests how much of the world is beyond the control of human beings even though almost all of the space on view there is encompassed by man-made architecture.

It is with a lifting of the spirit that one returns to *The School of Athens* after having had to face up to underlying "reality" in *The School of Rome.* In our reading of Raphael's masterpiece we are encouraged and instructed by Tomasso Laureti's graphic "commentary" upon it, which reminds us of how little we usually see even in those pictures and other great works of the mind with which we chance to be most familiar. (Photographs of the Laureti fresco discussed here may be found in (1) Aikin, *The Capitoline Hill During the Reign of Sixtus V,* pp. 102–3; (2) "Hall of the Captains," pp. 64–66; (3) Pietrangeli, "La Sala dei Capitani," pp. 641, 644; (4) *Il Campidoglio all'epoca di Raffaello* [Milan: Electa, 1984], pp. 34–35; (5) Luigi Spezzaferro, ed., *Il Campi doglio e Sisto V* [Rome: Carte Segrete, 1991], pp. 139, 154.)

Epilogue

[Simonides said,] *"I tell you, Hiero, your contest is against others who rule cities; if you make the city you rule the happiest of these, know well that you will be declared by herald the victor in the most noble and magnificent contest among human beings. . . . Enrich your friends with confidence, Hiero, for you will enrich yourself. Augment the city, for you attach power to yourself. . . . [If] you prove superior to your friends in beneficence, your enemies will be utterly unable to resist you. And if you do all these things, know well, of all things you will acquire the most noble and most blessed possessions to be met with among human beings, for while being happy, you will not be envied for being happy."*

—Xenophon

i

How do moderns tend to respond to the ancient authors discussed in this book? A critical modern challenge to much of what I have ventured to say here may have been anticipated in the work of an influential Italian "philosopher of history," Giambattista Vico (1668–1774). How, for example, did Vico read Homer, the first thinker considered at length in this book? One answer is that he practically read him out of existence.

The epigraph is taken from Xenophon, *Hiero* 11.7–15 (closing lines of the dialogue). See the headnote for the Prologue.

Another answer is that he did not read him very well. Still another answer combines these two to this effect: Since Vico did not read Homer very well, he practically read him out of existence.

We hear today of the divorce between the social sciences and the humanities, a divorce which the work of Vico can be said to have tried to avoid. A Vicoian reconciliation here tends to consist of the subjugation of the humanities to the social sciences (in the form of such sciences as anthropology, linguistics, history and sociology). "At the center of Vico's theory of poetic wisdom," it has been argued, "is his theory of 'imaginative universals'" (Verene, p. 412). It is such theories, which seem to look to something other than Plato's Ideas, around which the social sciences since Vico's time have developed in attempts to account for, among other things, artistic achievements. (See, e.g., Vico, *Autobiography*, p. 59.)

It may be, of course, that Vico was wrong in many, perhaps in all critical, parts of his attempt to use what we now call the social sciences to explain the humanities. Certainly, he had far less data to work with than his successors have had access to. But he does suggest an approach that remains significant, establishing him as a founder of the modern scientific schools of literary study. He himself was willing to have his "discovery of the true Homer" regarded as perhaps his greatest intellectual contribution. (See Vico, *The New Science*, p. 269.)

It is that discovery, including the presuppositions and method upon which it seems to depend, that I examine here. In order to do so, I must say more about the Homeric poems (supplementing what I have said in the prologue and opening chapter of this book). By doing so I hope to make useful suggestions about the proper relation between the humanities and the social sciences.

ii

Implicit in Vico's approach here is his unstated assumption that he is, in critical respects, superior to his ancient counterparts. After all, he relies upon "principles of philology" and "canons of mythology" which, although derived by him from materials evidently available to the ancients as well, simply did not occur to them. Is not Vico markedly modern in this kind of assumption of an essential superiority to the ancients?

(See Vico, *Autobiography*, pp. 159–60.) Whether Vico himself believed what he said about the Homeric poems is not my primary concern here. Rather, I consider the implications and consequences of the Vicoian approach, which seems to have had considerable influence on modernity.

It is Vico's innovative approach that permits him to conclude that neither the *Iliad* nor the *Odyssey* was made by a single poet but rather, in each case, by an entire people in the manner that myths and fairy tales are said to evolve. He places these two poetic developments half the Mediterranean and several centuries apart from each other. (Vico's mode has been followed by others—for example, F. A. Wolf and his school. See John A. Scott, *The Unity of Homer*, p. 39 f. See, also, Tagliacozzo and White, eds., *Gianbattista Vico: An International Symposium*, pp. 577–78.)

The more distinguished readers of the *Iliad* and *Odyssey* in antiquity, including Plato and Aristotle, took it for granted that individual poets had made them. Their only major question about authorship of the "Homeric poems" seems to have been as to whether it was one poet or two. (Seneca reports this difference of opinion. See Vico, *New Science*, p. 250.) Longinus, for example, suggested that the *Iliad* was written in Homer's youth, while the *Odyssey* was written in his old age, thus accounting for any stylistic and other differences there may be. (See ibid., pp. 253, 267, 270.)

Vico's position, on the other hand, is that "the true Homer" was "the Greek people of the heroic or poetic age, mythological in thought, barbaric in manners and completely ignorant of the 'recondite wisdom' of later philosophers" (Fisch, p. 1026). Vico could reach this conclusion even though he recognized that "Plato left firmly fixed the opinion that Homer was endowed with sublime esoteric wisdom (and all the other philosophers have followed in his train . . .)" (*New Science*, p. 245).

Vico can be taken to concede, however, that if the *Iliad* and the *Odyssey* did contain from their beginning the wisdom he refers to, then they could not have been made by "the Greek peoples" but rather must have been made by a man (or men) of genius, since (he says) "esoteric wisdom appertains to but few individual men." But, he argues, "the meanings of esoteric wisdom" long associated with these poems "were intruded into the Homeric fables by the philosophers who came later" (ibid., p. 262).

In addition, Vico suggests, the *Iliad* and the *Odyssey* must have been "a confused mass of material" before the editors commissioned by the Athenian tyrants (the Pisistratids) took charge of them (ibid., p. 264). He further suggests that "the reason why the Greek peoples so vied with each other for the honor of being [Homer's] fatherland, and why almost all claimed him as citizen, is that the Greek peoples were themselves Homer" (ibid., p. 270).

iii

The modern re-ordering of the great works of the past may be seen in how Greek texts are amended as well as accounted for and in how the Bible is analyzed (with various "layers" of texts having been posited). Critical to such an approach to texts may be the modern tendency to re-duce works of the mind, including works of art, to something less ele-vated than had been traditionally assumed. "The spirit of the age," "material causes," and "forces," rather than "inspiration" and "reason," are looked to in order to account for the thing being examined. The work of the mind being examined is not grasped as it was regarded by either its maker or its original audience. Rather, an "anthropological," "linguistic," or "sociological" (in short, a social science) approach is re-lied upon. (See the Leo Strauss epigraph at the front of this book.)

The most appealing forms today of such an approach, which is more or less materialistic at bottom (and probably historicist and relativistic in inclination) may be seen in the Marxist and the Freudian accounts of why things are as they are. These accounts, which are currently in eclipse, can seem for some so illuminating as to take on the character of revelations. Common to all such forms is the assumption that "non-lit-erary" principles can be used to explain the construction and the appeal of a story. (See, for an anticipation of the Marxist notion that economic development is reflected in the ideas of an age, Vico, *New Science,* p. 270.)

Critical to the appeal of the Vico account is the control by scholars that is either assumed or promised. Thus, it has been noticed (Fisch, p. 1026):

> Vico approached his new science through a new theory of knowledge. . . .
> We know in mathematics because, by abstraction and definition, we have

made the objects of our knowledge. We have a quasi-knowledge of the world of nature just so far as we are able to carry the experimental method by which, as it were, we make what we know; but, to speak more strictly and as a whole, the world of nature is known only by God, who made it. On the other hand, we can know the civil world or world of nations, the institutions of human culture, because we have made that world and "its principles are therefore to be found within the modifications of our own human mind."

Is not such an emphasis upon *our knowing only what we make* reflected in how Vico can speak of Homer? After all, has not he himself made the Homer that he speaks of? This is related to the tendency of the educated in modern times to consider themselves superior to the ancients—since they, as moderns, can put the ancients in their place, revising their texts and otherwise accounting for them according to whatever "theory" of history or literary evolution happens to be fashionable.

iv

Chance may largely determine what data are available and what theories or approaches are brought to bear upon the interpretation of a well-crafted work. But is not a truly well-crafted work one which has, as much as possible in the circumstances, eliminated the influence of chance in its make-up? This is not to deny that chance may affect conditions and hence whether the work is seen for what it is or whether it is or can be interpreted and applied as it was intended to be.

Consider, for example, how the Declaration of Independence has been read at times. During the Lincoln-Douglas debates of 1858, Stephen Douglas insisted upon trying to read its "created equal" language in the light of the undoubted fact that some of the men who signed the Declaration (with such language in it) continued to hold slaves. Actions, or material manifestations, were taken by Douglas to be authoritative in determining what the "created equal" language in the Declaration said or was intended to mean. Abraham Lincoln, on the other hand, argued that this language held up a standard by which the country could be guided until such time as circumstances permitted realization of the goal thus set forth. (See, e.g., Anastaplo, "Slavery and the Constitution,"

p. 677; *The Amendments to the Constitution,* pp. 125, 135, 168; "'Racism,' Political Correctness, and Constitutional Law.")

Similar observations can be made about the way that the Constitution of the United States has been read, or rather mis-read, over the past two centuries, so much so at times that the misapprehension of one part has led to chronic distortions elsewhere in the interpretation of that instrument. For example, because the Commerce Clause was unduly limited by judicial interpretation in the latter half of the nineteenth century and the first half of the twentieth century, the required sensible governing of the economy had to be secured by distorting other parts of the Constitution in addition to the Commerce Clause, including the Treaty Power provision—with such results as that seen in the curious case of *Missouri v. Holland* (1920). Something of the modern attitude I have been referring to may be seen in an observation by the all-too-modern Oliver Wendell Holmes, Jr. in the course of his opinion for the Court in *Missouri v. Holland:* "The case before us must be considered in the light of our whole experience and not merely in that of what was said a hundred years ago" (252 U.S. 433). Deeds and circumstances (that is to say, "history") are thus said to take precedence over words (that is to say, ideas or principles). (See, on the Commerce Clause, Crosskey, pp. 1387–88; Anastaplo, *The Constitution of 1787,* p. 332. The discussion of "equipment," in chapter 12 of this book, is also relevant here.)

One reason moderns tend to disregard or to distort the work of their distant predecessors is that they do not appreciate how well crafted such work can be. The fashionable response to the American Constitution provides, again, a case in point. It has yet to be recognized by most American judges and constitutional scholars that that instrument is remarkably suited, and was intended from the beginning to be suited, for use in quite varying circumstances. Modern experts have to manipulate various provisions of the Constitution to do what does need to be done but which, unbeknownst to them, was originally intended to be taken care of elsewhere in the instrument. Or consider such work as the *Alice* stories by Lewis Carroll: it is not noticed how well crafted these stories are in the vital sequences of challenges facing the intrepid Alice underground and behind the looking glass. (See, e.g., Anastaplo, *The Artist as Thinker,* p. 166.) In short, modern intellectuals tend to ignore, or at least to underestimate, the manifestations of the thinker in the superb craftsman, especially if he should happen to be "inspired."

Much the same can be said about Vico's reading of Homer, a reading which depends (as we have seen) upon his assumption that there is nothing particularly recondite or esoteric (that is to say, truly thoughtful) about the Homeric stories. He argues, as we have seen, that it is the philosophers who have read complexities into the fairly simple and straightforward expressions of the collective mind of the Greek people that these stories represent. Thus, he observed, "The complete absence of philosophy which we have shown in Homer, and our discoveries concerning his fatherland and his age, arouse in us a strong suspicion that he may perhaps have been quite simply a man of the people" (*New Science*, p. 254). Plato can be said by Vico to have supplied, rather than to have found and confirmed, the esoteric wisdom now seen in Homer's poems, poems which in themselves exhibit no more than a common wisdom. (See Vico, *Autobiography*, p. 154. See, also, *New Science*, pp. xlvi, 69 f., 133, 223 f., 262, 270 f., 273. Vico insists that philosophy and poetry are so different in principle that the practitioner of one cannot do the other. See ibid., p. 261; Isaiah Berlin, "Vico and the Ideal of Enlightenment, pp. 648–49. Consider, however, the range exhibited by authors such as Lucretius and Shakespeare. The authorship of the *Iliad* is assigned by Vico to peoples in Asia Minor, the authorship of the *Odyssey* to peoples in the west of Greece.)

The people-as-poet seem, according to Vico, to work by a kind of instinct. A considerable emphasis must be placed by Vico upon Homer's work as a reflection of its times—this is an emphasis, in effect, upon chance—and all this in the name of greater rationality in criticism. It has been observed that "Vico's *New Science* is a science of origins" (Verene, p. 411). Does not this kind of emphasis upon origins mean that material causes and process are made more of than forms or ends? Or, put another way, does not this mean (to apply Leo Strauss's caution) that the high (especially in matters cultural) is systematically to be seen in terms of the low, thereby keeping us from seeing the high fully or truly as it is? The high is given its due, as is the intimate relation between thinker and artist, in the passage with which Mark Van Doren opens his fine discussion of the *Iliad* (*The Noble Voice*, p. 1): "Homer, with Shakespeare at his side, is still the sovereign poet. The phrase is Dante's, who is third in this strict company which excludes all others. Only these three—yet Chaucer is a fourth—are masters of the main art a poet must learn: the art of standing at the right distance from his matter, of keeping the right relation to it, and of using, along with the knowledge he brings, the knowledge he gains while he goes." (See, for Dante's salutes to Homer, *Inferno*, 4.85–90, 26.52–142.)

Modern readers of Vico praise his pioneering effort to account for the Homeric poems as he does, even as they criticize the data and the analyses of the data he relied upon. They use variations of Vico's approach in employing modern methods and information in trying to account for what is to be seen in great works of art. They would, for example, make more of the unconscious than Vico does. (He does tend to make more use than they do of the surface of the poems.) What Vico's modern critics rarely do, it seems to me, is to question the principal assumption upon which much of his work rests, the assumption that he has indeed read Homer well enough to be justified in categorizing him as lacking "sublime esoteric wisdom."

This is not to suggest that one cannot learn from such efforts as those by Vico. I am reminded again of the work of Samuel Butler in his efforts to prove that the author of the *Odyssey* was a woman. However questionable his conclusions, Butler does call to our attention features ("feminine" features) of the poem which we might otherwise neglect. (One thing which Butler does not sufficiently appreciate is that the *Odyssey* can be seen as the older Homer "playing" with the young Homer evident in the *Iliad*, whether it be the same man or not. See Butler, *The Authoress of the Odyssey*, e.g., pp. 247–48. We can see such playfulness in Sappho [in chapter 2 of this book] and in Plato [at the end of chapter 11 of this book]. See, on Delphi identifying Homer as Odysseus' grandson, Anastaplo, *The Artist as Thinker*, p. 248.)

I have yet to establish, or at least to begin to establish in this context, that Vico is incorrect in what he says about the *Iliad* and the *Odyssey*, however useful his suggestions may be for investigating folk tales and other probable emanations of the collective mind. Vico himself, we should notice, does relatively little analysis of Homer's plots and lines. Perhaps if he had done more he might have recognized in each of them a single mind at work rather than a people. (He does concede, it should be remembered, that a truly thoughtful account presupposes an exceptional rather than a collective mind.) We, then, must return to Homer's poems—or, rather, to samples of them—to remind ourselves of the level of the thinking that went into them.

Critical to both poems is the storytelling that goes on by characters within the poems. Individuals are shown telling stories. Odysseus, of course, can be shown as presenting quite elaborate (often quite contrived) stories, some of which I have examined in the prologue and in chapter 1 of this book. In addition, Zeus himself is shown as having to "plot" out carefully what is to happen among the Achaeans in order to achieve the complicated effects he intends. (See, e.g., *Iliad* 2.1 f.) Whoever made up these poems considered it plausible that such stories as are told by characters in the poems (after all, Odysseus' tale to the Phaecians occupies several books) can be presented as having been devised by single minds. If this is so, why not the entire poems, the *Iliad* and the *Odyssey*?

We should notice as well that it is the artist of exceptional mind who can have the grasp of a craft which permits him to vary it as he wishes for the effect he wants to achieve. Plutarch observed, for example (*Moralia* 1:429), "But Homer felt no repugnance against making the very first of his lines unmetrical; so abounding was his confidence regarding the rest on account of his ability." Does not Homer suggest that he is not bound by chance as others may be? Besides, is it not fitting that his lines become metrical after the Muse has been invoked at the outset?

v

Let us begin our sampling of the Homeric texts in this context by looking once again at the Catalogue of Ships, in book 2 of the *Iliad*. (See, for an echo of the Catalogue of Ships, Herodotus, *History* 7.60–99.) This is a long passage which is generally regarded, even by those who see "Homer" as clearly a single man, as material that comes from a bardic tradition incorporated wholesale by the poet into the *Iliad*.

Whatever the sources for the names and descriptions in the Catalogue of Ships may have been, consider once more the use to which the poet of the *Iliad* puts them. The catalogue must appear a meticulous, even pedantic, and, to most readers, uninteresting account of the various contingents of Achaeans who had come to besiege Troy under the command of Agamemnon. I observe in part 2 of chapter 1 of this book that in this inventory of contingents, the contingent of the prudent

Odysseus is central to the array of Achaean ships, and that the contingents of the two great rivals, Agamemnon and Achilles (each with special claim to preeminence), are at an equal distance (in terms of number of contingents) on either side of the unifying Odysseus. It is the quarrel of Agamemnon and Achilles, the reader of the *Iliad* must not forget, that is said to be largely responsible for what happens in the *Iliad*.

Are not such facts, which become evident upon simple calculations, suggestive about Homer? Should they not put us on notice about much of what he does and does not say (and not only about the relations of Achilles and Agamemnon)? Should they alert us not to underestimate the subtlety, as well as the audacity, of a great artist? Thus, one can begin to understand, upon carefully examining the construction of Homer's poems, why he *could* be called by his countrymen "the wisest of all the Greeks." (Samuel Butler notices that Homer, in how he makes use of his sources, is like John Bunyan in his use of the Bible in *The Pilgrim's Progress*. The number of contingents among the Trojans, we again notice, is one-half of the number of contingents among the much more complicated, and hence much more interesting, Achaeans. See Anastaplo, *The Constitutionalist*, p. 807; *The Artist as Thinker*, p. 4.)

The importance of Odysseus is pointed up by this arrangement in book 2 of the *Iliad*. (I suggest, in part 2 of chapter 1, how the Catalogue of Ships in the *Iliad* may be connected with the Catalogue of Personages in the *Odyssey*.) Homer himself is aware that Odysseus' contingent *is* central in the *Iliad*, for he makes that explicit later on. (See *Iliad* 8.212 f.)

The Odysseus of the *Iliad* speaks quite craftily, very much in the fashion of the hero of the *Odyssey*. In fact, it can be said, all of the principal characters appear to be consistent from one poem to the other—characters such as Achilles, Agamemnon (both of whom Odysseus reports talking with in Hades, in the *Odyssey*), Menelaus, Helen (both of whom Telemachus meets in Sparta), and Ajax (who refuses to talk to Odysseus in Hades). Does not this, too, tend to undercut the arguments of both Vico and Butler with respect to the different makers of the two poems?

Furthermore, there are other elements of each poem in the other. Thus, in the *Iliad*, the poet takes his bearings by a time of peace; certainly, he seems much more dubious about the war, and the consequences of wrath, than Vico gives him credit for. (Critical to the Vicoian position is the assumption that the maker of the *Iliad* is himself swept along by the barbaric passions of his time.) And in the *Odyssey,* which is more a poem of peace, there can be fierce fighting from time to time. (This ability to mix the elements of tragedy and comedy may be seen as well in Shakespeare—who is also one poet, whoever he may be said to have been.)

It should further be noticed that the arrangements employed in the *Iliad,* and in the *Odyssey* also, *are* those of a great poet. They are, in both poems, quite sophisticated and highly selective arrangements. It is hardly likely, for example, that any "folk mind" would, in developing the story of the Trojan War (as in the *Iliad*), have postponed the telling of the memorable Trojan Horse story to the *Odyssey* (although it is evident in the *Iliad* that the story is already known to the poet). Did he anticipate that he would be able to deal with it elsewhere? In any event, that maker of the *Iliad* dared *not* to tell it when a lesser poet would have "had to."

Similar observations can be made about the *Odyssey.* No one telling the story of the *Odyssey* from memory would be likely to organize it as Homer does (with four books passing before Odysseus himself comes on stage). There are anticipations of things to come, and there is a remarkable use of what we call "flashbacks." Are not these signs of a particularly confident, and thoughtful, poetic mind at work here, as in the *Iliad*? ("The entrance of Odysseus is not until the fifth book [of the *Odyssey*]; not, that is to say, until it has been prepared with all the skill available to Homer, which means all the skill there is" [Van Doren, p. 81].)

vi

Let us now look further into the *Odyssey,* with Vico's provocative analyses and conclusions in mind.

That which is merely suggested in the Catalogue of Ships about Odysseus and his prudence, and which is evident elsewhere in the *Iliad* as well, is developed even more in the *Odyssey.* Central to the *Odyssey* is the concluding episode in the very long tale told by Odysseus in the Phaeacian court of Alcinous. The centrality in the *Odyssey* of this episode should become apparent to anyone who consults the number of pages in any standard edition of the *Odyssey.* (This is in book 12 of the twenty-four books established by editors.) One can see in this central episode of the *Odyssey* that character and hence conduct do matter in one's life, that one chooses meaningfully.

This episode is about the slaughter of the Cattle of the Sun and the effect of that sacrilegious slaughter on Odysseus' men, something touched upon in part 2 of chapter 2 of this book. Only Odysseus survives the ensuing storm at sea—because, we are given to understand, only he had restrained himself and chosen properly. We have noticed that only Odysseus refrained from killing and eating the Cattle of the Sun, although he was as hungry as his men. Is it only retroactively that Odysseus attributes his men's destruction to their sacrilege? This raises a deeper question: what "really happened" on that occasion? Are we to understand that Odysseus is making up all this to entertain his royal audience? Is all this his fantasy (a kind of dream), designed to appeal to his pious (or at least impressionable) audience, whose help he needs, explaining why it is that only he has survived to invoke their aid? (I have noticed that Homer does seem, in the opening lines of the *Odyssey,* to ratify the story about the Herd of the Sun. But does Homer intend *that* to be understood as a miraculous episode? I have also noticed that Odysseus himself reveals how his curiosity, if not also his greed, had led to the deadly encounter with the Cyclops.)

It has always been suspected by some, I have noticed as well, that Odysseus made up much of what he reports in the Court of Alcinous. (Such an argument proceeds on the assumption that Homer intends the overall story told by the narrator of the *Odyssey,* as distinguished from the stories told here and there by Odysseus, to be about things that do or at least can happen among human beings.) Even so, whether or not the tale told by Odysseus in the court of Alcinous "really happened," the account does reflect the character of Odysseus—of wily Odysseus (or of an Odysseus-like Homer)—and, as such, it is both revealing and appropriate. We can see, under either understanding, why it is that Odysseus does prevail: he is a prudent man able to discipline himself; he is a man of considerable rhetorical gifts, who is able to adapt himself to circumstances. (Edgar of Shakespeare's *King Lear,* with his ability to use one disguise after another, is Odyssean. One also sees in Edgar the subordination of the noble, or the fine appearances of things, to the just. The juxtaposition of this noble and the just, or at least the useful, may be seen as well in the combination of Don Quixote and Sancho Panza, with the noble the more attractive of the pair. I have found instructive for this section the work of Laurence Berns and Amy A. Kass.)

I have argued that Homer is far more than a gifted storyteller reworking old stories. We must be careful, if we are to understand what permits art to have its enduring effects, not to underestimate the disciplined intelligence of the better artists. Behind whatever inspiration or beneath whatever unconscious Homer drew upon, a surpassing intelligence may be discerned, an intelligence which grasps the natures of things, human and non-human alike. Is it not prudent to assume, therefore, that the intelligence evident in the works of the greatest artists is not simply that of imaginative critics but rather that of the artists themselves—and that their greatness consists, in part, in their ability to see and to describe what *is,* or (to use an old-fashioned phrase) in their ability to imitate nature? (See Anastaplo, *The Artist as Thinker,* pp. 5–6.)

I have been noticing the organization of the entire *Odyssey* by Homer. But consider also how Odysseus himself organizes the stories he tells in the Court of Alcinous, the stories which stretch across several books of the Odyssey. *His* principle of organization can be shown by a Homer to be different from Homer's, if only because Homer and Odysseus have different audiences and purposes. (See Anastaplo, *The Artist as Thinker,* p. 357. The stories told by Odysseus seem to have been triggered by the songs sung by a local bard in the Court of Alcinous, with the second of the bard's songs leading to the third, which was requested by Odysseus, and that in turn leading to Odysseus' long series of stories. The first and third songs by the bard are about the Trojan War.)

Of the dozen or so stories told by Odysseus on this occasion, the central one is about his visit to Hades (which includes his masterly character sketches of the old Trojan War comrades he meets there). It must have made quite an impression upon Odysseus' Phaeacian audience, and must have reinforced their sense of hospitality and good will toward him, that he can describe himself as a man who had visited Hades. The Hades visit is framed, so to speak, by visits to Circe's island, which take place both before and after the reported visit to Hades. (Elpenor's burial is used to bring Odysseus back to Circe's island.)

The stories told by Odysseus in the court of Alcinous are perhaps the most fanciful in the entire *Odyssey.* I have already observed that it is

Odysseus, and definitely not Homer in his own name, who tells these stories. That is, Homer does not himself say that such things do happen (however much he is prepared to have us caught up, as we are, by Odysseus' account). Homer is also prepared to have a few of his audience —his best or real audience?—reflect upon what these stories, if contrived by Odysseus, say about Odysseus and about how he sees his own career. (A similar detachment is seen in the way Homer leaves it to Menelaus to tell of a remarkable encounter with Proteus. Once again, Homer does not vouch for the truth of what Menelaus reports, however significant the Proteus myth may be, if only as a representation of the transformations that a poet goes through.)

I believe it highly unlikely, therefore, that a "folk mind" or anyone but a poet of genius would have been as careful, and as ingenious, as the maker of the *Iliad* or of the *Odyssey* is in what is said by him in his own name. The truth very much matters to him, even as he uses fictions to tell his stories and to make his points. His scrupulousness in this respect may most dramatically be seen in how the gods are presented, especially their interventions in human affairs. Are not all, or almost all, such interventions readily explainable as "natural" (that is, not-divine) things —if one can step back to see what is and is not being said by the poet? Vico is quite critical of belief in these gods, but there is no indication, so far as I can tell, that Vico is aware of the distance Homer carefully places between himself and such gods. Certainly, it is difficult to imagine any folk mind, or the people as poet, consistently refusing to vouch for the accuracy of these accounts of these gods' interventions in human affairs. What Homer himself truly believed about the gods is, we have noticed, difficult to say. One could well begin, in thinking further about him, by considering what he indicates about that fate by which the gods themselves are evidently bound. (Fate is, in Homer and elsewhere among the Greeks, a mysterious combination of character and chance. Does not a proper understanding of chance depend upon a grasp of the natural? The single use of *nature* in Homer [*Odyssey* 9.303] is indeed curious. See section ix of chapter 2 of this book.)

The careful reader of these poems can well conclude, I have suggested, that Homer is a man of surpassing intelligence as well as a quite sophisticated observer of the world. If he is as careful and astute as I have suggested he is, why should he be any more likely to "believe in" these gods than *we* are, however useful he may find it to tell the stories about them that he does? Certainly, he is aware of the skepticism that some express now and then (and even within the poems) about various signs, omens, and other supposed evidence of divine interventions.

The popular mind, in hearing these stories, was apt to accept them as presented on the surface of the poems. This may be seen in how these stories were repeated in various forms by the Greeks for centuries after Homer, with even popular worship built around them. Is there any reason to believe that the popular mind which could make such poems would be apt to feel about them differently from the popular mind which accepted them?

This is not to suggest that the popular mind is never correct. After all, it has long been accepted, by almost everyone (the few and the many alike), that the *Iliad* and the *Odyssey* were made close enough in time and place to each other to be the work of one poet or at least to be the work of two poets within one or two generations of each other.

Vico, a distinguished forerunner of modern critics, probably did not know enough about Greek history or the Greek language to be able to speak with the assurance he did about the dating and the geographical placing of the makings of these two poems. Indeed, I am told on very good authority, there still is not enough linguistic, archaeological, or other such information available to permit anyone to determine that the *Iliad* and the *Odyssey* were *not* made by the same poet. Perhaps, then, Vico's principal failing here was that he did not know how much he would have had to know in order to be entitled to be as certain as he made himself out to be (in opposition to long-established opinion) about the authorship of these poems. That is, it is important to know when one does not yet know enough to be entitled to be revolutionary in one's responses. But then, it is still another manifestation of modern social science, if not of modernity itself, that it should be believed that the received opinions of the community should enjoy no privileged status, that everything is always up for reconsideration. It has even become fashionable to believe that there is something dubious about any opinion that has been long accepted. It remains to be seen what will happen to *this* belief, or opinion, if it in turn should become long accepted.

vii

I believe that what may be fundamental to my critique of Vico's "discovery of the true Homer" is the judgment that he simply is not prepared to read, with the care that they deserve and require, the best works of the mind. In this failing, Vico does seem very much a modern. Still, we can wonder, what came first—the inability to read with the utmost care or the assumption that there really is nothing worthy of such care? There may be here a reciprocal effect—and so the possibility of a rigorous grasp of the truly best is steadily diminished. Here, too, we can see how chance developments may affect the conditions required for the recognition and establishment of the good.

The profound failing here, I should at once add, is not exclusively that of the social sciences. The humanities must share the blame, of which there is plenty to go around. After all, the humanities *should* provide authoritative guidance to social scientists (and to physical scientists as well) as to what the best way of life is. This should include guidance to what is truly worth knowing and how, including challenging instruction in what it means to know. But all too often the humanities (including poetry, philosophy, and theology) have become trivial, or at least merely private, pursuits. Either they do not have or they no longer manifest the confidence required for a sustained and elevating exercise of the guidance they, and perhaps they alone, are equipped to provide us all. One consequence of the modern approach to these matters is the virtual deification of chance in human affairs (which may be related, by the way, to the gambling mania being exploited these days by one government after another in the western world). (See, on the not-unrelated Deconstructionist movement, Anastaplo, *The Artist as Thinker,* pp. 470–72.)

I have returned in this book to some of the greatest works of the mind that have shaped and challenged us from antiquity. Each such work, I must repeat, invites study on its own terms, however instructive it can be to weave them all together. These works reveal what can and cannot be sensibly said by the thinker as artist, in matters divine as well as human, about the discovery and conquest of chance, about an understanding and imitation of nature, and about the domain and reign of reason.

Selected Bibliography

The only texts listed here are those for which the translations quoted from or the citations given in the text of this book are keyed to particular editions.

The Adams-Jefferson Letters. Edited by Lester J. Cappon. New York: Clarion Books, Simon and Schuster, 1972.

Aeschylus. *Oresteia (Agamemnon, The Libation Bearers, and The Eumenides).* Translated by Richmond Lattimore. Chicago: University of Chicago Press, 1969.

Aikin, Robert Cushing. *The Capitoline Hill During the Reign of Sixtus V.* Ph.D. diss., University of California, Berkeley, 1977.

Alvis, John. *Shakespeare's Understanding of Honor.* Durham, N.C.: Carolina Academic Press, 1991.

Anastaplo, George. "The Ambiguity of Justice in Plato's *Republic.*" In *Original Intent and the Framers of the Constitution,* edited by Harry V. Jaffa. Washington, D.C.: Regnery Gateway, 1994.

———. *The Amendments to the Constitution: A Commentary.* Baltimore: Johns Hopkins University Press, 1995.

———. *The American Moralist: On Law, Ethics, and Government.* Athens: Ohio University Press, 1992.

———. *The Artist as Thinker: From Shakespeare to Joyce.* Athens: Ohio University Press, 1983.

———. *Brief on the Merits* (1960), *In re Anastaplo,* 366 U.S. 82 (1961).

———. "Can Beauty 'Hallow Even the Bloodiest Tomahawk'?" *The Critic,* vol. 48 (Winter 1993).

———. "Church and State: Explorations." *Loyola University of Chicago Law Journal,* vol. 19 (1987).

———. *The Constitution of 1787: A Commentary.* Baltimore: Johns Hopkins University Press, 1989.

———. *The Constitutionalist: Notes on the First Amendment.* Dallas: Southern Methodist University Press, 1971.

———. "Freedom of Speech and the First Amendment: Explorations." *Texas Tech Law Review,* vol. 21 (1990).

————. "How to Read the Constitution of the United States." *Loyola University of Chicago Law Journal,* vol. 17 (1985).

————. *Human Being and Citizen: Essays on Virtue, Freedom, and the Common Good.* Chicago: Swallow Press, 1975.

————. "An Introduction to 'Ancient' African Thought." *The Great Ideas Today* (*Encyclopedia Britannica*) (1995).

————. "An Introduction to Hindu Thought: The *Bhagavad Gita.*" *The Great Ideas Today* (*Encyclopedia Britannica*) (1985).

————. "Lessons for the Student of Law: The Oklahoma Lectures." *Oklahoma City University Law Review,* vol. 20 (1995).

————. "Natural Law or Natural Right?" *Loyola University of New Orleans Law Review,* vol. 38 (1993).

————. "On Crime, Criminal Lawyers, and O. J. Simpson: Plato's *Gorgias* Revisited." *Loyola University of Chicago Law Journal,* vol. 26 (1995).

————. "On Freedom: Explorations." *Oklahoma City University Law Review,* vol. 17 (1992).

————. "On How Eric Voegelin Has Read Plato and Aristotle." *Independent Journal of Philosophy,* vol. 5/6 (1988).

————. "On Plato's *Meno,*" *Review of Metaphysics,* vol. 32 (1979).

————. "On the Use, Neglect, and Abuse of Veils: The Parliaments of the World's Religions, 1893, 1993." *The Great Ideas Today* (*Encyclopedia Britannica*) (1994).

————. "On Trial: Explorations." *Loyola University of Chicago Law Journal,* vol. 22 (1991).

————. "'Racism,' Political Correctness, and Constitutionalism Law: A Law School Case Study." *South Dakota Law Review,* vol. 42 (1996–97).

————. "Rome, Piety, and Law: Explorations." *Loyola University of New Orleans Law Review,* vol. 39 (1993).

————. "Shadia Drury on 'Leo Strauss.'" *The Vital Nexus,* vol. 1 (1990).

————. "Slavery and the Constitution: Explorations." *Texas Tech Law Review,* vol. 20 (1989).

Anastaplo, Sara Prince. *Poems.* In *Law and Philosophy,* edited by John A. Murley, Robert L. Stone, and William T. Braithwaite, 2:1033. Athens: Ohio University Press, 1992.

Aristophanes. *Birds.* Translated by Benjamin B. Rogers. In Loeb Classical Library, *Aristophanes,* vol. 2. Reprint, Cambridge, Mass.: Harvard University Press, 1978.

————. *Clouds.* In *Four Texts on Socrates,* translated by Thomas G. West and Grace Starry West. Ithaca: Cornell University Press, 1984.

Aristotle. *Metaphysics.* Translated by W. D. Ross. In *The Basic Works of Aristotle,* edited by Richard P. McKeon. New York: Random House, 1941.

————. *Nicomachean Ethics.* Translated by W. D. Ross. In *The Basic Works of Aristotle,* edited by Richard P. McKeon. New York: Random House, 1941.

———. *Poetics.* Translated by Ingram Bywater. In *The Basic Works of Aristotle,* edited by Richard P. McKeon. New York: Random House, 1941.

———. *Politics.* Translated by Carnes Lord. Chicago: University of Chicago Press, 1984.

Arnhart, Larry. *Aristotle on Political Reasoning: A Commentary on the "Rhetoric."* DeKalb: Northern Illinois University Press, 1981.

Arrian, *The Campaigns of Alexander.* Penguin Books.

Arrowsmith, William. Foreword to *Rhesus,* by Euripides, translated by Richard Emil Braun. The Greek Tragedy in New Translations. New York: Oxford University Press, 1992.

———. Introduction to *The Birds,* by Aristophanes, translated by William Arrowsmith. Ann Arbor: University of Michigan Press, 1961.

Augustine. *The City of God.* Modern Library.

Aurelius, Marcus. *Meditations.* Translated and introduced by G. M. A. Grube. The Library of Liberal Arts 173. Indianapolis: Bobbs-Merrill, [1963].

Bacchylides. *The Poems and Fragments.* Edited by Richard C. Jebb. Cambridge: University Press, 1905.

Benardete, Seth. "Euripides' *Hippolytus.*" In *Essays in Honor of Jacob Klein.* Annapolis: St. John's College Press, 1976.

———. *Herodotean Inquiries.* The Hague: Martinus Nijhoff, 1969.

———. "On Plato's *Timaeus* and Timaeus' Science Fiction." *Interpretation,* vol. 2 (1971).

Berlin, Isaiah. "Vico and the Ideal of Enlightenment." *Social Research,* vol. 43 (1976).

Berns, Gisela. "*Nomos* and *Physis* (An Interpretation of Euripides' *Hippolytos*)." *Hermes,* vol. 101 (1973).

Berns, Laurence. "Aristotle's *Poetics.*" In *Ancients and Moderns: Essays on the Tradition of Political Philosophy in Honor of Leo Strauss,* edited by Joseph Cropsey. New York: Basic Books, 1964.

Blackstone, William. *Commentaries on the Laws of England.* Edited by Stanley N. Katz. Chicago: University of Chicago Press, 1979.

Boethius. *The Consolation of Philosophy.* Translated and introduction by Richard Green. The Library of Liberal Arts 86. Indianapolis: Bobbs-Merrill, [1962].

Bowra, C. M. *Pindar.* Oxford: Clarendon Press, 1964.

Brann, Eva T. H. Introduction to *The Republic, by Plato,* translated by Raymond Larson. Northbrook, Ill.: Crofts Classics, 1979.

"Brutus, Lucius Brutus." In *New Century Cyclopedia of Names* 1:687. New York: Appleton-Century-Croft, 1954.

Burn, A. R., ed. *Histories,* by Herodotus. Penguin Books, 1974.

Burnet, John. *Greek Philosophy.* New York: St. Martin's Press, 1968.

Butler, Samuel. *The Authoress of the Odyssey.* Chicago: University of Chicago Press, 1967.

Camesasca, Ettore. *All the Frescoes of Raphael.* New York: Hawthorn Books, 1963.

Cather, Willa. *On Writing.* New York: Alfred A. Knopf, 1949.

Catullus, Gaius Valerius. *The Complete Poems.* New York: E. P. Dutton & Co., 1970.

Chamberlain, Samuel E. *My Confession: Recollections of a Rogue.* Lincoln: University of Nebraska Press, 1987.

Churchill, Winston S. *Great Contemporaries.* London: Thornton Butterworth Ltd., 1937.

———. *My Early Life: A Roving Commission.* London: Thornton Butterworth, 1930.

Cicero. *On the Commonwealth.* Library of Liberal Arts.

———. *On the Nature of the Gods.* Translated by Hubert M. Poteat. Chicago: University of Chicago Press, 1950.

Clark, Kenneth. *Another Part of the Wood: A Self-Portrait.* London: John Murray, 1974.

The Concise Oxford Companion to Classical Literature. Edited by M. C. Howatson and Ian Chilvers. Oxford: Oxford University Press, 1993.

Cox, Edwin M. *The Poems of Sappho.* London: Williams & Norgate, 1925.

Crosskey, William W. *Politics and the Constitution.* Chicago: University of Chicago Press, 1953.

de Alvarez, Leo Paul S., ed. *Abraham Lincoln, The Gettysburg Address, and American Constitutionalism.* Irving; Texas: University of Dallas Press, 1976.

Diogenes Laertius *Lives of Eminent Philosophers.* Translated by R. D. Hicks. 2 vols. Loeb Classical Library. New York: G. P. Putnam's, 1925; reprint, Cambridge, Mass.: Harvard University Press, 1942–.

Edmonds, J. M., ed. and trans. *Lyra Graeca.* 3 vols. The Loeb Classical Library. New York: G. P. Putnam's, 1922–1927.

Euripides. *Hippolytus.* Translated by David Grene. In *The Complete Greek Tragedies,* edited by David Grene and Richmond Lattimore. Chicago: University of Chicago Press, 1992.

Fisch, Max H. "Giambattista Vico." *Encyclopedia Britannica,* 14th edition.

Fortescue, John. *De Laudibus Legum Anglie.* Cambridge: University Press, 1942.

Freeman, Kathleen. *Ancilla to the Pre-Socratic Philosophers.* Oxford: Basil Blackwell, 1952.

Freud, Sigmund. *Basic Writings.* Modern Library.

Fritzsche, Hellmut. "Of Things That Are Not." In *Law and Philosophy,* edited by John A. Murley, Robert L. Stone, and William T. Braithwaite, 1:3. Athens: Ohio University Press, 1992.

Goodman, Nathan G. *A Benjamin Franklin Reader.* New York: Thomas Y. Crowell Co., 1945.

Gorgias. *See* Sprague, *The Older Sophists.*

Grene, David. "The Interpretation of the *Hippolytus* of Euripides." *Classical Philology,* vol. 34 (1939).

Groden, Suzy Q., ed. *The Poems of Sappho.* Library of Liberal Arts.

Grube, G. M. A. *The Drama of Euripides.* London: Metheun & Co., 1941.

Halkin, Abraham, and David Hartman, eds. *Crisis and Leadership: Epistles of Maimonides.* Philadelphia: Jewish Publication Society, 1985.

"Hall of the Captains." *Capitoline Museums, Rome.* Federico Garolla Editore, 1984.

Hawthorne, John G. "Gorgias of Leontini." Ph.D. diss., University of Chicago, 1949.

Heidegger, Martin. *An Introduction to Metaphysics.* Garden City, N. Y.: Doubleday & Co., 1961.

Herodotus. *History.* Translated by David Grene. Chicago: University of Chicago Press, 1987.

Hollis, Christopher. *Sir Thomas More.* London: Steed & Ward, 1934.

Holmes, O. W. "Natural Law." *Harvard Law Review,* vol. 39 (1918).

Homer. *Iliad.* Translated by Richmond Lattimore. Chicago: University of Chicago Press, 1951.

———. *Odyssey.* Translated by Richmond Lattimore. New York: HarperCollins, 1965.

How, W. W., and J. Wells. *A Commentary on Herodotus.* Oxford: Clarendon Press, 1912, 1961.

Hus, Alain. *Greek and Roman Religion.* New York: Hawthorn Books, 1962.

Jaffa, Harry V. *Statesmanship.* Durham, N.C.: Carolina Academic Press, 1981.

James, William. *Writings.* Edited by John J. McDermott. Chicago: University of Chicago Press, 1967.

Josephson, Brian D. "The Elusivity of Nature and the Mind-Matter Problem." In *The Interrelationship Between Mind and Matter,* edited by Beverly Rubik. Philadelphia: The Center for Frontier Sciences, Temple University, 1992.

Kazantzakis, Nikos. *Serpent and Lily.* Translated by Theodora Vasils. Berkeley: University of California Press, 1980.

Kerferd, G. B. "Gorgias of Leontini." *Encyclopedia of Philosophy* 3:374. New York: Macmillan, 1967.

———. "Gorgias on nature, or that which is not." *Phronesis,* vol. 1 (1955).

Klein, Jacob. "Socrates and Aristophanes." *Massachusetts Review,* vol. 9 (1968).

———. *Lectures and Essays.* Annapolis: St. John's College Press, 1985.

Lattimore, Richmond. *Greek Lyrics.* Chicago: University of Chicago Press, 1955.

Lattimore, Richmond, trans. *Rhesus,* by Euripides. In *Compete Greek Tragedies.* Chicago: University of Chicago Press, 1958.

———. *The Odyssey of Homer.* New York: HarperCollins, 1967.

Lavin, Marilyn Aronberg, and Sara Maria Anastaplo. "Heart and Soul and the Pulmonary Tree in Two Paintings by Piero della Francesca." *Artibus et Historiae,* no. 31 (1995).

Levey, Michael. *From Giotto to Cézanne.* London: Thames and Hudson, 1968.

Lyra Graeca. Edited by J. M. Edmonds. Loeb Classical Library.

Machiavelli, Niccolò. *The Prince.* Edited by Leo Paul S. de Alvarez. Irving, Texas: University of Dallas Press, 1980.

Mackail, J. W. *Lectures on Greek Poetry.* London: Longmans, Green and Co., 1910.

Masson, Georgina. *The Comprehensive Guide to Rome.* London: Collins, 1972.

Masugi, Ken, ed. *Interpreting Tocqueville's "Democracy in America."* Savage, Md.: Rowman and Littlefield, Publishers, 1991.

Mencken, H. L., ed. *A New Dictionary of Quotations.* New York: Alfred A. Knopf, 1962.

Missouri v. Holland, 252 U.S. 416 (1920).

Mourelatos, Alexander P. D. *The Pre-Socratics.* New York: Anchor Books, Doubleday, 1974.

Mullen, William. *Choreia: Pindar and Dance.* Princeton, N.J.: Princeton University Press, 1982.

Murley, John A., Robert L. Stone, and William T. Braithwaite, eds. *Law and Philosophy: The Practice of Theory.* 2 vols. Athens: Ohio University Press, 1992.

Norwood, Gilbert. *Greek Tragedy.* London: Methuen and Co., 1920.

Oggins, Robin S., and Virginia Darrow Oggins. "Falconry and Medieval Social Status." *Mediaevalia,* vol. 12 (1989).

Page, Denys L. "Sappho." *Encyclopedia Britannica,* 14th edition.

Pietrangeli, Carlo. "La Sala dei Capitani." *Capitolium: Rassegna Mensile dei Communedi Roma,* vol. 37, no. 10 (October 1962).

Pindar. *Odes.* Translated by Roy Arthur Swanson. Library of Liberal Arts.

———. *The Odes of Pindar.* Translated by J. E. Sandys. 2nd, rev. ed. Loeb Classical Library No. 56. New York: Putnam, 1919; reprint, Cambridge, Mass.: Harvard University Press, 1978.

Plato. *The Apology of Socrates.* In *Four Texts on Socrates,* edited by West and West.

———. *Laws.* Translated by Thomas L. Pangle. New York: Basic Books, 1980.

———. *The Republic.* Translated by Allan Bloom. New York: Basic Books, 1968.

———. *Symposium.* Translated by Seth Benardete. In *The Dialogue of Plato,* edited by Erich Segal. New York: Bantam Books, 1986.

———. *Timaeus.* Translated by R. G. Bury. Loeb Classical Library.

Plutarch. *Moralia.* Loeb Classical Library.

Polyakov, A. M. *Gauge Fields and Strings.* Chur, Switzerland: Harwood Academic Publishers, 1987.

Rabelais, François. *The Histories of Gargantua and Pantagruel.* Translated and with an introduction by J. M. Cohen. Harmondsorth, Middlesex: Penguin Books, [1955].

Racine, Jean, *Phedre.* Translated by Margaret Rawlings. New York: E. P. Dutton & Co., 1962.

Redig de Campos, Deoclecio. *The "Stanze" of Raphael.* Rome: Edisioni dei Tuero, 1968.

Robinson, David M. *Sappho and Her Influence.* Boston: Marshall Jones Co., 1924.

Rose, H. J. *A Handbook of Greek Literature.* New York: E. P. Dutton & Co., 1960.

Sappho. *Poems.* See (1) Cox, (2) Groden, and (3) *Lyra Graeca.*

Scott, John A. *The Unity of Homer.* Berkeley: University of California Press, 1921.

Sealey, Raphael. *The Athenian Republic: Democracy or the Rule of Law.* University Park: Pennsylvania State University Press, 1987.

Shaw, Bernard. *In King Charles's Golden Days.* In *The Theater of Bernard Shaw,* edited by Allan S. Downer, vol. 2. New York: Dodd, Mead & Co., 1961.

Shorey, Paul. *Selected Papers.* New York: Garland Publishers, 1980.

Smith, Adam. *The Wealth of Nations.* Modern Library.

Snell, Bruno. *Poetry and Society.* Freeport, N.Y.: Books for Libraries Press, 1971.

Sophocles. *Antigone.* Translated by David Grene. University of Chicago Press Collection.

———. *Oedipus Tyrannus.* Translated by David Grene. University of Chicago Press Collection.

Sprague, Rosamond Kent. *The Older Sophists.* Columbia: University of South Carolina Press, 1972.

Stone, Robert L., ed. *Essays on "The Closing of the American Mind."* Chicago: Chicago Review Press, 1989.

Strauss, Leo. *The City and Man.* Chicago: Rand McNally, 1964.

———. *Natural Right and History.* Chicago: University of Chicago Press, 1953.

———. *On Plato's Banquet* (transcript of a University of Chicago course, 1959), 240 pages.

———. *Persecution and the Art of Writing.* Glencoe, Ill.: The Free Press, 1952.

———. "Plato." In *History of Political Philosophy,* edited by Leo Strauss and Joseph Cropsey. Chicago: Rand McNally, 1963.

———. *Socrates and Aristophanes.* New York: Basic Books, 1965.

———. *Spinoza's Critique of Religion.* New York: Schoken Book, 1965.

———. *What is Political Philosophy?* Glencoe, Ill.: The Free Press, 1959.

Symonds, John A. *Sudies of the Greek Poets.* New York: Harper & Brothers, 1901.

Tagliacozzo, Giorgio, and Hayden V. White, eds. *Giambattista Vico: An International Symposium.* Baltimore: Johns Hopkins University Press, 1969.

Taylor, A. E. *Varia Socratica.* First Series. Oxford: James Parker & Co., 1911.

"Theseus." *New Century Cyclopedia of Names,* vol. 3, p. 3838. New York: Appleton-Century-Croft, 1954.

Thucydides. *Peloponnesian War.* Translated by Richard Crawley and T. E. Wick. Modern Library.

Turner, Dawson W. *Notes on Herodotus.* London: Henry C. Bohn, 1853.

Van Doren, Mark. *The Noble Voice: A Study of Ten Great Poems.* New York: Henry Holt and Co., 1946.

Vasari, Giorgio. *Lives of the Artists.* Edited by Betty Burroughs. New York: Simon and Schuster, 1946.

The Vatican: Spirit and Art of Christian Rome. New York: The Metropolitan Museum of Art, 1982.

Verene, Donald P. "Vico's Philosophy of Imagination." *Social Research,* vol. 43 (1976).

Vico, Giambattista. *Autobiography.* Ithaca: Cornell University Press, 1944.

————. *The New Science.* New York: Doubleday, Anchor Books, 1962.

Ward, Anne. G. *The Quest for Theseus.* New York: Praeger Publishers, 1970.

Weintraub, Karl Joachim. "1483 and all that." University of Chicago lecture, 1983.

West, Thomas G., and Grace Starry West, trans. *Four Texts on Socrates.* Ithaca: Cornell University Press, 1984.

Wharton, Henry Thorton. *Sappho.* London: John Lane, 1908.

Whitehead, Alfred North. *The Aims of Education.* New York: The Free Press, 1967.

————. *Science and the Modern World.* New York: The Free Press, 1967.

Willcock, Malcolm M. *A Companion to the Iliad.* Chicago: University of Chicago Press, 1976.

Wood, Henry. *The Histories of Herodotus: An Analysis of the Formal Structure.* The Hague: Mouton, 1972.

Wormell, Donald E. W. "Pindar." *Encyclopedia Britannica,* 15th edition.

Xenophon. *Hiero or Tyrannicus.* Translated by Marvin Kendrick. In *On Tyranny, edited* by Leo Strauss. New York: The Free Press, 1991.

Index

This index has been prepared with the able assistance of Elaine C. Gist of the Secretarial Staff of the Loyola University of Chicago School of Law.

A Note about the Author

George Anastaplo is Lecturer in the Liberal Arts at the University of Chicago, Professor Emeritus of Political Science and of Philosophy at Rosary College, and Professor of Law at Loyola University of Chicago.